ULTIMATE X-MEN

writer
MARK MILLAR

pencils
DAVID FINCH
AND **ADAM KUBERT**
WITH BEN AND RAY LAI

inks
ART THIBERT
AND **DANNY MIKI**
WITH BEN AND RAY LAI

colors
DAVE STEWART

letters
CHRIS ELIOPOULOS

cover art
DAVID FINCH

assistant editor
STEPHANIE MOORE

associate editors
C. B. CEBULSKI
AND **BRIAN SMITH**

editor
RALPH MACCHIO

collections editor
JEFF YOUNGQUIST

associate editor
CORY SEDLMEIER

assistant editor
JENNIFER GRÜNWALD

book designer
JEOF VITA

editor in chief
JOE QUESADA

president
BILL JEMAS

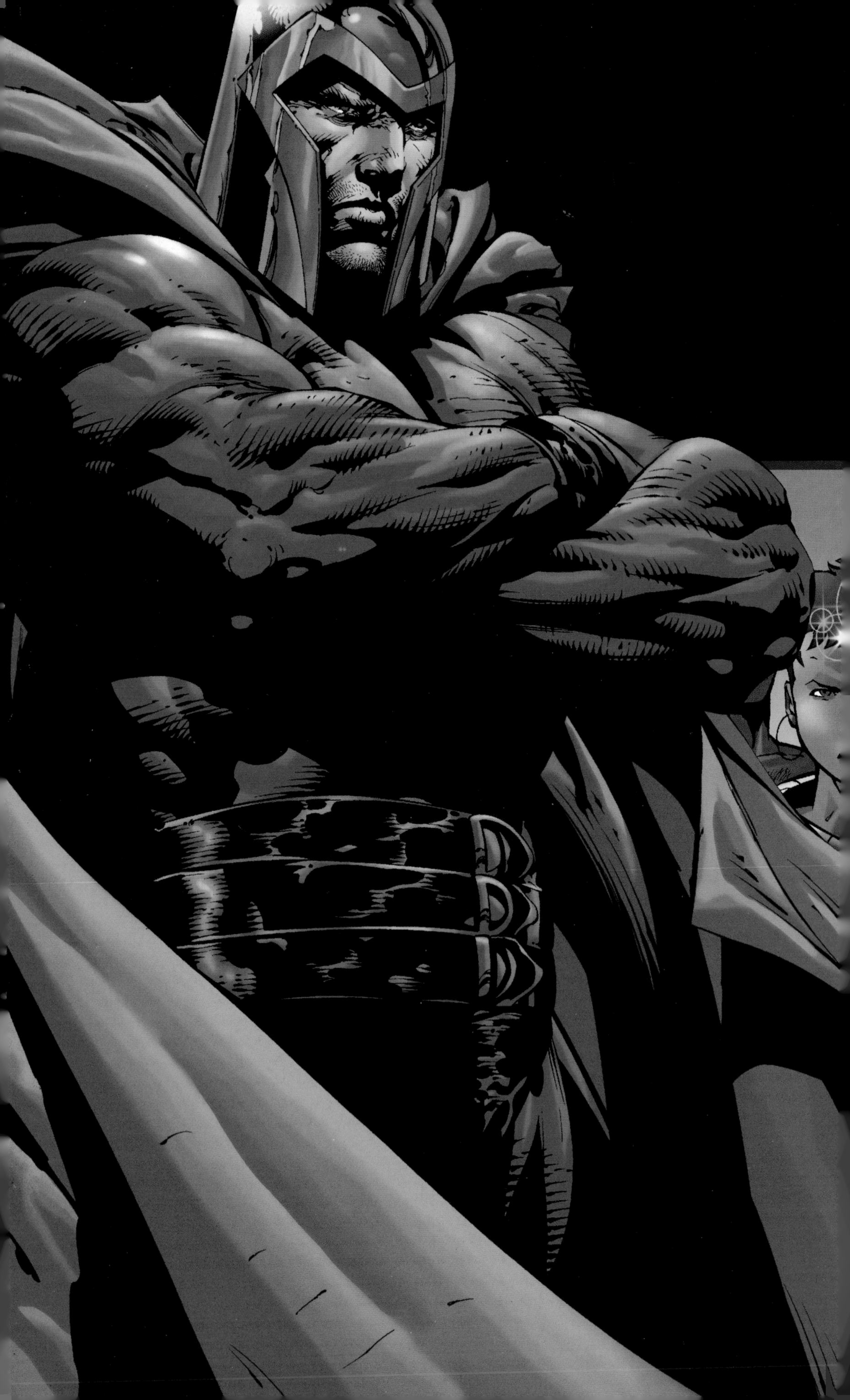

ULTIMATE X-MEN

RETURN of the KING

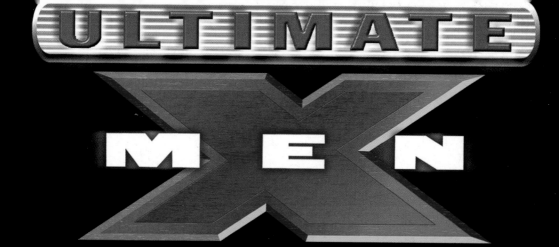

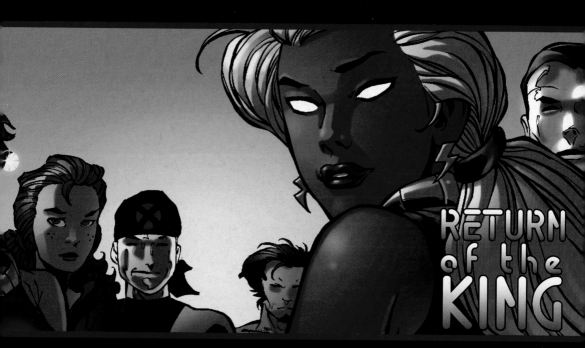

PREVIOUSLY IN ULTIMATE X-MEN:

Professor Charles Xavier brought them together to bridge the gap between man and mutant: Cyclops. Marvel Girl. Storm. Iceman. Beast. Colossus. Wolverine. They are the X-Men, soldiers for Xavier's dream of peaceful coexistence. This dream is slowly being forged into reality.

During his attack on Washington, D.C., the mutant master of magnetism, Magneto, was apparently killed by Professor Xavier. However, in actuality, Xavier would never take the life of another living creature and secretly spared Magneto's life while still allowing the world at large to believe he had died. Xavier placed mental blocks in Magneto's mind, and he has been living a simple existence as Erik Lensherr, completely unaware of his past life as a mutant terrorist.

However, the new Brotherhood of Mutants has discovered that Magneto is indeed still alive. With the aid of their psychics, they are able to remove the mental blocks Xavier placed in his mind.

Magneto has returned!

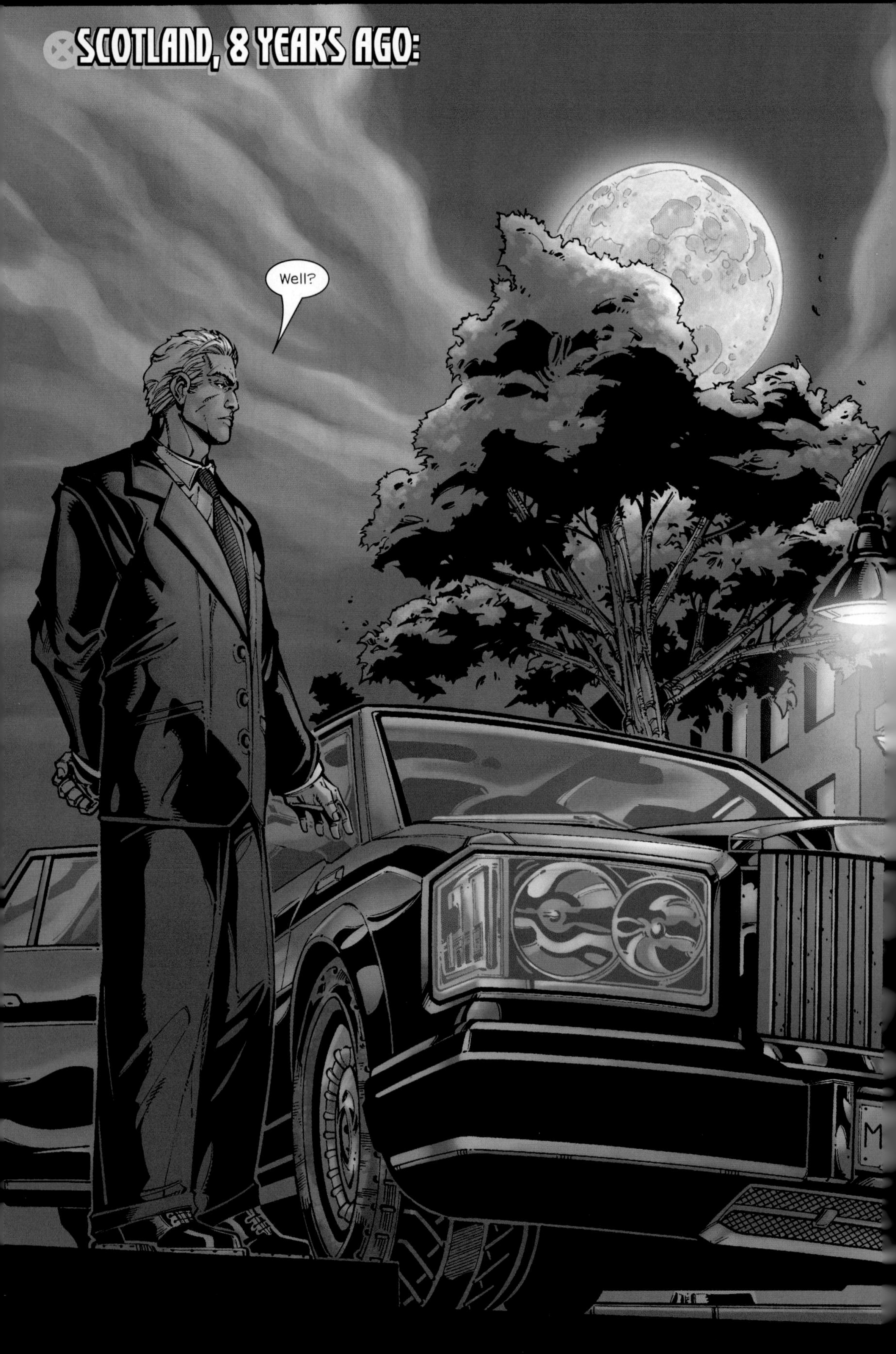
SCOTLAND, 8 YEARS AGO:
Well?

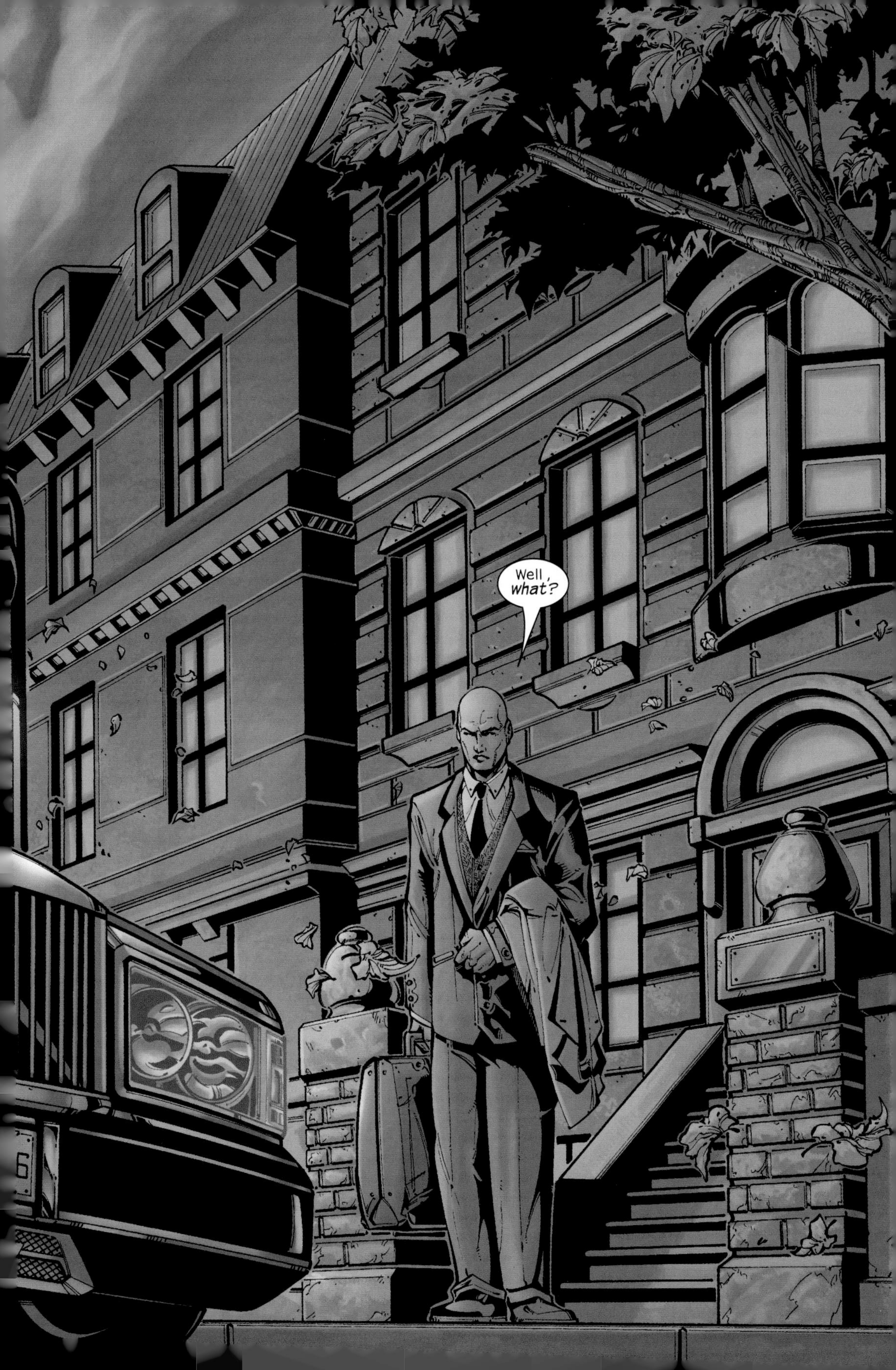
Well, what?

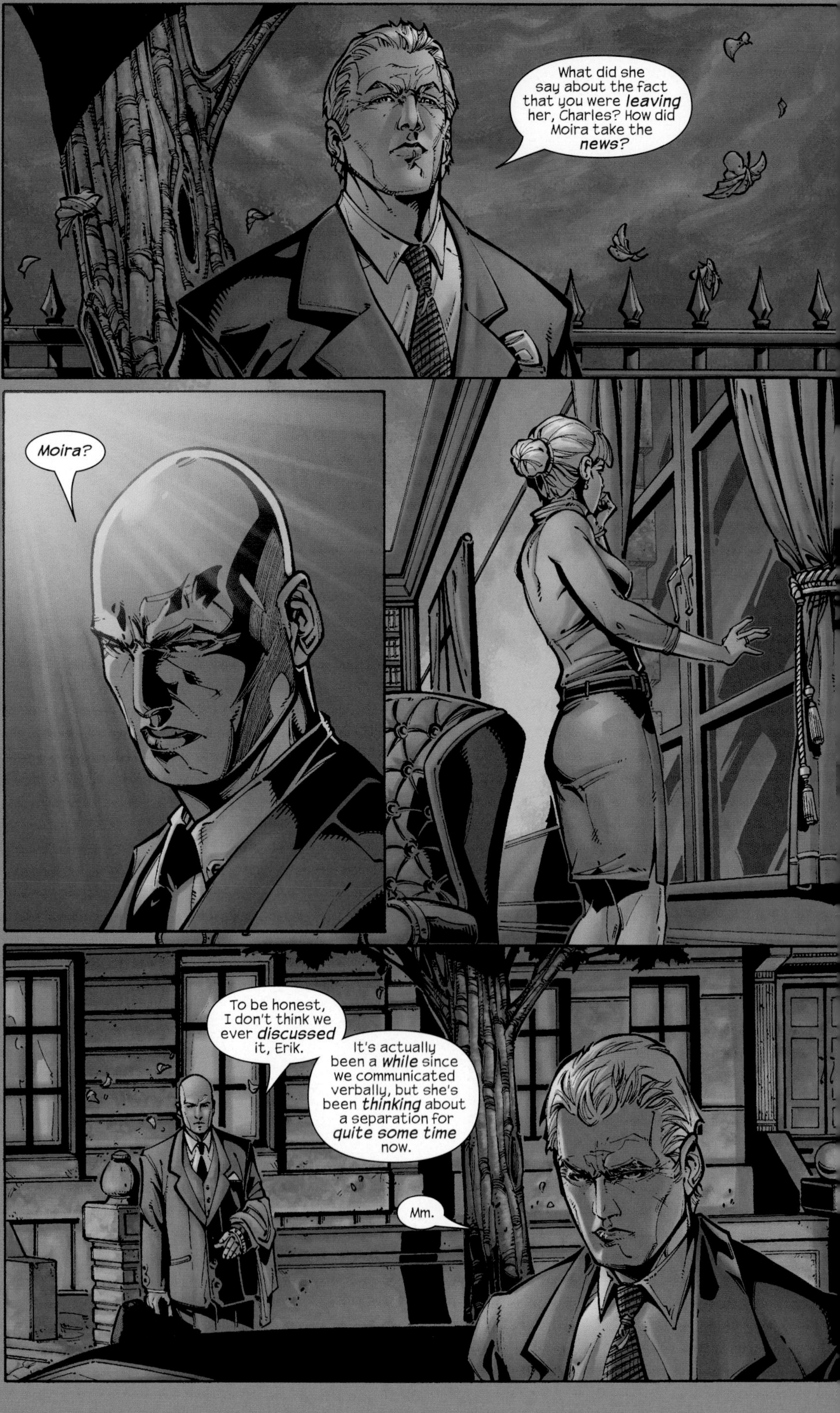
What did she say about the fact that you were *leaving* her, Charles? How did Moira take the *news?*
Moira?
To be honest, I don't think we ever *discussed* it, Erik.
It's actually been a *while* since we communicated verbally, but she's been *thinking* about a separation for *quite some time* now.
Mm.

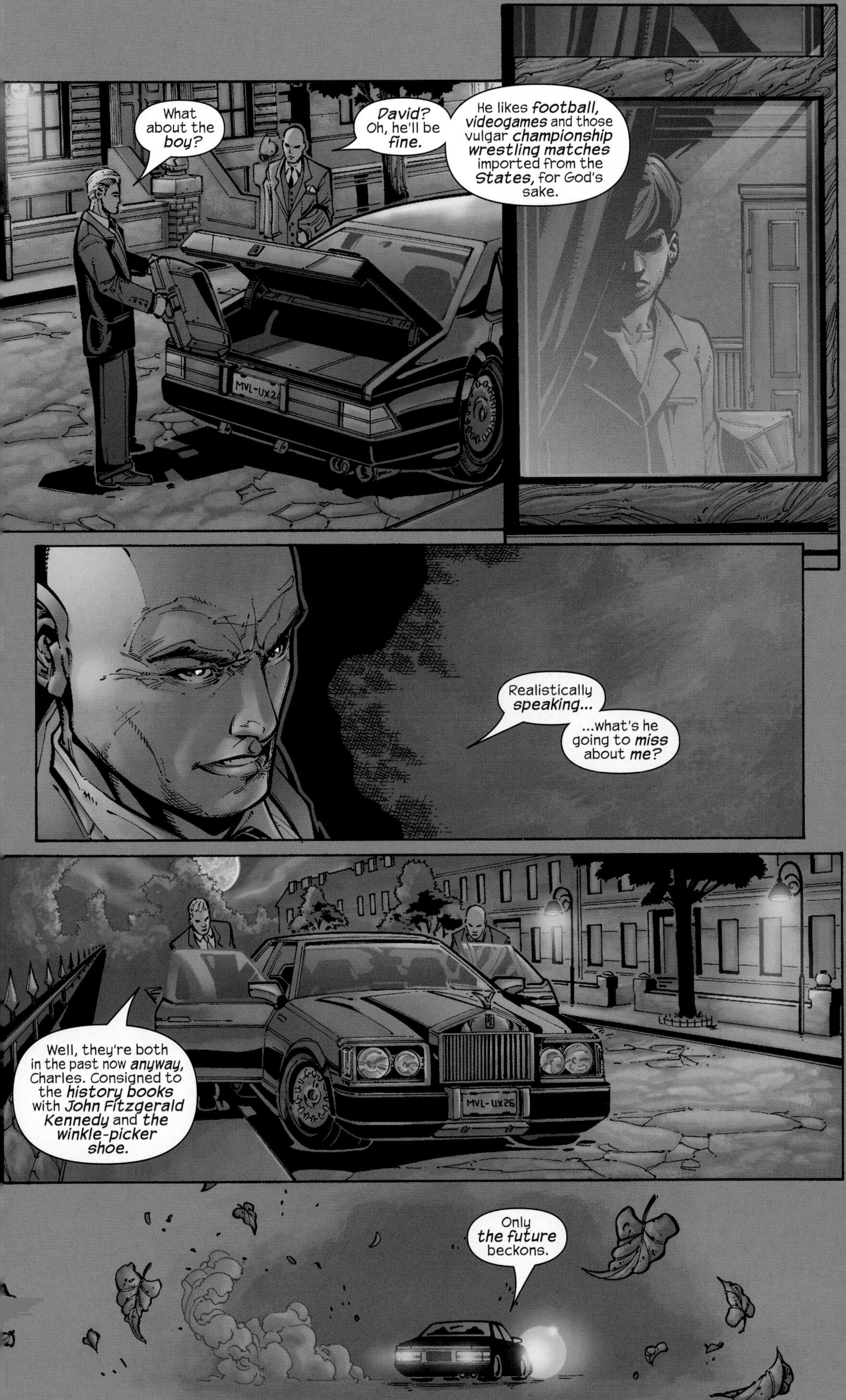

What about the boy?
David? Oh, he'll be fine.
He likes football, videogames and those vulgar championship wrestling matches imported from the States, for God's sake.
MVL-UX26
Realistically speaking...
...what's he going to miss about me?
Well, they're both in the past now anyway, Charles. Consigned to the history books with John Fitzgerald Kennedy and the winkle-picker shoe.
MVL-UX26
Only the future beckons.

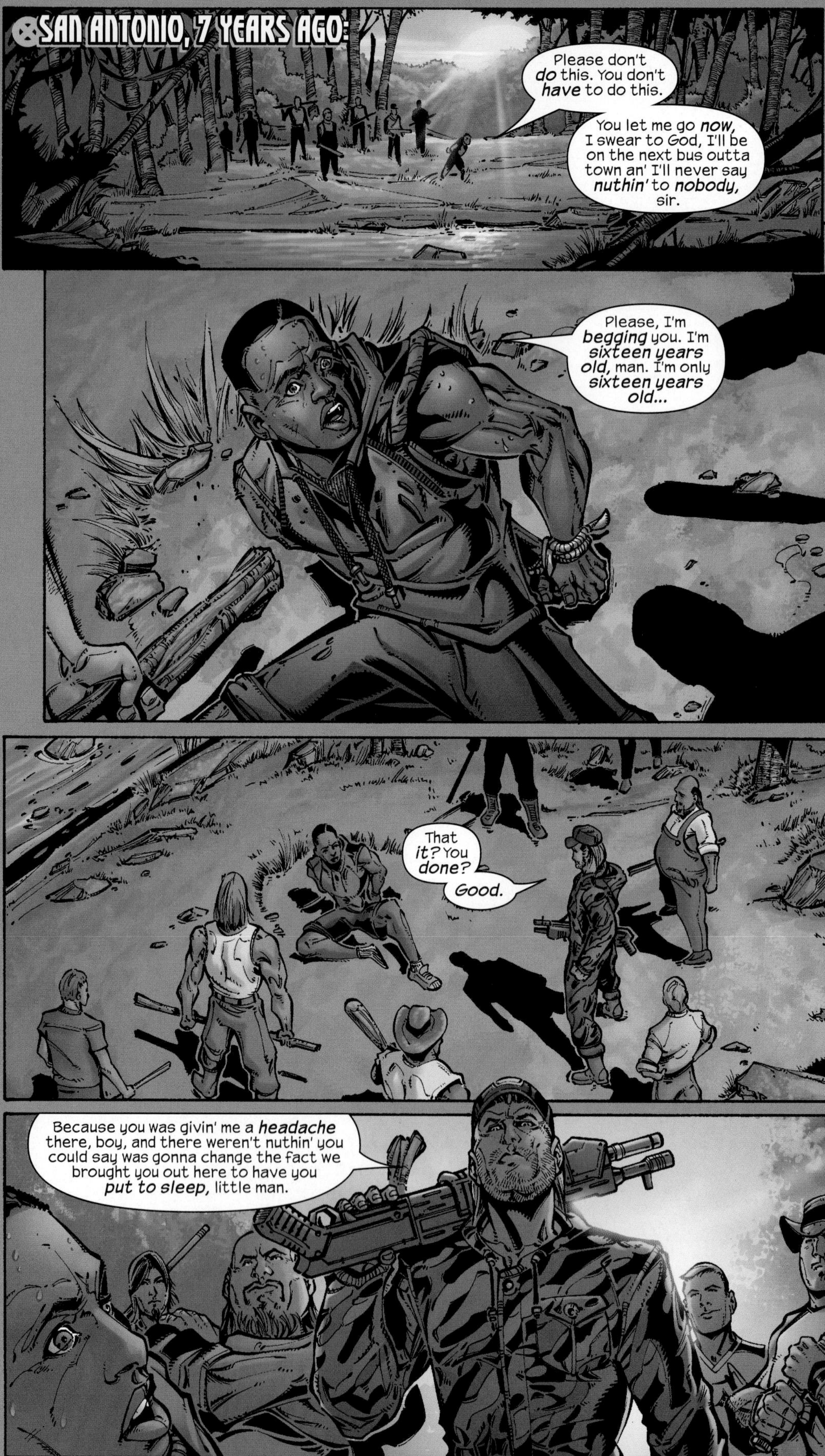
SAN ANTONIO, 7 YEARS AGO:
Please don't *do* this. You don't *have* to do this.
You let me go *now,* I swear to God, I'll be on the next bus outta town an' I'll never say *nuthin'* to *nobody,* sir.
Please, I'm *begging* you. I'm *sixteen years old,* man. I'm only *sixteen years old...*
That *it?* You *done?*
Good.
Because you was givin' me a *headache* there, boy, and there weren't nuthin' you could say was gonna change the fact we brought you out here to have you *put to sleep,* little man.

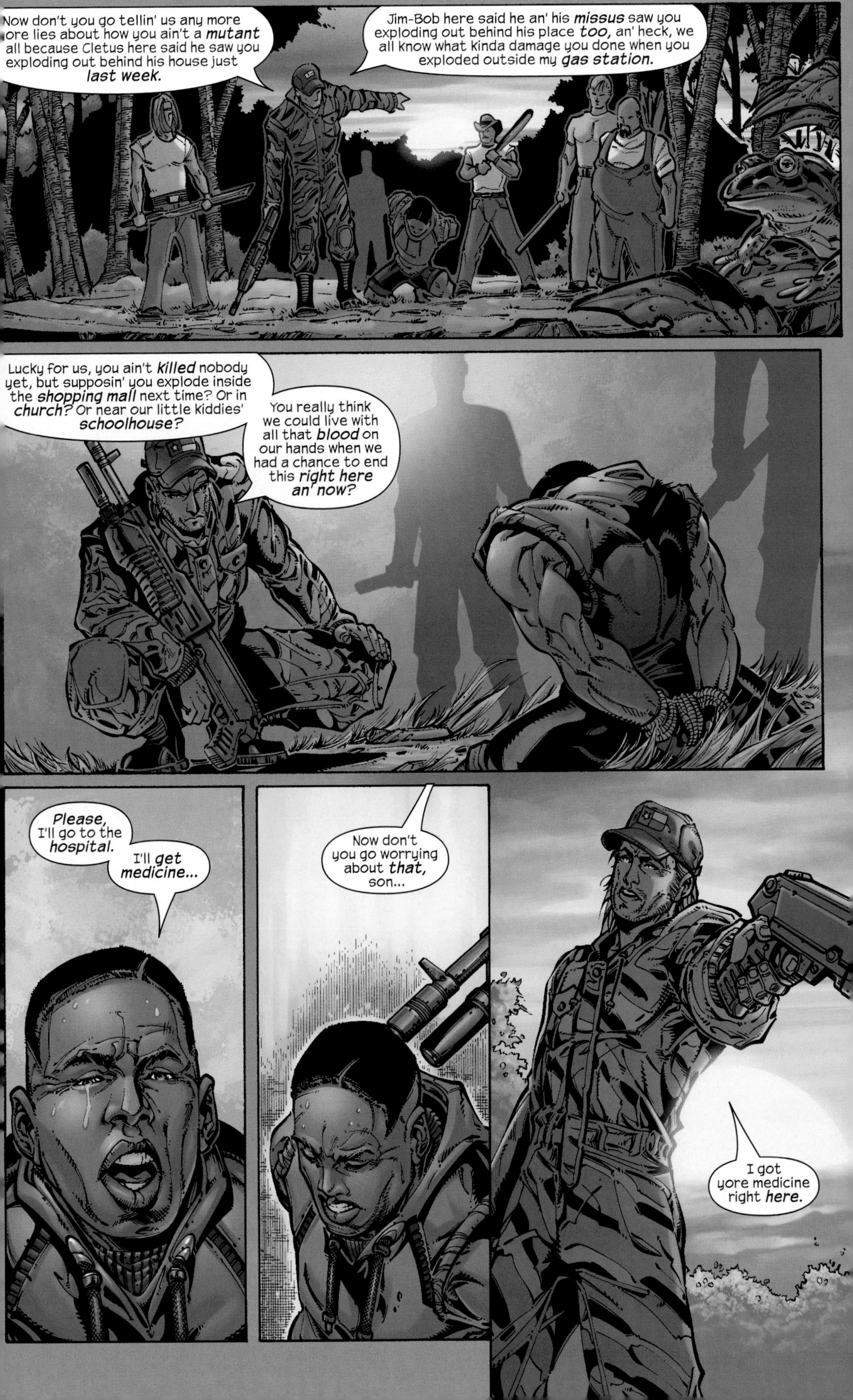

Now don't you go tellin' us any more ore lies about how you ain't a *mutant* all because Cletus here said he saw you exploding out behind his house just *last week.*
Jim-Bob here said he an' his *missus* saw you exploding out behind his place *too,* an' heck, we all know what kinda damage you done when you exploded outside my *gas station.*
Lucky for us, you ain't *killed* nobody yet, but supposin' you explode inside the *shopping mall* next time? Or in *church*? Or near our little kiddies' *schoolhouse?*
You really think we could live with all that *blood* on our hands when we had a chance to end this *right here an' now?*
Please, I'll go to the *hospital.*
I'll *get medicine...*
Now don't you go worrying about *that,* son...
I got yore medicine right *here.*

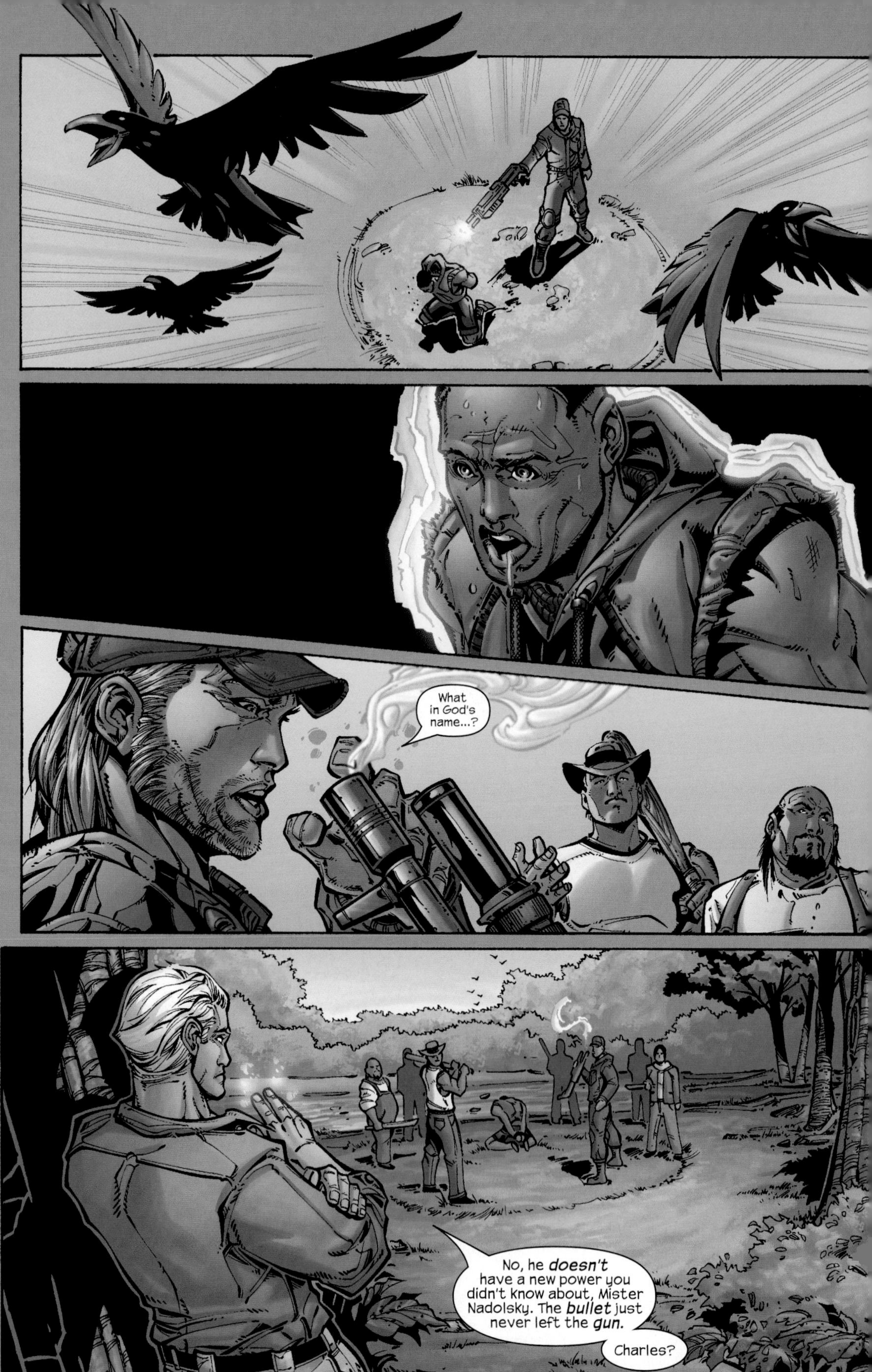
What in God's name...?
No, he *doesn't* have a new power you didn't know about, Mister Nadolsky. The *bullet* just never left the *gun*.
Charles?

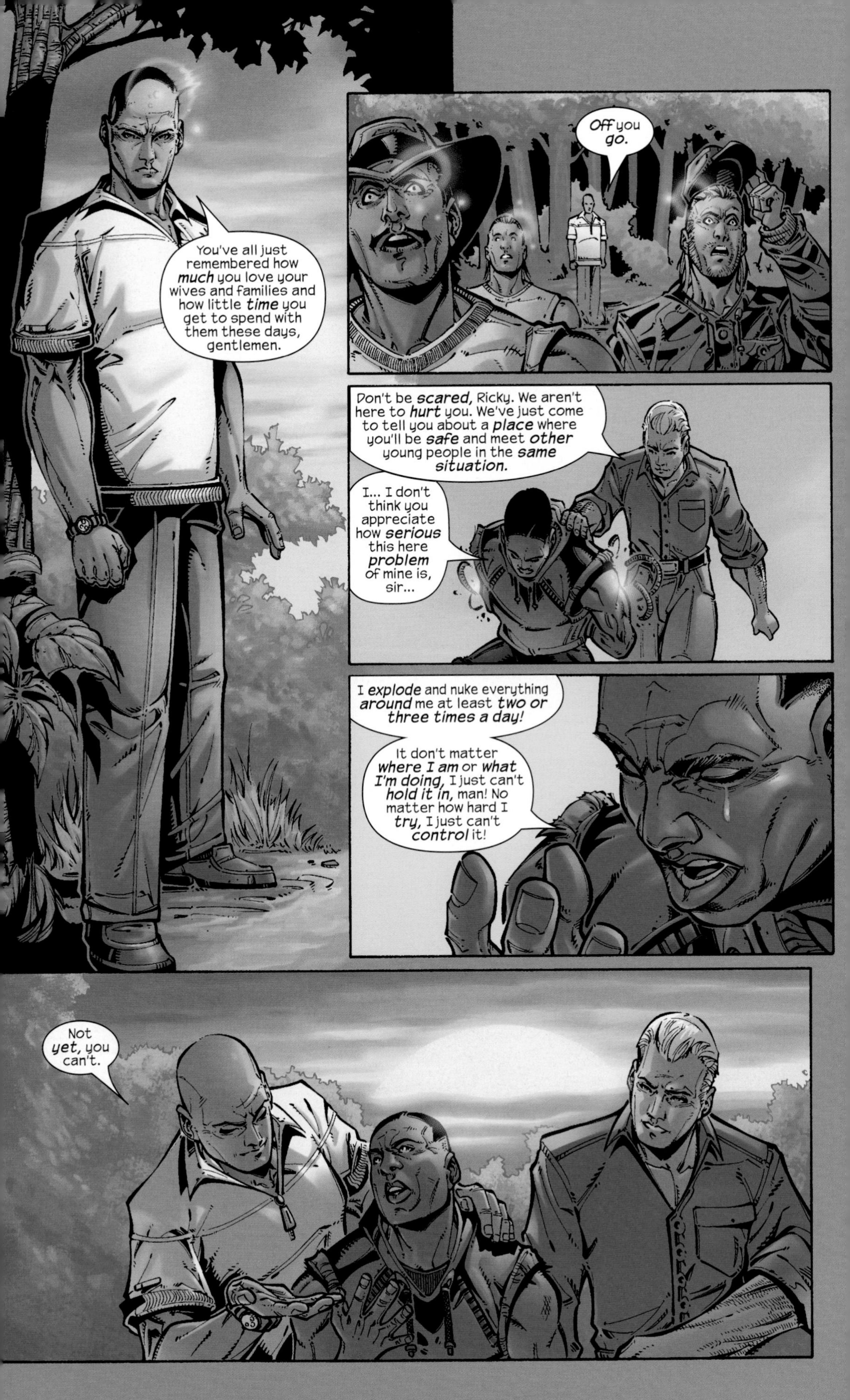

You've all just remembered how *much* you love your wives and families and how little *time* you get to spend with them these days, gentlemen.
Off you *go.*
Don't be *scared,* Ricky. We aren't here to *hurt* you. We've just come to tell you about a *place* where you'll be *safe* and meet *other* young people in the *same situation.*
I... I don't think you appreciate how *serious* this here *problem* of mine is, sir...
I *explode* and nuke everything *around* me at least *two or three times a day!*
It don't matter *where I am* or *what I'm doing,* I just can't *hold it in,* man! No matter how hard I *try,* I just can't *control* it!
Not *yet,* you can't.

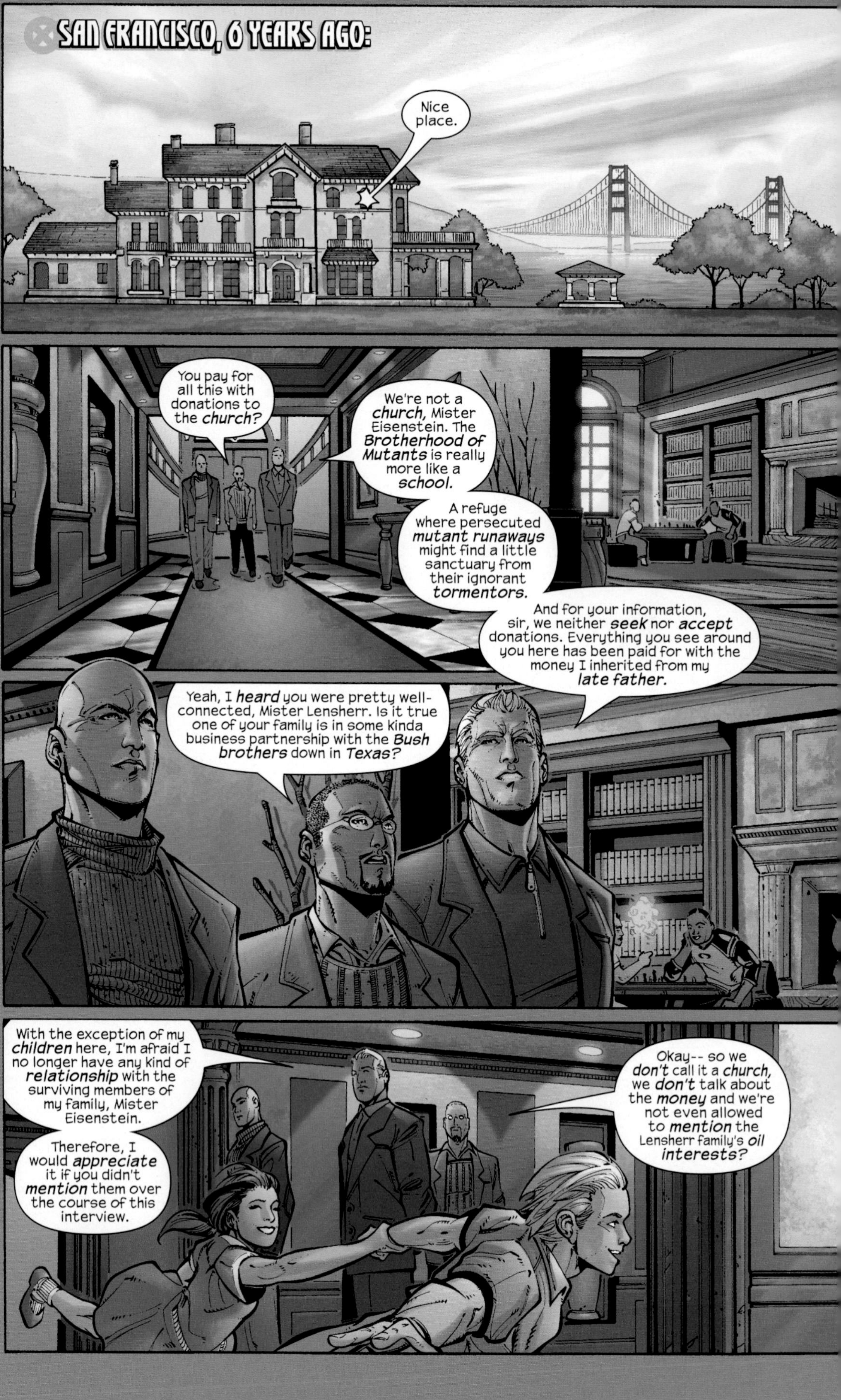
SAN FRANCISCO, 6 YEARS AGO:
Nice place.
You pay for all this with donations to the church?
We're not a church, Mister Eisenstein. The Brotherhood of Mutants is really more like a school.
A refuge where persecuted mutant runaways might find a little sanctuary from their ignorant tormentors.
And for your information, sir, we neither seek nor accept donations. Everything you see around you here has been paid for with the money I inherited from my late father.
Yeah, I heard you were pretty well-connected, Mister Lensherr. Is it true one of your family is in some kinda business partnership with the Bush brothers down in Texas?
With the exception of my children here, I'm afraid I no longer have any kind of relationship with the surviving members of my family, Mister Eisenstein.
Therefore, I would appreciate it if you didn't mention them over the course of this interview.
Okay-- so we don't call it a church, we don't talk about the money and we're not even allowed to mention the Lensherr family's oil interests?

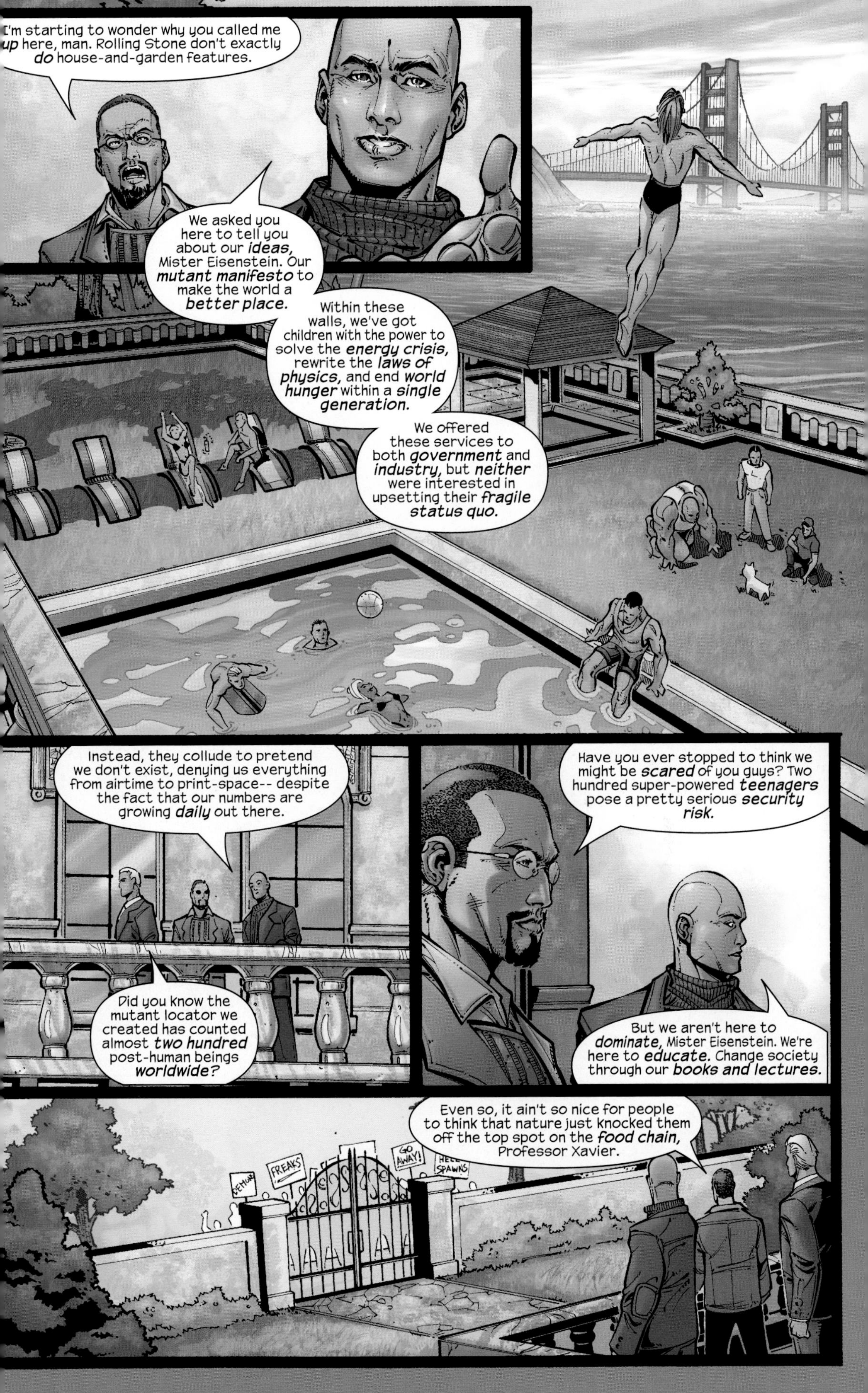

I'm starting to wonder why you called me up here, man. Rolling Stone don't exactly do house-and-garden features.
We asked you here to tell you about our ideas, Mister Eisenstein. Our mutant manifesto to make the world a better place.
Within these walls, we've got children with the power to solve the energy crisis, rewrite the laws of physics, and end world hunger within a single generation.
We offered these services to both government and industry, but neither were interested in upsetting their fragile status quo.
Instead, they collude to pretend we don't exist, denying us everything from airtime to print-space-- despite the fact that our numbers are growing daily out there.
Did you know the mutant locator we created has counted almost two hundred post-human beings worldwide?
Have you ever stopped to think we might be scared of you guys? Two hundred super-powered teenagers pose a pretty serious security risk.
But we aren't here to dominate, Mister Eisenstein. We're here to educate. Change society through our books and lectures.
Even so, it ain't so nice for people to think that nature just knocked them off the top spot on the food chain, Professor Xavier.
DEMON
FREAKS
GO AWAY!
SPAWNS

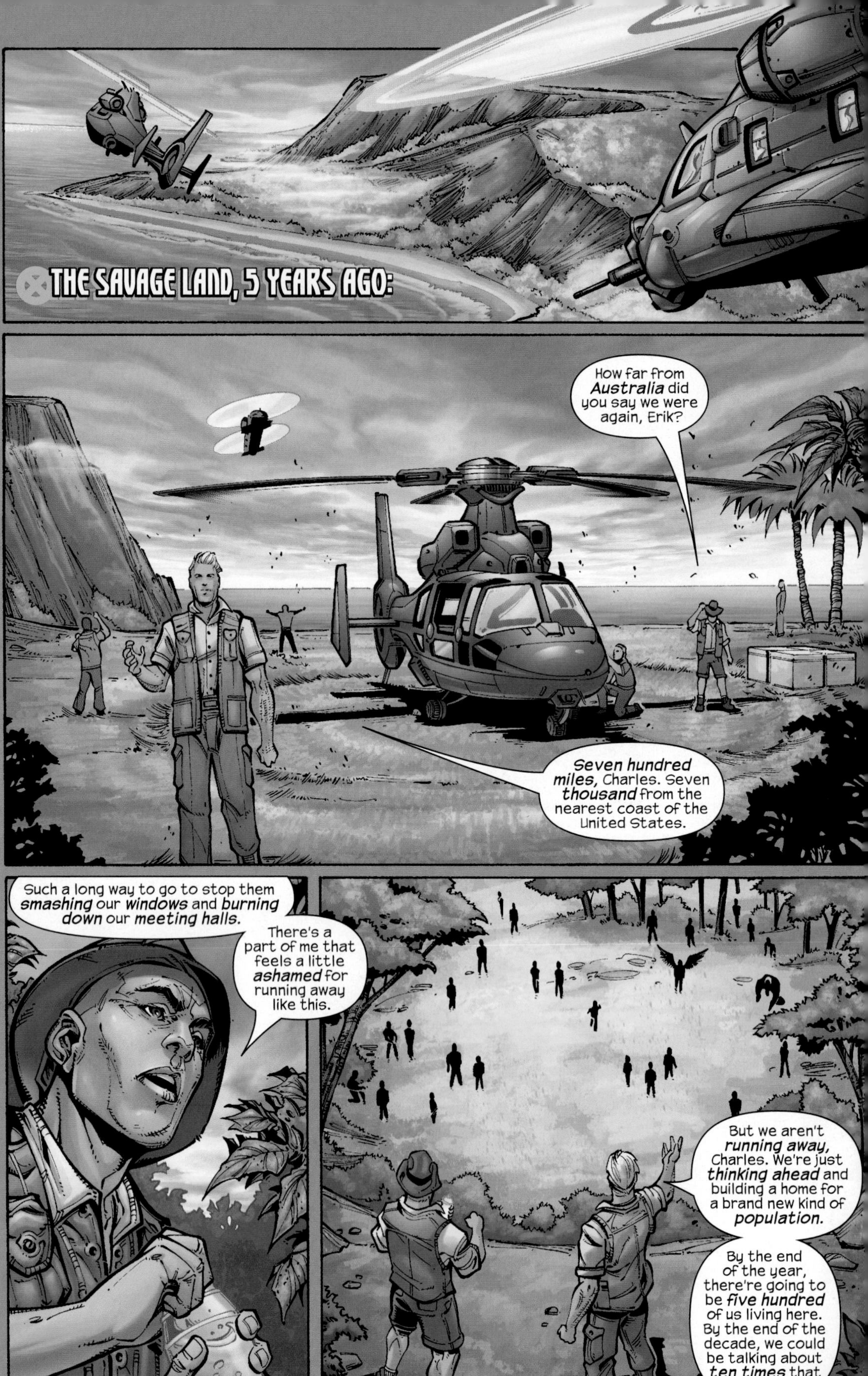
THE SAVAGE LAND, 5 YEARS AGO:
How far from *Australia* did you say we were again, Erik?
Seven hundred miles, Charles. Seven *thousand* from the nearest coast of the United States.
Such a long way to go to stop them *smashing* our *windows* and *burning down* our *meeting halls.*
There's a part of me that feels a little *ashamed* for running away like this.
But we aren't *running away,* Charles. We're just *thinking ahead* and building a home for a brand new kind of *population.*
By the end of the year, there're going to be *five hundred* of us living here. By the end of the decade, we could be talking about *ten times* that number.

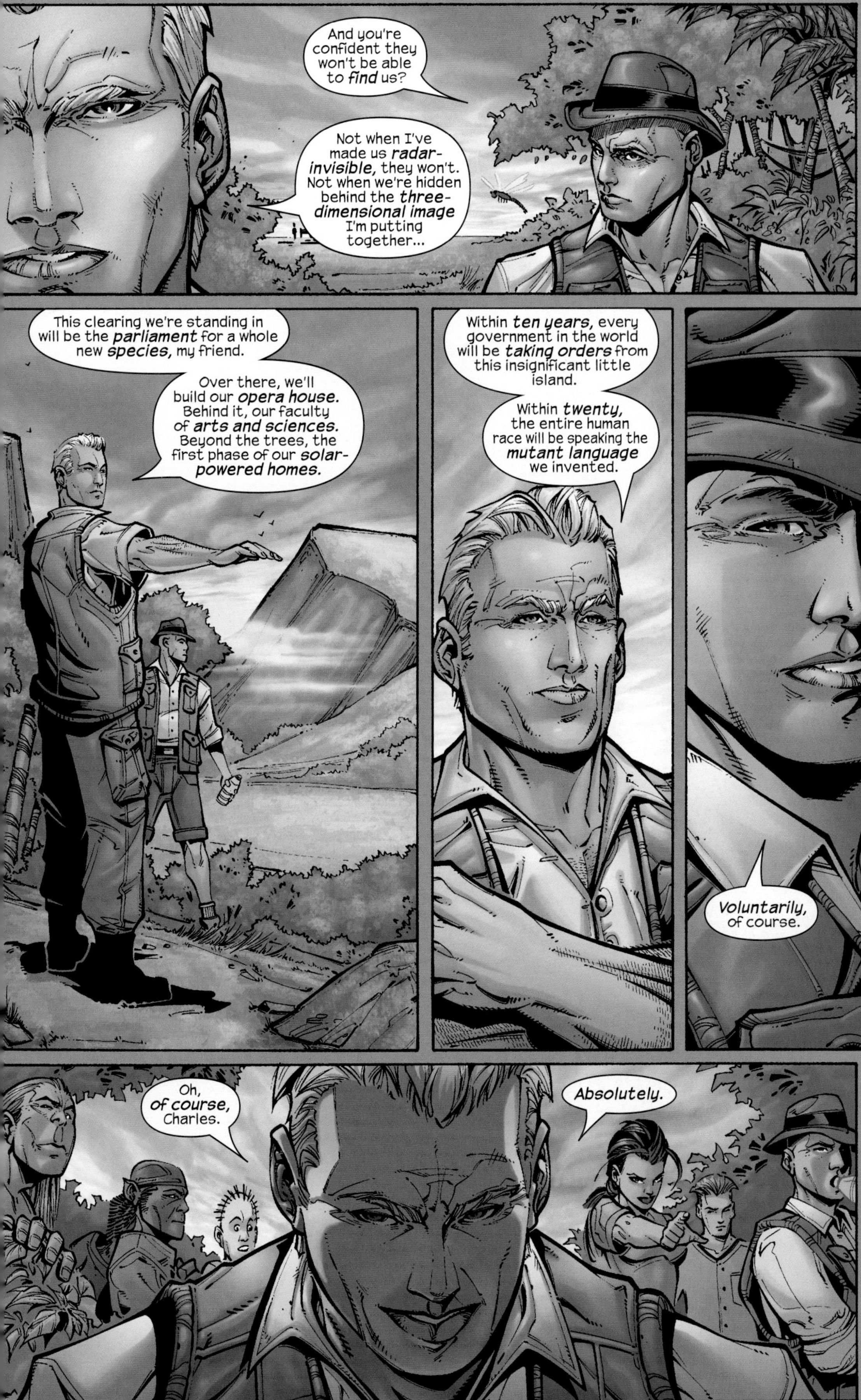
And you're confident they won't be able to *find* us?
Not when I've made us *radar-invisible,* they won't. Not when we're hidden behind the *three-dimensional image* I'm putting together...
This clearing we're standing in will be the *parliament* for a whole new *species,* my friend.
Over there, we'll build our *opera house.* Behind it, our faculty of *arts and sciences.* Beyond the trees, the first phase of our *solar-powered homes.*
Within *ten years,* every government in the world will be *taking orders* from this insignificant little island.
Within *twenty,* the entire human race will be speaking the *mutant language* we invented.
Voluntarily, of course.
Oh, *of course,* Charles.
Absolutely.

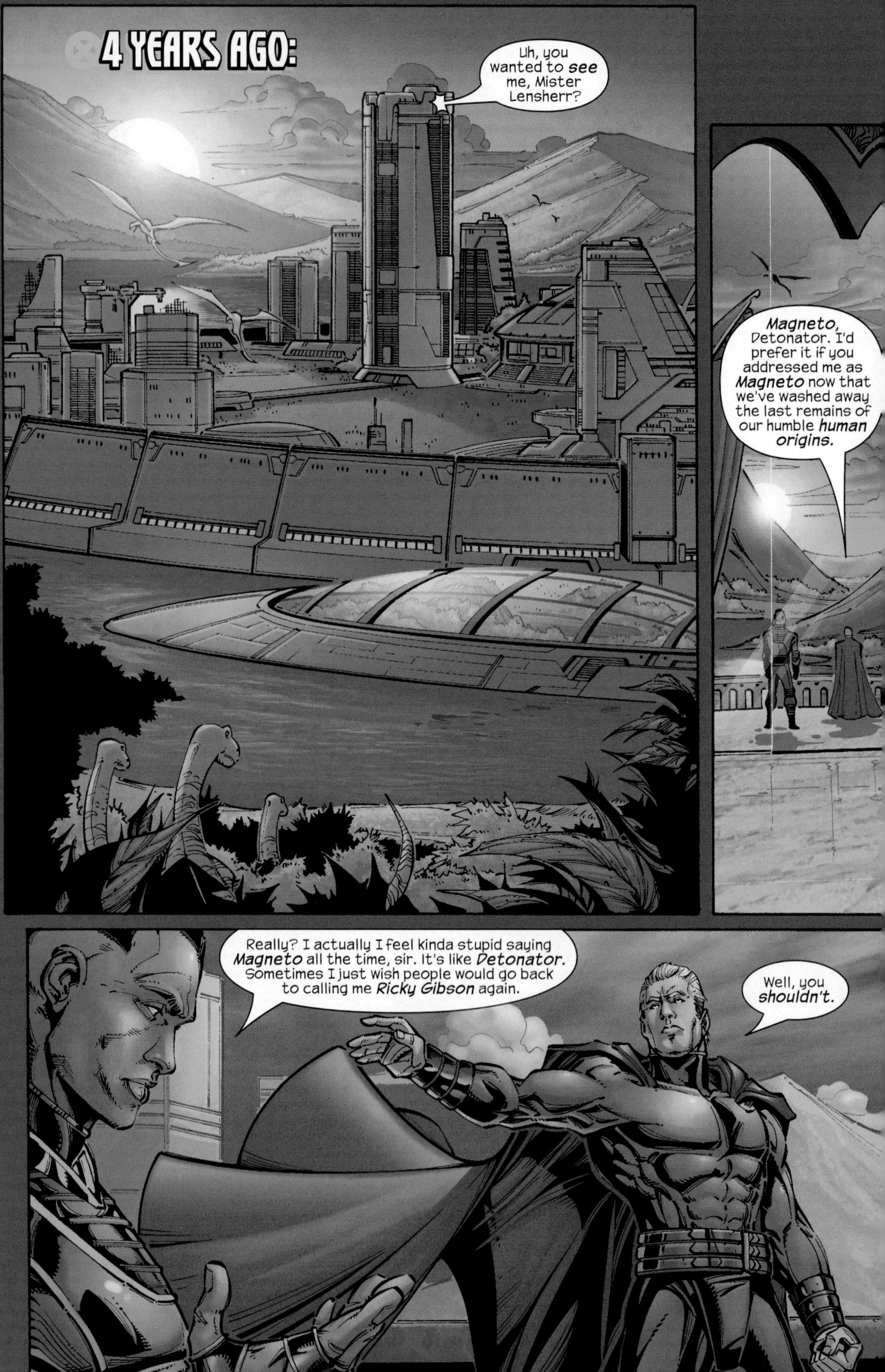
4 YEARS AGO:
Uh, you wanted to see me, Mister Lensherr?
Magneto, Detonator. I'd prefer it if you addressed me as Magneto now that we've washed away the last remains of our humble human origins.
Really? I actually I feel kinda stupid saying Magneto all the time, sir. It's like Detonator. Sometimes I just wish people would go back to calling me Ricky Gibson again.
Well, you shouldn't.

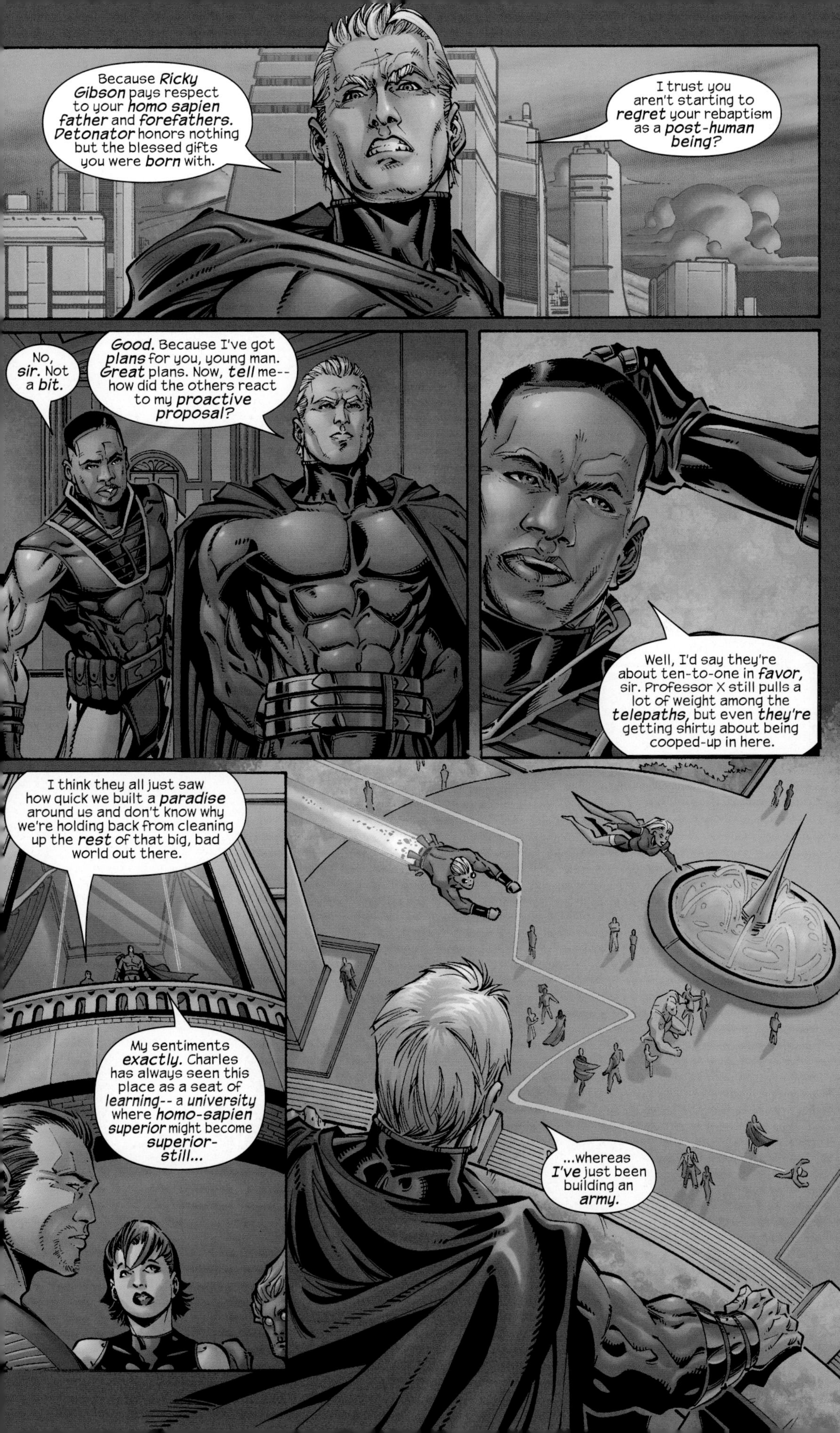

Because Ricky Gibson pays respect to your homo sapien father and forefathers. Detonator honors nothing but the blessed gifts you were born with.
I trust you aren't starting to regret your rebaptism as a post-human being?
No, sir. Not a bit.
Good. Because I've got plans for you, young man. Great plans. Now, tell me-- how did the others react to my proactive proposal?
Well, I'd say they're about ten-to-one in favor, sir. Professor X still pulls a lot of weight among the telepaths, but even they're getting shirty about being cooped-up in here.
I think they all just saw how quick we built a paradise around us and don't know why we're holding back from cleaning up the rest of that big, bad world out there.
My sentiments exactly. Charles has always seen this place as a seat of learning-- a university where homo-sapien superior might become superior-still...
...whereas I've just been building an army.

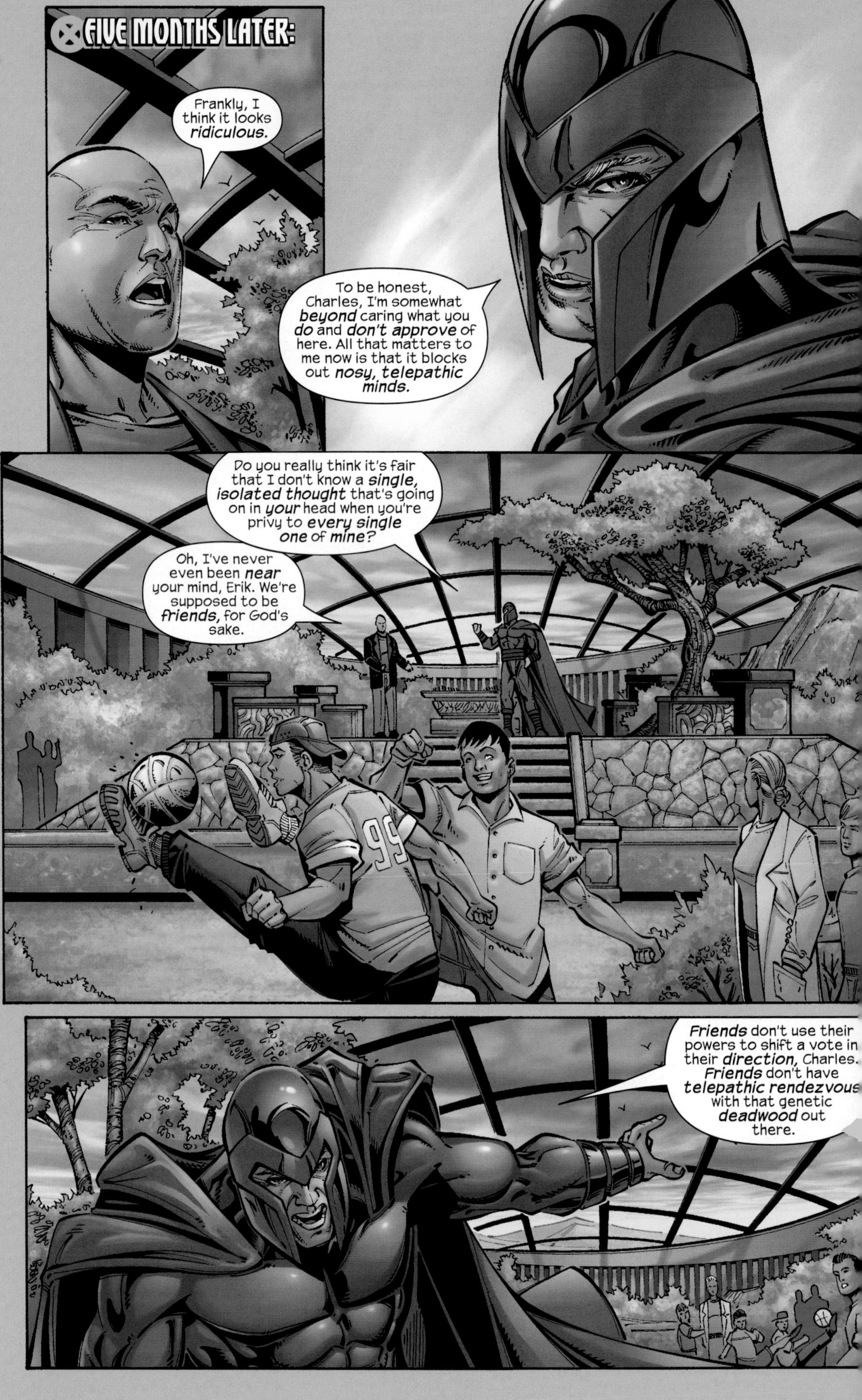
FIVE MONTHS LATER:
Frankly, I think it looks ridiculous.
To be honest, Charles, I'm somewhat beyond caring what you do and don't approve of here. All that matters to me now is that it blocks out nosy, telepathic minds.
Do you really think it's fair that I don't know a single, isolated thought that's going on in your head when you're privy to every single one of mine?
Oh, I've never even been near your mind, Erik. We're supposed to be friends, for God's sake.
99
Friends don't use their powers to shift a vote in their direction, Charles. Friends don't have telepathic rendezvous with that genetic deadwood out there.

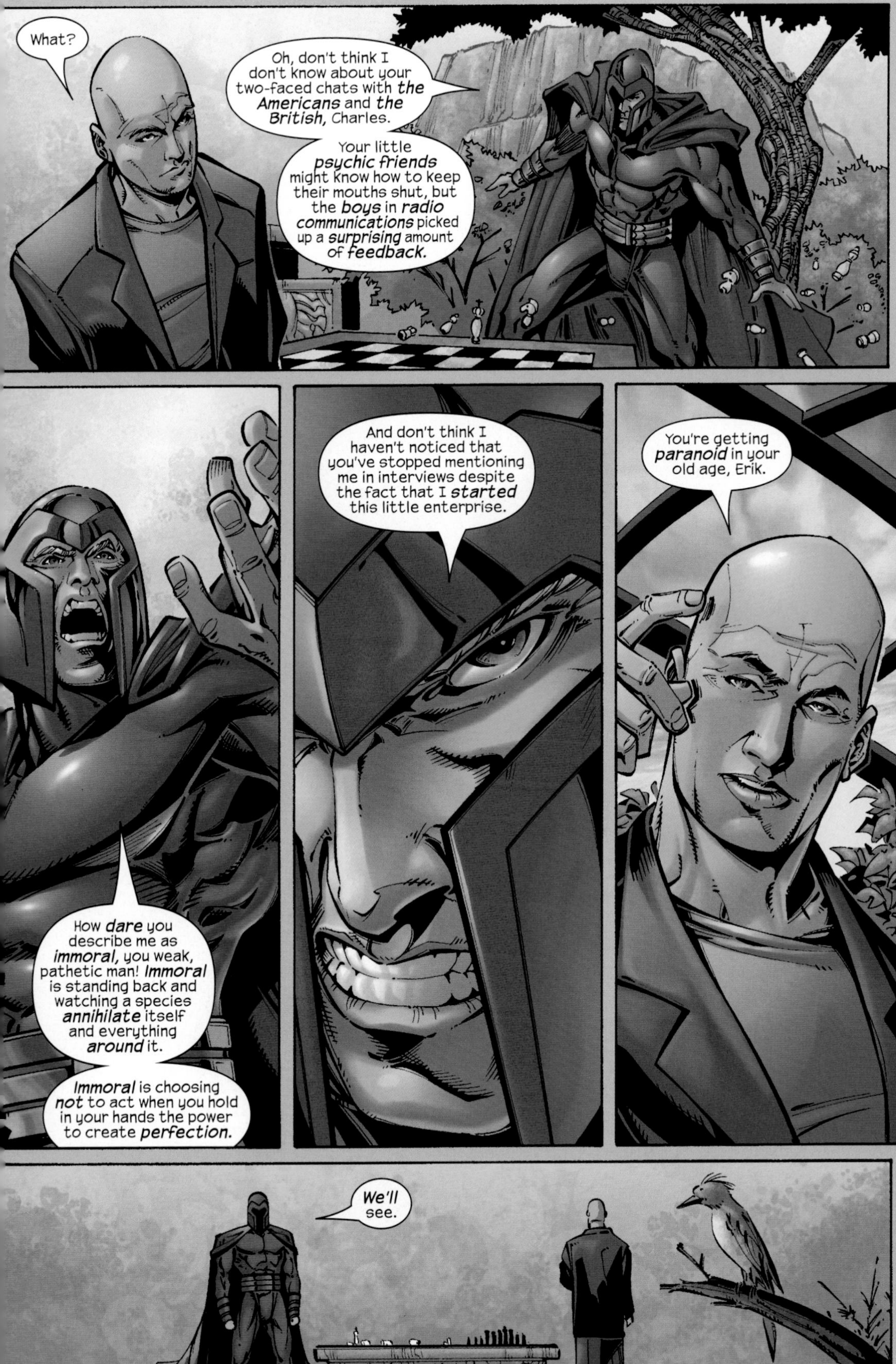
What?
Oh, don't think I don't know about your two-faced chats with the Americans and the British, Charles.
Your little psychic friends might know how to keep their mouths shut, but the boys in radio communications picked up a surprising amount of feedback.
How dare you describe me as immoral, you weak, pathetic man! Immoral is standing back and watching a species annihilate itself and everything around it.
Immoral is choosing not to act when you hold in your hands the power to create perfection.
And don't think I haven't noticed that you've stopped mentioning me in interviews despite the fact that I started this little enterprise.
You're getting paranoid in your old age, Erik.
We'll see.

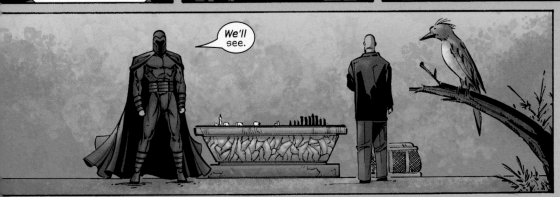

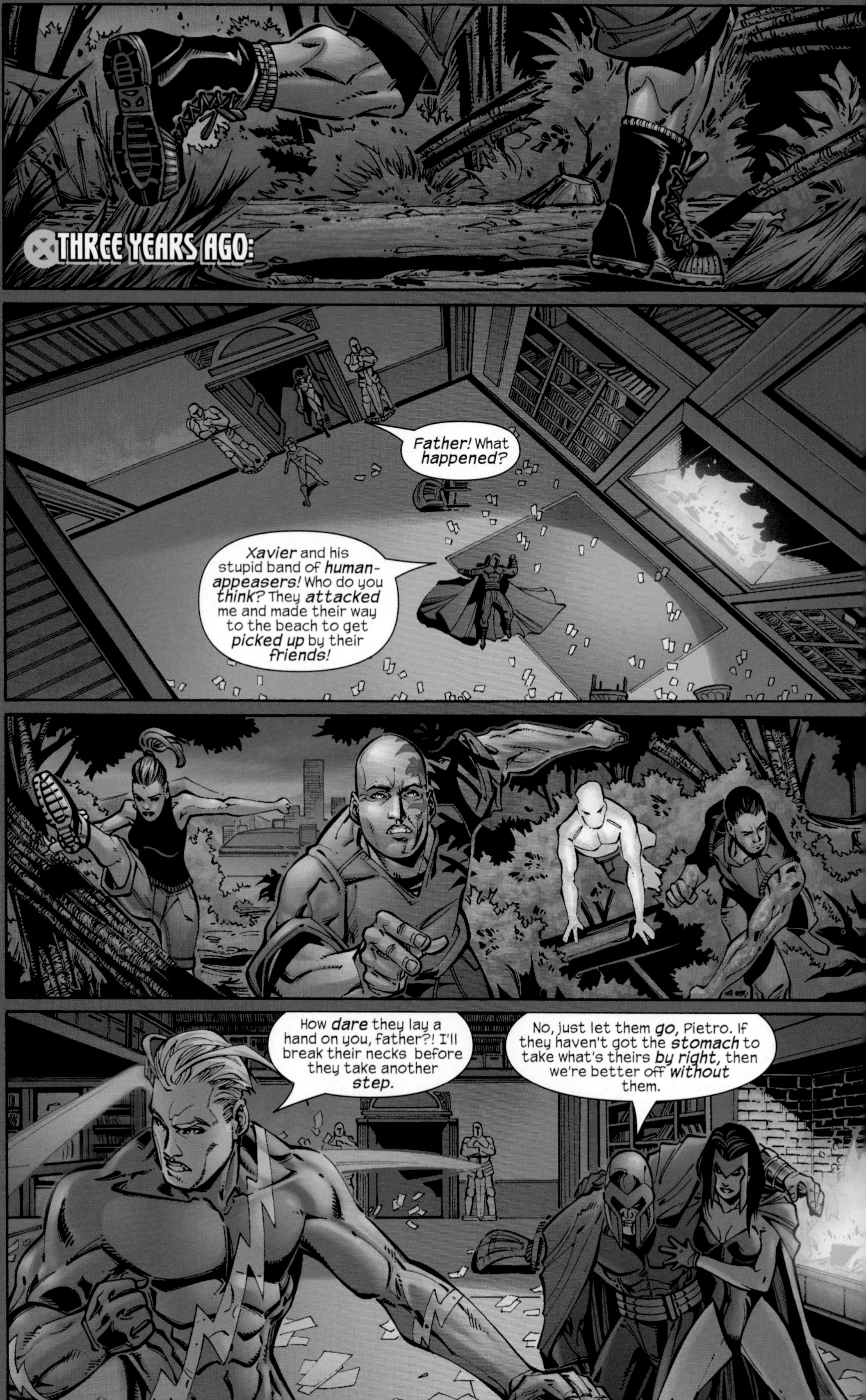
THREE YEARS AGO:
Father! What happened?
Xavier and his stupid band of human-appeasers! Who do you think? They attacked me and made their way to the beach to get picked up by their friends!
How dare they lay a hand on you, father?! I'll break their necks before they take another step.
No, just let them go, Pietro. If they haven't got the stomach to take what's theirs by right, then we're better off without them.

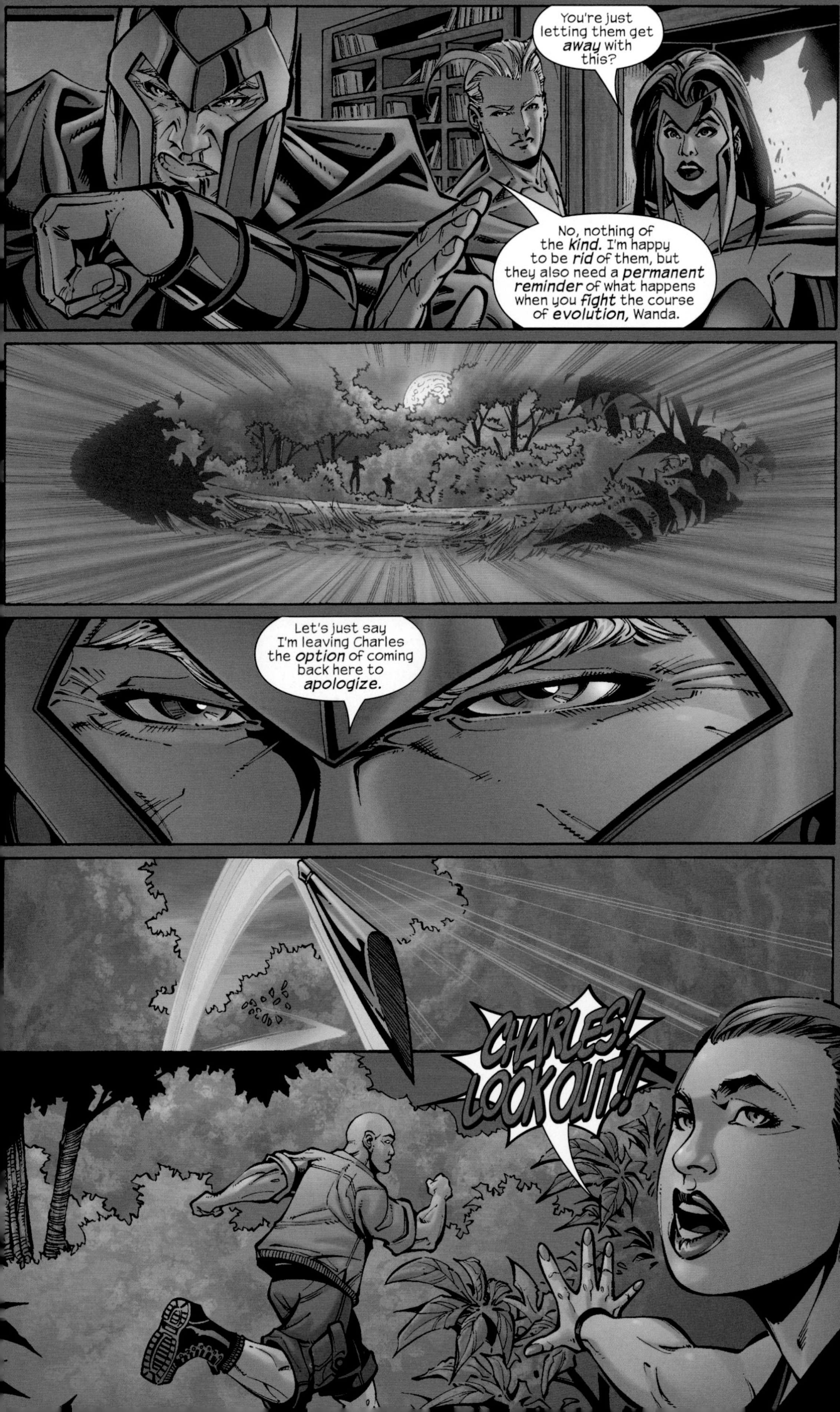
You're just letting them get *away* with this?
No, nothing of the *kind.* I'm happy to be *rid* of them, but they also need a *permanent reminder* of what happens when you *fight* the course of *evolution,* Wanda.
Let's just say I'm leaving Charles the *option* of coming back here to *apologize.*
CHARLES! LOOK OUT!!

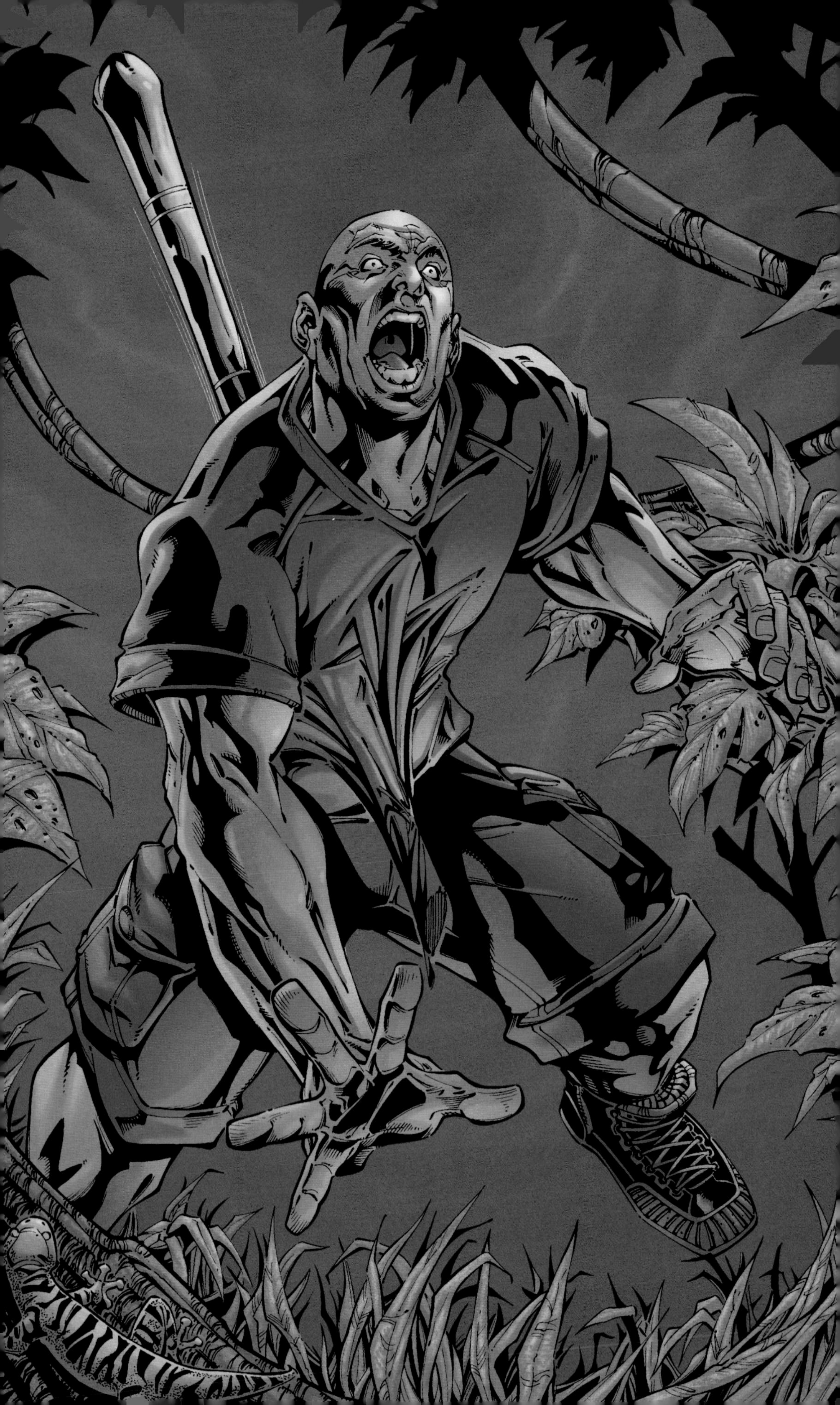

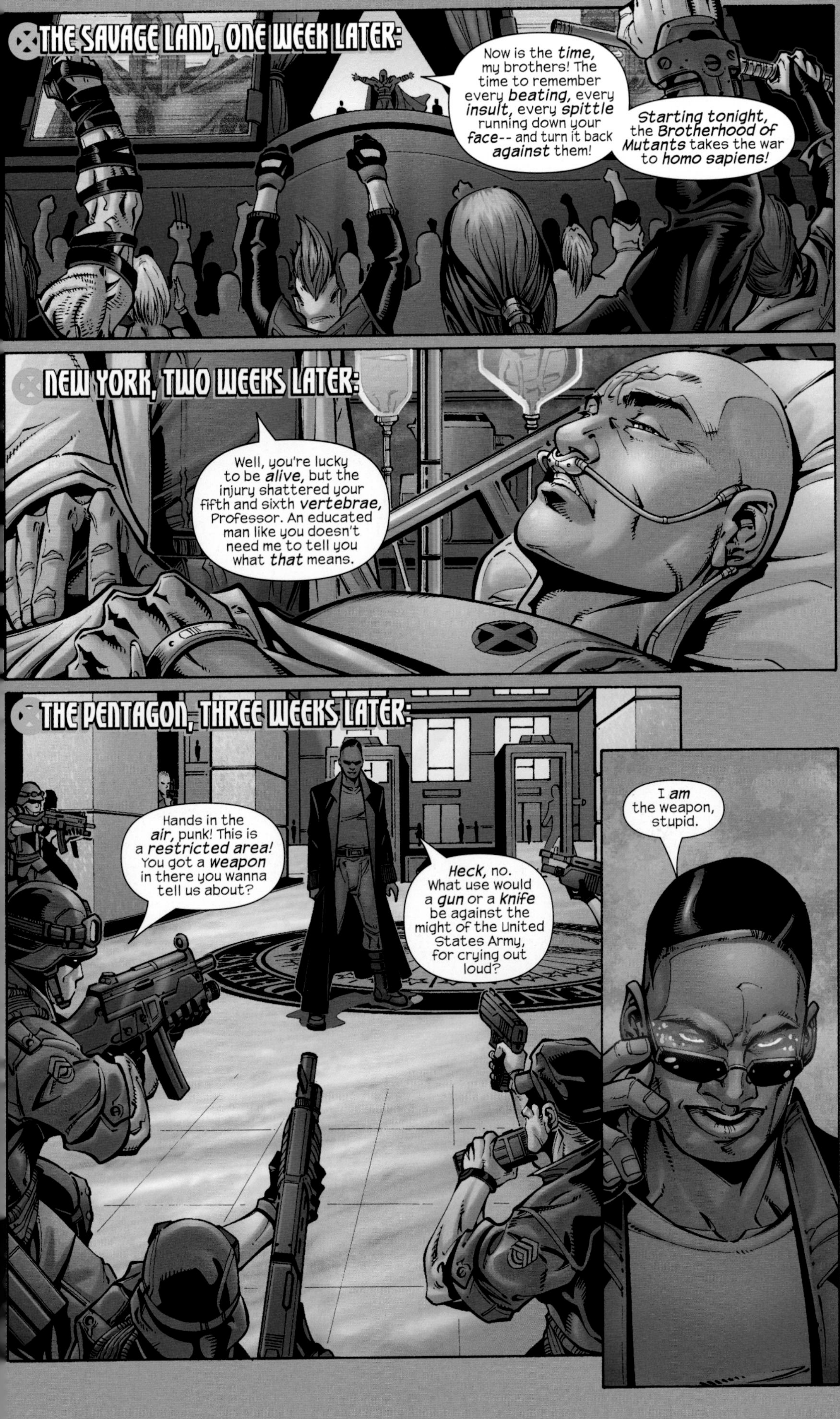
THE SAVAGE LAND, ONE WEEK LATER:
Now is the time, my brothers! The time to remember every beating, every insult, every spittle running down your face-- and turn it back against them!
Starting tonight, the Brotherhood of Mutants takes the war to homo sapiens!
NEW YORK, TWO WEEKS LATER:
Well, you're lucky to be alive, but the injury shattered your fifth and sixth vertebrae, Professor. An educated man like you doesn't need me to tell you what that means.
THE PENTAGON, THREE WEEKS LATER:
Hands in the air, punk! This is a restricted area! You got a weapon in there you wanna tell us about?
Heck, no. What use would a gun or a knife be against the might of the United States Army, for crying out loud?
I am the weapon, stupid.

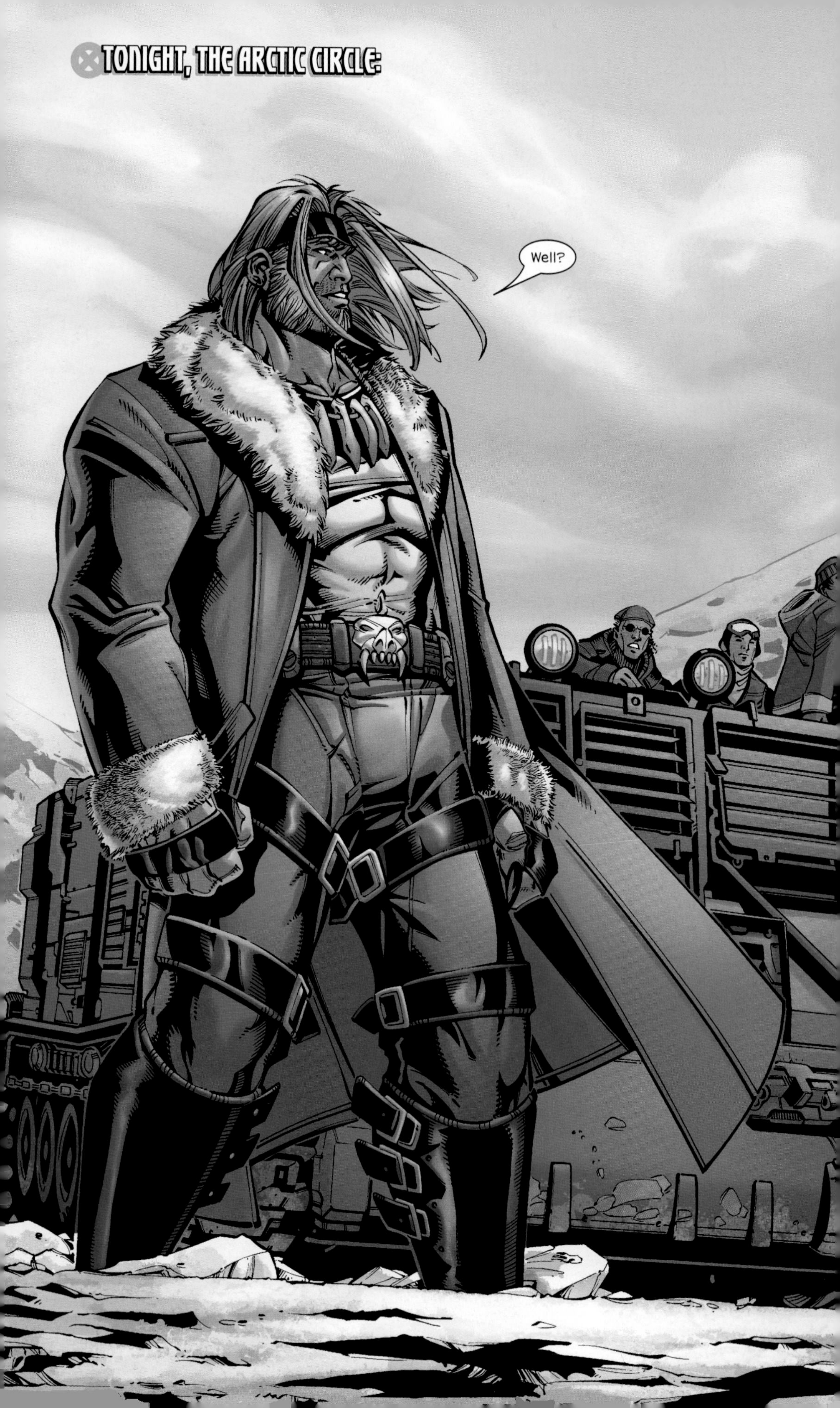
TONIGHT, THE ARCTIC CIRCLE:
Well?

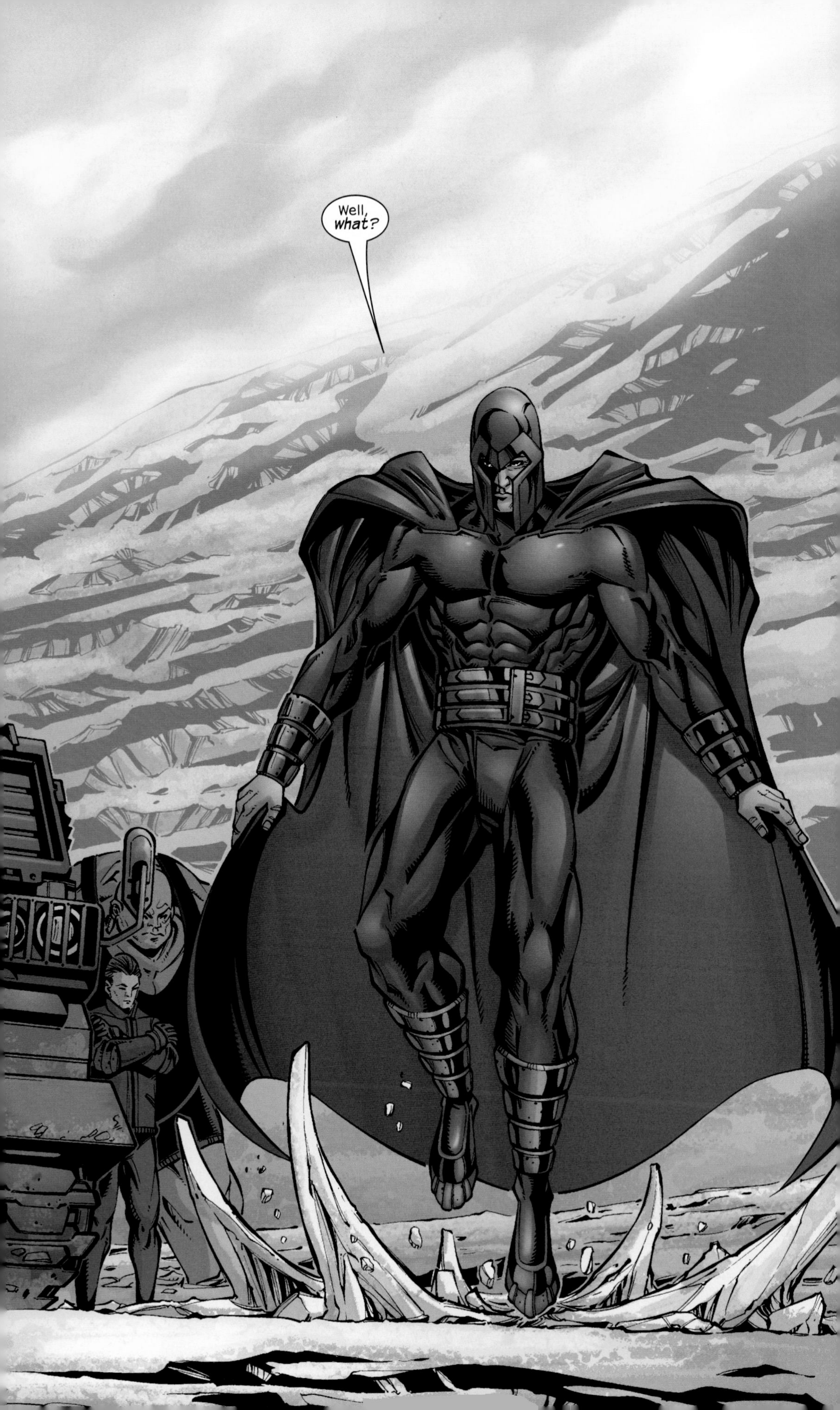
Well, *what?*

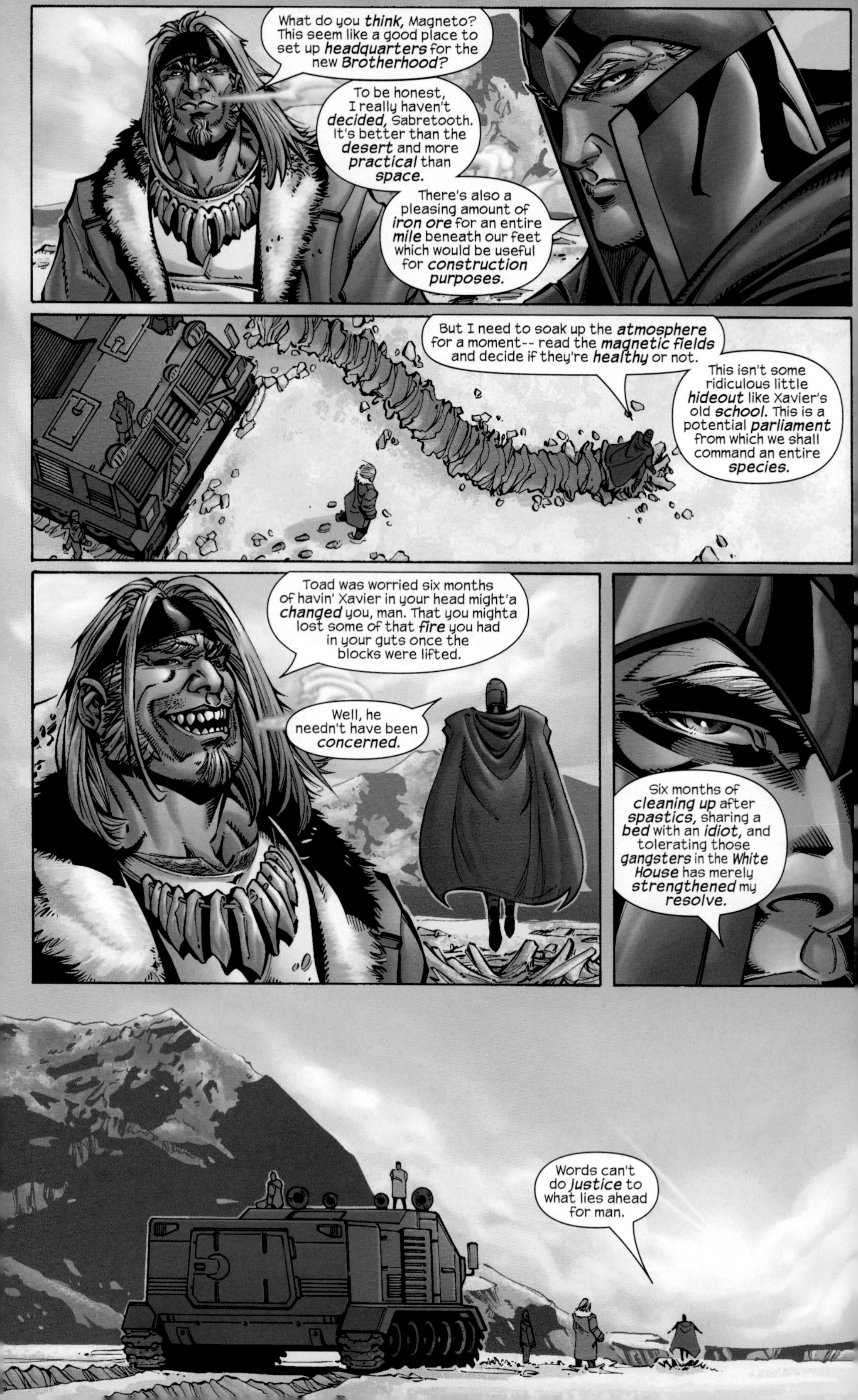
What do you think, Magneto? This seem like a good place to set up headquarters for the new Brotherhood?
To be honest, I really haven't decided, Sabretooth. It's better than the desert and more practical than space.
There's also a pleasing amount of iron ore for an entire mile beneath our feet which would be useful for construction purposes.
But I need to soak up the atmosphere for a moment-- read the magnetic fields and decide if they're healthy or not.
This isn't some ridiculous little hideout like Xavier's old school. This is a potential parliament from which we shall command an entire species.
Toad was worried six months of havin' Xavier in your head might'a changed you, man. That you mighta lost some of that fire you had in your guts once the blocks were lifted.
Well, he needn't have been concerned.
Six months of cleaning up after spastics, sharing a bed with an idiot, and tolerating those gangsters in the White House has merely strengthened my resolve.
Words can't do justice to what lies ahead for man.

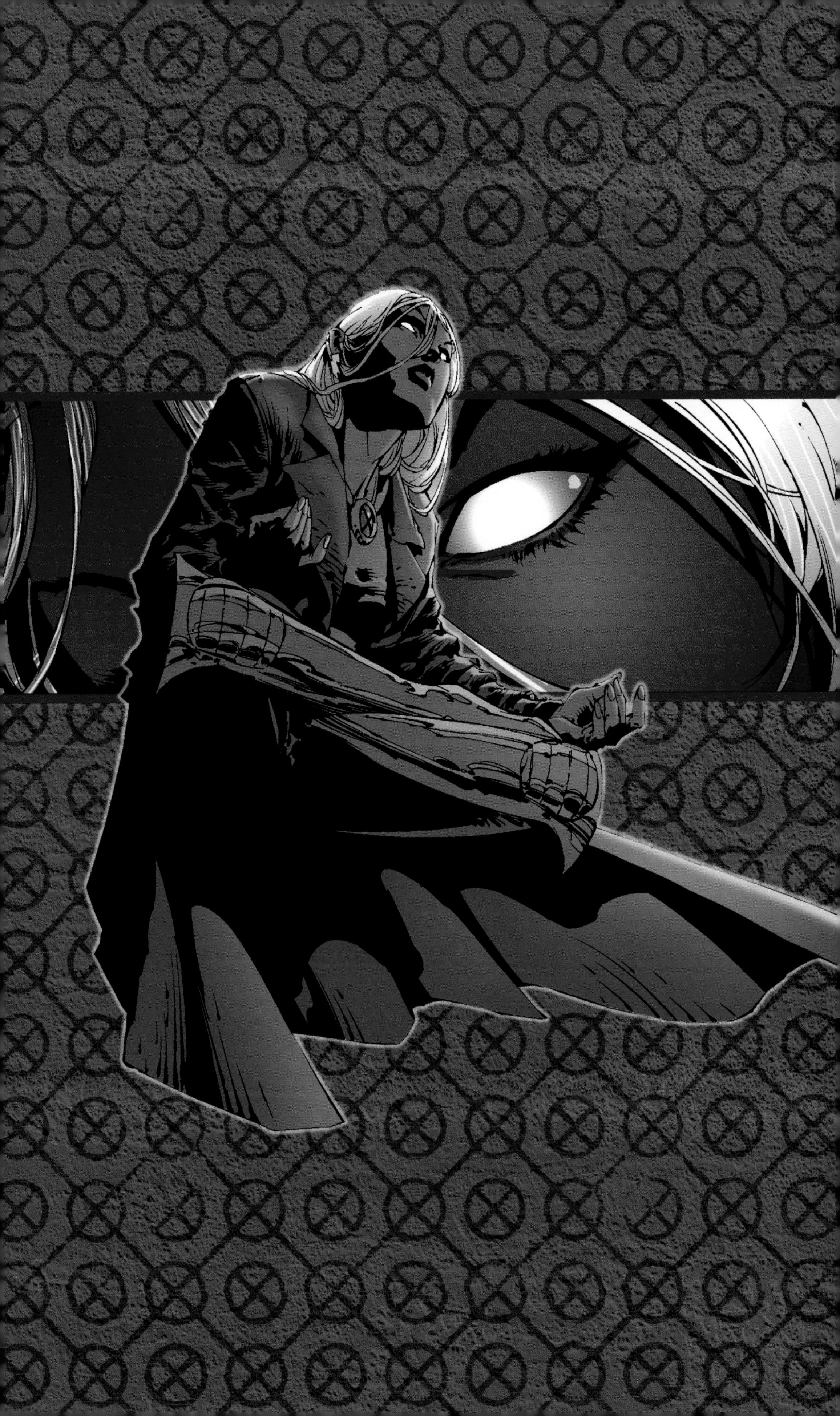

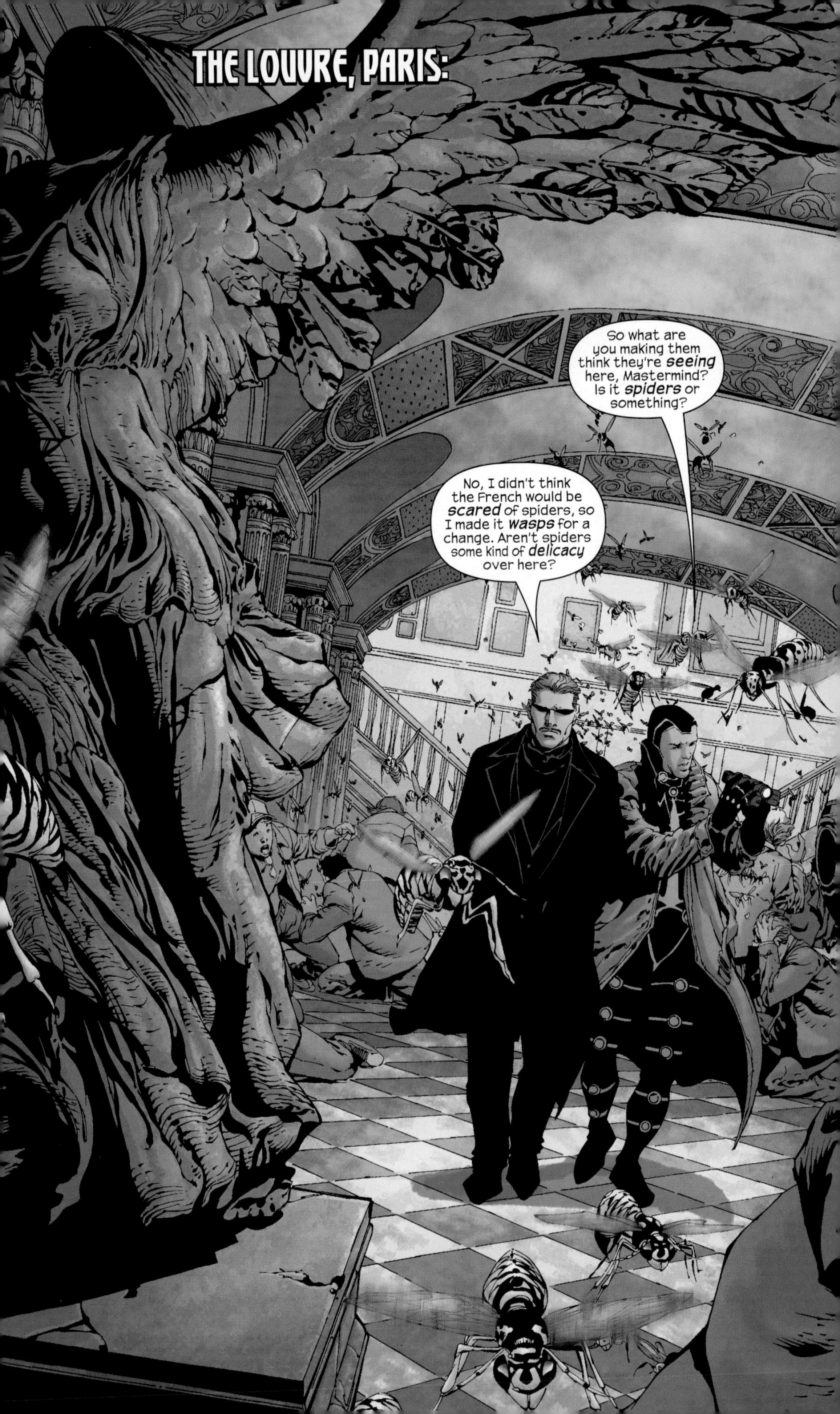
THE LOUVRE, PARIS:
So what are you making them think they're *seeing* here, Mastermind? Is it *spiders* or something?
No, I didn't think the French would be *scared* of spiders, so I made it *wasps* for a change. Aren't spiders some kind of *delicacy* over here?

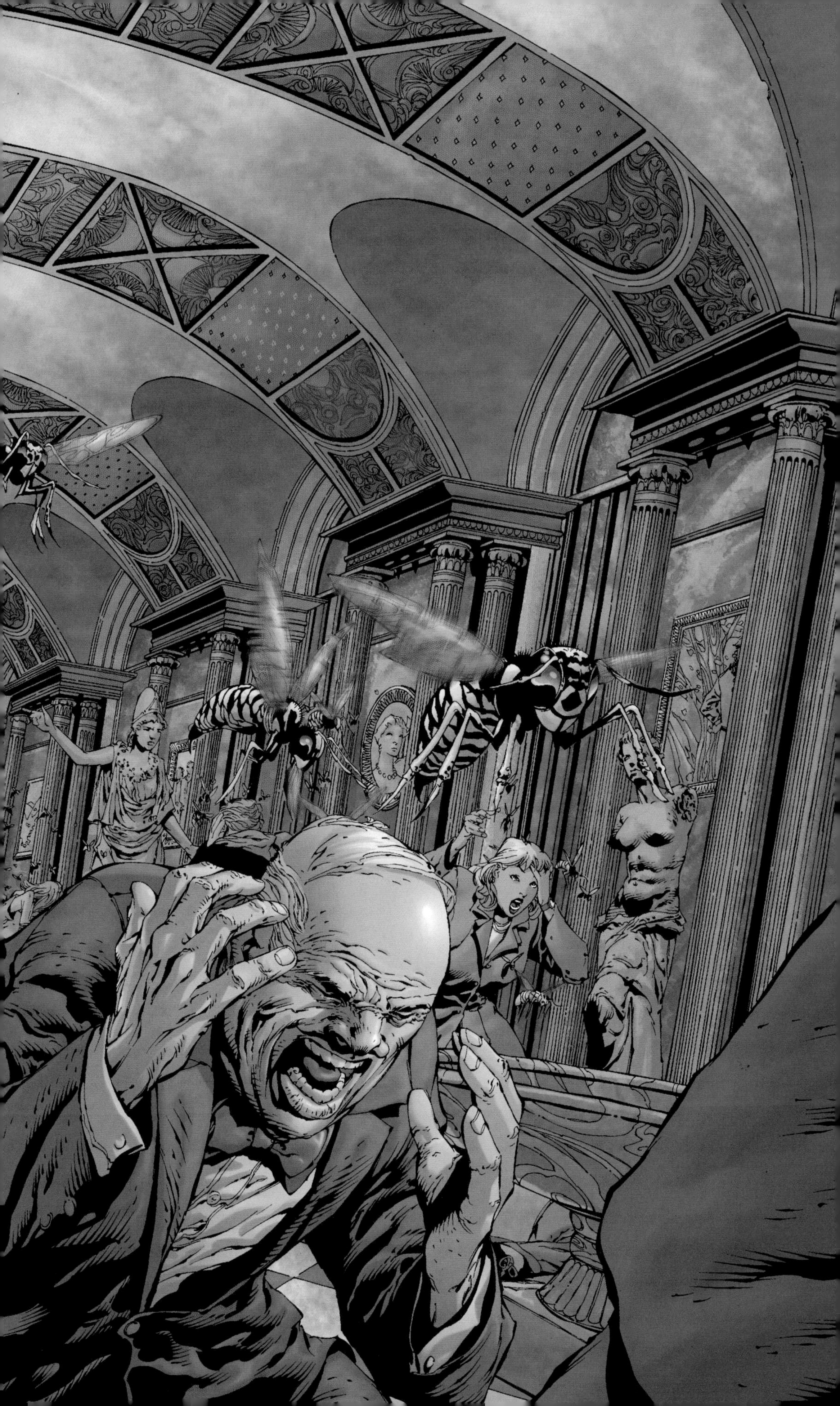

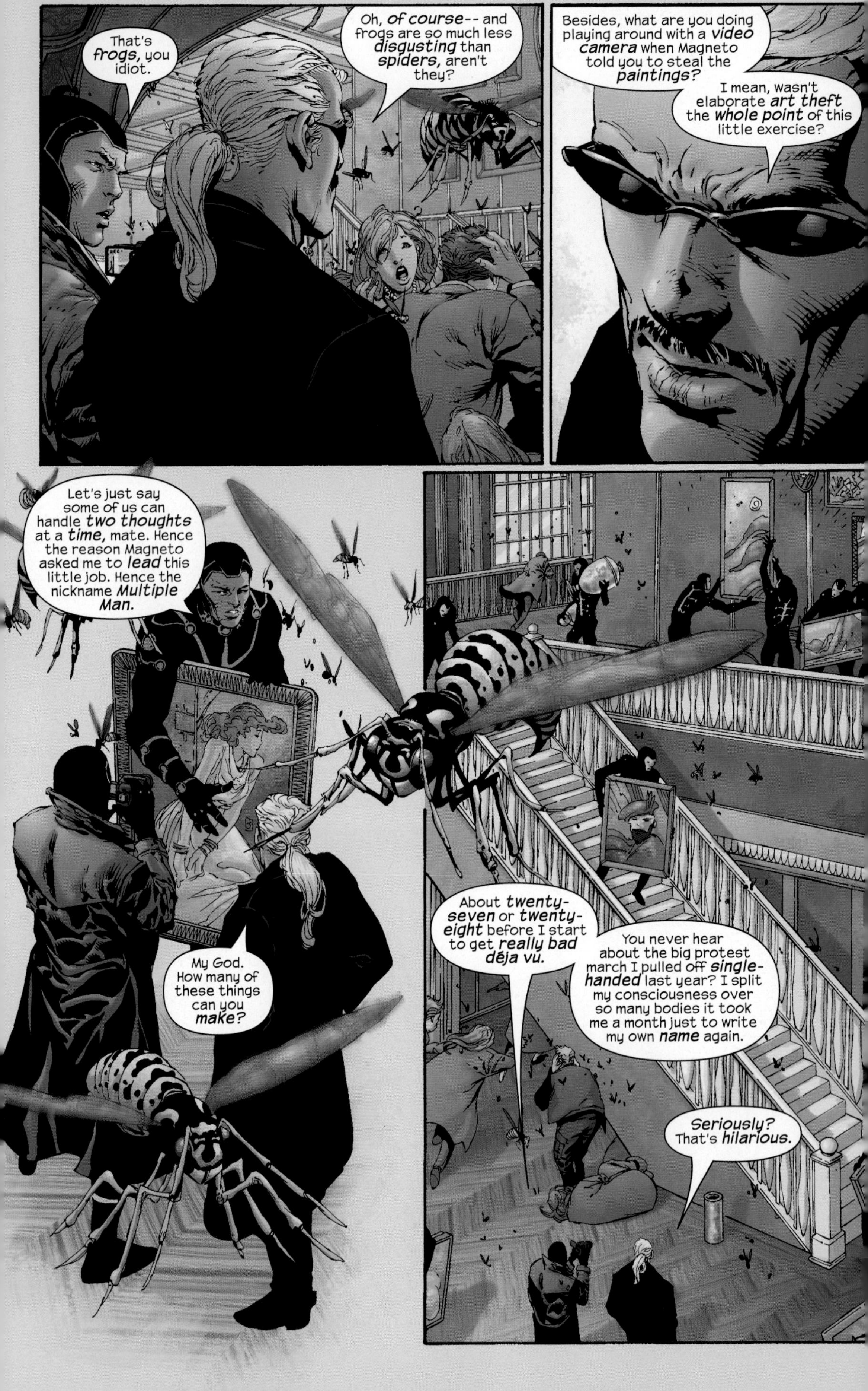
That's frogs, you idiot.
Oh, of course-- and frogs are so much less disgusting than spiders, aren't they?
Besides, what are you doing playing around with a video camera when Magneto told you to steal the paintings?
I mean, wasn't elaborate art theft the whole point of this little exercise?
Let's just say some of us can handle two thoughts at a time, mate. Hence the reason Magneto asked me to lead this little job. Hence the nickname Multiple Man.
My God. How many of these things can you make?
About twenty-seven or twenty-eight before I start to get really bad déja vu.
You never hear about the big protest march I pulled off single-handed last year? I split my consciousness over so many bodies it took me a month just to write my own name again.
Seriously? That's hilarious.

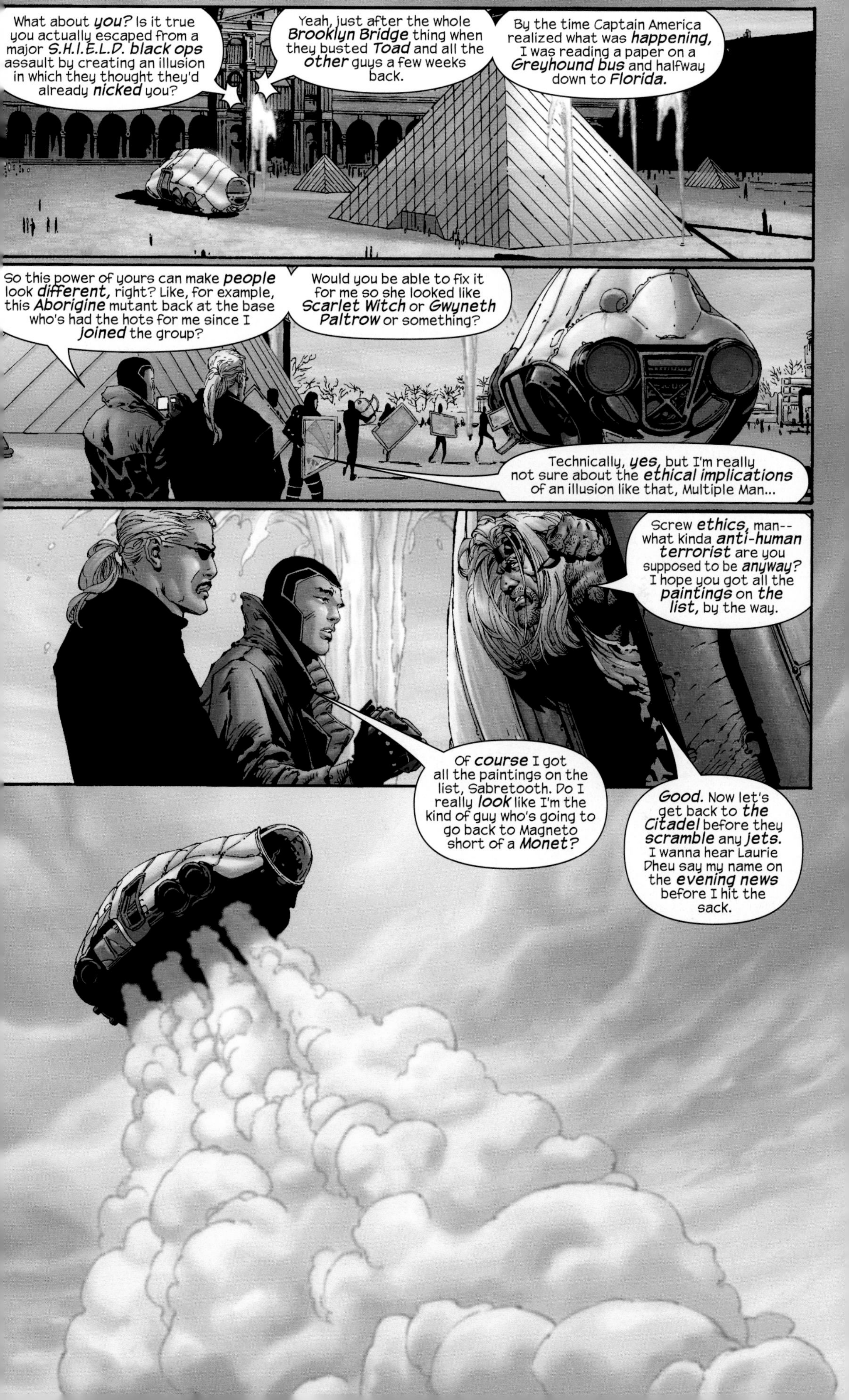
What about you? Is it true you actually escaped from a major S.H.I.E.L.D. black ops assault by creating an illusion in which they thought they'd already nicked you?
Yeah, just after the whole Brooklyn Bridge thing when they busted Toad and all the other guys a few weeks back.
By the time Captain America realized what was happening, I was reading a paper on a Greyhound bus and halfway down to Florida.
So this power of yours can make people look different, right? Like, for example, this Aborigine mutant back at the base who's had the hots for me since I joined the group?
Would you be able to fix it for me so she looked like Scarlet Witch or Gwyneth Paltrow or something?
Technically, yes, but I'm really not sure about the ethical implications of an illusion like that, Multiple Man...
Screw ethics, man-- what kinda anti-human terrorist are you supposed to be anyway? I hope you got all the paintings on the list, by the way.
Of course I got all the paintings on the list, Sabretooth. Do I really look like I'm the kind of guy who's going to go back to Magneto short of a Monet?
Good. Now let's get back to the Citadel before they scramble any jets. I wanna hear Laurie Dheu say my name on the evening news before I hit the sack.

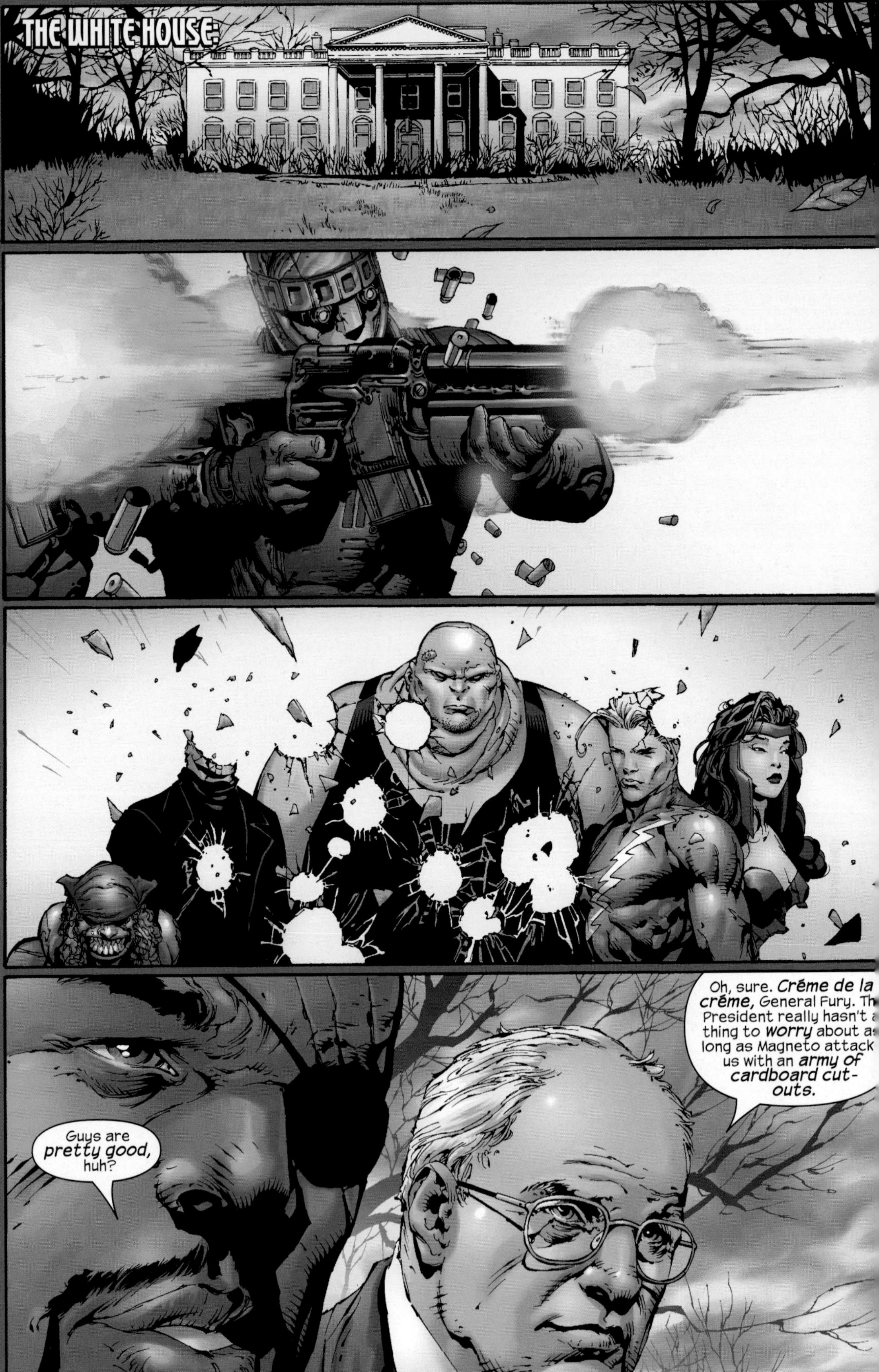
THE WHITE HOUSE:
Oh, sure. *Crême de la crême,* General Fury. Th President really hasn't thing to *worry* about a long as Magneto attack us with an *army of cardboard cut-outs.*
Guys are *pretty good,* huh?

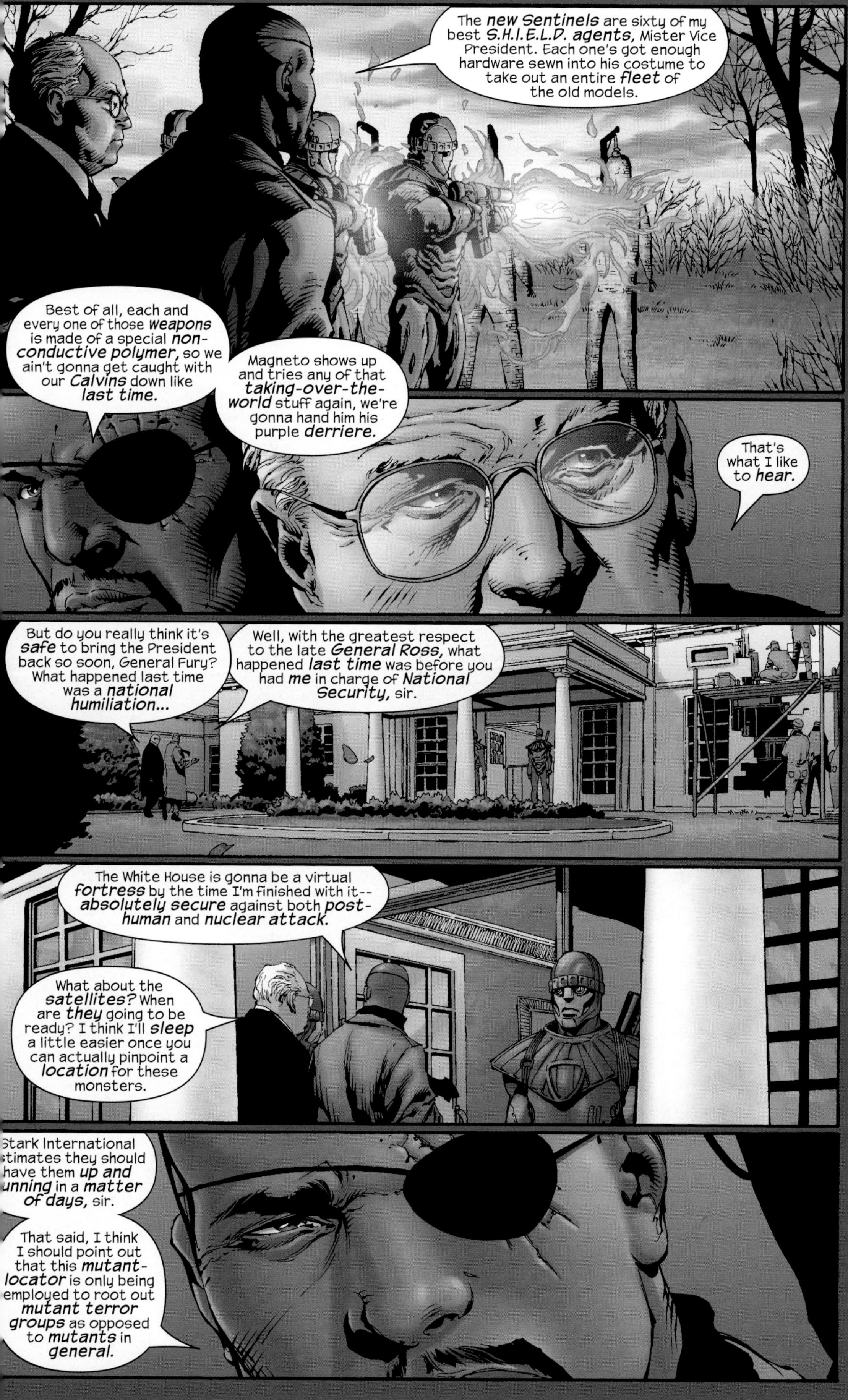

The new Sentinels are sixty of my best S.H.I.E.L.D. agents, Mister Vice President. Each one's got enough hardware sewn into his costume to take out an entire fleet of the old models.
Best of all, each and every one of those weapons is made of a special non-conductive polymer, so we ain't gonna get caught with our Calvins down like last time.
Magneto shows up and tries any of that taking-over-the-world stuff again, we're gonna hand him his purple derriere.
That's what I like to hear.
But do you really think it's safe to bring the President back so soon, General Fury? What happened last time was a national humiliation...
Well, with the greatest respect to the late General Ross, what happened last time was before you had me in charge of National Security, sir.
The White House is gonna be a virtual fortress by the time I'm finished with it-- absolutely secure against both post-human and nuclear attack.
What about the satellites? When are they going to be ready? I think I'll sleep a little easier once you can actually pinpoint a location for these monsters.
Stark International estimates they should have them up and running in a matter of days, sir.
That said, I think I should point out that this mutant-locator is only being employed to root out mutant terror groups as opposed to mutants in general.

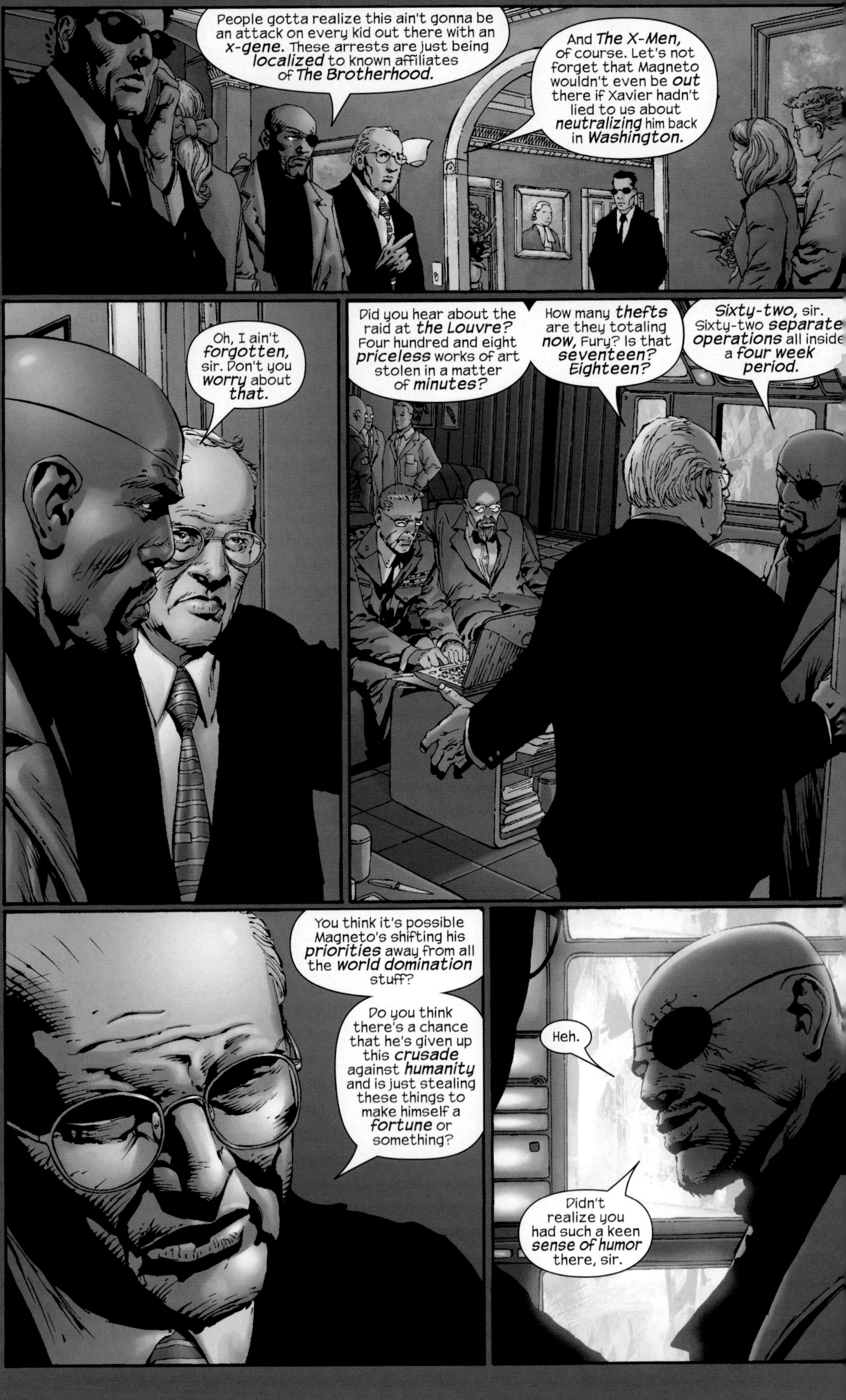

People gotta realize this ain't gonna be an attack on every kid out there with an x-gene. These arrests are just being localized to known affiliates of The Brotherhood.
And The X-Men, of course. Let's not forget that Magneto wouldn't even be out there if Xavier hadn't lied to us about neutralizing him back in Washington.
Oh, I ain't forgotten, sir. Don't you worry about that.
Did you hear about the raid at the Louvre? Four hundred and eight priceless works of art stolen in a matter of minutes?
How many thefts are they totaling now, Fury? Is that seventeen? Eighteen?
Sixty-two, sir. Sixty-two separate operations all inside a four week period.
You think it's possible Magneto's shifting his priorities away from all the world domination stuff?
Do you think there's a chance that he's given up this crusade against humanity and is just stealing these things to make himself a fortune or something?
Heh.
Didn't realize you had such a keen sense of humor there, sir.

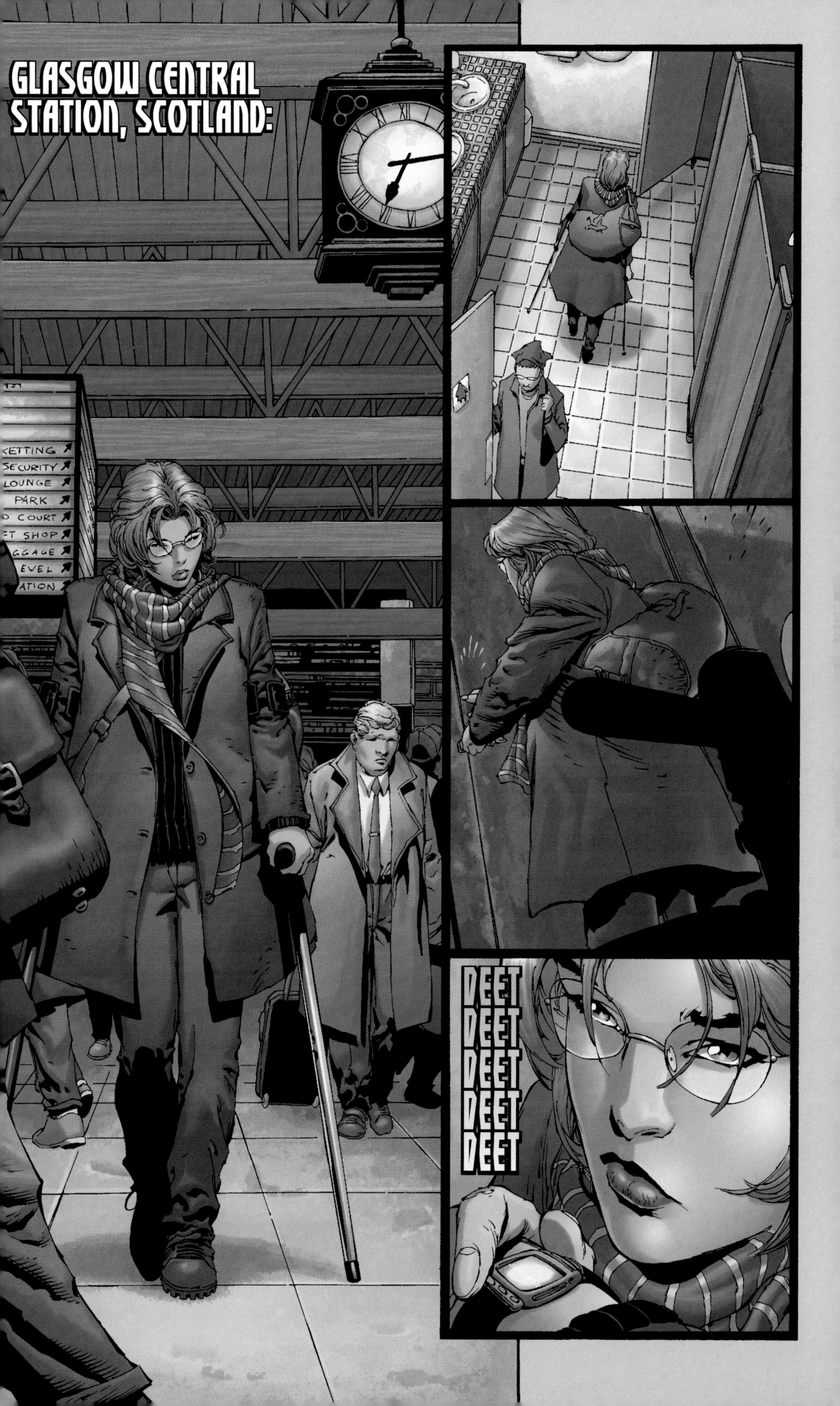
GLASGOW CENTRAL STATION, SCOTLAND:
SECURITY
LOUNGE
PARK
DEET
DEET
DEET
DEET
DEET

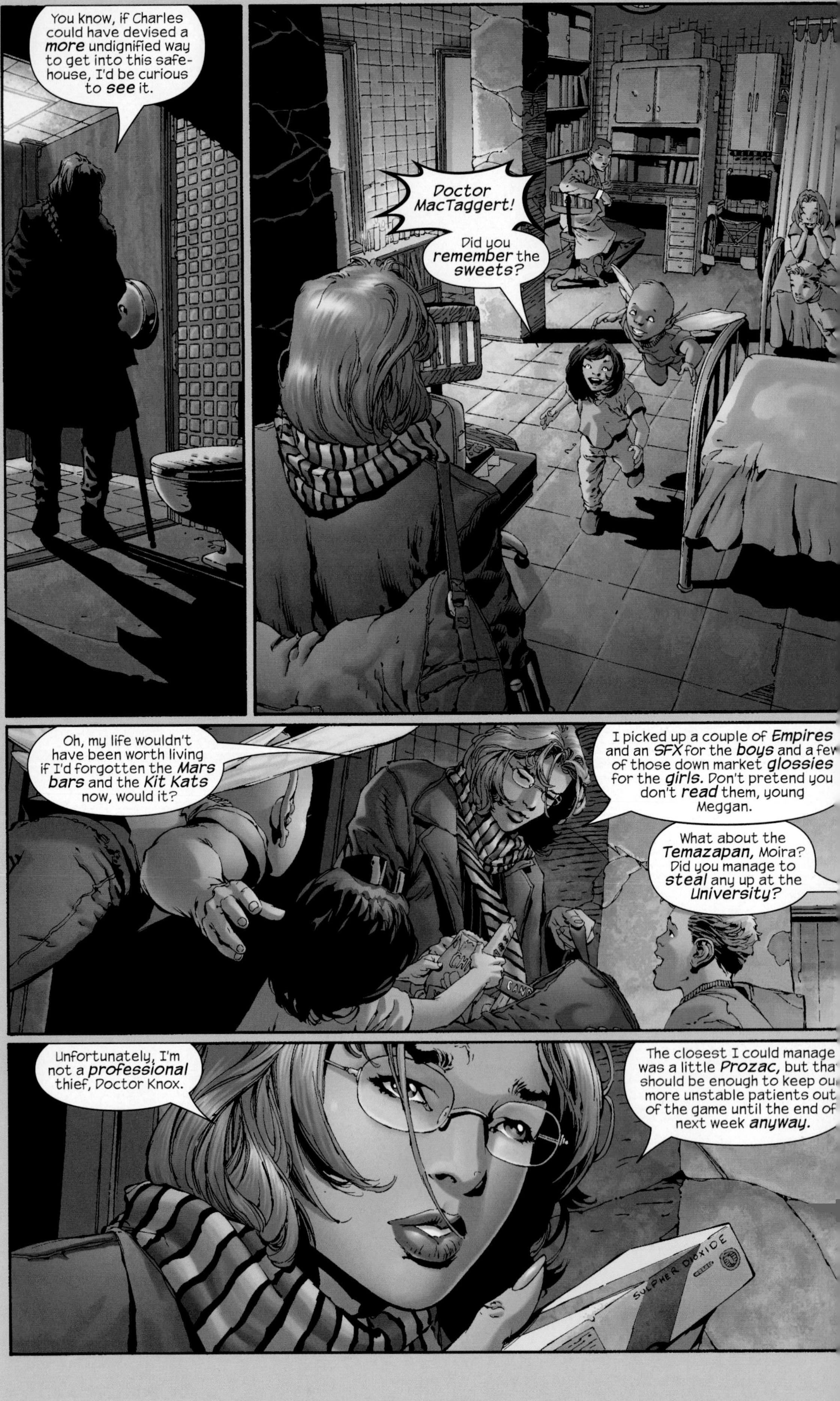

You know, if Charles could have devised a more undignified way to get into this safe-house, I'd be curious to see it.
Doctor MacTaggert!
Did you remember the sweets?
Oh, my life wouldn't have been worth living if I'd forgotten the Mars bars and the Kit Kats now, would it?
I picked up a couple of Empires and an SFX for the boys and a few of those down market glossies for the girls. Don't pretend you don't read them, young Meggan.
What about the Temazapan, Moira? Did you manage to steal any up at the University?
Unfortunately, I'm not a professional thief, Doctor Knox.
The closest I could manage was a little Prozac, but that should be enough to keep our more unstable patients out of the game until the end of next week anyway.
SULPHER DIOXIDE

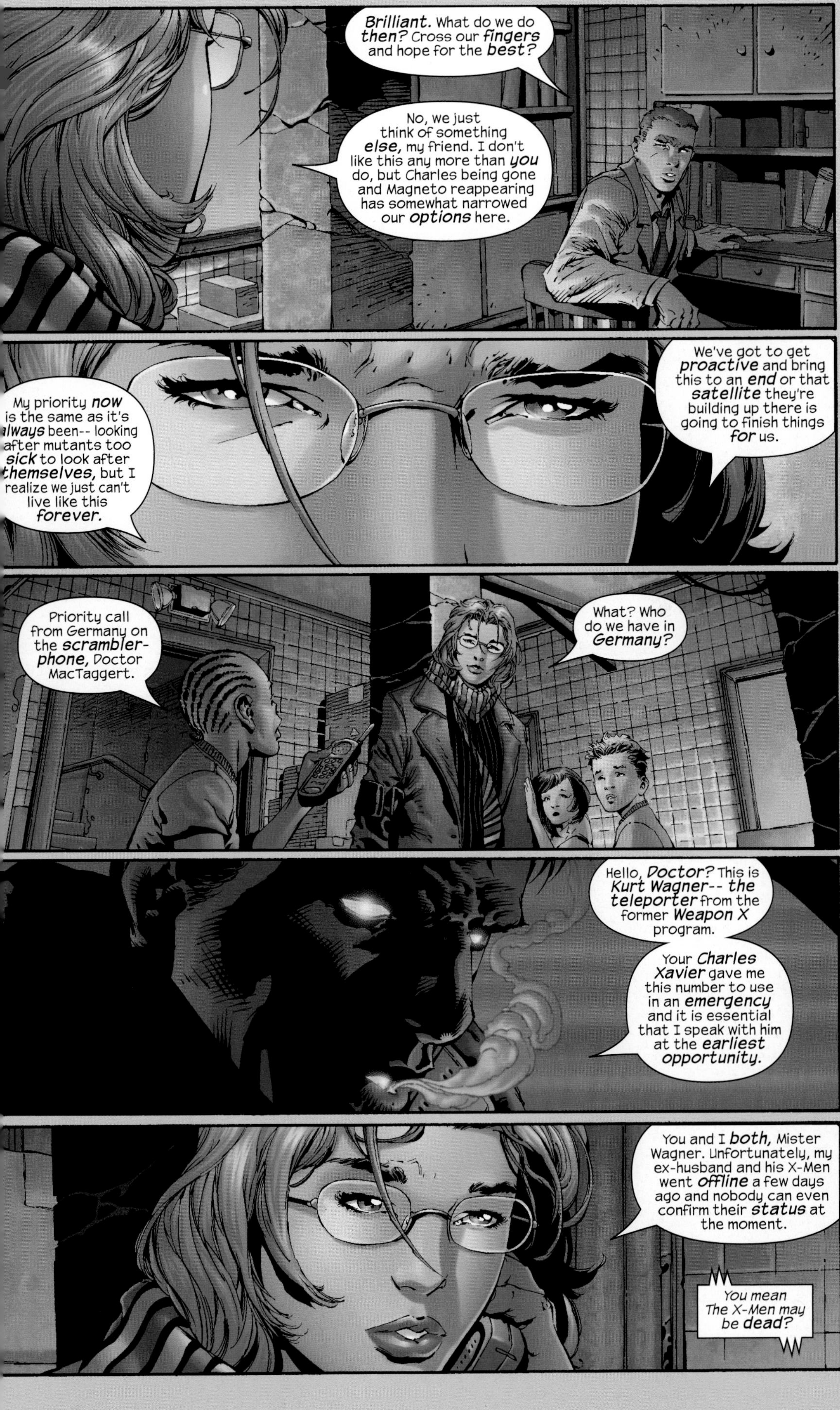
Brilliant. What do we do then? Cross our fingers and hope for the best?
No, we just think of something else, my friend. I don't like this any more than you do, but Charles being gone and Magneto reappearing has somewhat narrowed our options here.
My priority now is the same as it's always been-- looking after mutants too sick to look after themselves, but I realize we just can't live like this forever.
We've got to get proactive and bring this to an end or that satellite they're building up there is going to finish things for us.
Priority call from Germany on the scrambler-phone, Doctor MacTaggert.
What? Who do we have in Germany?
Hello, Doctor? This is Kurt Wagner-- the teleporter from the former Weapon X program.
Your Charles Xavier gave me this number to use in an emergency and it is essential that I speak with him at the earliest opportunity.
You and I both, Mister Wagner. Unfortunately, my ex-husband and his X-Men went offline a few days ago and nobody can even confirm their status at the moment.
You mean The X-Men may be dead?

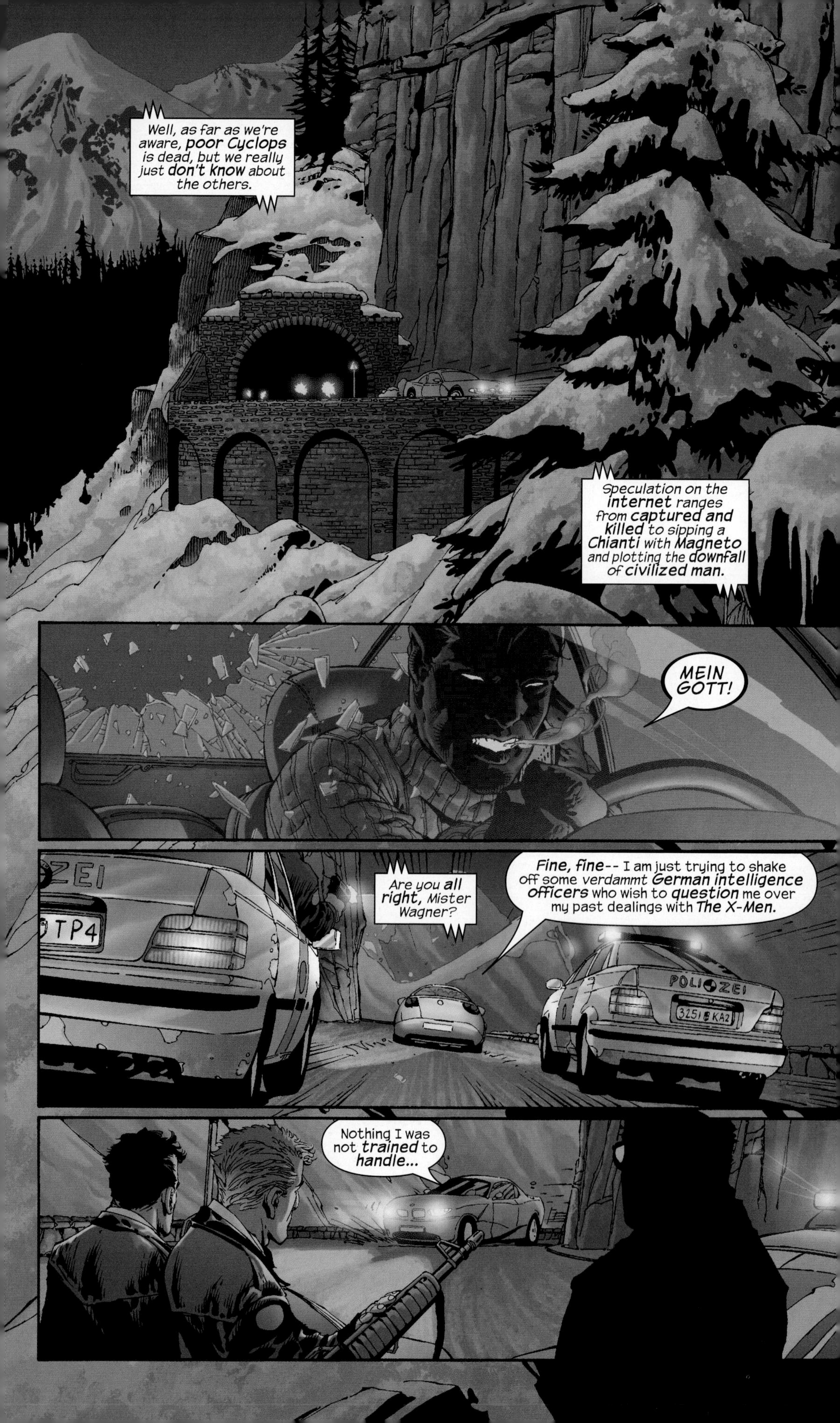
Well, as far as we're aware, poor Cyclops is dead, but we really just don't know about the others.
Speculation on the internet ranges from captured and killed to sipping a Chianti with Magneto and plotting the downfall of civilized man.
MEIN GOTT!
Are you all right, Mister Wagner?
Fine, fine-- I am just trying to shake off some verdammt German intelligence officers who wish to question me over my past dealings with The X-Men.
POLIZEI
Nothing I was not trained to handle...

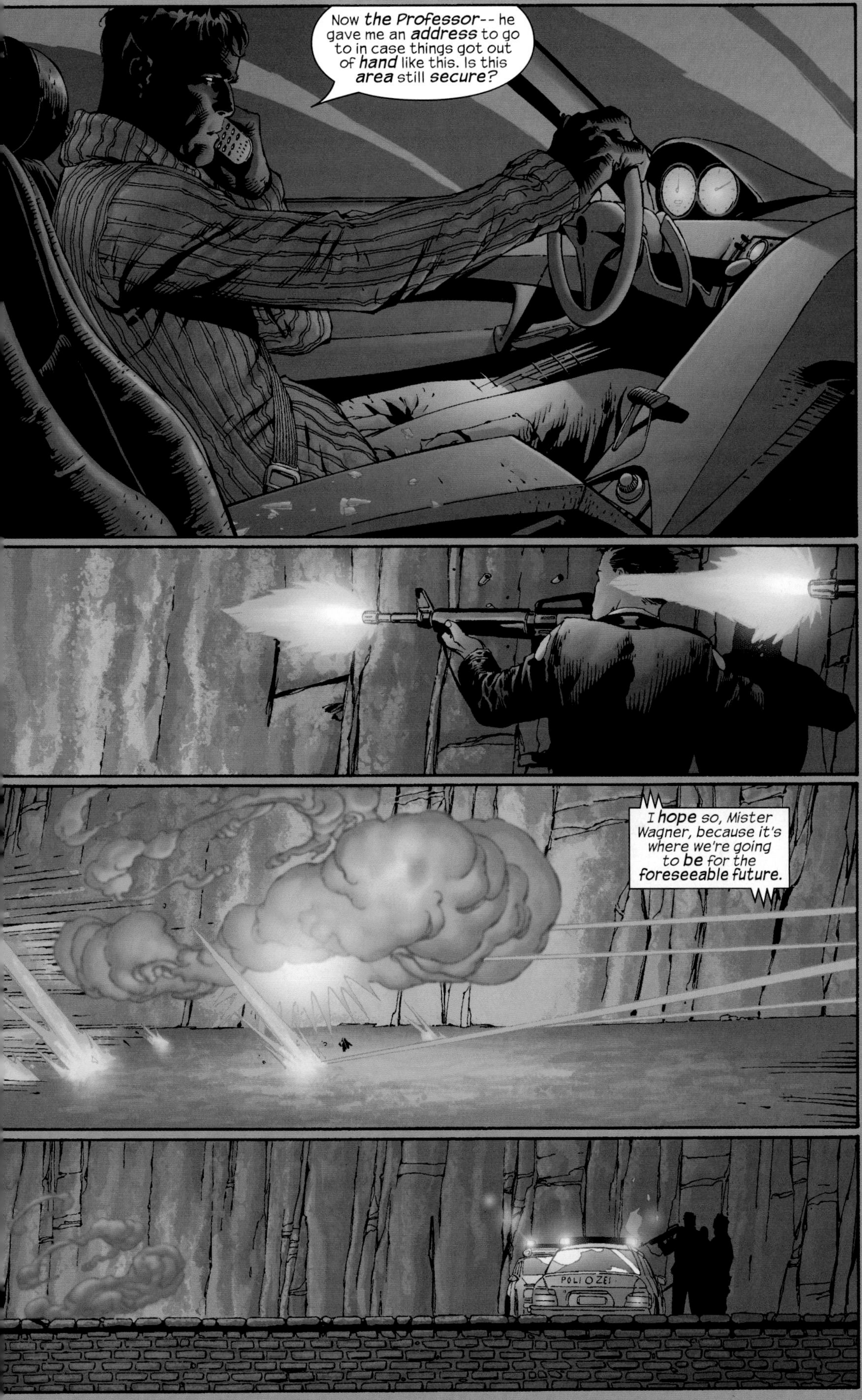
Now the Professor-- he gave me an address to go to in case things got out of hand like this. Is this area still secure?
I hope so, Mister Wagner, because it's where we're going to be for the foreseeable future.

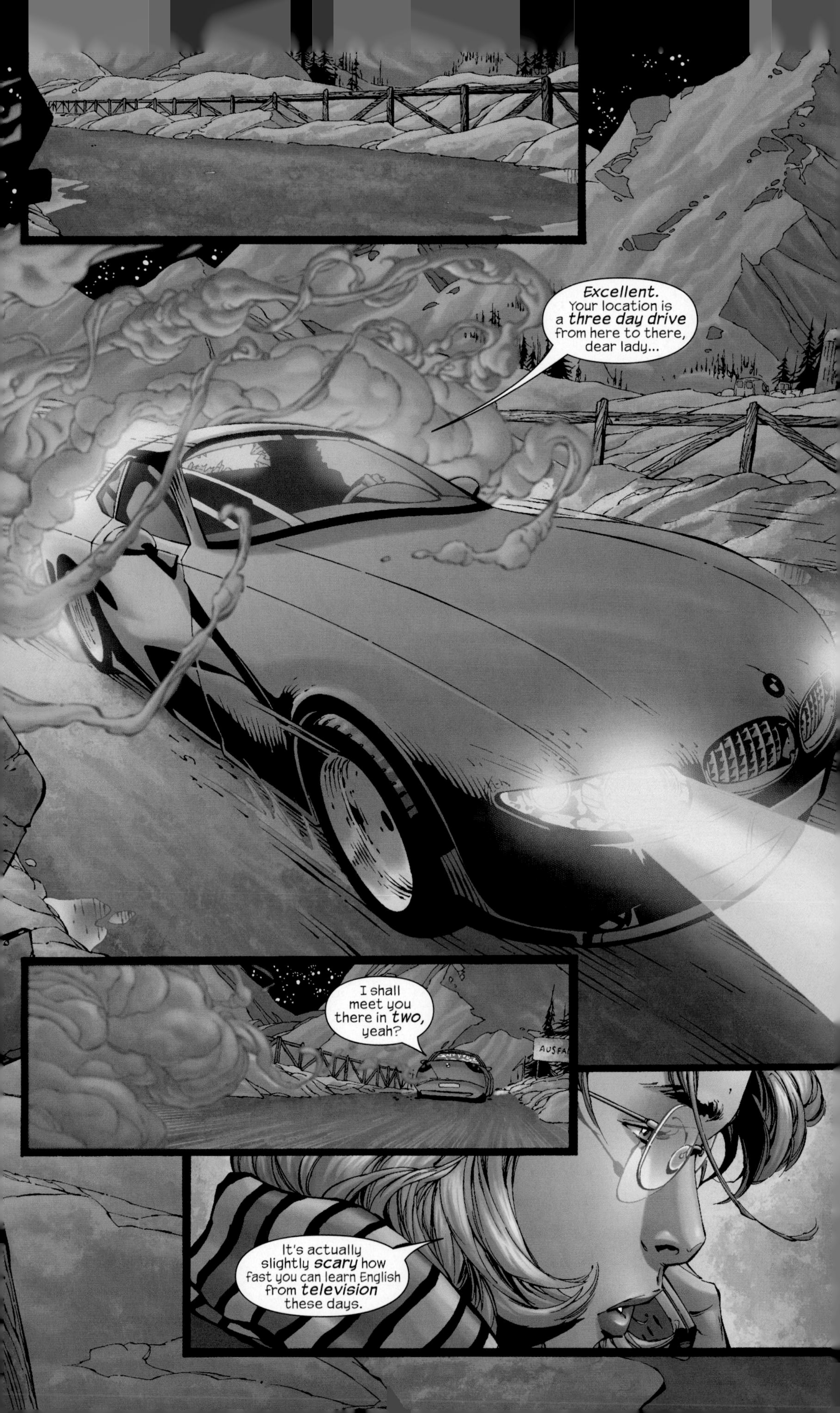
Excellent. Your location is a three day drive from here to there, dear lady...
I shall meet you there in two, yeah?
AUSFA
It's actually slightly scary how fast you can learn English from television these days.

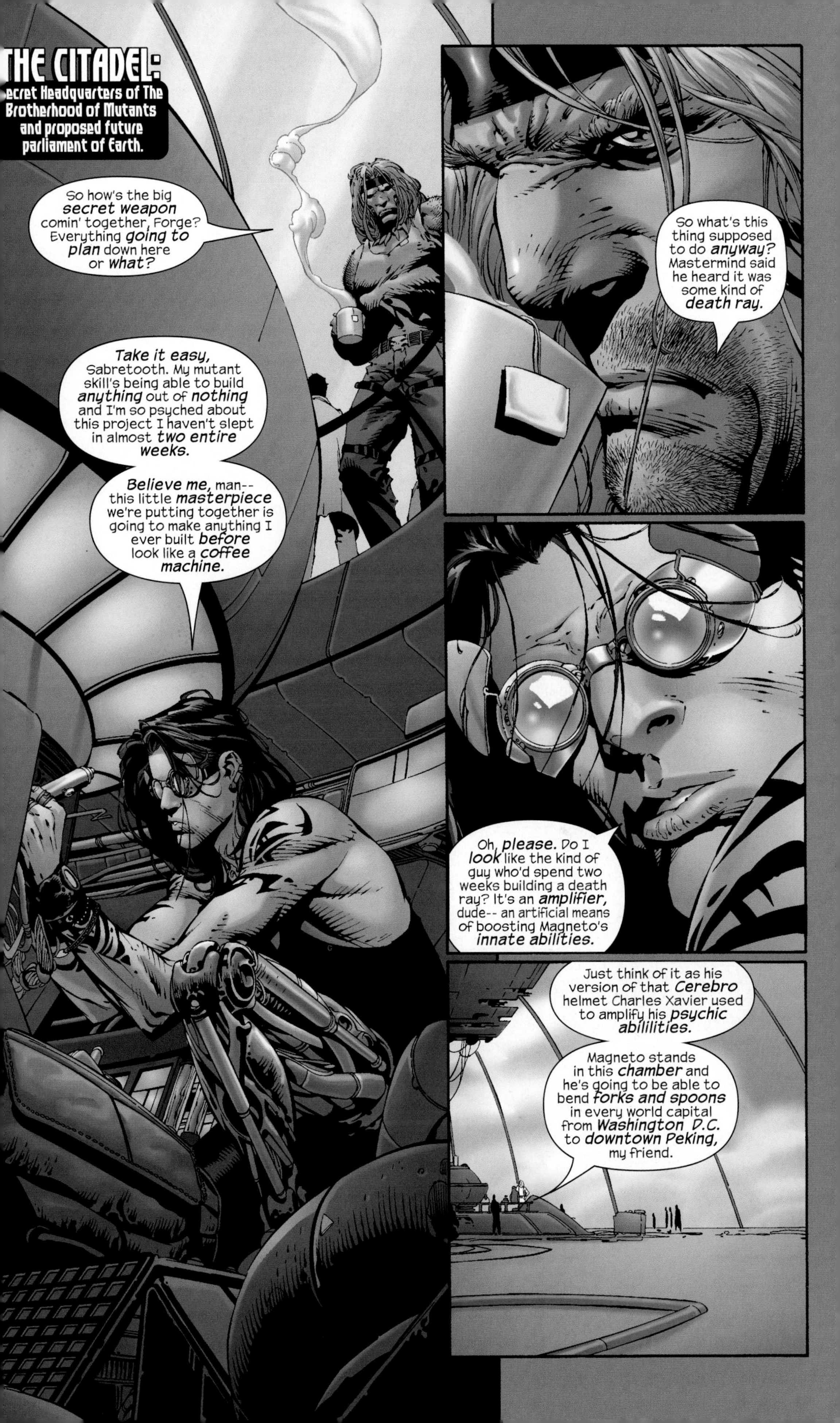
THE CITADEL:
ecret Headquarters of The Brotherhood of Mutants and proposed future parliament of Earth.
So how's the big secret weapon comin' together, Forge? Everything going to plan down here or what?
Take it easy, Sabretooth. My mutant skill's being able to build anything out of nothing and I'm so psyched about this project I haven't slept in almost two entire weeks.
Believe me, man-- this little masterpiece we're putting together is going to make anything I ever built before look like a coffee machine.
So what's this thing supposed to do anyway? Mastermind said he heard it was some kind of death ray.
Oh, please. Do I look like the kind of guy who'd spend two weeks building a death ray? It's an amplifier, dude-- an artificial means of boosting Magneto's innate abilities.
Just think of it as his version of that Cerebro helmet Charles Xavier used to amplify his psychic abililities.
Magneto stands in this chamber and he's going to be able to bend forks and spoons in every world capital from Washington D.C. to downtown Peking, my friend.

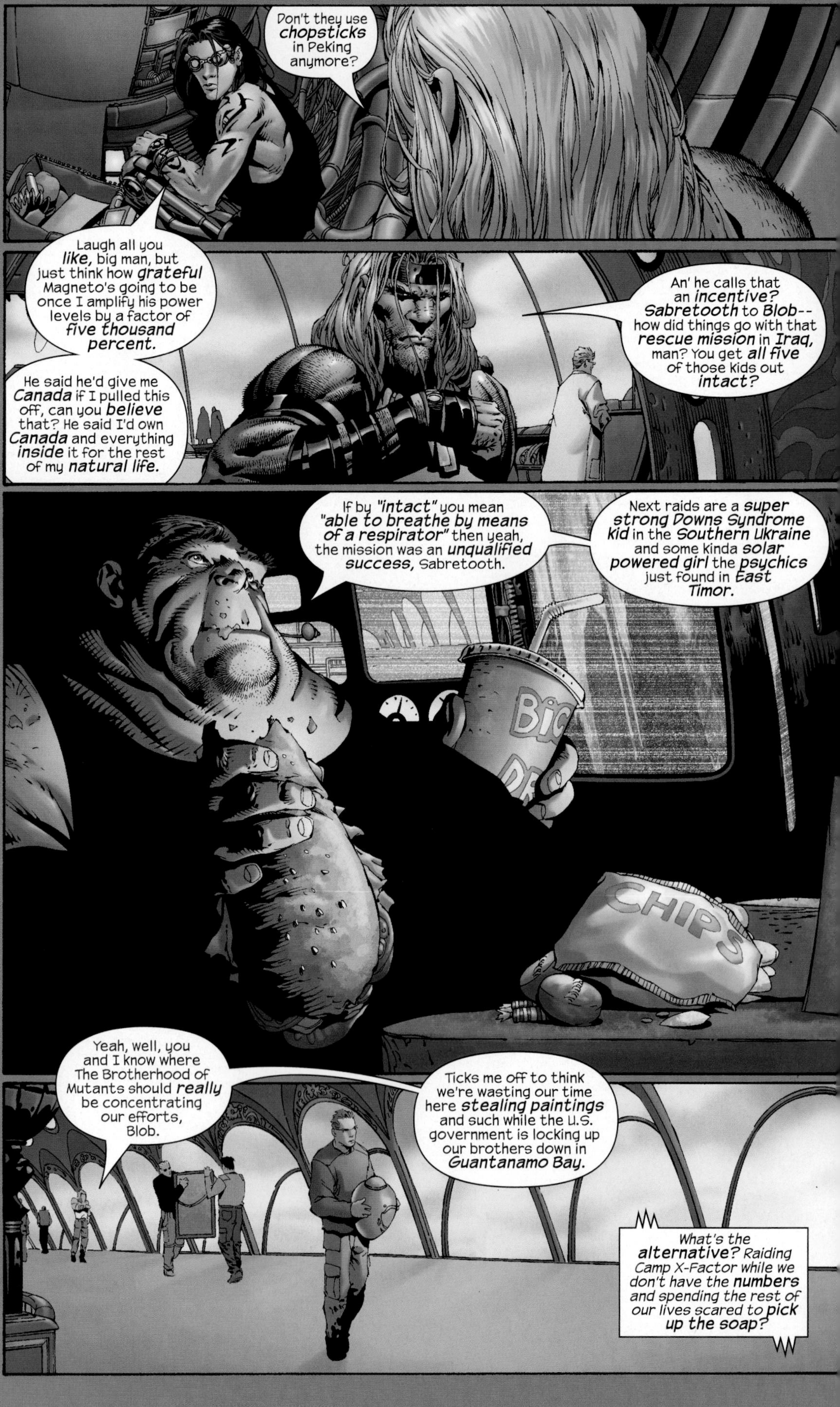

Don't they use chopsticks in Peking anymore?
Laugh all you like, big man, but just think how grateful Magneto's going to be once I amplify his power levels by a factor of five thousand percent.
He said he'd give me Canada if I pulled this off, can you believe that? He said I'd own Canada and everything inside it for the rest of my natural life.
An' he calls that an incentive? Sabretooth to Blob-- how did things go with that rescue mission in Iraq, man? You get all five of those kids out intact?
If by "intact" you mean "able to breathe by means of a respirator" then yeah, the mission was an unqualified success, Sabretooth.
Next raids are a super strong Downs Syndrome kid in the Southern Ukraine and some kinda solar powered girl the psychics just found in East Timor.
CHIPS
Yeah, well, you and I know where The Brotherhood of Mutants should really be concentrating our efforts, Blob.
Ticks me off to think we're wasting our time here stealing paintings and such while the U.S. government is locking up our brothers down in Guantanamo Bay.
What's the alternative? Raiding Camp X-Factor while we don't have the numbers and spending the rest of our lives scared to pick up the soap?

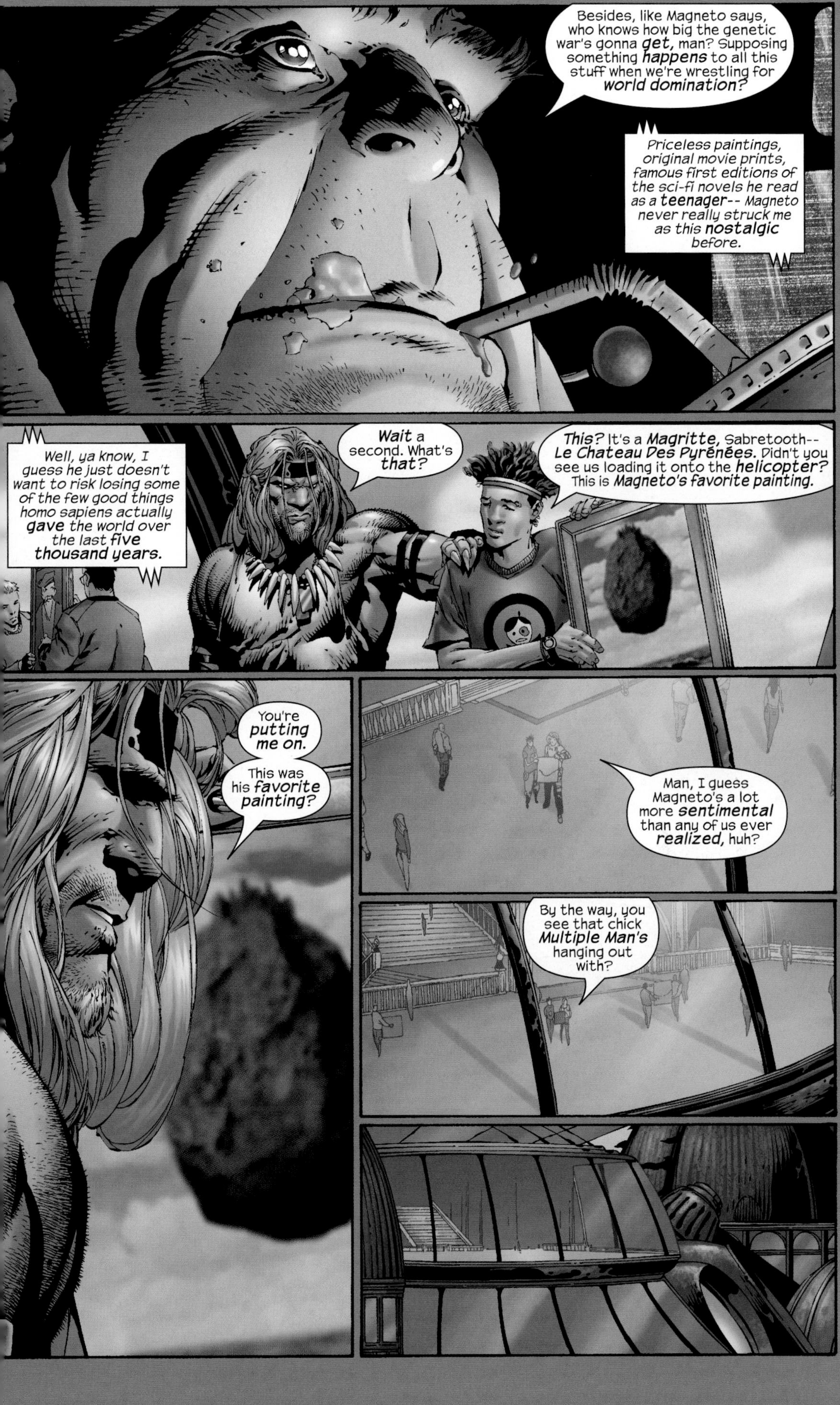

Besides, like Magneto says, who knows how big the genetic war's gonna get, man? Supposing something happens to all this stuff when we're wrestling for world domination?
Priceless paintings, original movie prints, famous first editions of the sci-fi novels he read as a teenager-- Magneto never really struck me as this nostalgic before.
Well, ya know, I guess he just doesn't want to risk losing some of the few good things homo sapiens actually gave the world over the last five thousand years.
Wait a second. What's that?
This? It's a Magritte, Sabretooth-- Le Chateau Des Pyrénées. Didn't you see us loading it onto the helicopter? This is Magneto's favorite painting.
You're putting me on.
This was his favorite painting?
Man, I guess Magneto's a lot more sentimental than any of us ever realized, huh?
By the way, you see that chick Multiple Man's hanging out with?

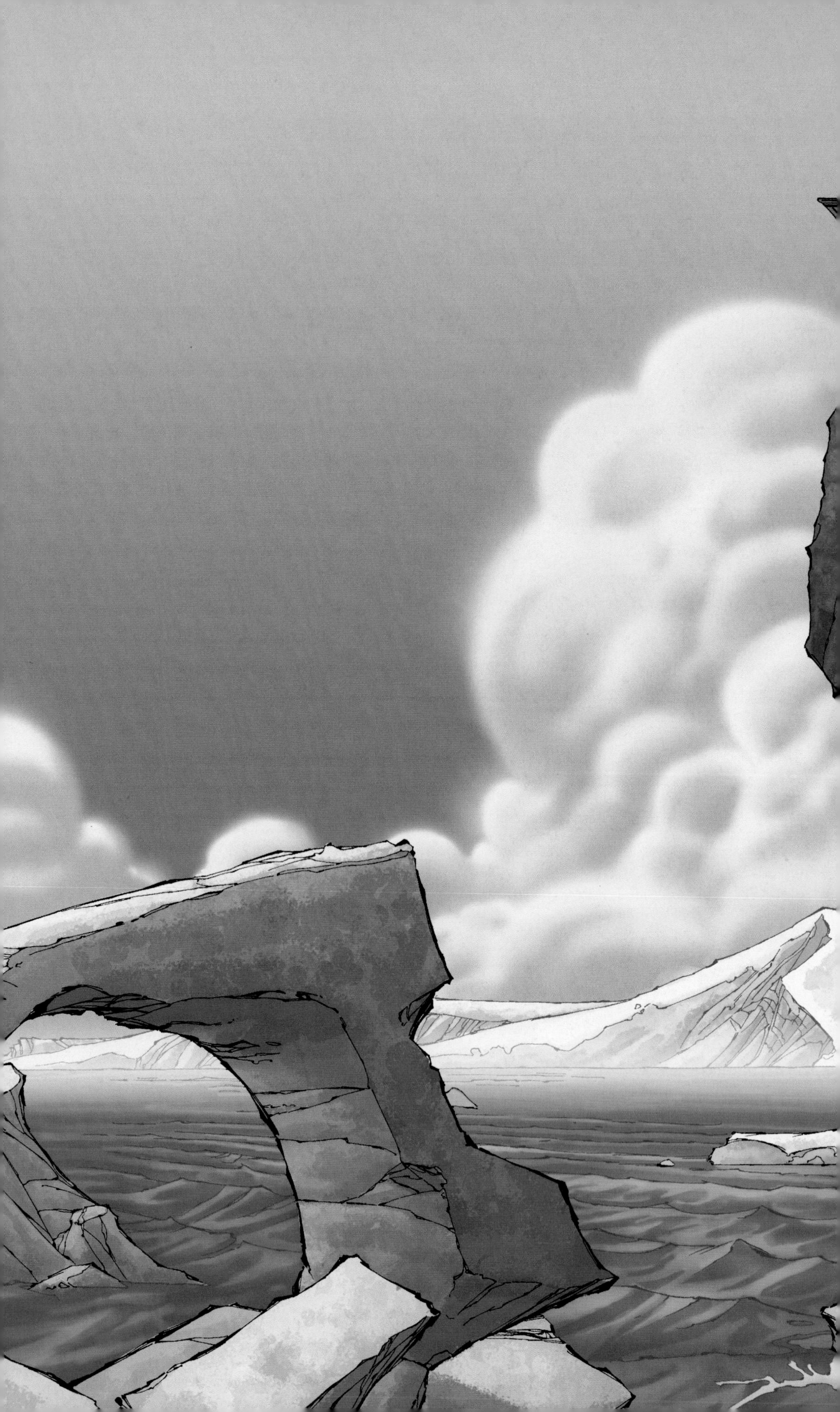

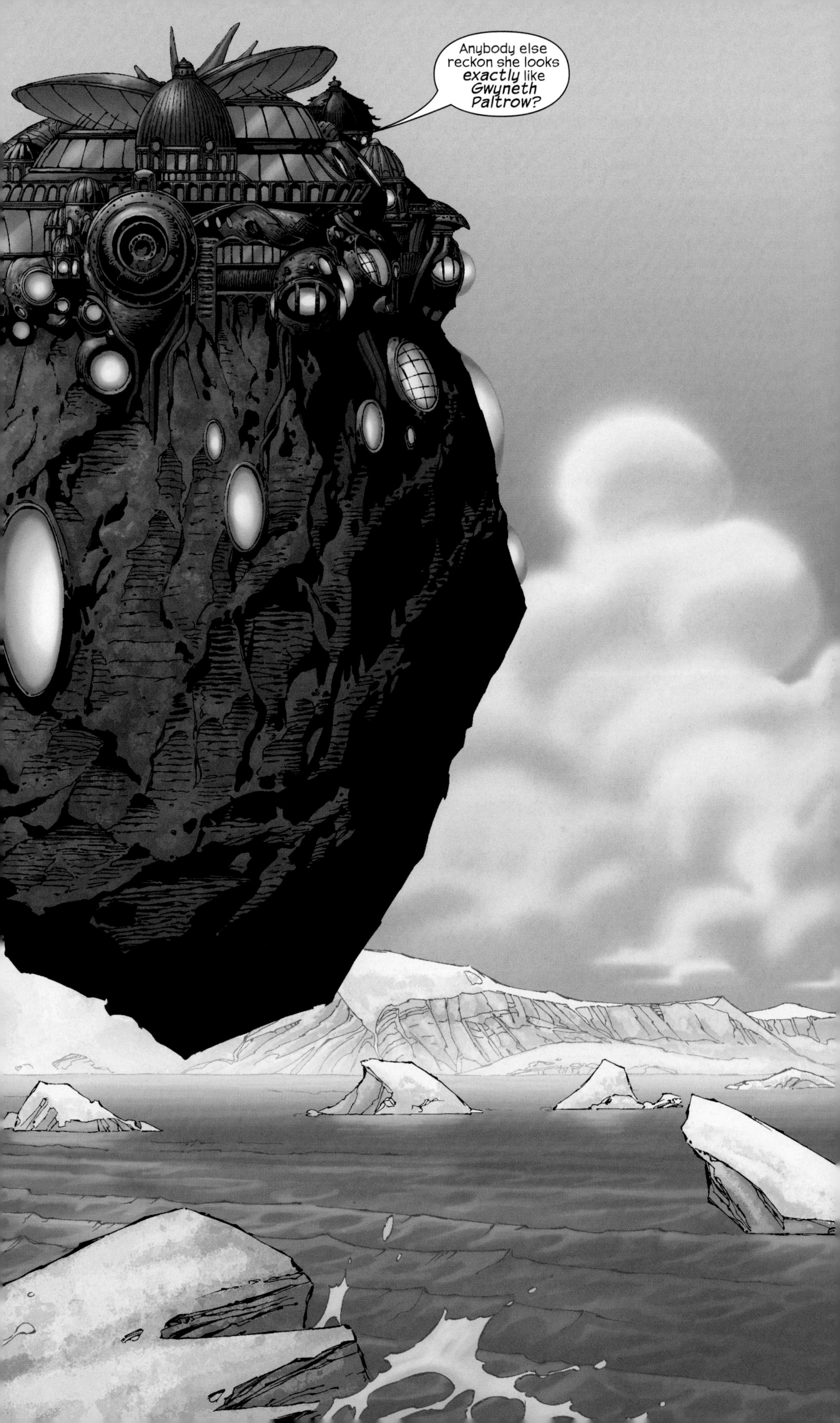
Anybody else reckon she looks exactly like Gwyneth Paltrow?

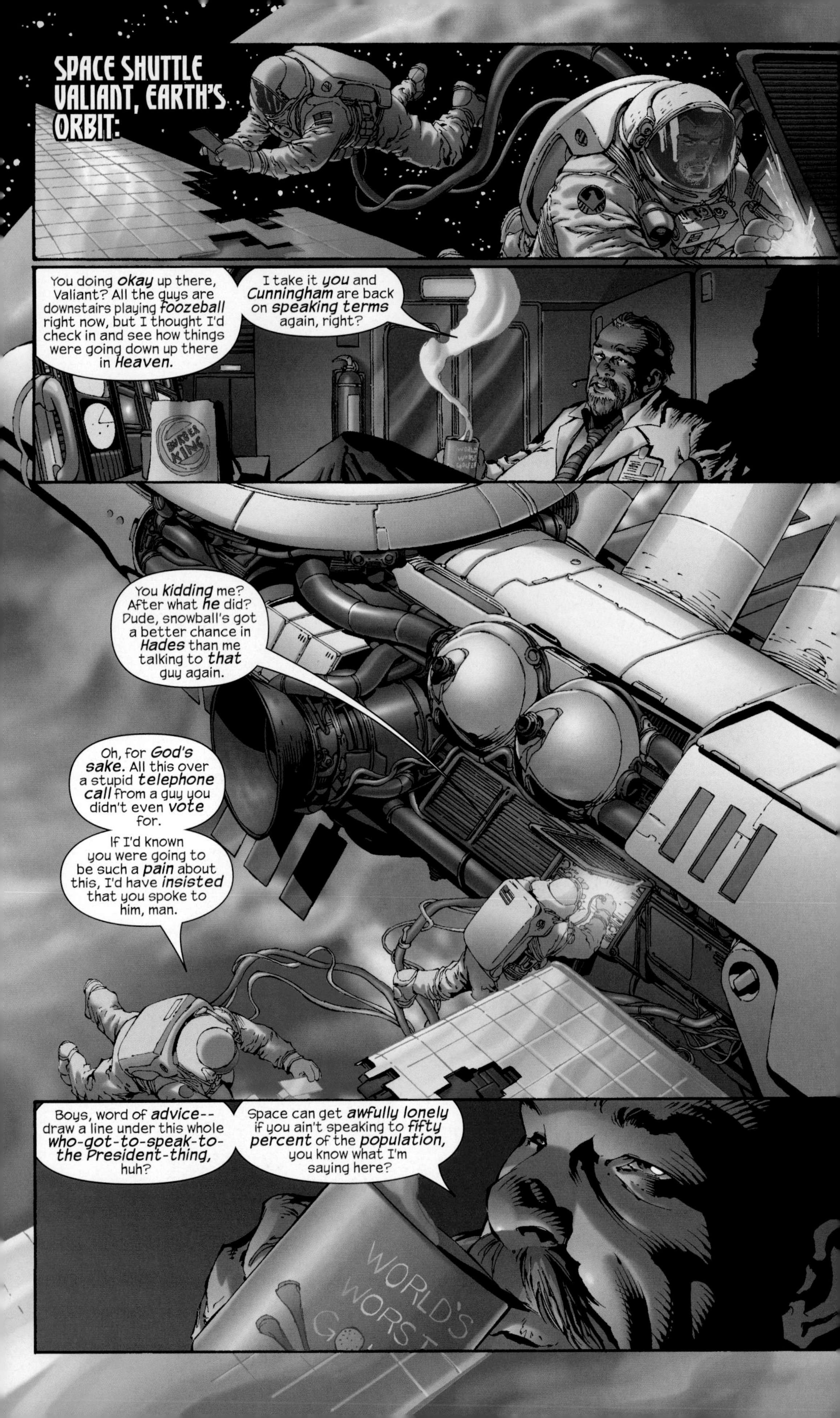
SPACE SHUTTLE VALIANT, EARTH'S ORBIT:
You doing okay up there, Valiant? All the guys are downstairs playing foozeball right now, but I thought I'd check in and see how things were going down up there in Heaven.
I take it you and Cunningham are back on speaking terms again, right?
You kidding me? After what he did? Dude, snowball's got a better chance in Hades than me talking to that guy again.
Oh, for God's sake. All this over a stupid telephone call from a guy you didn't even vote for.
If I'd known you were going to be such a pain about this, I'd have insisted that you spoke to him, man.
Boys, word of advice-- draw a line under this whole who-got-to-speak-to-the President-thing, huh?
Space can get awfully lonely if you ain't speaking to fifty percent of the population, you know what I'm saying here?
WORLD'S WORST GOLF

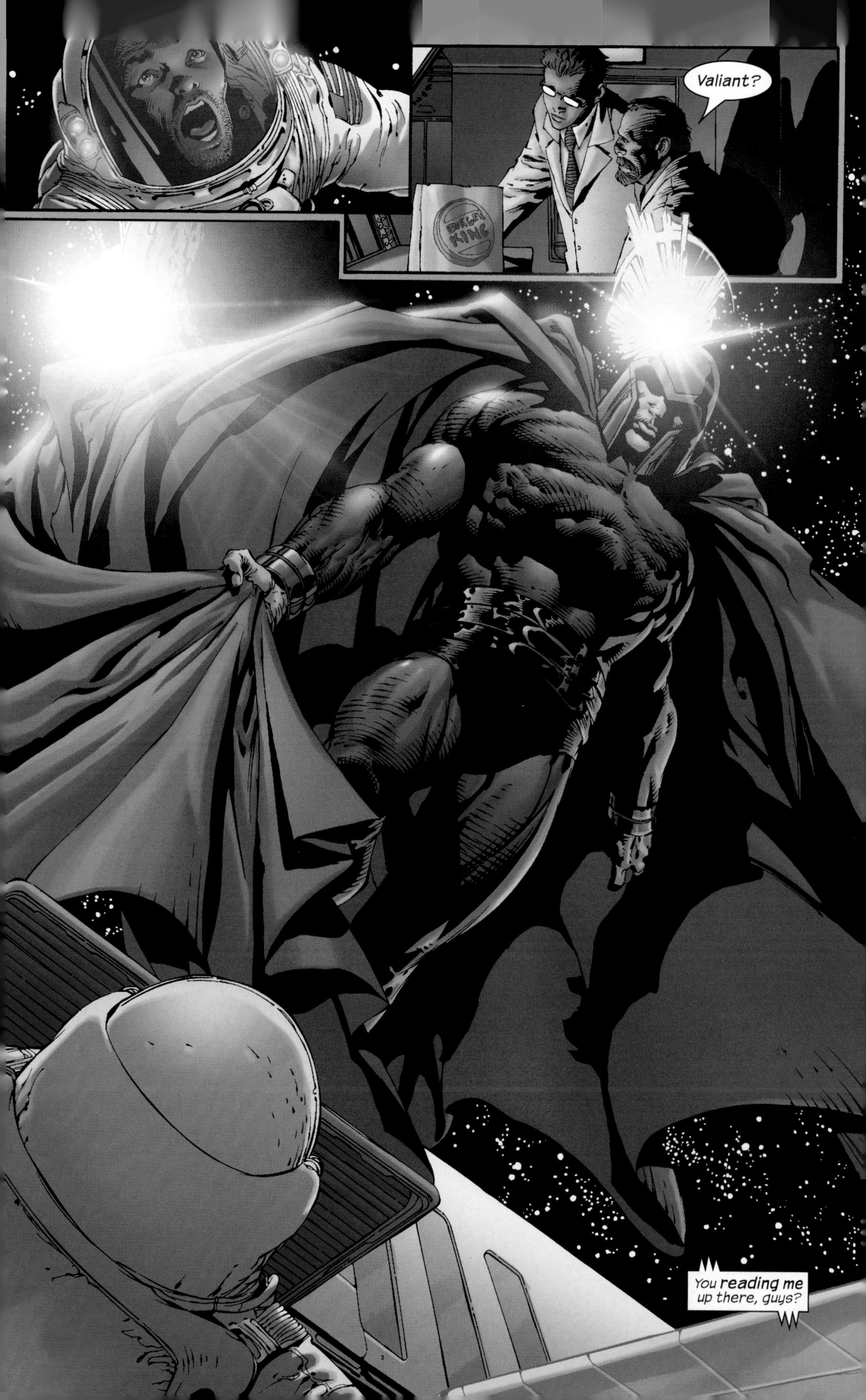
Valiant?
BURGER KING
You reading me up there, guys?

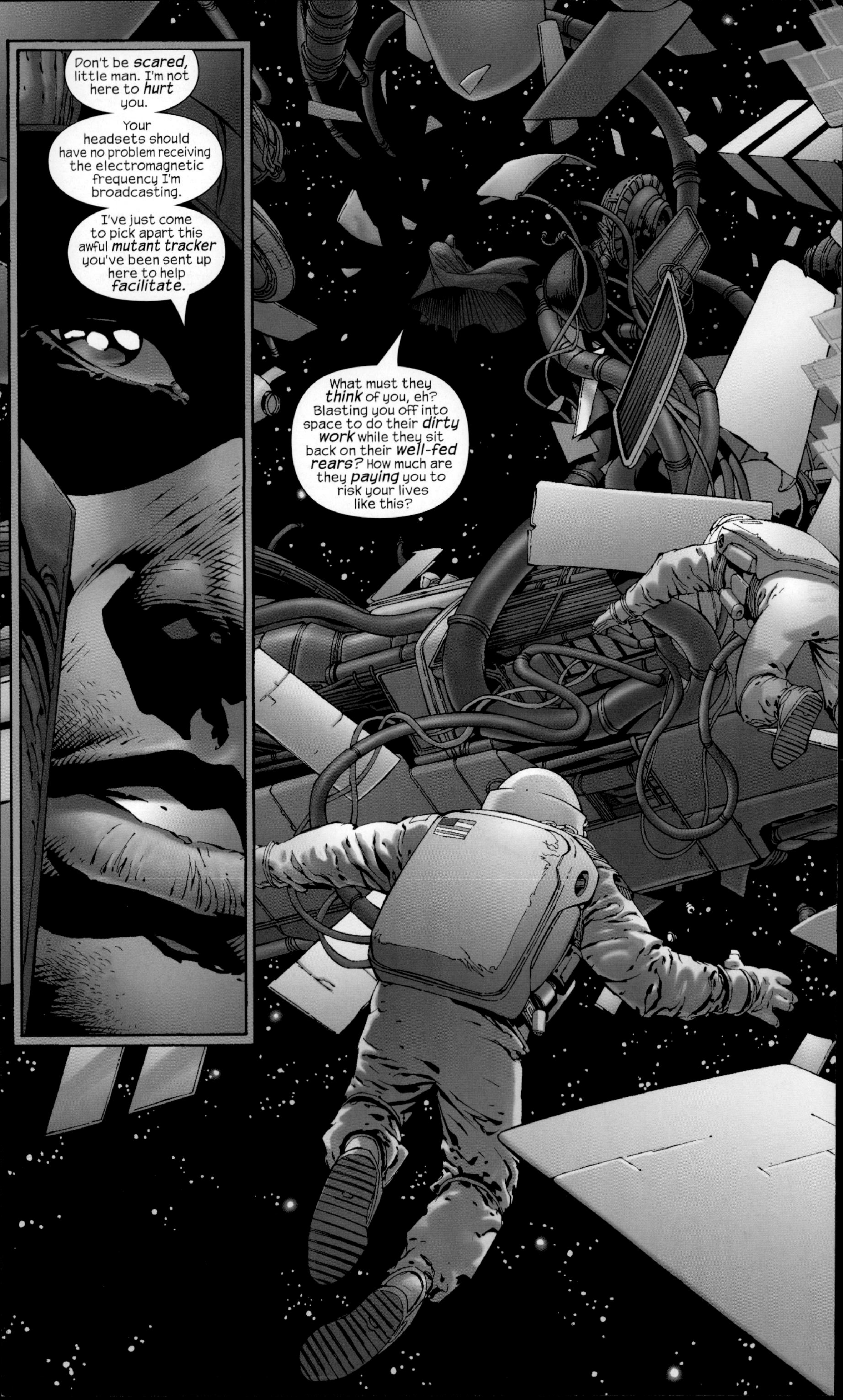
Don't be scared, little man. I'm not here to hurt you.
Your headsets should have no problem receiving the electromagnetic frequency I'm broadcasting.
I've just come to pick apart this awful mutant tracker you've been sent up here to help facilitate.
What must they think of you, eh? Blasting you off into space to do their dirty work while they sit back on their well-fed rears? How much are they paying you to risk your lives like this?

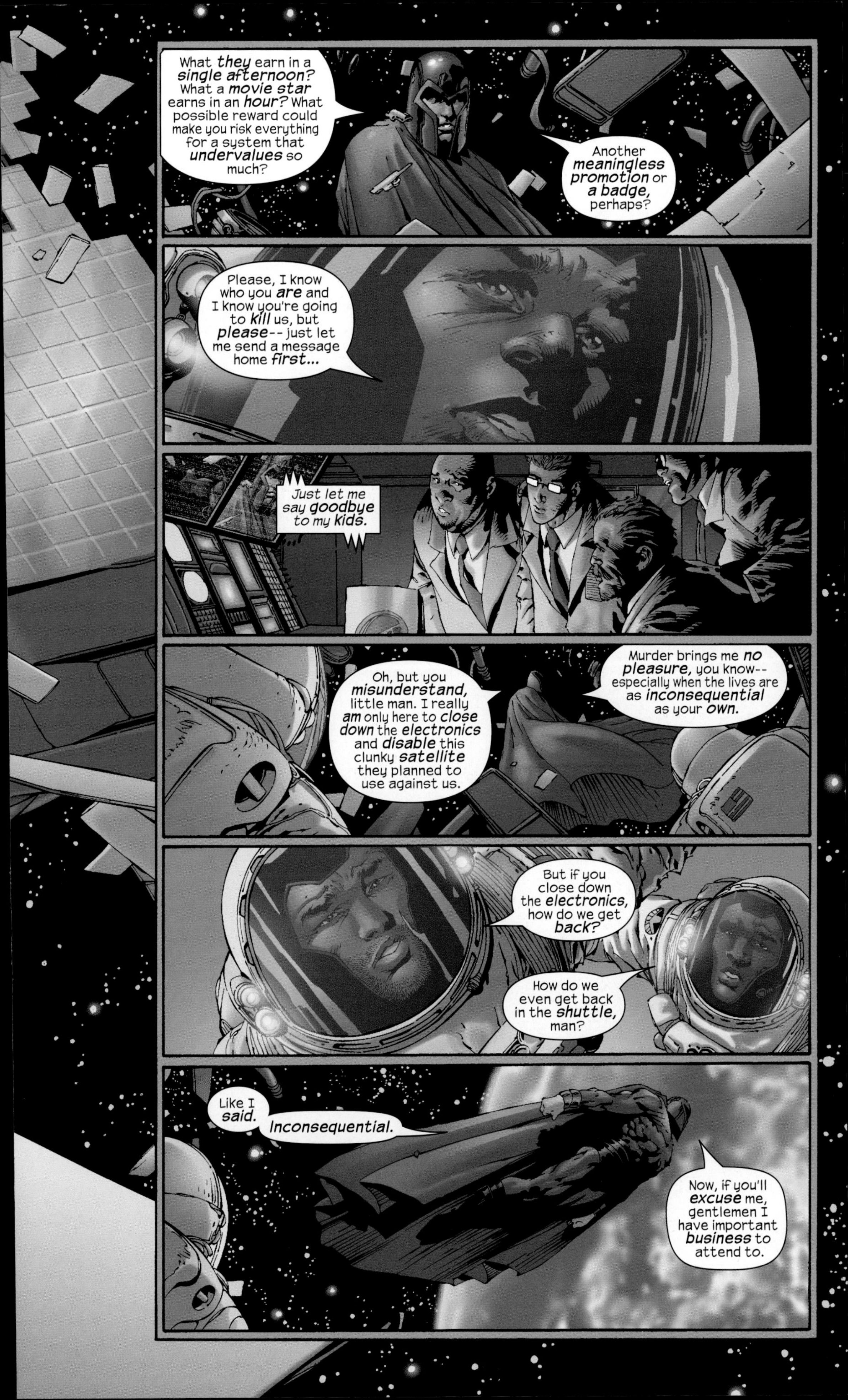

What they earn in a single afternoon? What a movie star earns in an hour? What possible reward could make you risk everything for a system that undervalues so much?
Another meaningless promotion or a badge, perhaps?
Please, I know who you are and I know you're going to kill us, but please-- just let me send a message home first...
Just let me say goodbye to my kids.
Oh, but you misunderstand, little man. I really am only here to close down the electronics and disable this clunky satellite they planned to use against us.
Murder brings me no pleasure, you know-- especially when the lives are as inconsequential as your own.
But if you close down the electronics, how do we get back?
How do we even get back in the shuttle, man?
Like I said.
Inconsequential.
Now, if you'll excuse me, gentlemen I have important business to attend to.

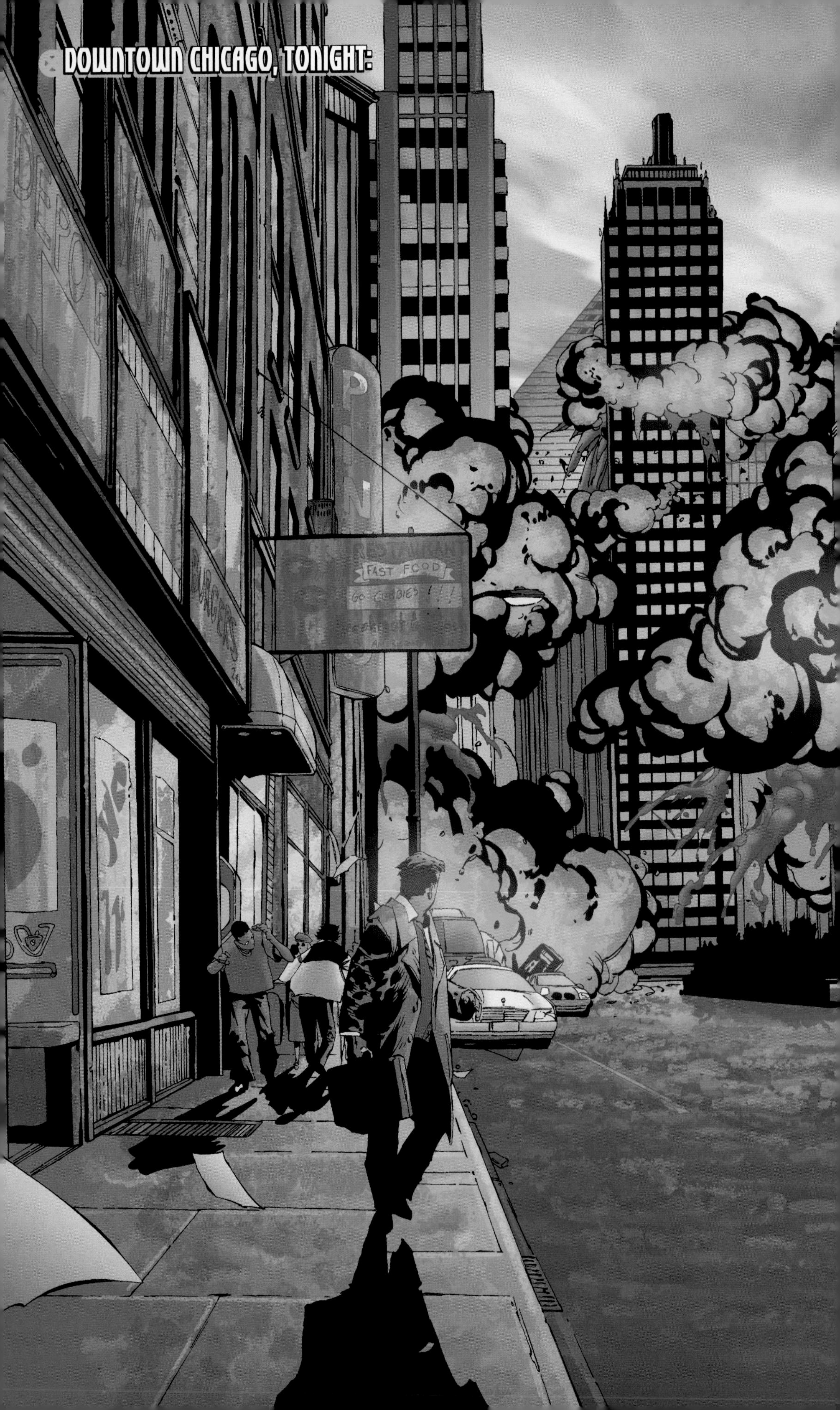
DOWNTOWN CHICAGO, TONIGHT:
RESTAURANT
FAST FOOD
GO CUBBIES!!!
BURGERS

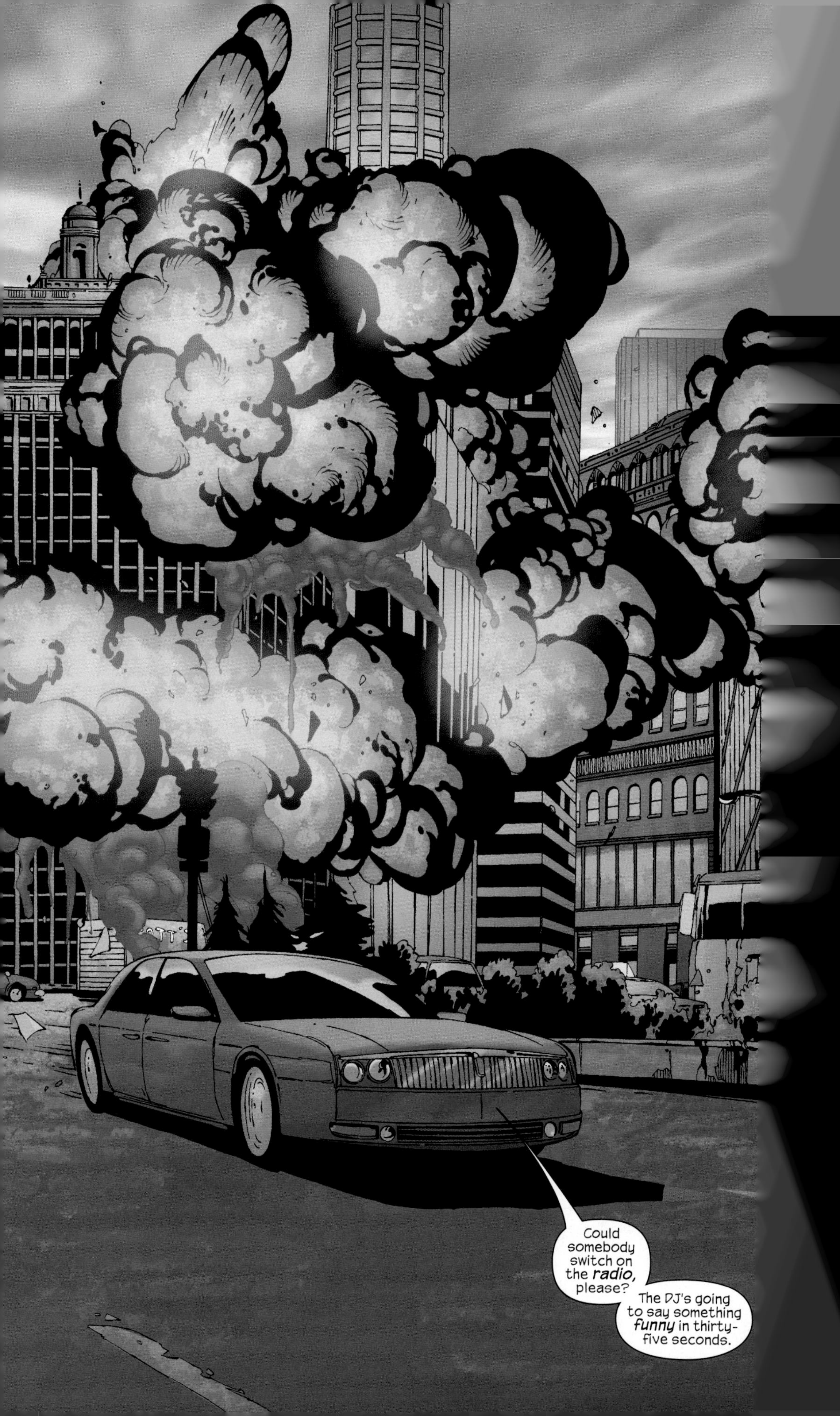
Could somebody switch on the *radio*, please?
The DJ's going to say something *funny* in thirty-five seconds.

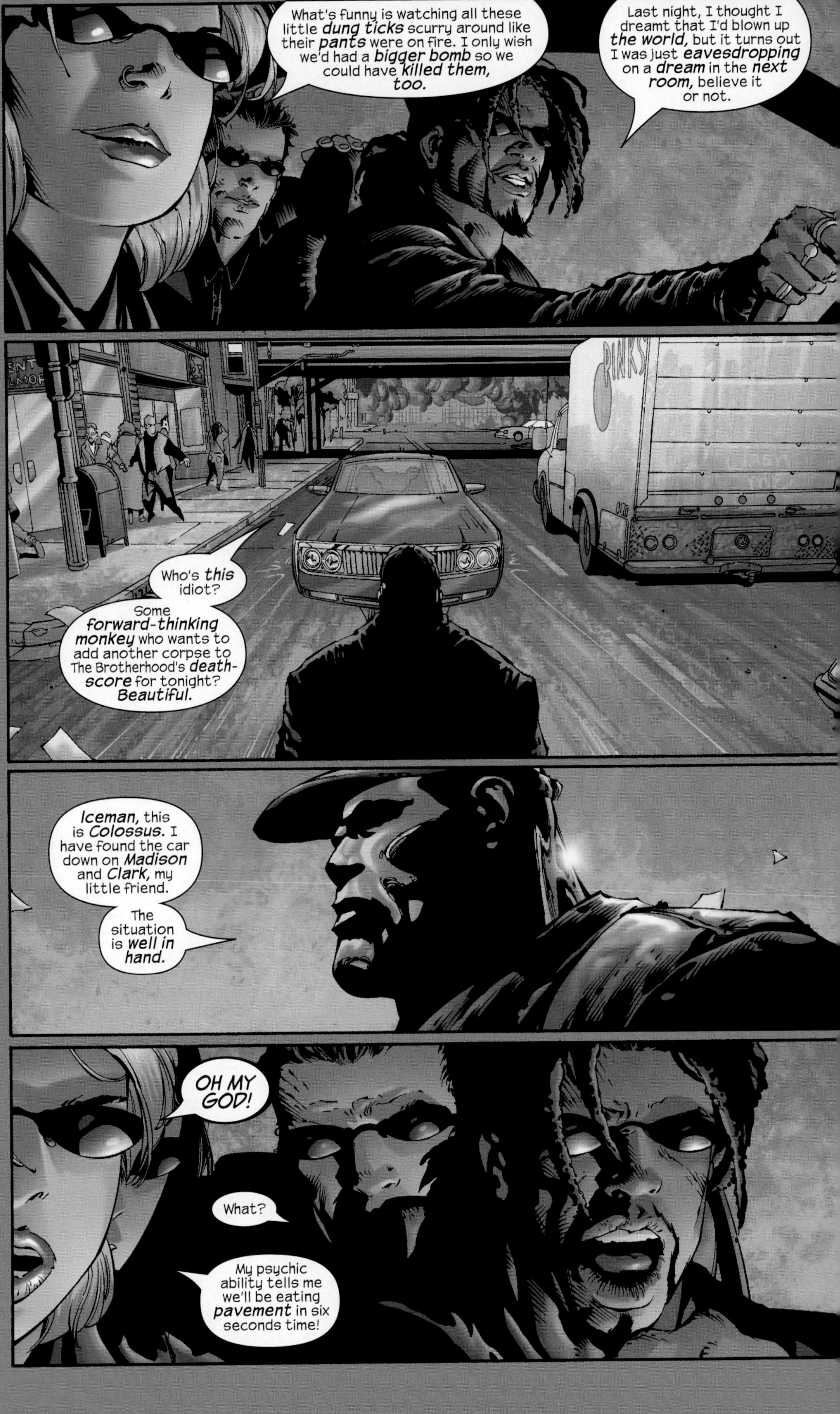
What's funny is watching all these little dung ticks scurry around like their pants were on fire. I only wish we'd had a bigger bomb so we could have killed them, too.
Last night, I thought I dreamt that I'd blown up the world, but it turns out I was just eavesdropping on a dream in the next room, believe it or not.
PINKS
Who's this idiot?
Some forward-thinking monkey who wants to add another corpse to The Brotherhood's death-score for tonight? Beautiful.
Iceman, this is Colossus. I have found the car down on Madison and Clark, my little friend.
The situation is well in hand.
OH MY GOD!
What?
My psychic ability tells me we'll be eating pavement in six seconds time!

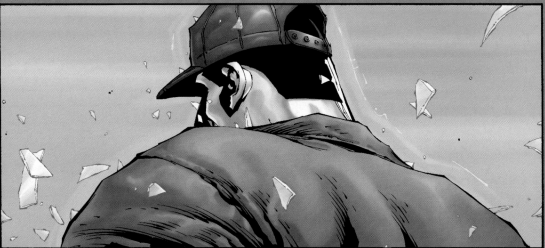

AAAGH!!

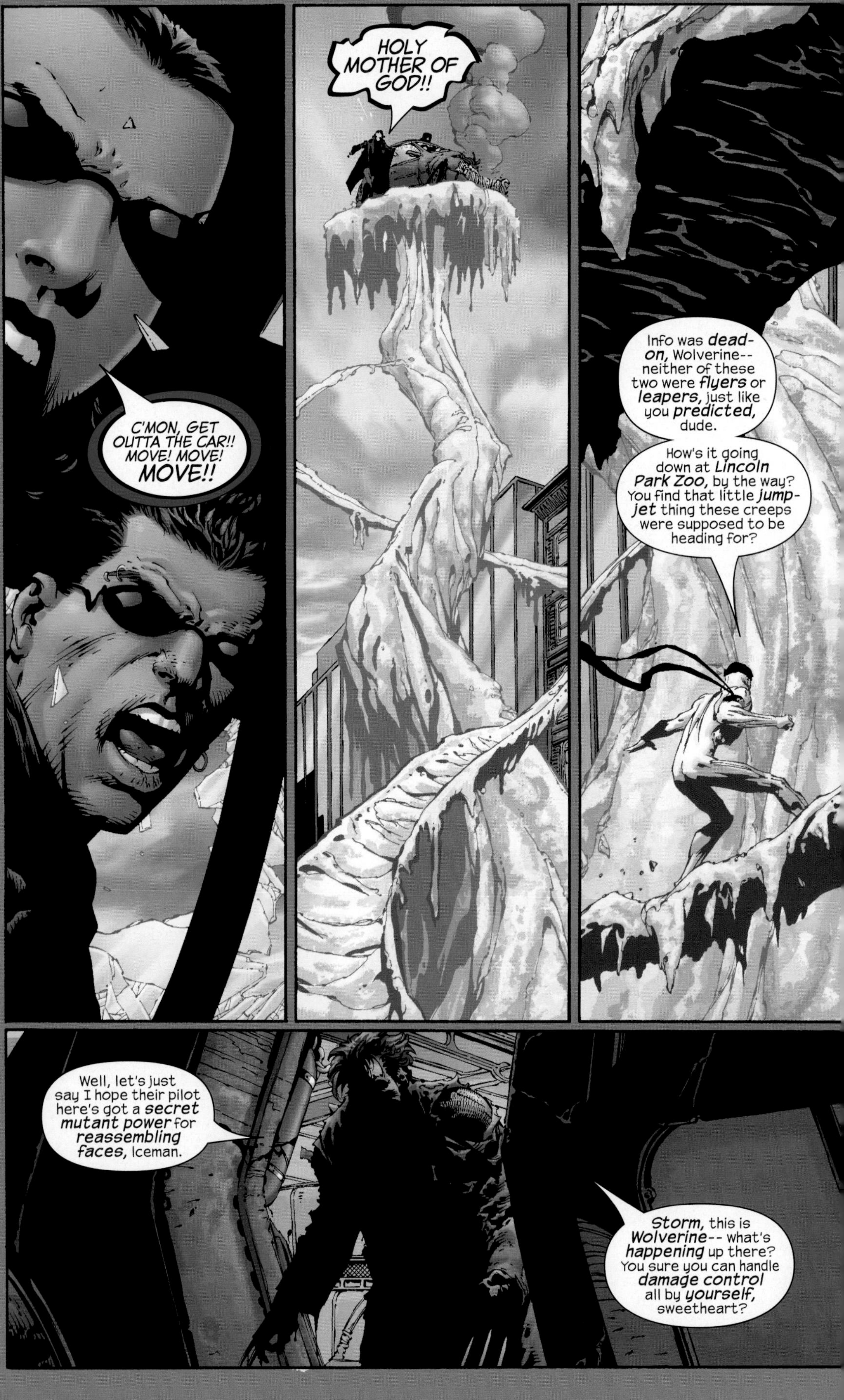
C'MON, GET OUTTA THE CAR!! MOVE! MOVE! MOVE!!
HOLY MOTHER OF GOD!!
Info was dead-on, Wolverine--neither of these two were flyers or leapers, just like you predicted, dude.
How's it going down at Lincoln Park Zoo, by the way? You find that little jump-jet thing these creeps were supposed to be heading for?
Well, let's just say I hope their pilot here's got a secret mutant power for reassembling faces, Iceman.
Storm, this is Wolverine-- what's happening up there? You sure you can handle damage control all by yourself, sweetheart?

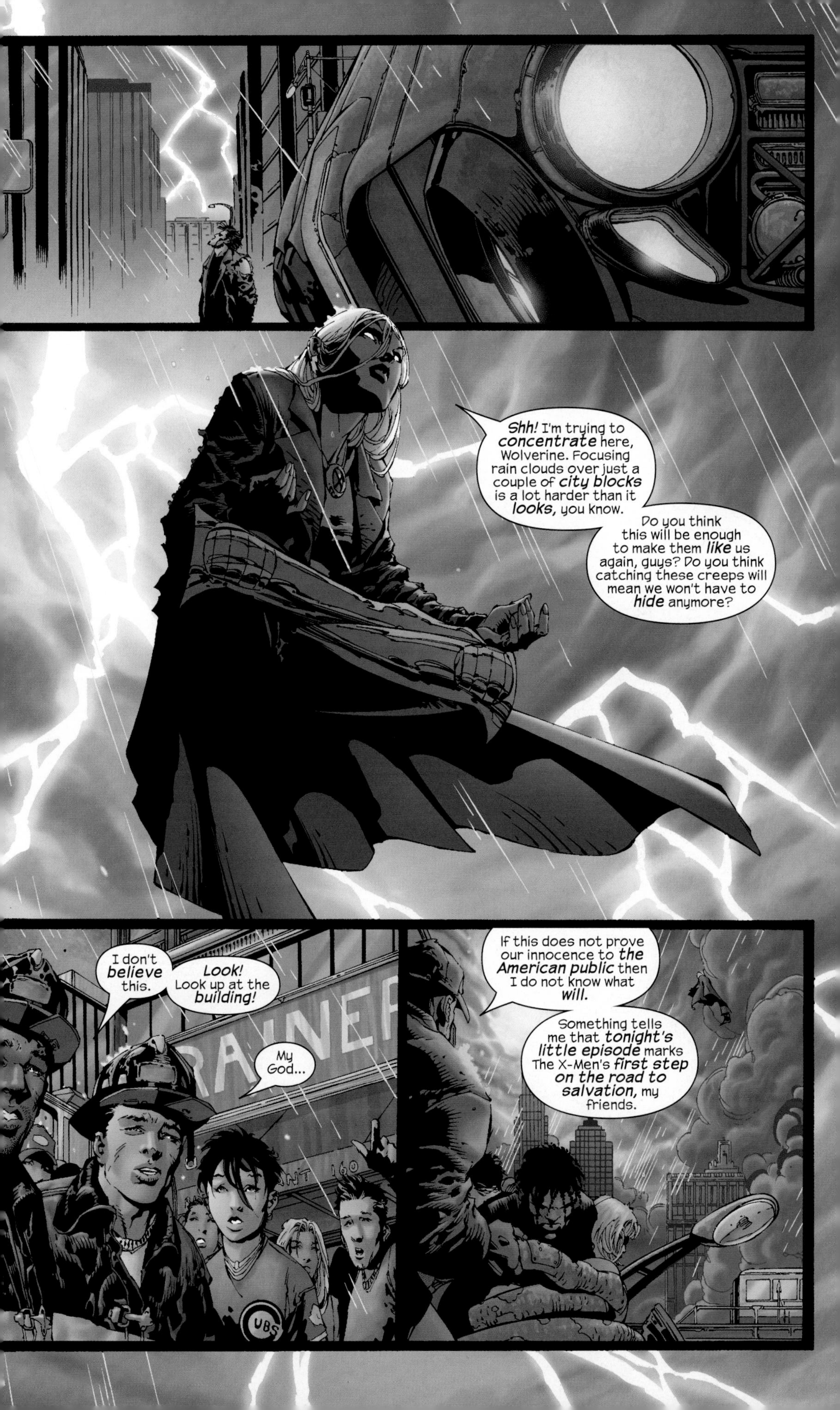

Shh! I'm trying to concentrate here, Wolverine. Focusing rain clouds over just a couple of city blocks is a lot harder than it looks, you know.
Do you think this will be enough to make them like us again, guys? Do you think catching these creeps will mean we won't have to hide anymore?
I don't believe this.
Look! Look up at the building!
My God...
If this does not prove our innocence to the American public then I do not know what will.
Something tells me that tonight's little episode marks The X-Men's first step on the road to salvation, my friends.

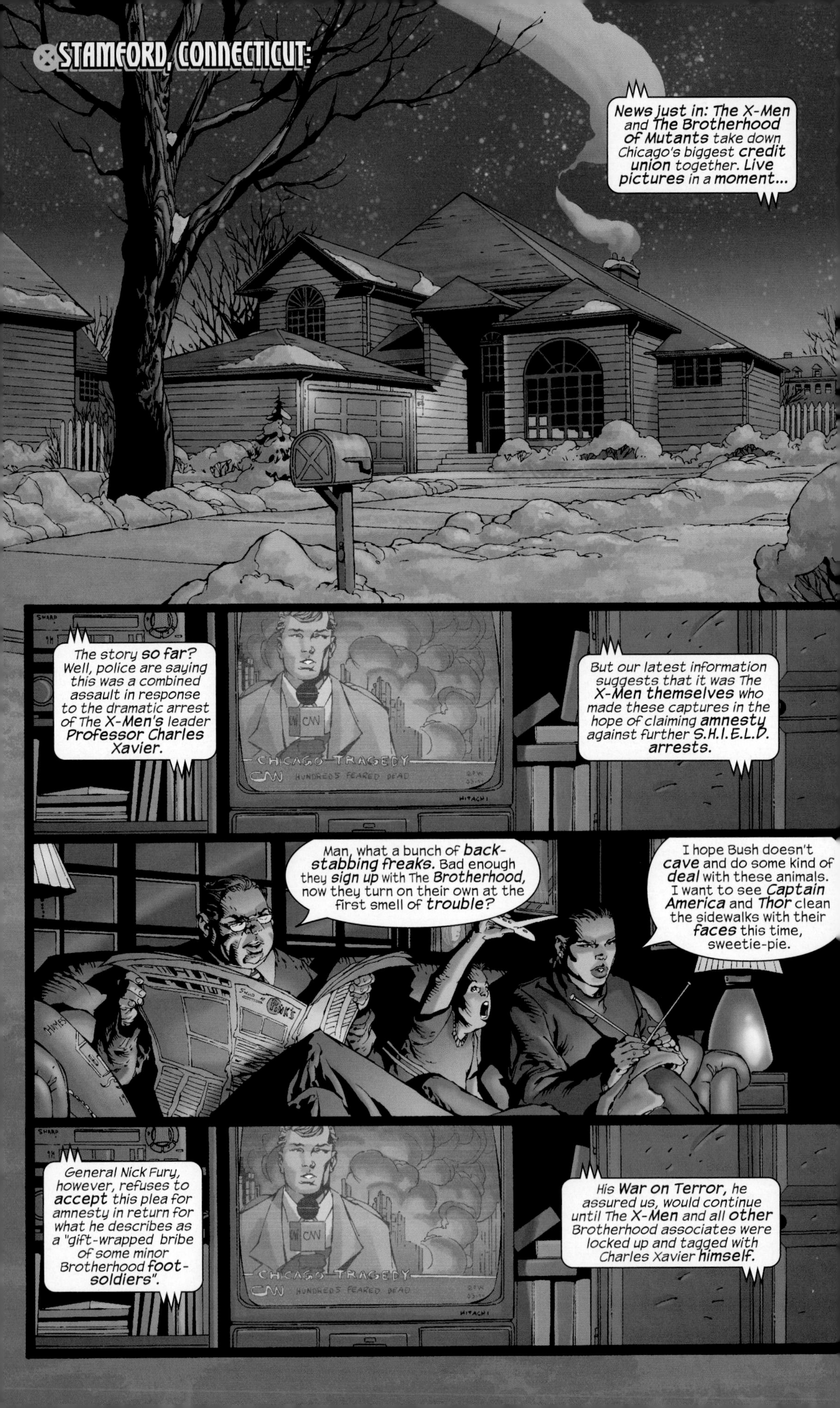
STAMFORD, CONNECTICUT:
News just in: The X-Men and The Brotherhood of Mutants take down Chicago's biggest credit union together. Live pictures in a moment...
The story so far? Well, police are saying this was a combined assault in response to the dramatic arrest of The X-Men's leader Professor Charles Xavier.
CHICAGO TRAGEDY
HUNDREDS FEARED DEAD
But our latest information suggests that it was The X-Men themselves who made these captures in the hope of claiming amnesty against further S.H.I.E.L.D. arrests.
Man, what a bunch of back-stabbing freaks. Bad enough they sign up with The Brotherhood, now they turn on their own at the first smell of trouble?
I hope Bush doesn't cave and do some kind of deal with these animals. I want to see Captain America and Thor clean the sidewalks with their faces this time, sweetie-pie.
General Nick Fury, however, refuses to accept this plea for amnesty in return for what he describes as a "gift-wrapped bribe of some minor Brotherhood foot-soldiers".
CHICAGO TRAGEDY
HUNDREDS FEARED DEAD
His War on Terror, he assured us, would continue until The X-Men and all other Brotherhood associates were locked up and tagged with Charles Xavier himself.

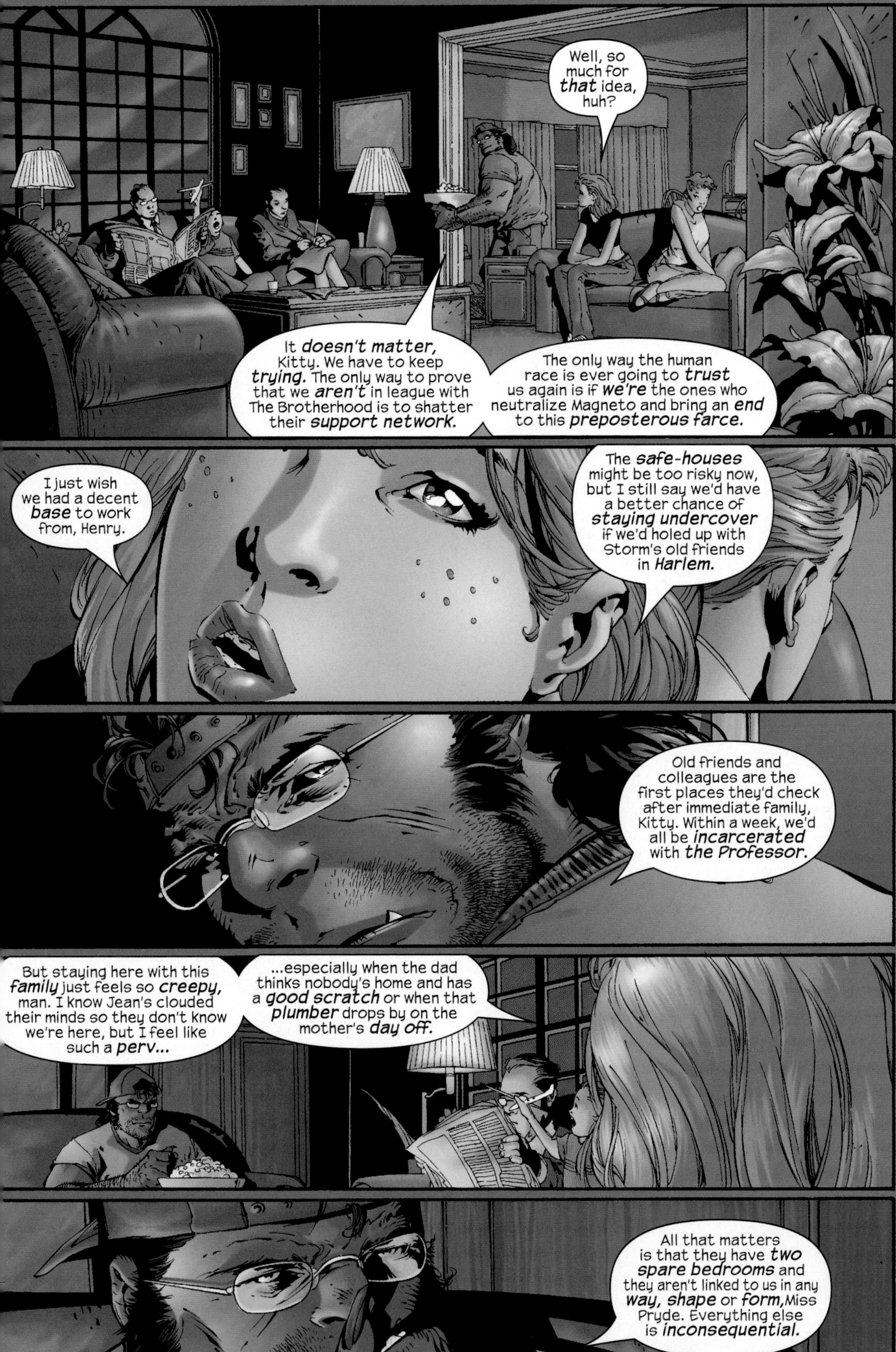
Well, so much for *that* idea, huh?
It *doesn't matter,* Kitty. We have to keep *trying.* The only way to prove that we *aren't* in league with The Brotherhood is to shatter their *support network.*
The only way the human race is ever going to *trust* us again is if *we're* the ones who neutralize Magneto and bring an *end* to this *preposterous farce.*
I just wish we had a decent *base* to work from, Henry.
The *safe-houses* might be too risky now, but I still say we'd have a better chance of *staying undercover* if we'd holed up with Storm's old friends in *Harlem.*
Old friends and colleagues are the first places they'd check after immediate family, Kitty. Within a week, we'd all be *incarcerated* with *the Professor.*
But staying here with this *family* just feels so *creepy,* man. I know Jean's clouded their minds so they don't know we're here, but I feel like such a *perv...*
...especially when the dad thinks nobody's home and has a *good scratch* or when that *plumber* drops by on the mother's *day off.*
All that matters is that they have *two spare bedrooms* and they aren't linked to us in any *way, shape* or *form,* Miss Pryde. Everything else is *inconsequential.*

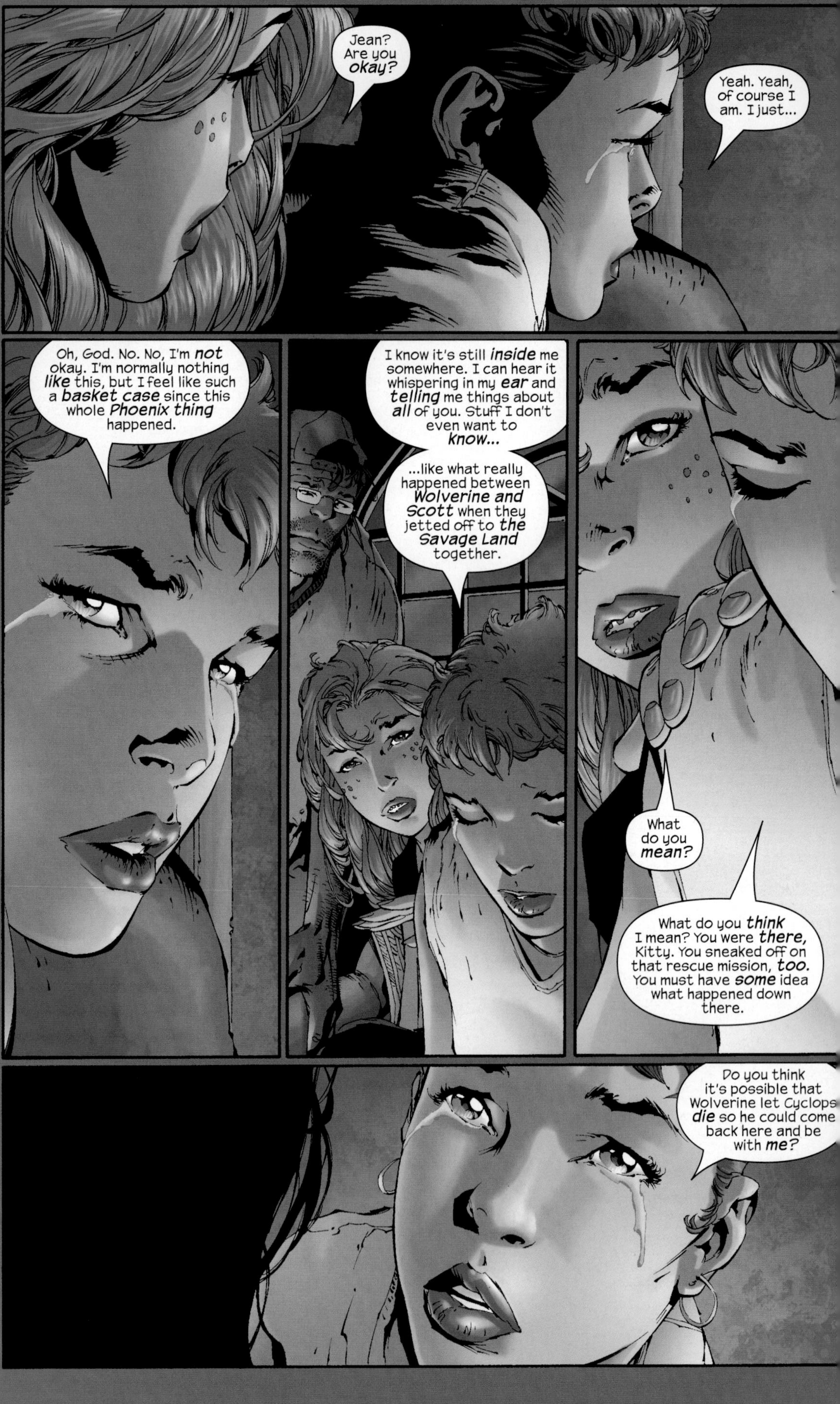
Jean? Are you okay?
Yeah. Yeah, of course I am. I just...
Oh, God. No. No, I'm not okay. I'm normally nothing like this, but I feel like such a basket case since this whole Phoenix thing happened.
I know it's still inside me somewhere. I can hear it whispering in my ear and telling me things about all of you. Stuff I don't even want to know...
...like what really happened between Wolverine and Scott when they jetted off to the Savage Land together.
What do you mean?
What do you think I mean? You were there, Kitty. You sneaked off on that rescue mission, too. You must have some idea what happened down there.
Do you think it's possible that Wolverine let Cyclops die so he could come back here and be with me?

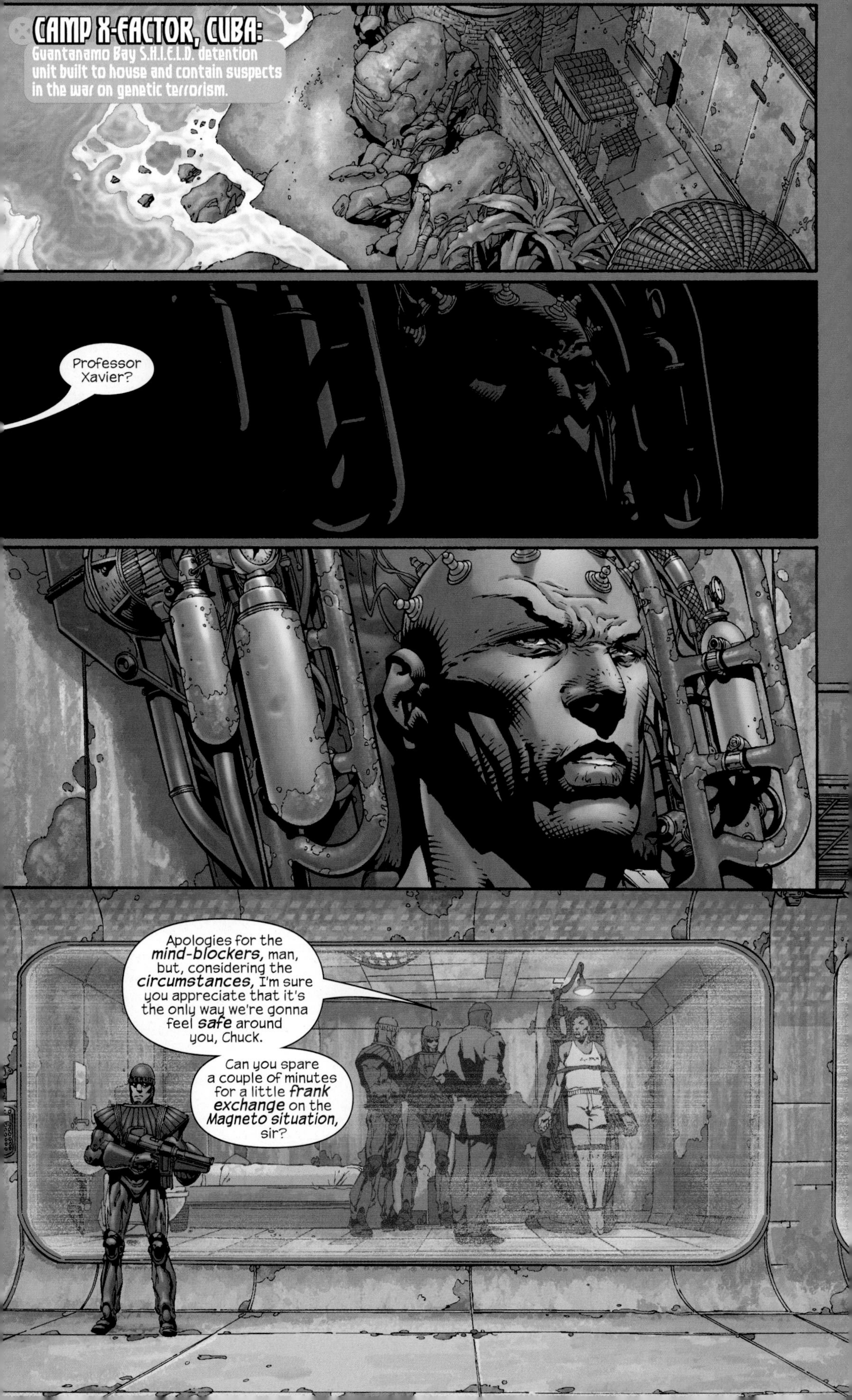
CAMP X-FACTOR, CUBA:
Guantanamo Bay S.H.I.E.L.D. detention unit built to house and contain suspects in the war on genetic terrorism.
Professor Xavier?
Apologies for the mind-blockers, man, but, considering the circumstances, I'm sure you appreciate that it's the only way we're gonna feel safe around you, Chuck.
Can you spare a couple of minutes for a little frank exchange on the Magneto situation, sir?

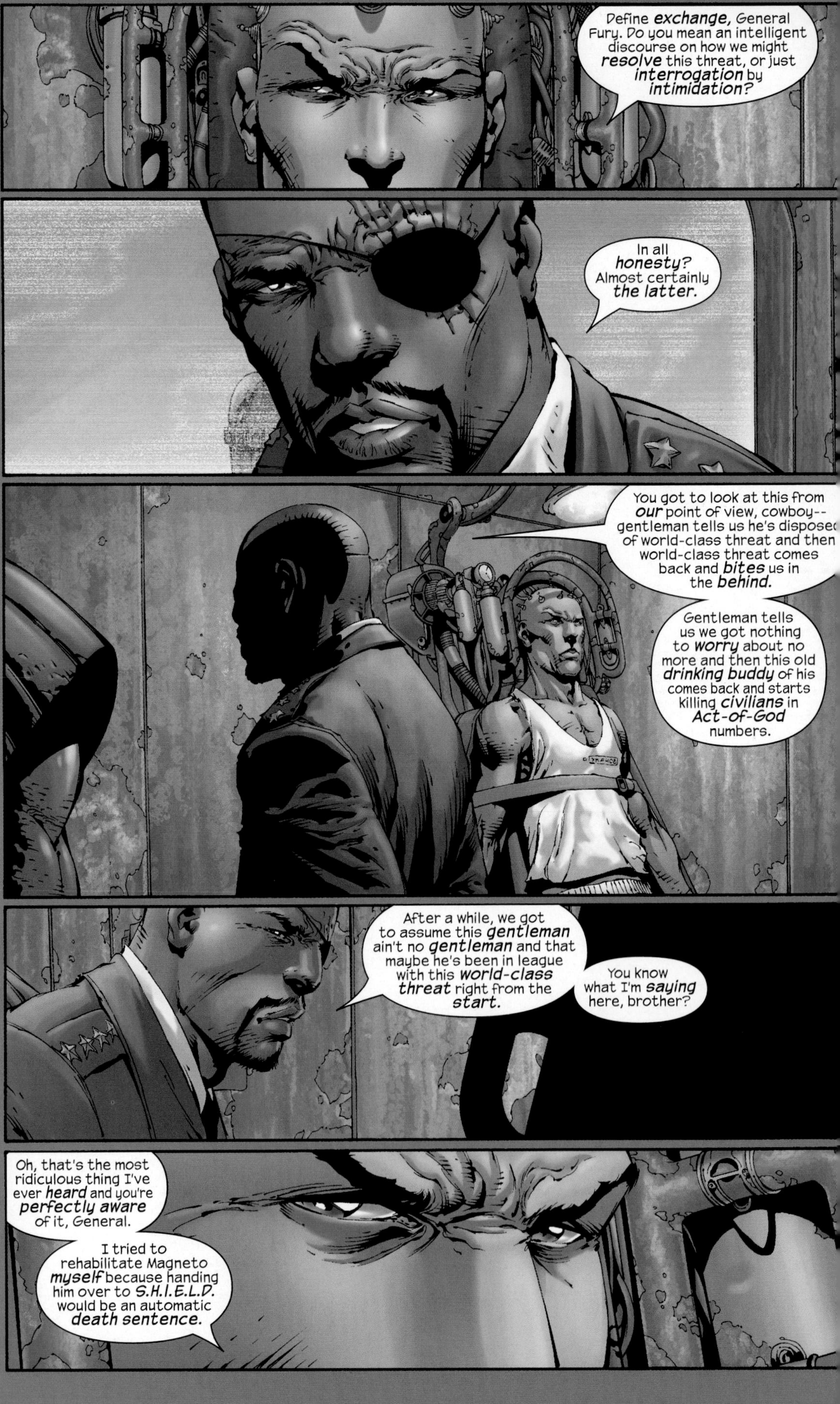
Define exchange, General Fury. Do you mean an intelligent discourse on how we might resolve this threat, or just interrogation by intimidation?
In all honesty? Almost certainly the latter.
You got to look at this from our point of view, cowboy-- gentleman tells us he's disposed of world-class threat and then world-class threat comes back and bites us in the behind.
Gentleman tells us we got nothing to worry about no more and then this old drinking buddy of his comes back and starts killing civilians in Act-of-God numbers.
After a while, we got to assume this gentleman ain't no gentleman and that maybe he's been in league with this world-class threat right from the start.
You know what I'm saying here, brother?
Oh, that's the most ridiculous thing I've ever heard and you're perfectly aware of it, General.
I tried to rehabilitate Magneto myself because handing him over to S.H.I.E.L.D. would be an automatic death sentence.

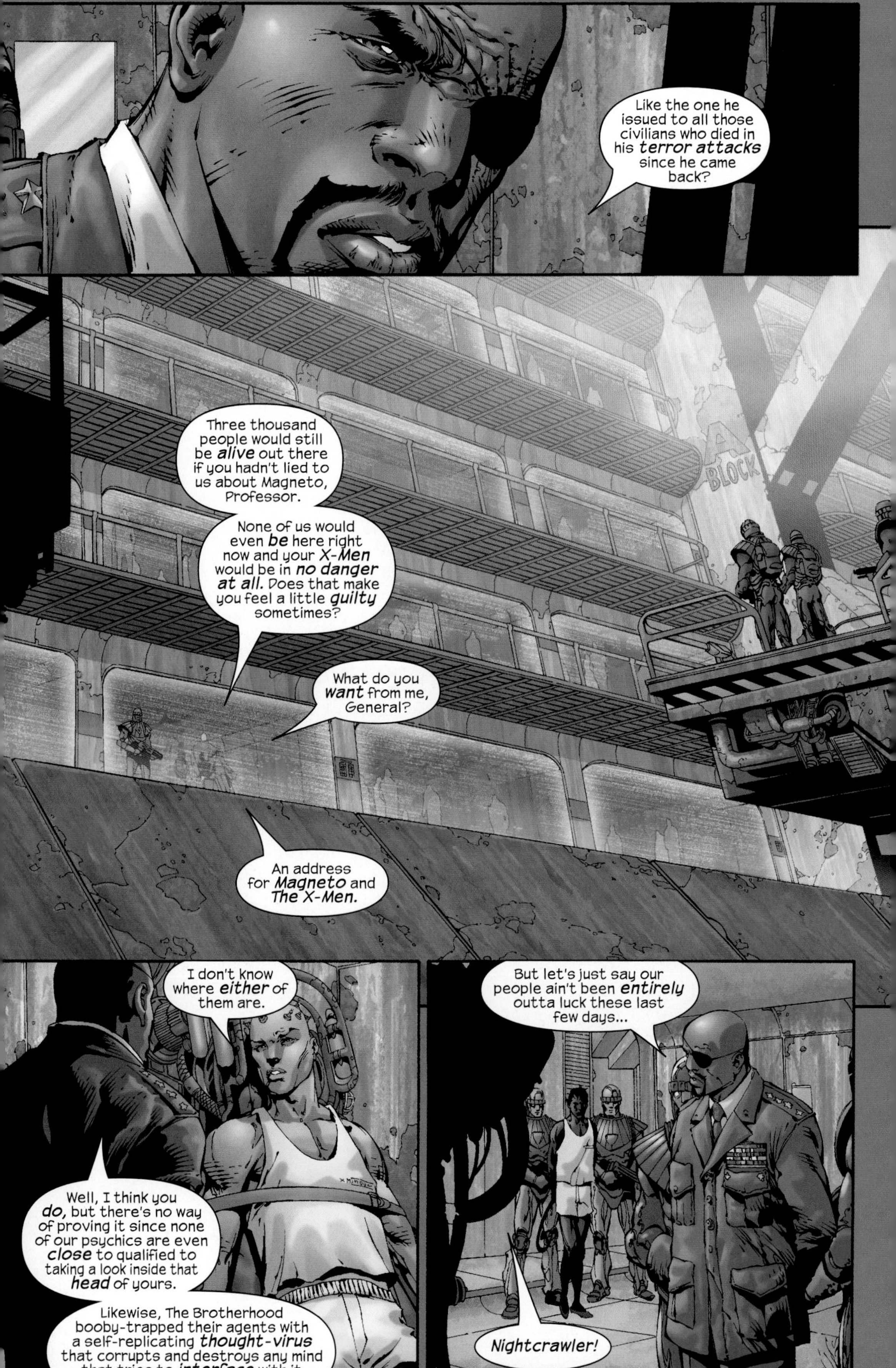
Like the one he issued to all those civilians who died in his *terror attacks* since he came back?
A BLOCK
Three thousand people would still be *alive* out there if you hadn't lied to us about Magneto, Professor.
None of us would even *be* here right now and your *X-Men* would be in *no danger at all.* Does that make you feel a little *guilty* sometimes?
What do you *want* from me, General?
An address for *Magneto* and *The X-Men.*
I don't know where *either* of them are.
Well, I think you *do,* but there's no way of proving it since none of our psychics are even *close* to qualified to taking a look inside that *head* of yours.
Likewise, The Brotherhood booby-trapped their agents with a self-replicating *thought-virus* that corrupts and destroys any mind that tries to *interface* with it.
But let's just say our people ain't been *entirely* outta luck these last few days...
Nightcrawler!

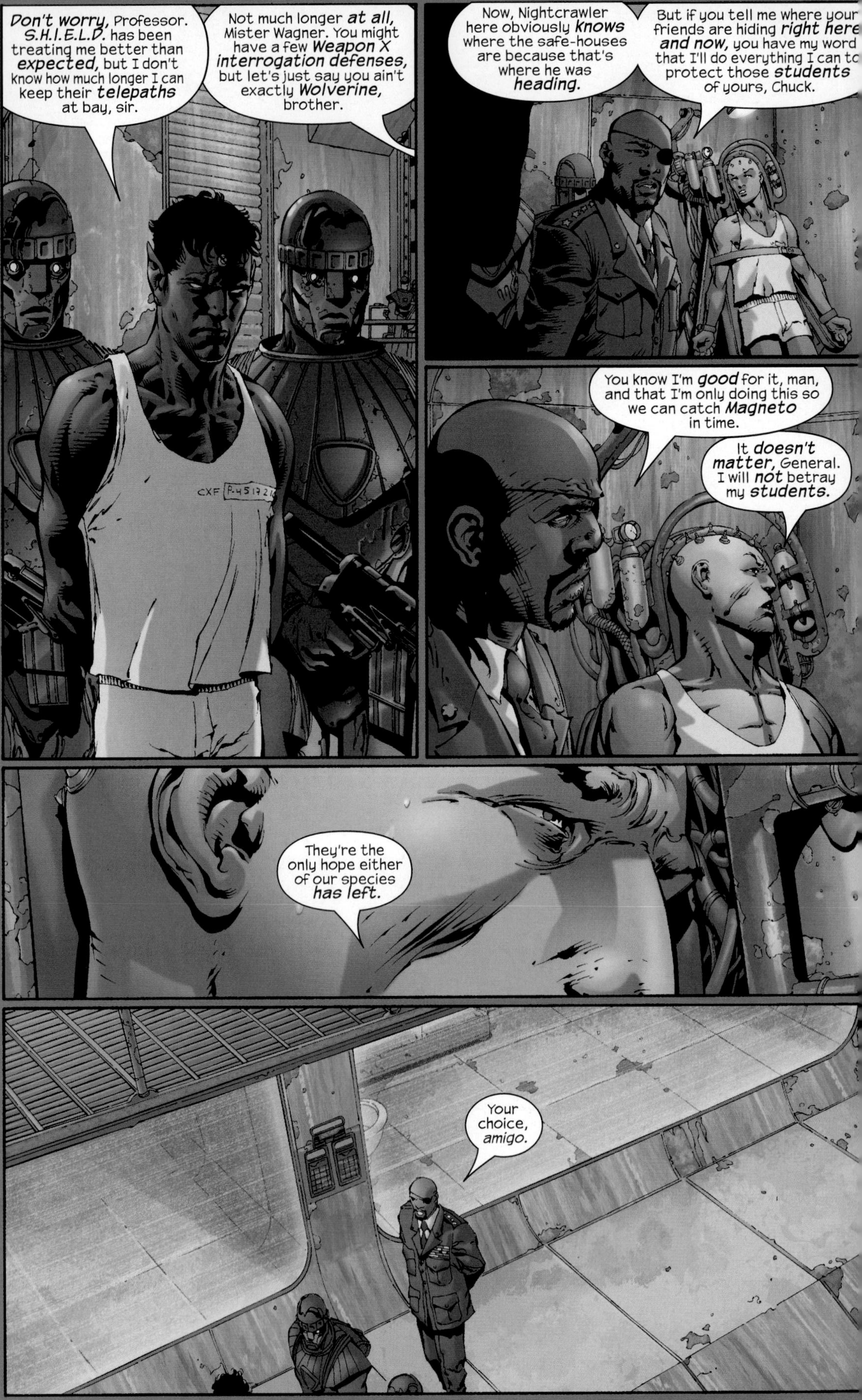

Don't worry, Professor. S.H.I.E.L.D. has been treating me better than expected, but I don't know how much longer I can keep their telepaths at bay, sir.
Not much longer at all, Mister Wagner. You might have a few Weapon X interrogation defenses, but let's just say you ain't exactly Wolverine, brother.
CXF P-4517216
Now, Nightcrawler here obviously knows where the safe-houses are because that's where he was heading.
But if you tell me where your friends are hiding right here and now, you have my word that I'll do everything I can to protect those students of yours, Chuck.
You know I'm good for it, man, and that I'm only doing this so we can catch Magneto in time.
It doesn't matter, General. I will not betray my students.
They're the only hope either of our species has left.
Your choice, amigo.

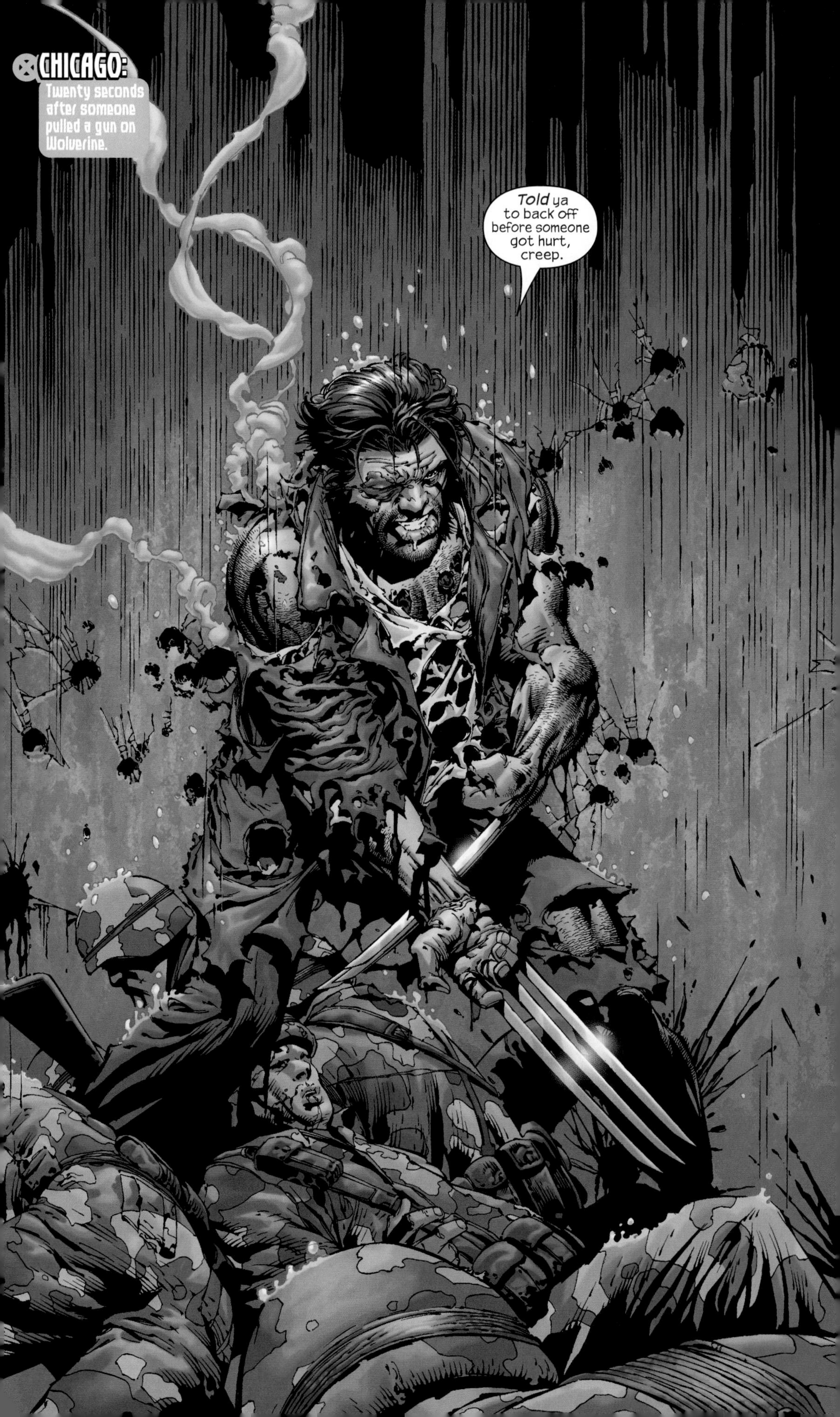
CHICAGO:
Twenty seconds after someone pulled a gun on Wolverine.
Told ya to back off before someone got hurt, creep.

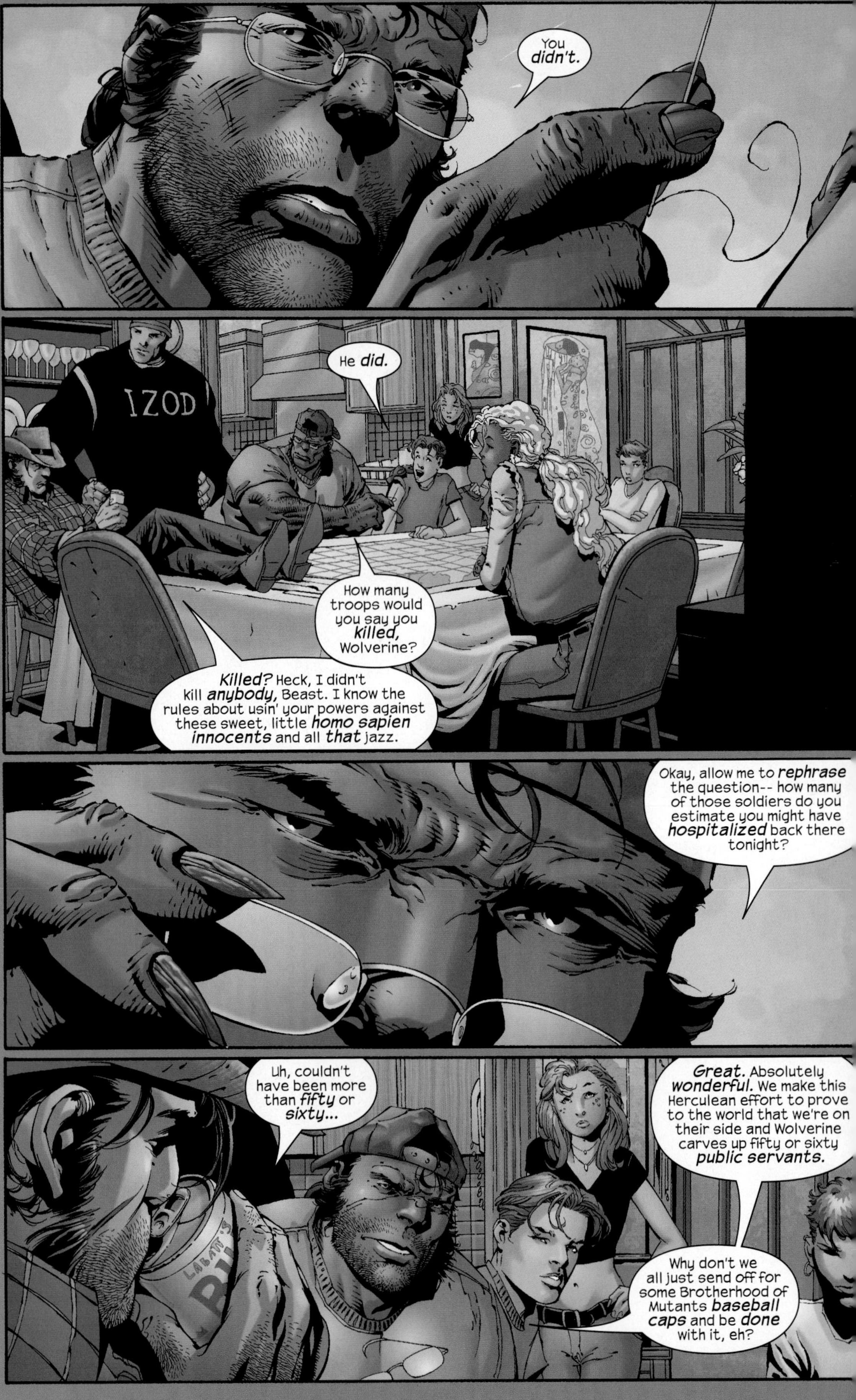

You didn't.
He did.
How many troops would you say you killed, Wolverine?
Killed? Heck, I didn't kill anybody, Beast. I know the rules about usin' your powers against these sweet, little homo sapien innocents and all that jazz.
Okay, allow me to rephrase the question-- how many of those soldiers do you estimate you might have hospitalized back there tonight?
Uh, couldn't have been more than fifty or sixty...
Great. Absolutely wonderful. We make this Herculean effort to prove to the world that we're on their side and Wolverine carves up fifty or sixty public servants.
Why don't we all just send off for some Brotherhood of Mutants baseball caps and be done with it, eh?

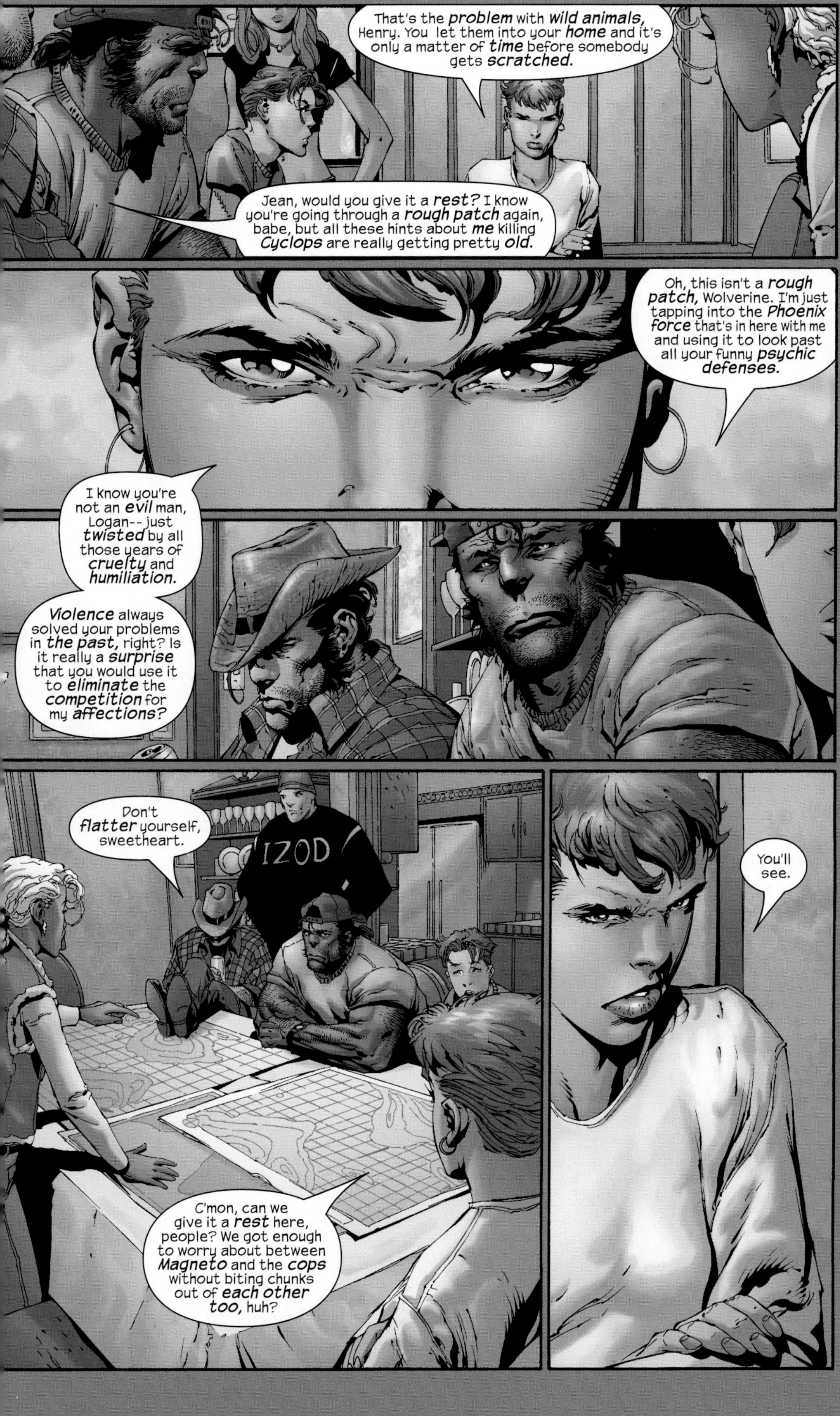
That's the problem with wild animals, Henry. You let them into your home and it's only a matter of time before somebody gets scratched.
Jean, would you give it a rest? I know you're going through a rough patch again, babe, but all these hints about me killing Cyclops are really getting pretty old.
Oh, this isn't a rough patch, Wolverine. I'm just tapping into the Phoenix force that's in here with me and using it to look past all your funny psychic defenses.
I know you're not an evil man, Logan--just twisted by all those years of cruelty and humiliation.
Violence always solved your problems in the past, right? Is it really a surprise that you would use it to eliminate the competition for my affections?
Don't flatter yourself, sweetheart.
IZOD
C'mon, can we give it a rest here, people? We got enough to worry about between Magneto and the cops without biting chunks out of each other too, huh?
You'll see.

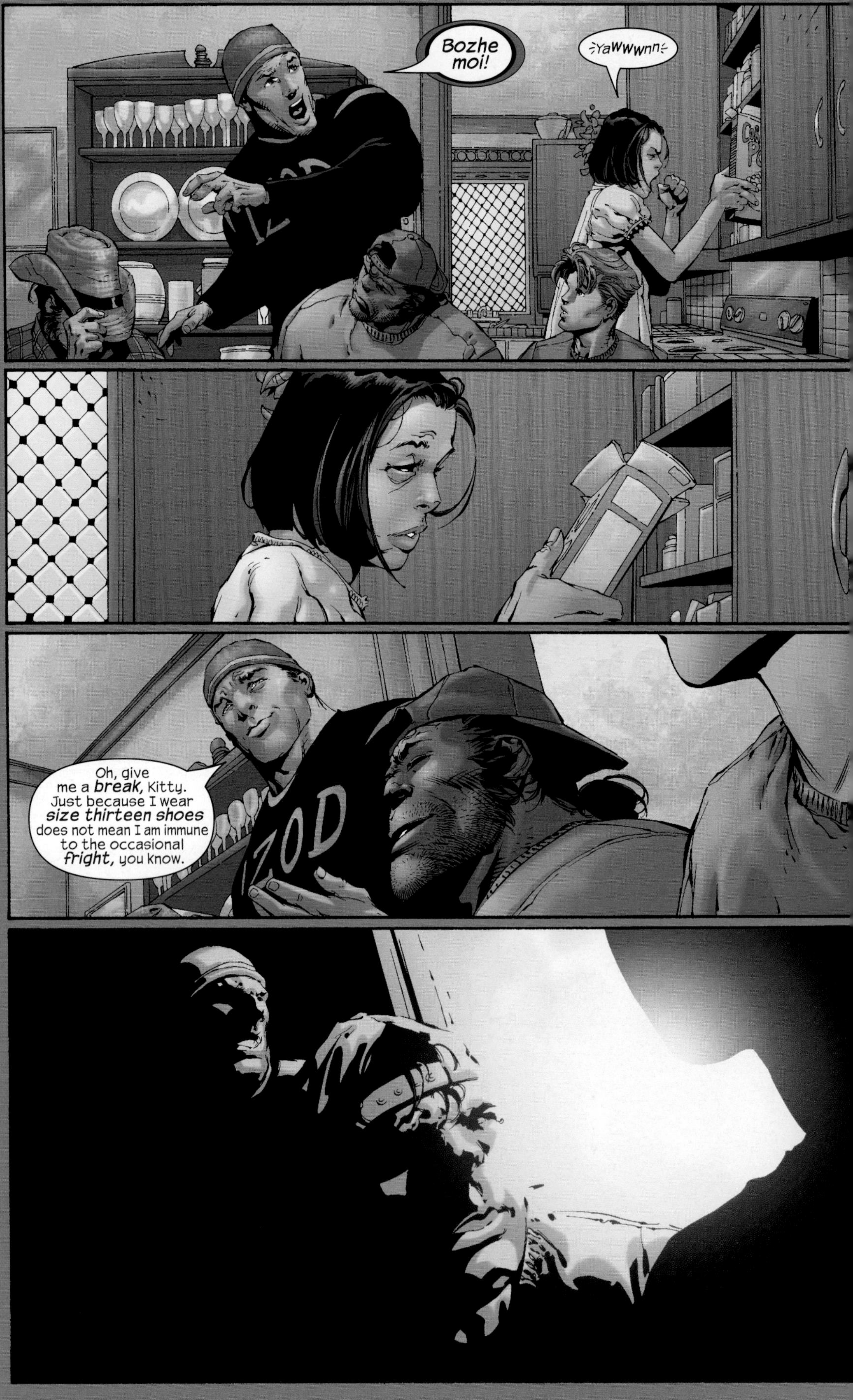
Bozhe moi!
-YaWWWnn-
Oh, give me a break, Kitty. Just because I wear size thirteen shoes does not mean I am immune to the occasional fright, you know.

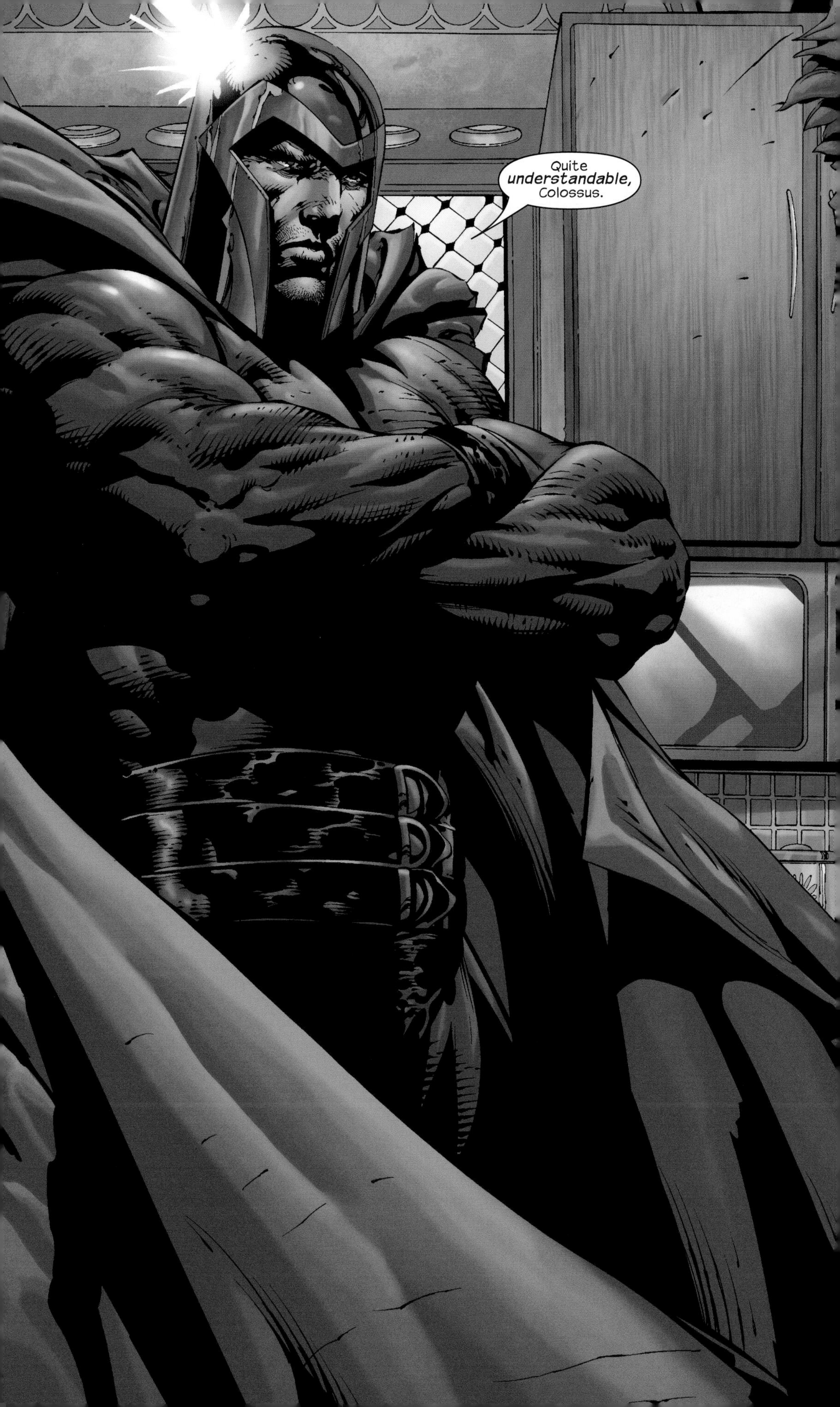
Quite *understandable,* Colossus.

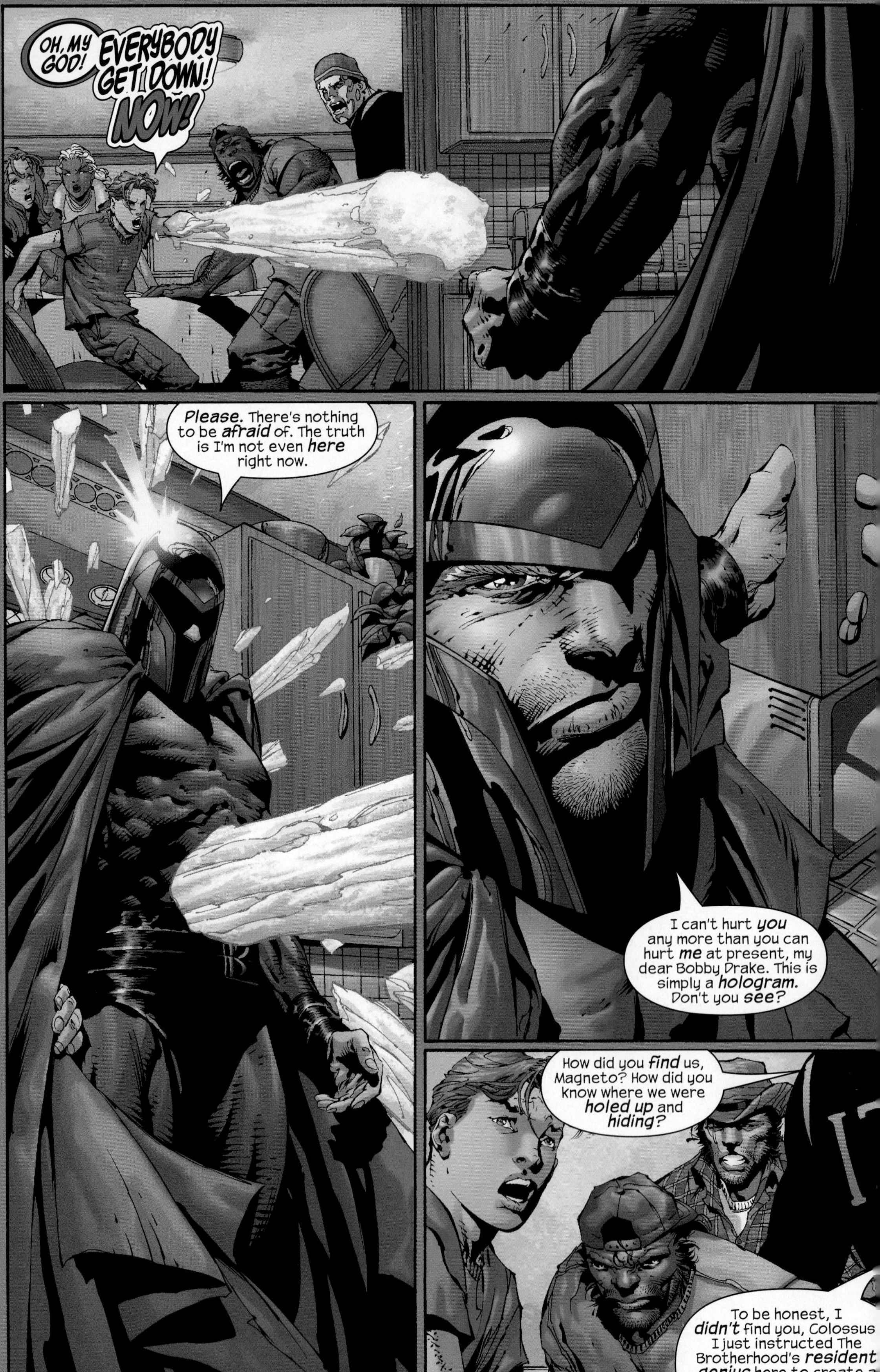

OH, MY GOD!
EVERYBODY GET DOWN! NOW!
Please. There's nothing to be afraid of. The truth is I'm not even here right now.
I can't hurt you any more than you can hurt me at present, my dear Bobby Drake. This is simply a hologram. Don't you see?
How did you find us, Magneto? How did you know where we were holed up and hiding?
To be honest, I didn't find you, Colossus. I just instructed The Brotherhood's resident genius here to create a means of contacting you wherever you were.

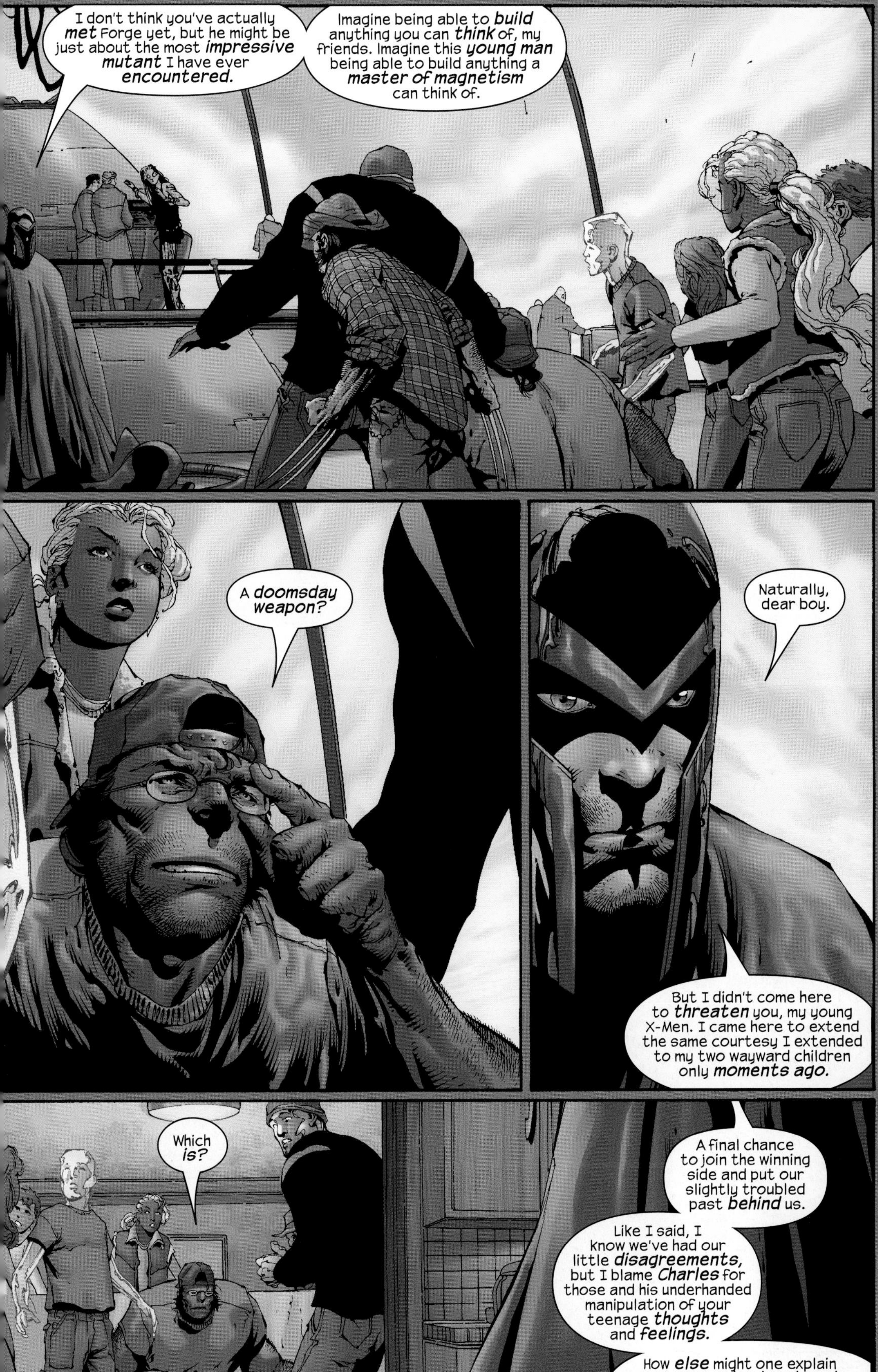

I don't think you've actually met Forge yet, but he might be just about the most impressive mutant I have ever encountered.
Imagine being able to build anything you can think of, my friends. Imagine this young man being able to build anything a master of magnetism can think of.
A doomsday weapon?
Naturally, dear boy.
But I didn't come here to threaten you, my young X-Men. I came here to extend the same courtesy I extended to my two wayward children only moments ago.
Which is?
A final chance to join the winning side and put our slightly troubled past behind us.
Like I said, I know we've had our little disagreements, but I blame Charles for those and his underhanded manipulation of your teenage thoughts and feelings.
How else might one explain a group of mutant outcasts who would fight to save a world that hates and fears them, eh?

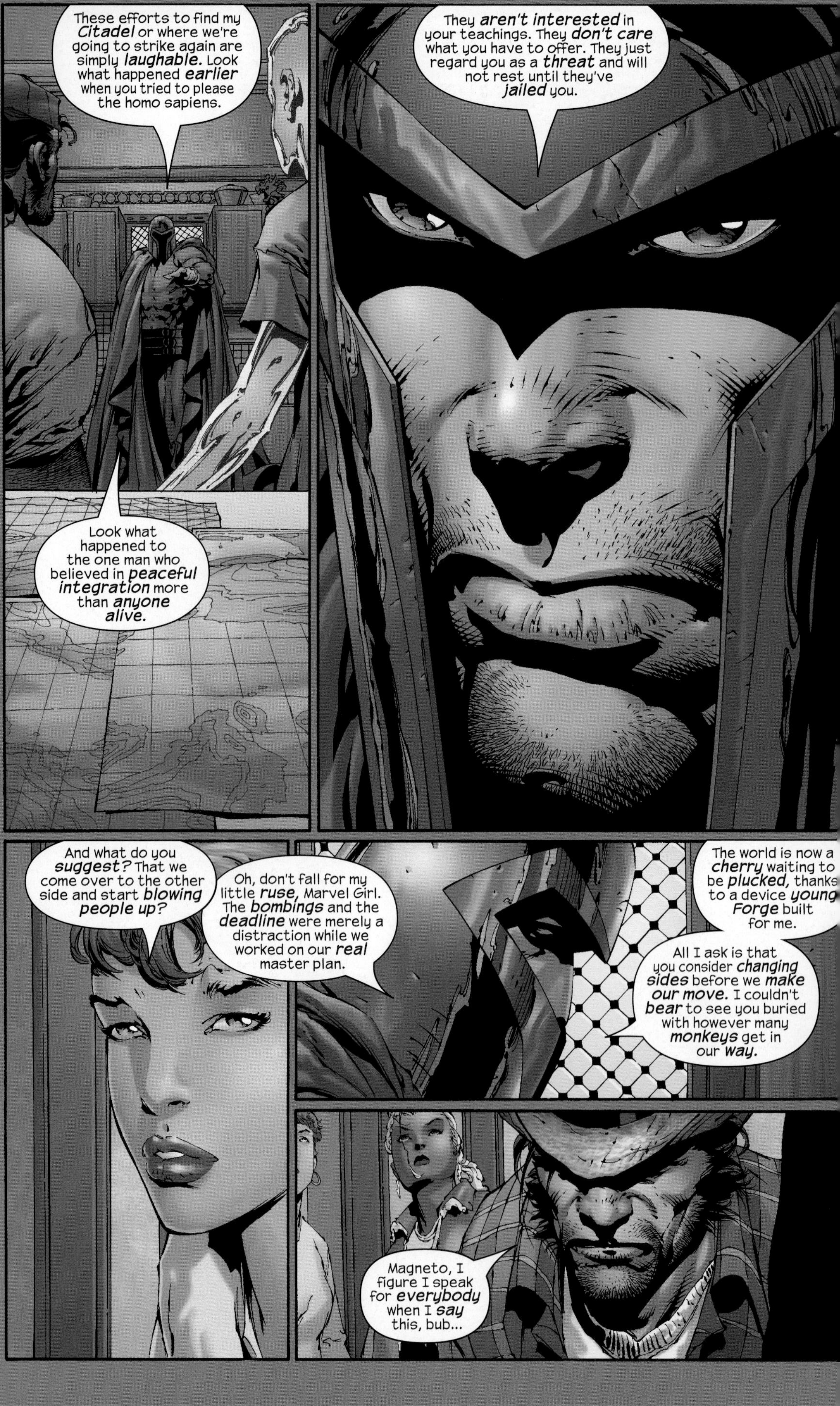
These efforts to find my Citadel or where we're going to strike again are simply laughable. Look what happened earlier when you tried to please the homo sapiens.
Look what happened to the one man who believed in peaceful integration more than anyone alive.
They aren't interested in your teachings. They don't care what you have to offer. They just regard you as a threat and will not rest until they've jailed you.
And what do you suggest? That we come over to the other side and start blowing people up?
Oh, don't fall for my little ruse, Marvel Girl. The bombings and the deadline were merely a distraction while we worked on our real master plan.
The world is now a cherry waiting to be plucked, thanks to a device young Forge built for me.
All I ask is that you consider changing sides before we make our move. I couldn't bear to see you buried with however many monkeys get in our way.
Magneto, I figure I speak for everybody when I say this, bub...

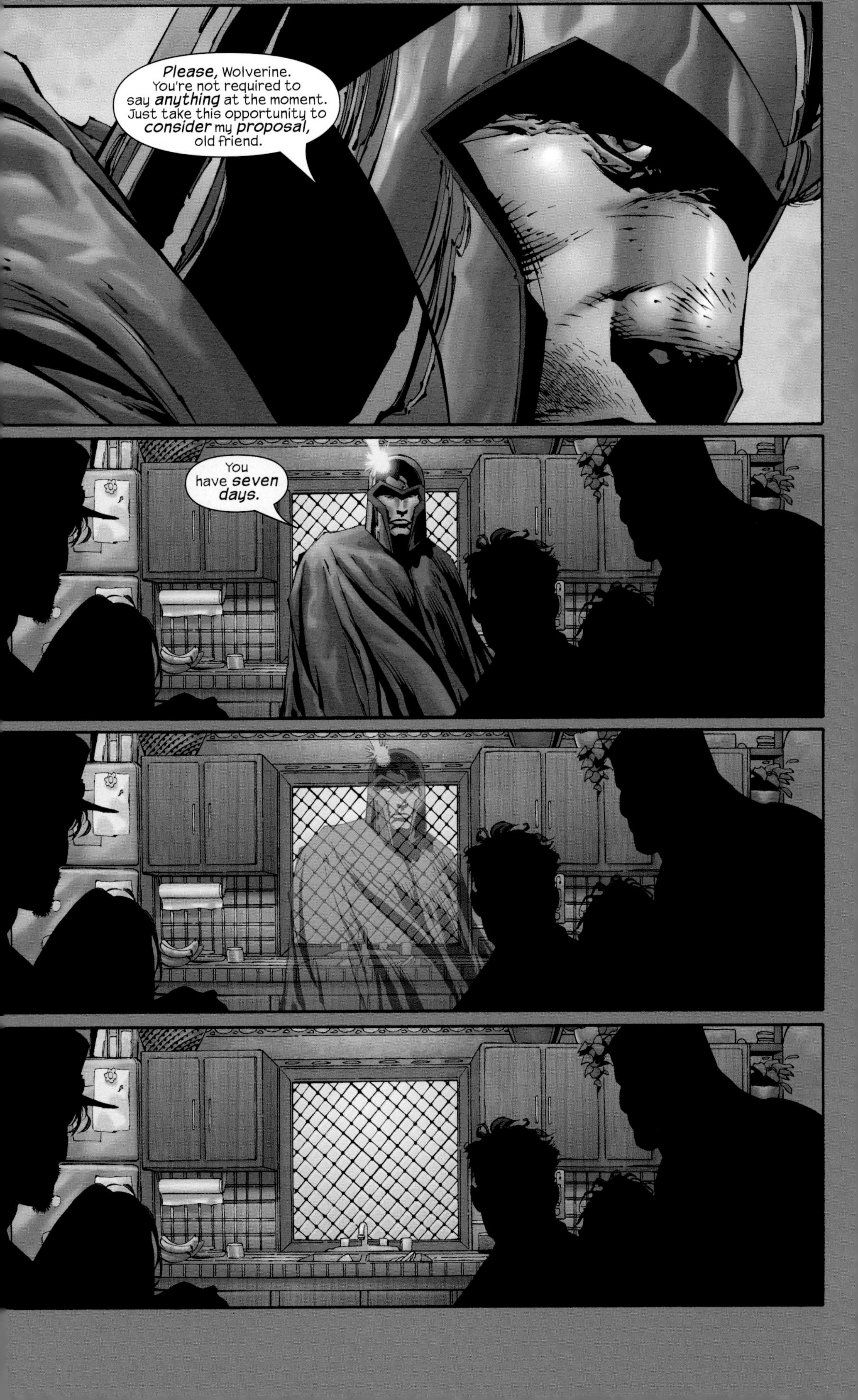
Please, Wolverine. You're not required to say anything at the moment. Just take this opportunity to consider my proposal, old friend.
You have seven days.

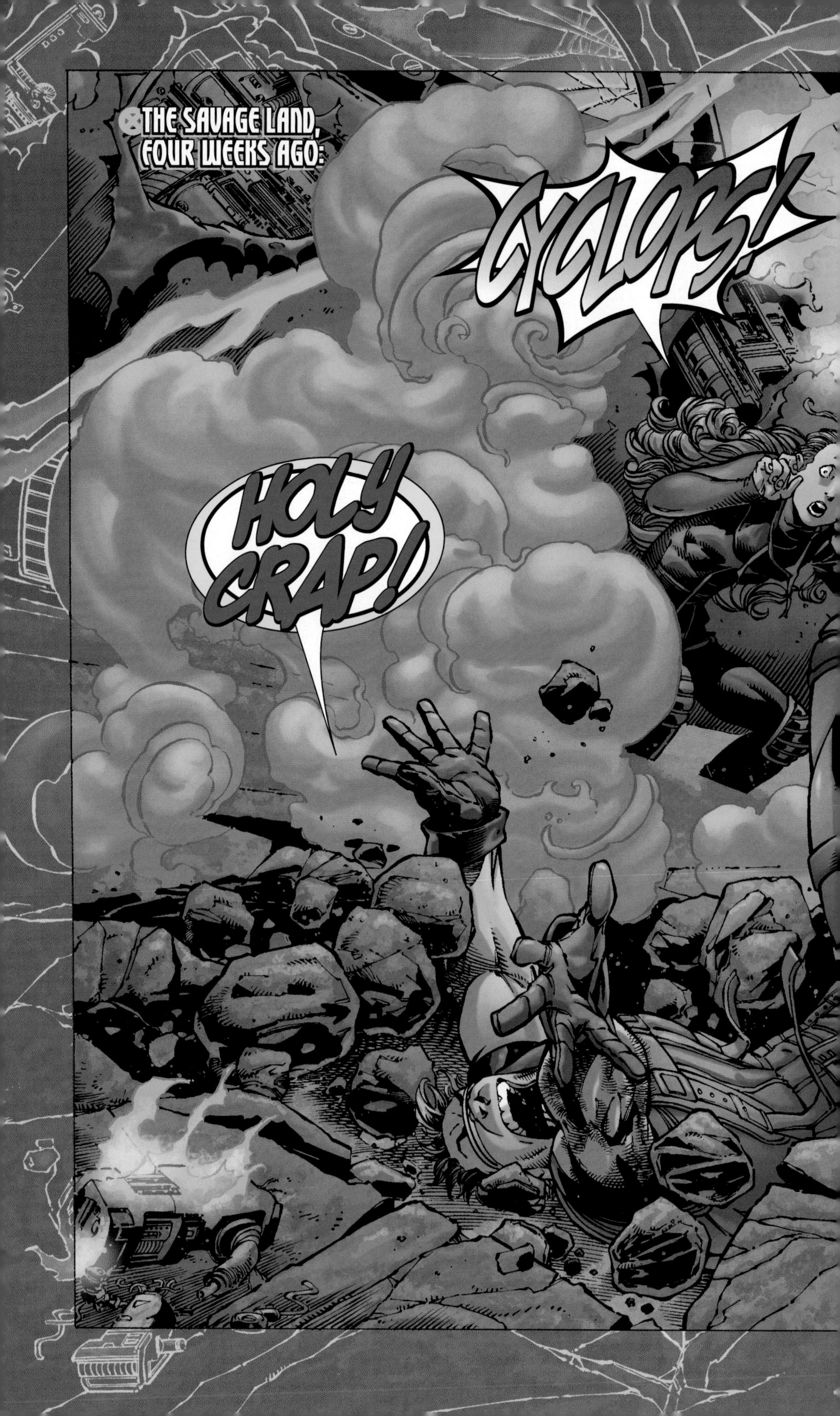
THE SAVAGE LAND, FOUR WEEKS AGO:
CYCLOPS!
HOLY CRAP!

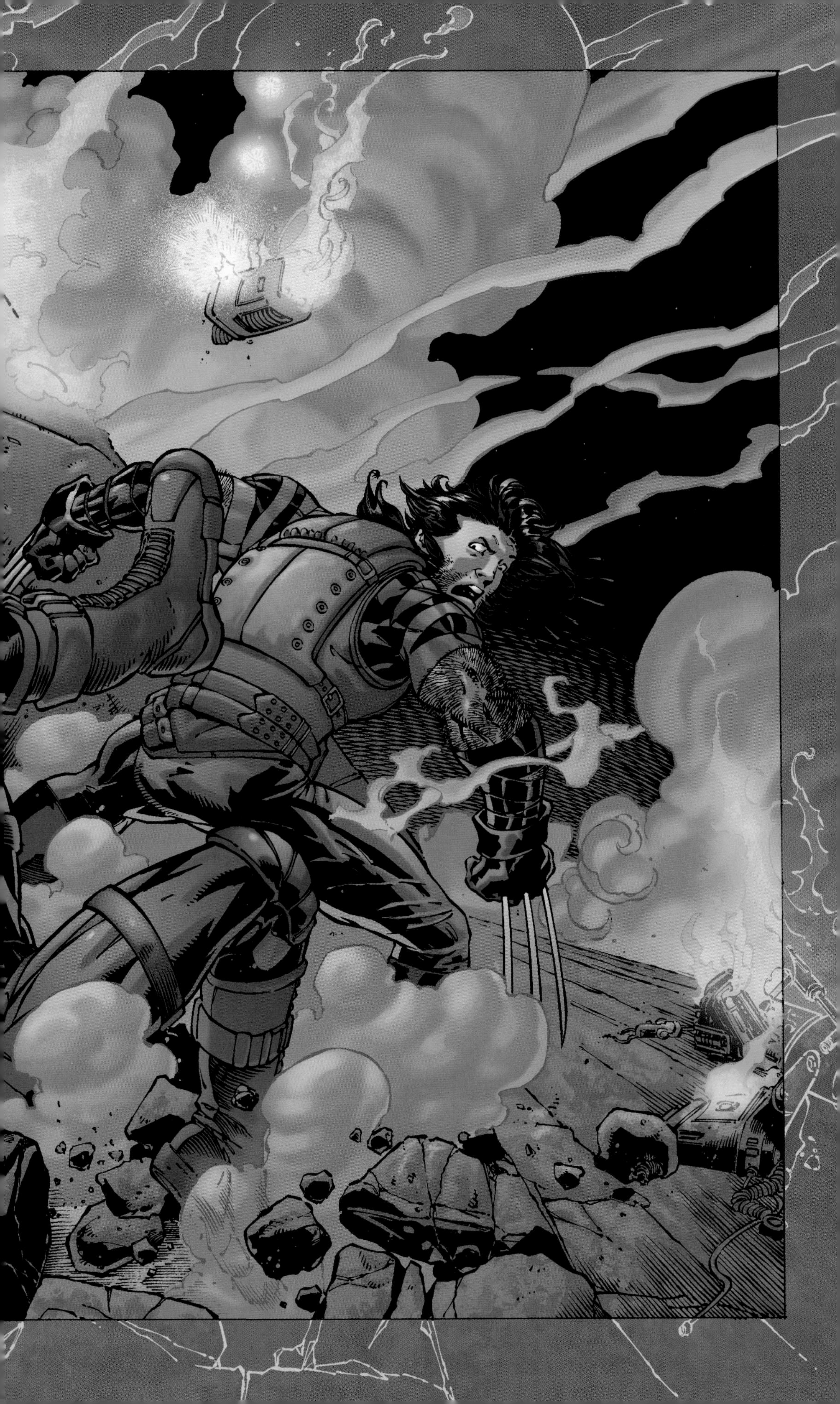

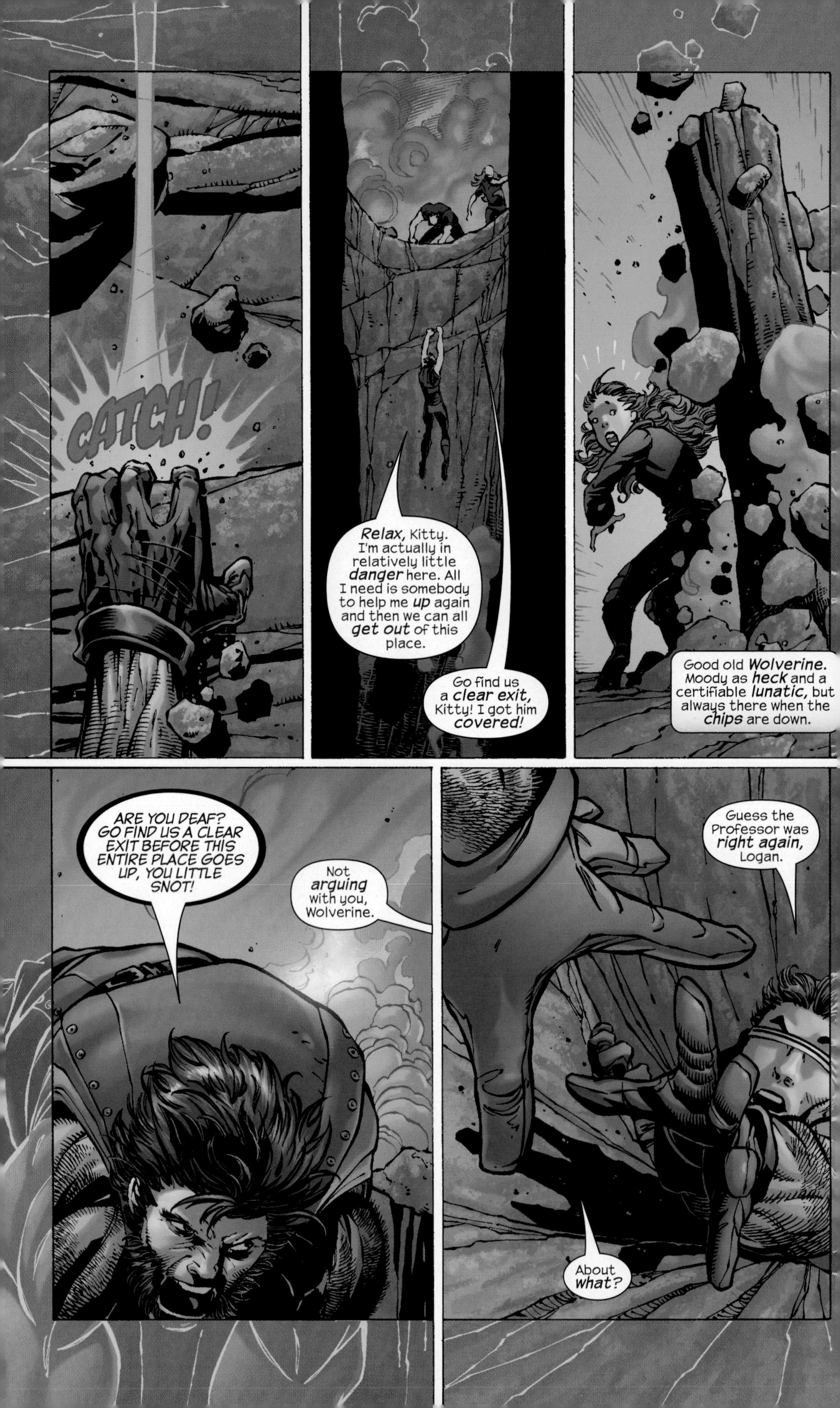
CATCH!
Relax, Kitty. I'm actually in relatively little danger here. All I need is somebody to help me up again and then we can all get out of this place.
Go find us a clear exit, Kitty! I got him covered!
Good old Wolverine. Moody as heck and a certifiable lunatic, but always there when the chips are down.
ARE YOU DEAF? GO FIND US A CLEAR EXIT BEFORE THIS ENTIRE PLACE GOES UP, YOU LITTLE SNOT!
Not arguing with you, Wolverine.
Guess the Professor was right again, Logan.
About what?

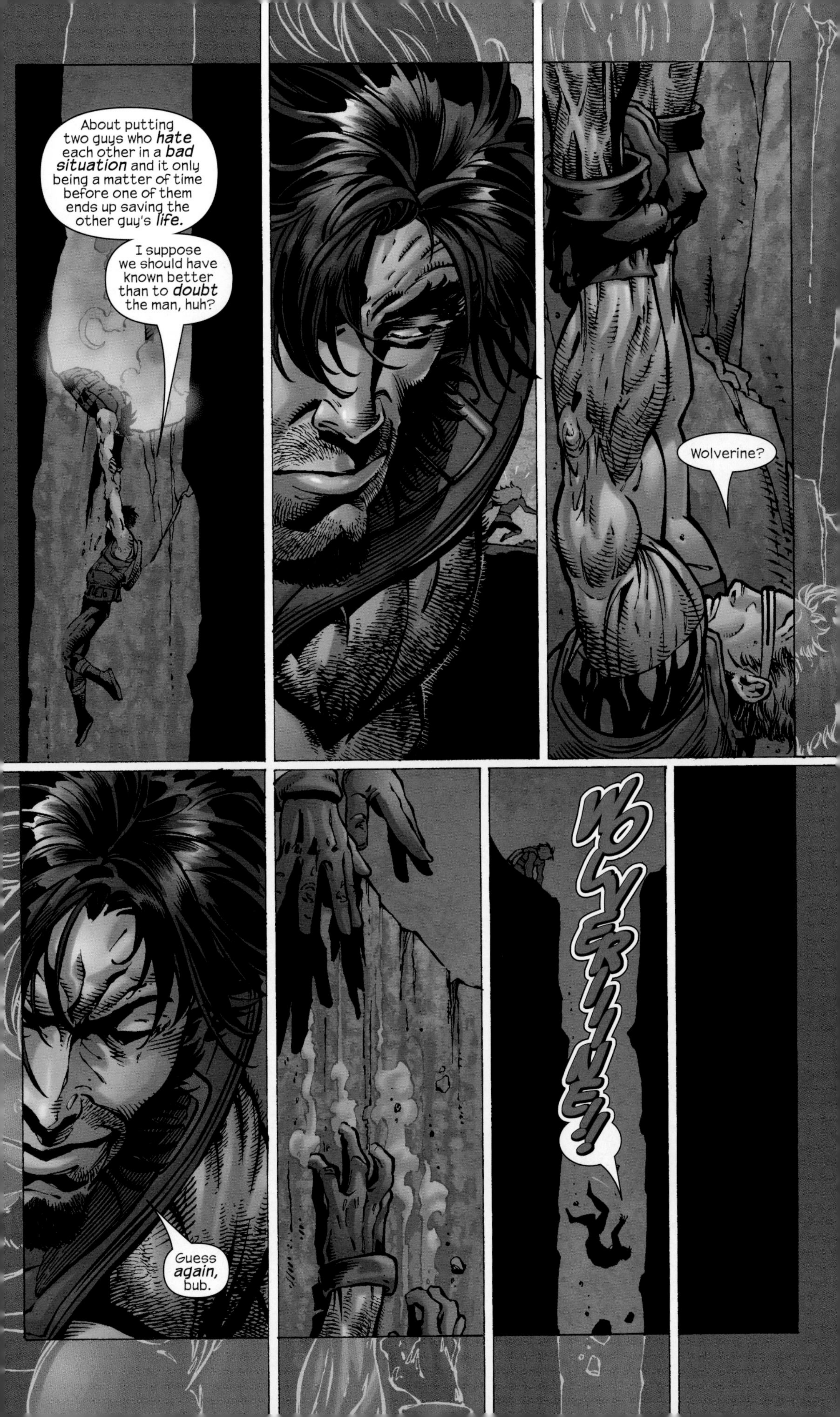
About putting two guys who hate each other in a bad situation and it only being a matter of time before one of them ends up saving the other guy's life.
I suppose we should have known better than to doubt the man, huh?
Wolverine?
Guess again, bub.
WOLVERIIINE!!

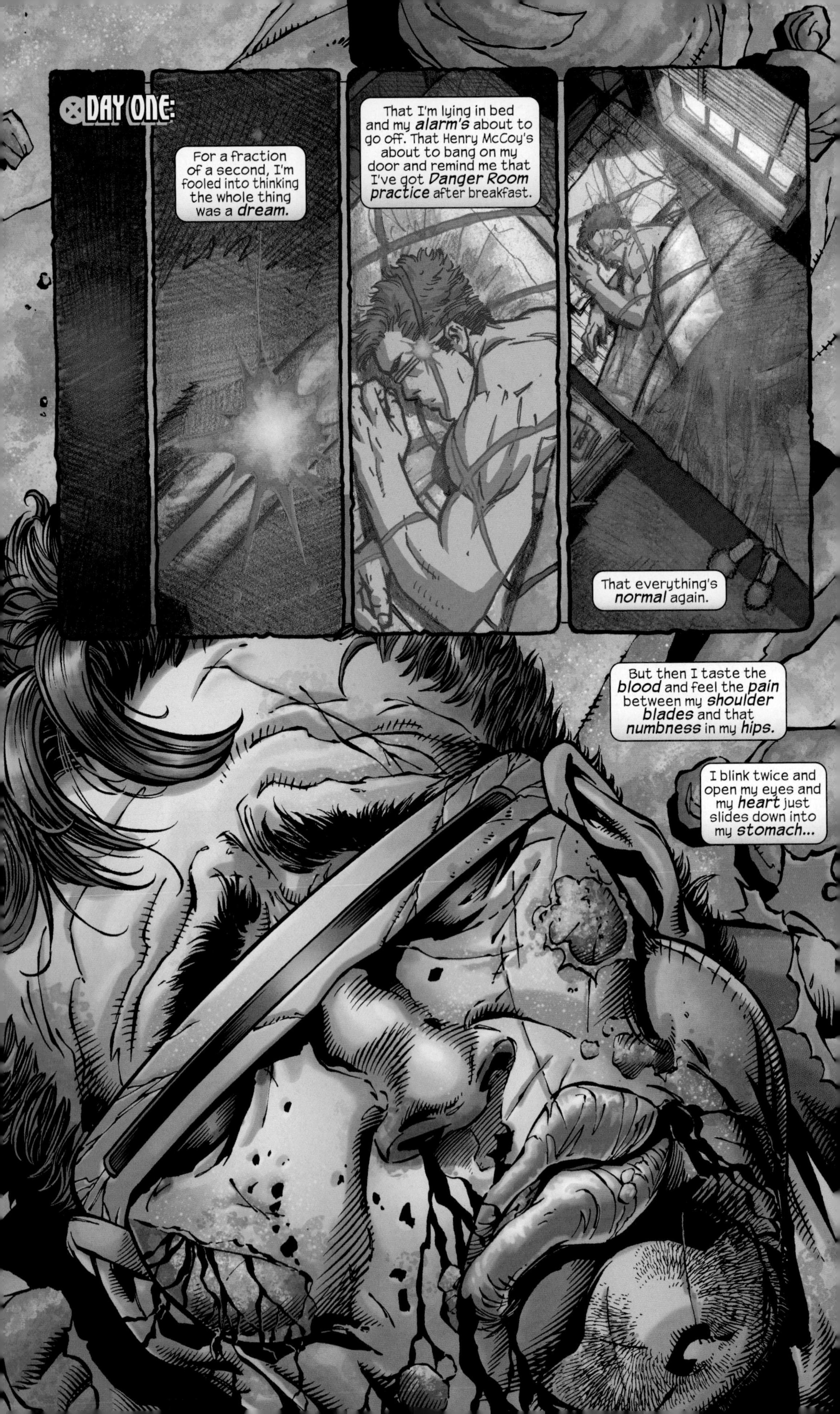
DAY ONE:
For a fraction of a second, I'm fooled into thinking the whole thing was a *dream.*
That I'm lying in bed and my *alarm's* about to go off. That Henry McCoy's about to bang on my door and remind me that I've got *Danger Room practice* after breakfast.
That everything's *normal* again.
But then I taste the *blood* and feel the *pain* between my *shoulder blades* and that *numbness* in my *hips.*
I blink twice and open my eyes and my *heart* just slides down into my *stomach...*

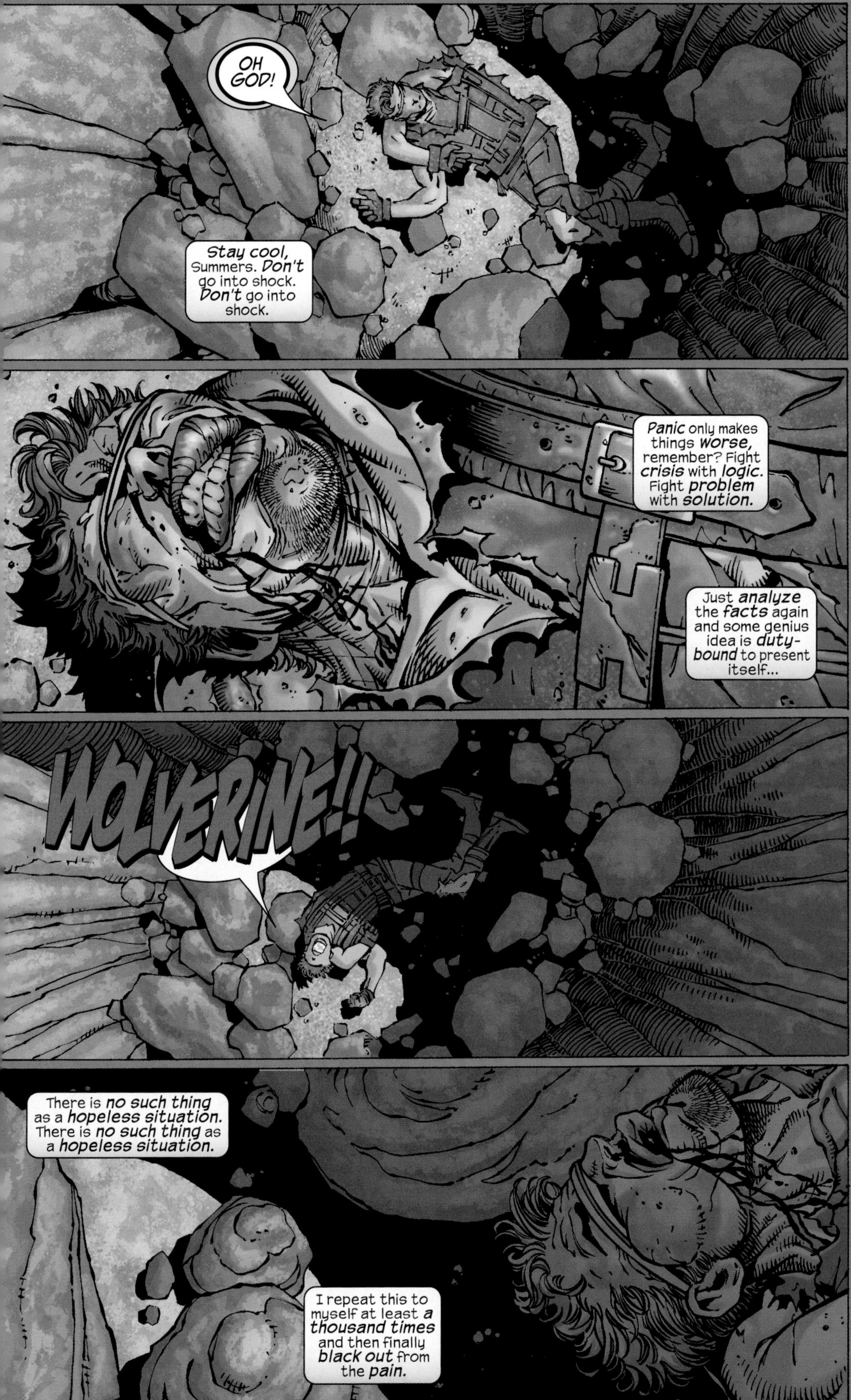
OH GOD!
Stay cool, Summers. Don't go into shock. Don't go into shock.
Panic only makes things worse, remember? Fight crisis with logic. Fight problem with solution.
Just analyze the facts again and some genius idea is duty-bound to present itself...
WOLVERINE!!
There is no such thing as a hopeless situation. There is no such thing as a hopeless situation.
I repeat this to myself at least a thousand times and then finally black out from the pain.

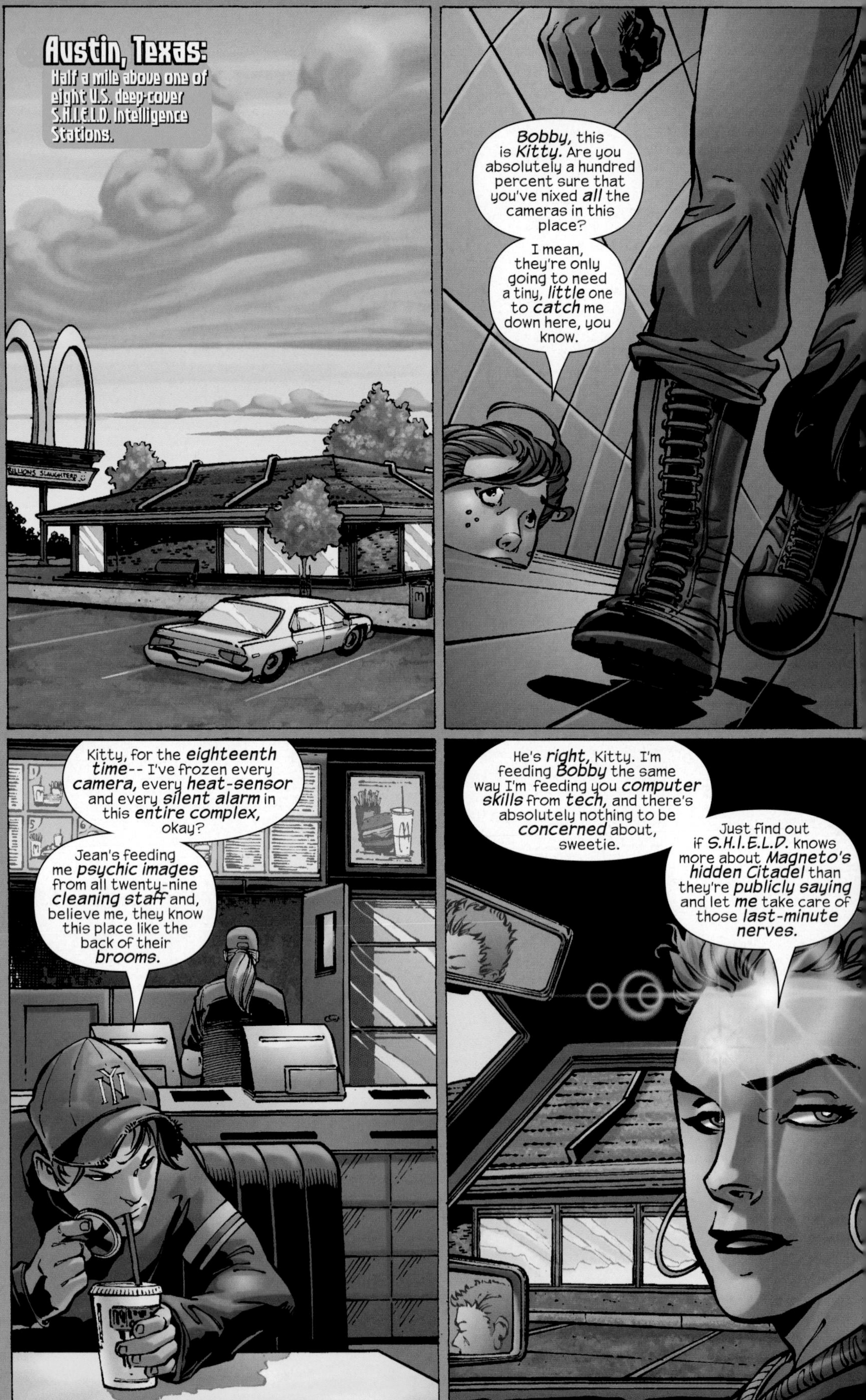
Austin, Texas:
Half a mile above one of eight U.S. deep-cover S.H.I.E.L.D. Intelligence Stations.
Bobby, this is Kitty. Are you absolutely a hundred percent sure that you've nixed all the cameras in this place?
I mean, they're only going to need a tiny, little one to catch me down here, you know.
Kitty, for the eighteenth time-- I've frozen every camera, every heat-sensor and every silent alarm in this entire complex, okay?
Jean's feeding me psychic images from all twenty-nine cleaning staff and, believe me, they know this place like the back of their brooms.
He's right, Kitty. I'm feeding Bobby the same way I'm feeding you computer skills from tech, and there's absolutely nothing to be concerned about, sweetie.
Just find out if S.H.I.E.L.D. knows more about Magneto's hidden Citadel than they're publicly saying and let me take care of those last-minute nerves.

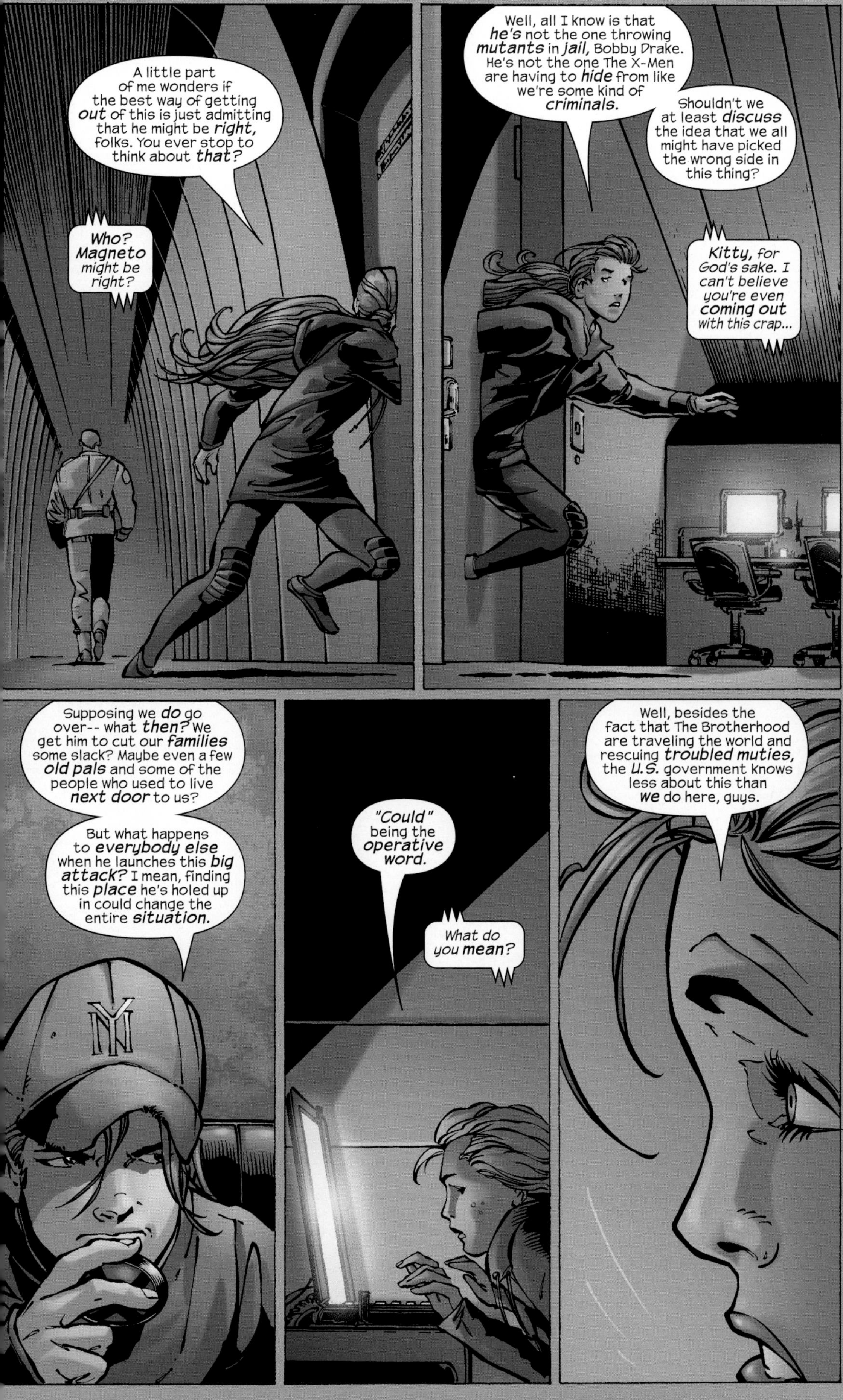
A little part of me wonders if the best way of getting out of this is just admitting that he might be right, folks. You ever stop to think about that?
Who? Magneto might be right?
Well, all I know is that he's not the one throwing mutants in jail, Bobby Drake. He's not the one The X-Men are having to hide from like we're some kind of criminals.
Shouldn't we at least discuss the idea that we all might have picked the wrong side in this thing?
Kitty, for God's sake. I can't believe you're even coming out with this crap...
Supposing we do go over-- what then? We get him to cut our families some slack? Maybe even a few old pals and some of the people who used to live next door to us?
But what happens to everybody else when he launches this big attack? I mean, finding this place he's holed up in could change the entire situation.
"Could" being the operative word.
What do you mean?
Well, besides the fact that The Brotherhood are traveling the world and rescuing troubled muties, the U.S. government knows less about this than we do here, guys.

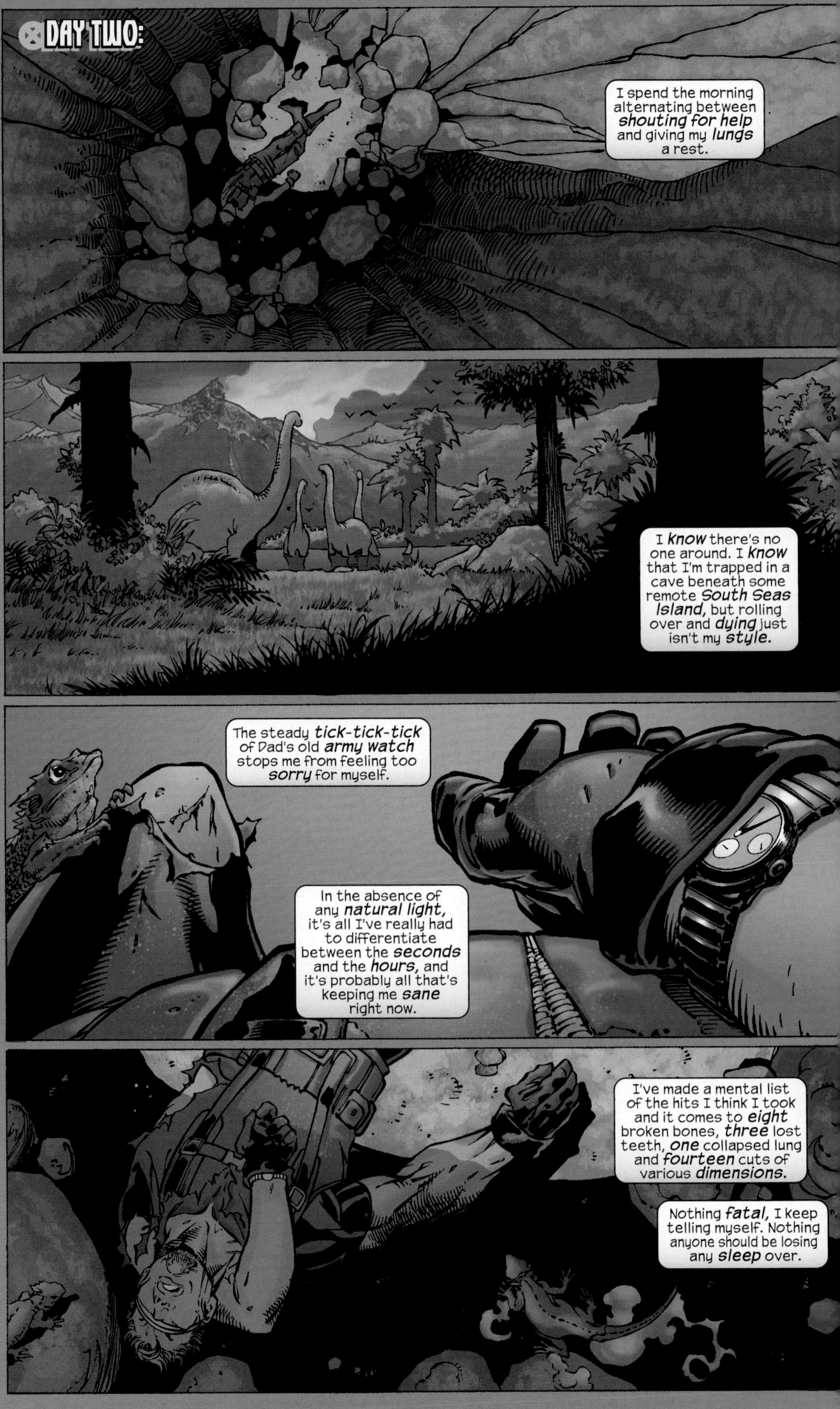
DAY TWO:
I spend the morning alternating between shouting for help and giving my lungs a rest.
I know there's no one around. I know that I'm trapped in a cave beneath some remote South Seas Island, but rolling over and dying just isn't my style.
The steady tick-tick-tick of Dad's old army watch stops me from feeling too sorry for myself.
In the absence of any natural light, it's all I've really had to differentiate between the seconds and the hours, and it's probably all that's keeping me sane right now.
I've made a mental list of the hits I think I took and it comes to eight broken bones, three lost teeth, one collapsed lung and fourteen cuts of various dimensions.
Nothing fatal, I keep telling myself. Nothing anyone should be losing any sleep over.

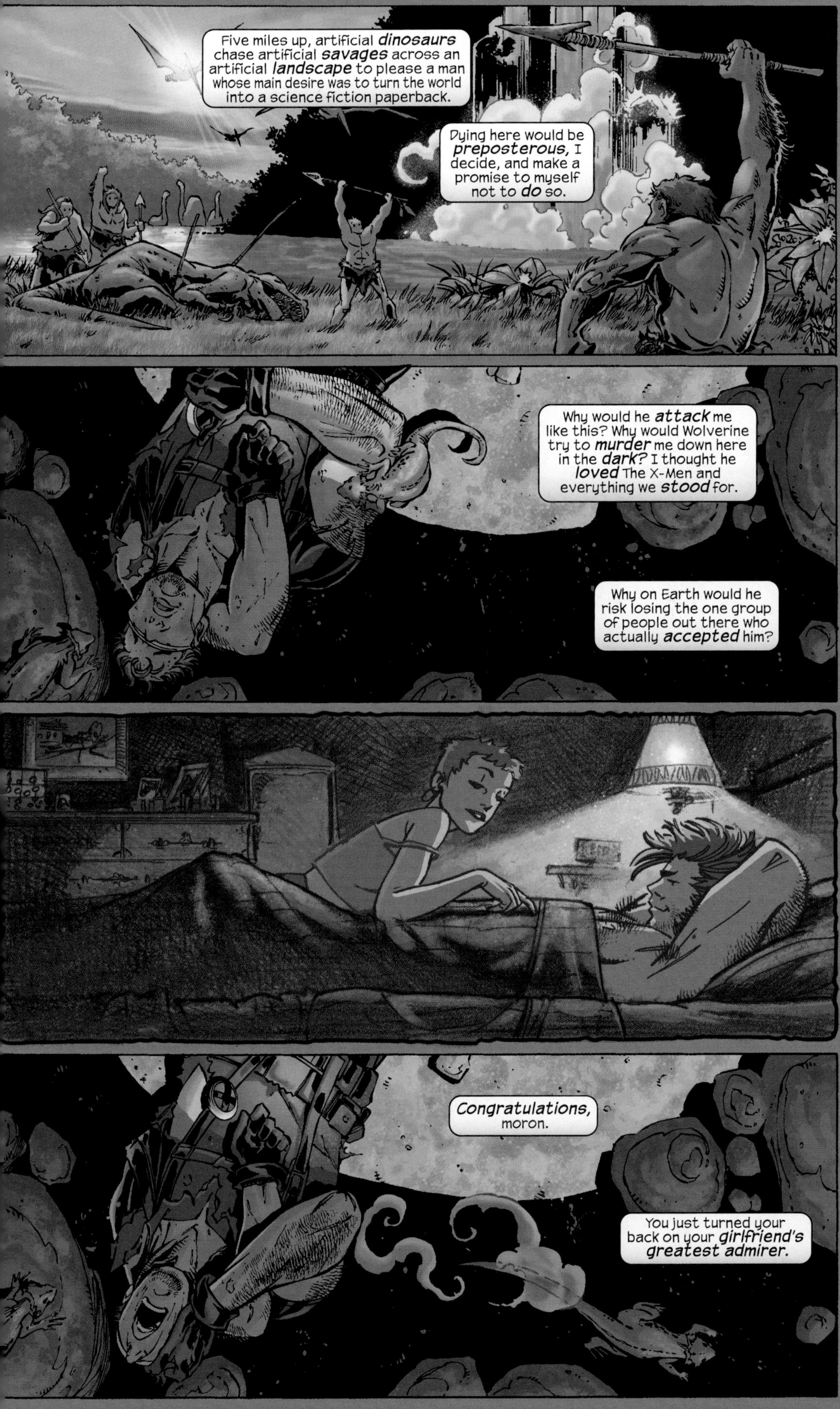
Five miles up, artificial dinosaurs chase artificial savages across an artificial landscape to please a man whose main desire was to turn the world into a science fiction paperback.
Dying here would be preposterous, I decide, and make a promise to myself not to do so.
Why would he attack me like this? Why would Wolverine try to murder me down here in the dark? I thought he loved The X-Men and everything we stood for.
Why on Earth would he risk losing the one group of people out there who actually accepted him?
Congratulations, moron.
You just turned your back on your girlfriend's greatest admirer.

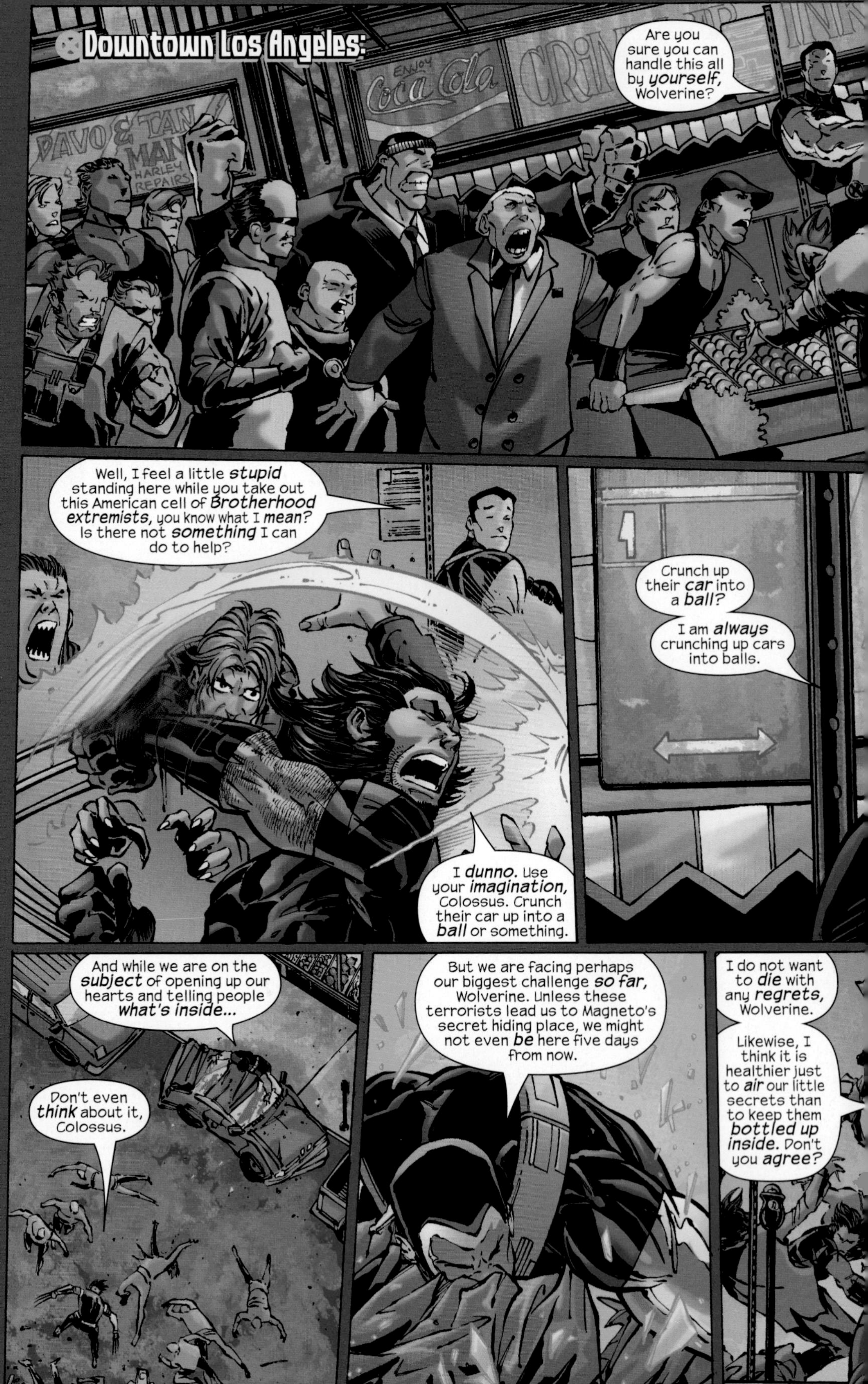
Downtown Los Angeles:
ENJOY Coca-Cola
DAVO & TAN MAN HARLEY REPAIRS
Are you sure you can handle this all by *yourself,* Wolverine?
Well, I feel a little *stupid* standing here while you take out this American cell of *Brotherhood extremists,* you know what I *mean?* Is there not *something* I can do to help?
I *dunno.* Use your *imagination,* Colossus. Crunch their car up into a *ball* or something.
Crunch up their *car* into a *ball?*
I am *always* crunching up cars into balls.
And while we are on the *subject* of opening up our hearts and telling people *what's inside...*
Don't even *think* about it, Colossus.
But we are facing perhaps our biggest challenge *so far,* Wolverine. Unless these terrorists lead us to Magneto's secret hiding place, we might not even *be* here five days from now.
I do not want to *die* with any *regrets,* Wolverine.
Likewise, I think it is healthier just to *air* our little secrets than to keep them *bottled up inside.* Don't you *agree?*

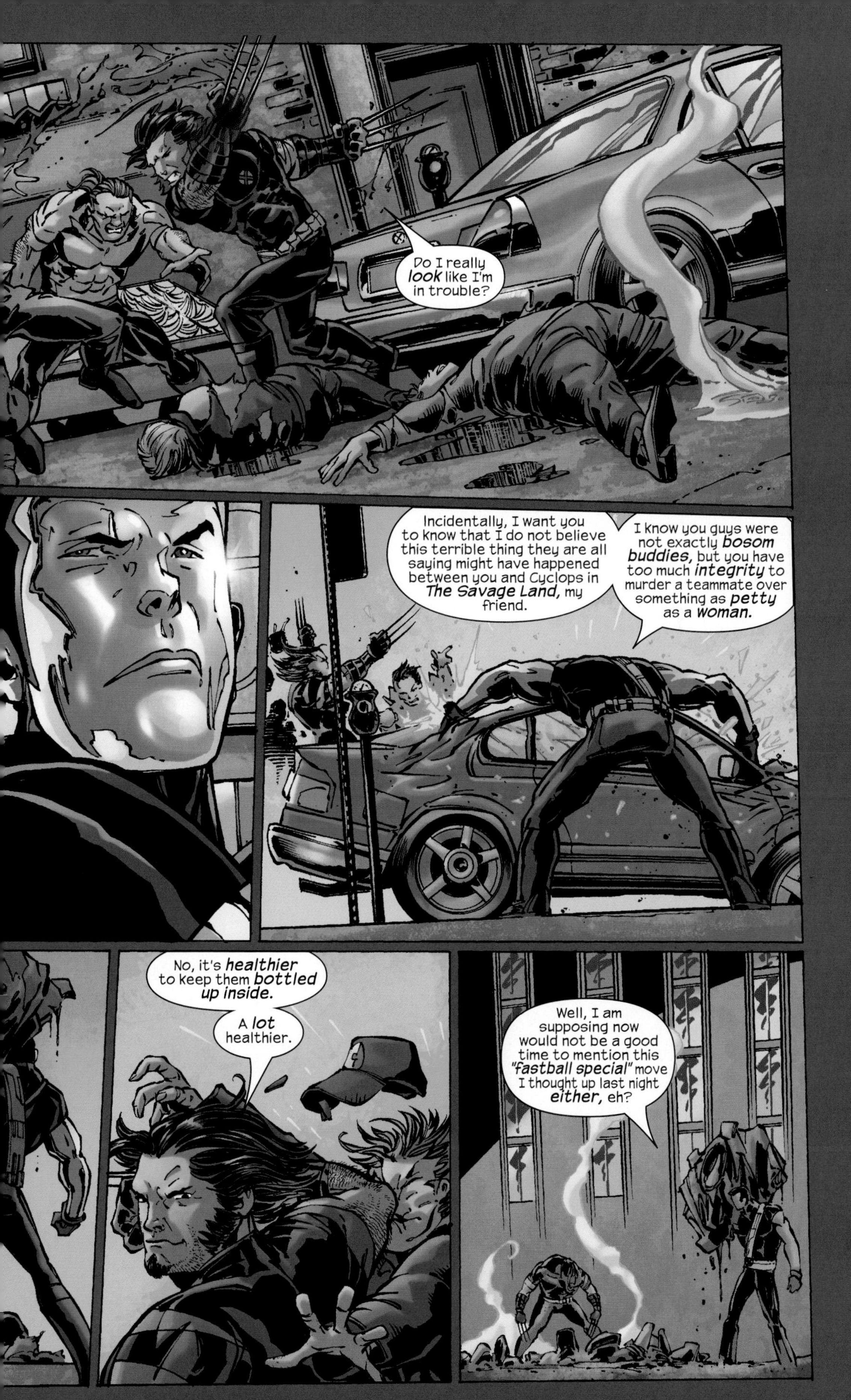

Do I really *look* like I'm in trouble?
Incidentally, I want you to know that I do not believe this terrible thing they are all saying might have happened between you and Cyclops in *The Savage Land,* my friend.
I know you guys were not exactly ***bosom buddies,*** but you have too much ***integrity*** to murder a teammate over something as ***petty*** as a ***woman.***
No, it's ***healthier*** to keep them ***bottled up inside.***
A *lot* healthier.
Well, I am supposing now would not be a good time to mention this *"fastball special"* move I thought up last night ***either,*** eh?

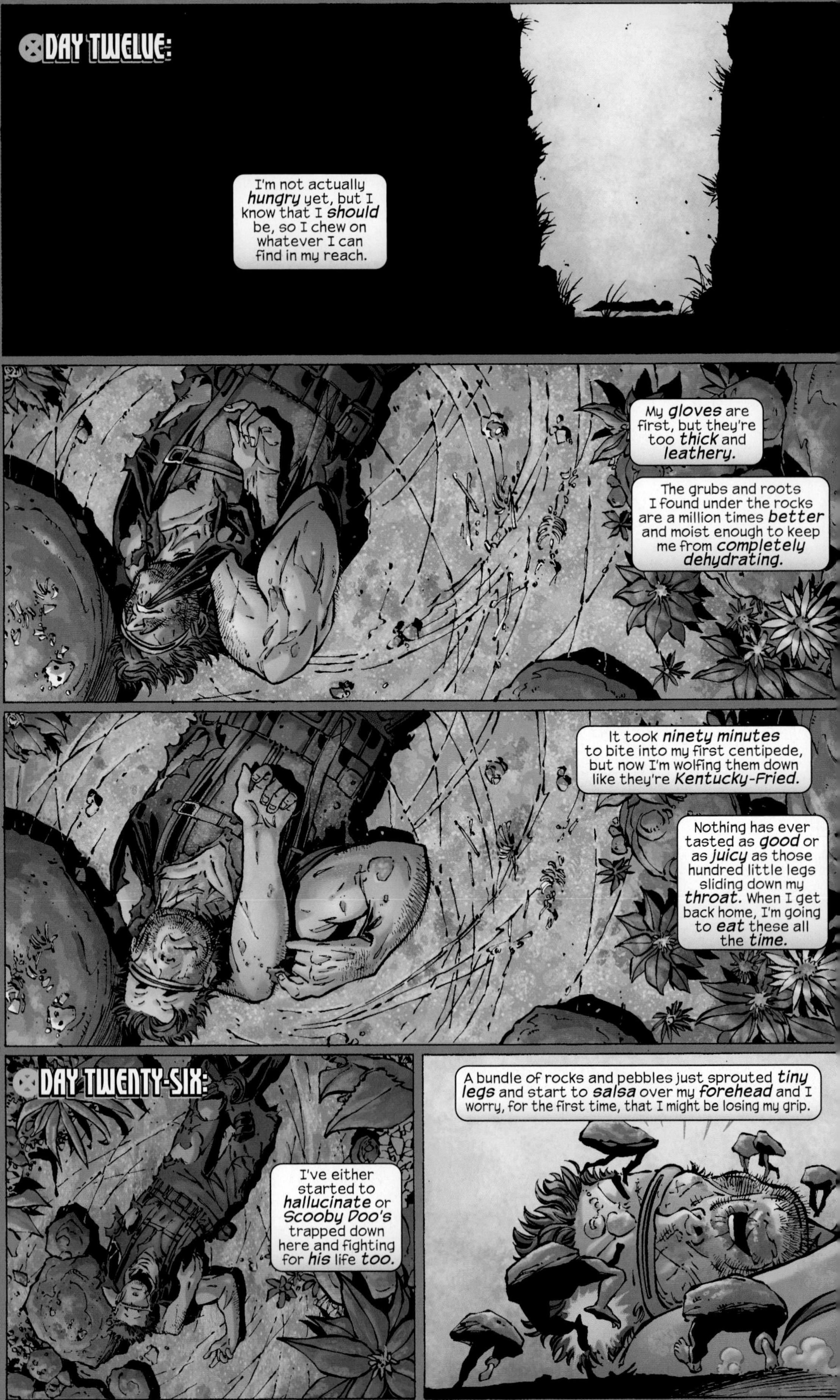

DAY TWELVE:
I'm not actually *hungry* yet, but I know that I *should* be, so I chew on whatever I can find in my reach.
My *gloves* are first, but they're too *thick* and *leathery*.
The grubs and roots I found under the rocks are a million times *better* and moist enough to keep me from *completely dehydrating*.
It took *ninety minutes* to bite into my first centipede, but now I'm wolfing them down like they're *Kentucky-Fried*.
Nothing has ever tasted as *good* or as *juicy* as those hundred little legs sliding down my *throat*. When I get back home, I'm going to *eat* these all the *time*.
DAY TWENTY-SIX:
I've either started to *hallucinate* or *Scooby Doo's* trapped down here and fighting for *his* life *too*.
A bundle of rocks and pebbles just sprouted *tiny legs* and start to *salsa* over my *forehead* and I worry, for the first time, that I might be losing my grip.

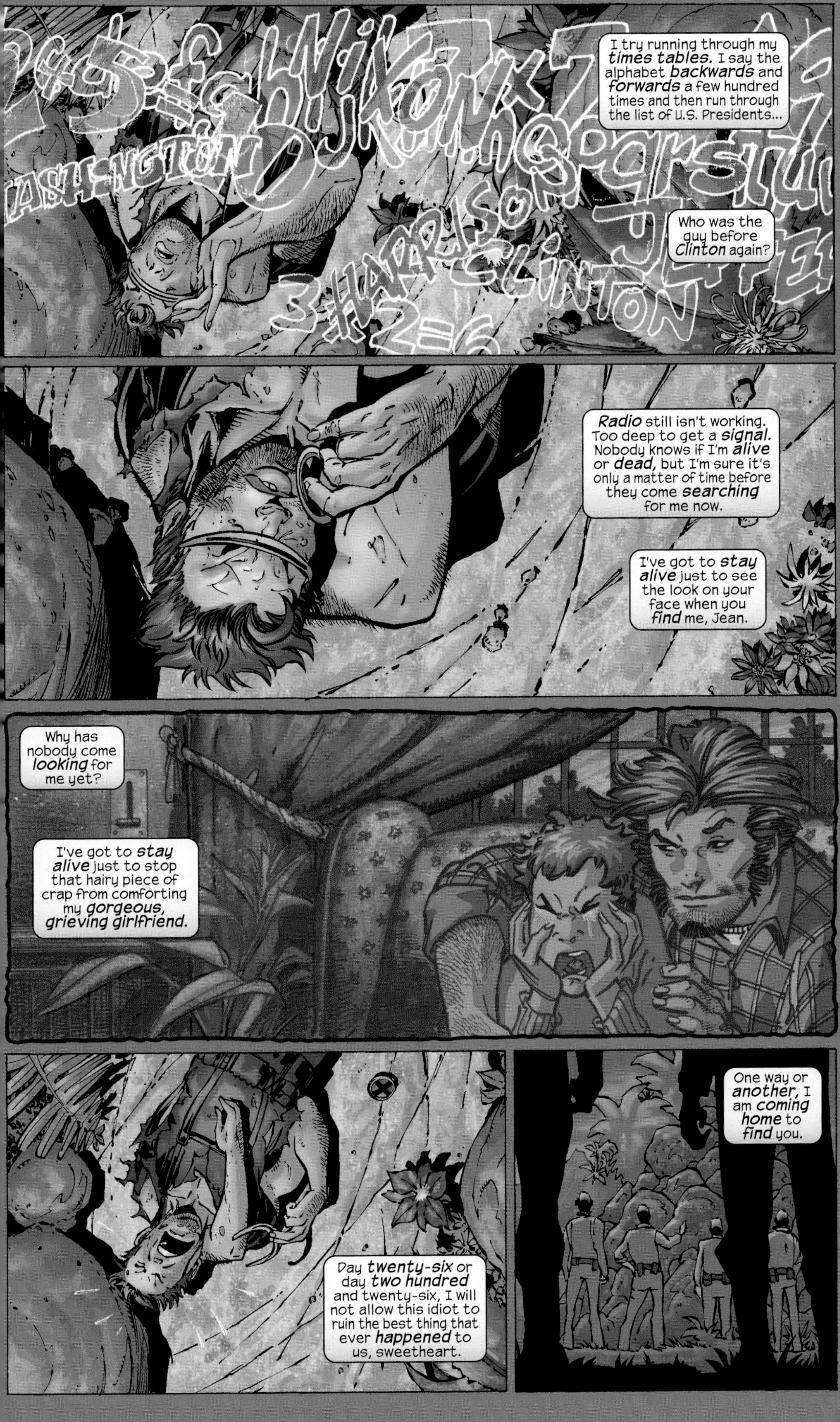
I try running through my times tables. I say the alphabet backwards and forwards a few hundred times and then run through the list of U.S. Presidents...
Who was the guy before Clinton again?
Radio still isn't working. Too deep to get a signal. Nobody knows if I'm alive or dead, but I'm sure it's only a matter of time before they come searching for me now.
I've got to stay alive just to see the look on your face when you find me, Jean.
Why has nobody come looking for me yet?
I've got to stay alive just to stop that hairy piece of crap from comforting my gorgeous, grieving girlfriend.
Day twenty-six or day two hundred and twenty-six, I will not allow this idiot to ruin the best thing that ever happened to us, sweetheart.
One way or another, I am coming home to find you.

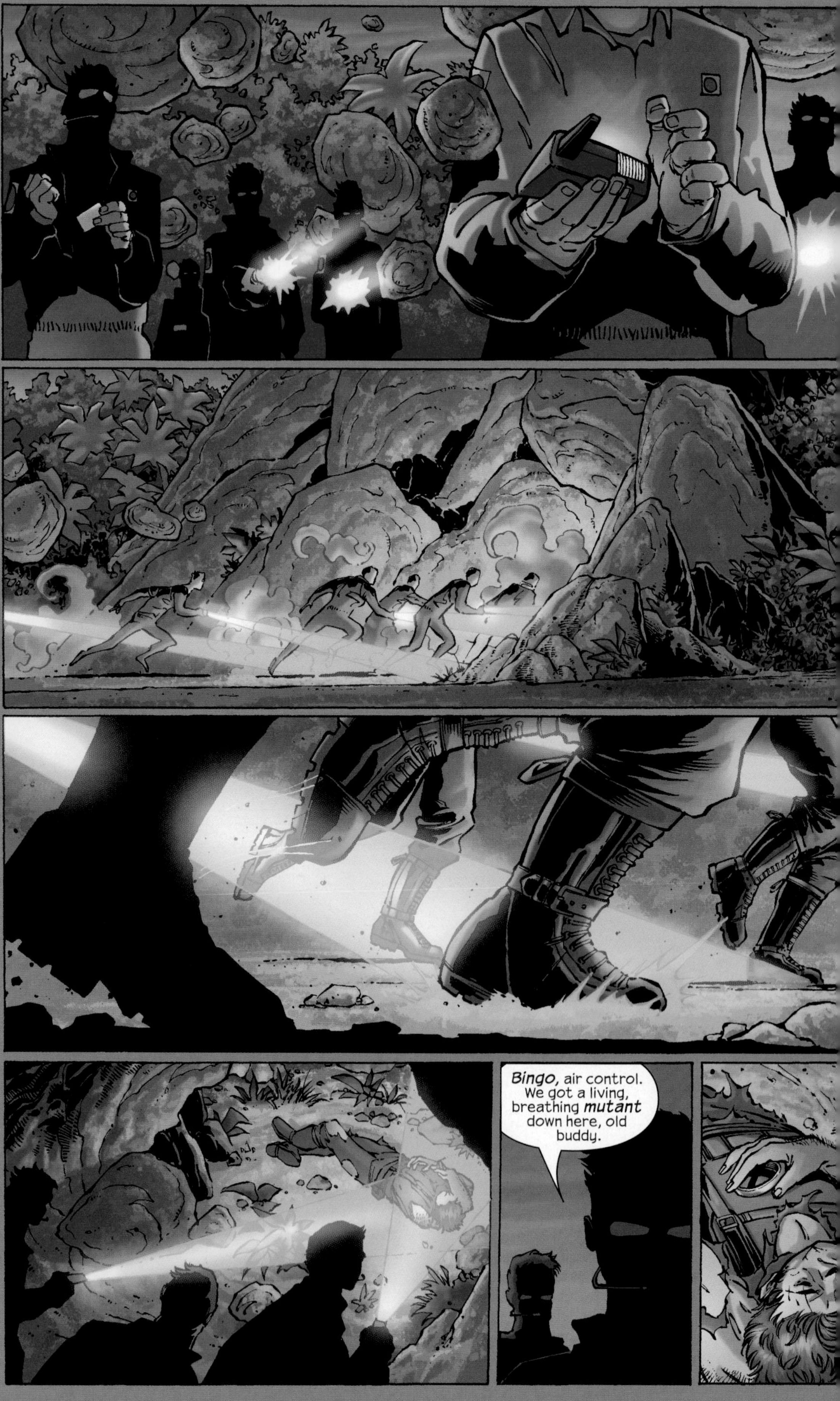
Bingo, air control. We got a living, breathing mutant down here, old buddy.

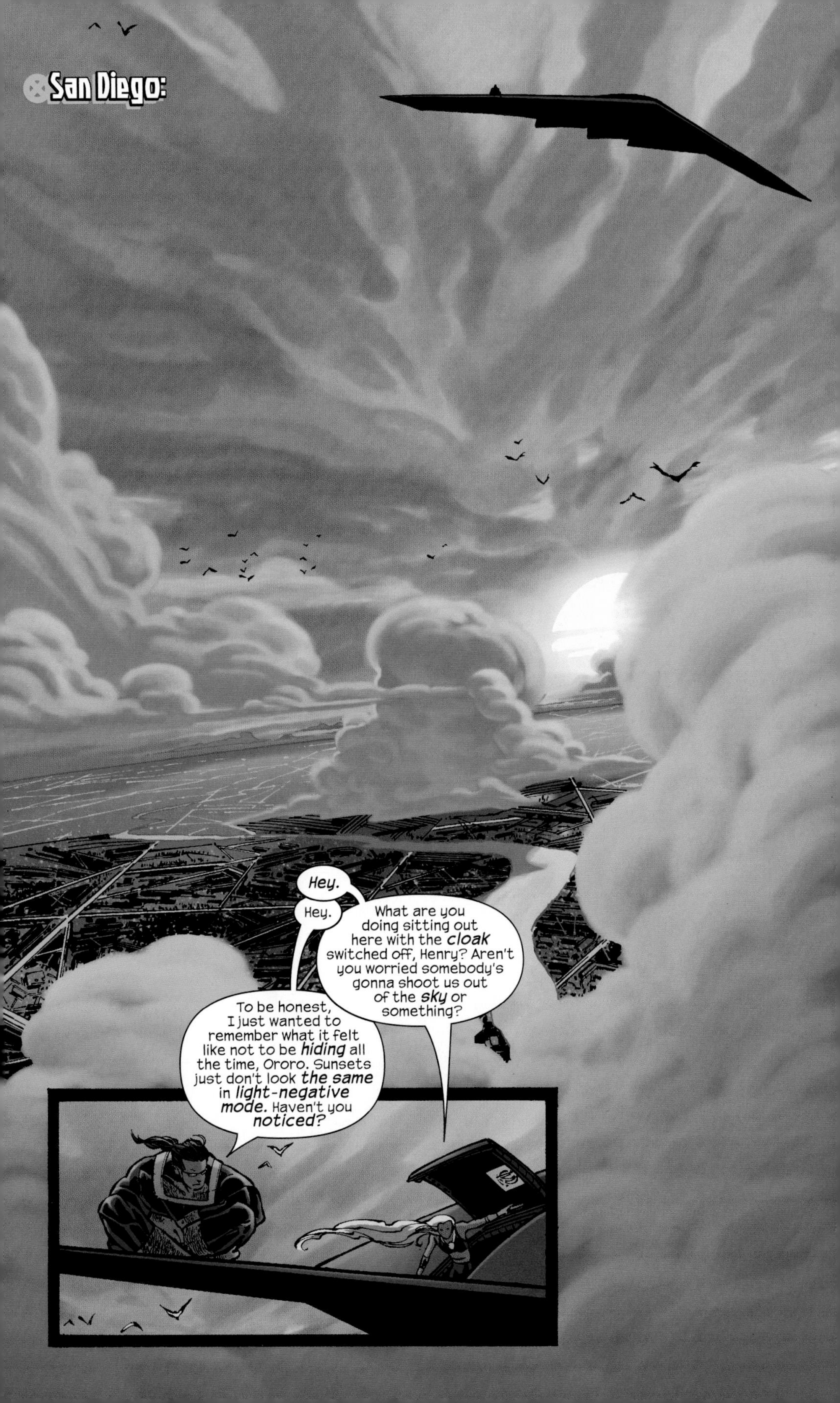
San Diego:
Hey.
Hey.
What are you doing sitting out here with the cloak switched off, Henry? Aren't you worried somebody's gonna shoot us out of the sky or something?
To be honest, I just wanted to remember what it felt like not to be hiding all the time, Ororo. Sunsets just don't look the same in light-negative mode. Haven't you noticed?

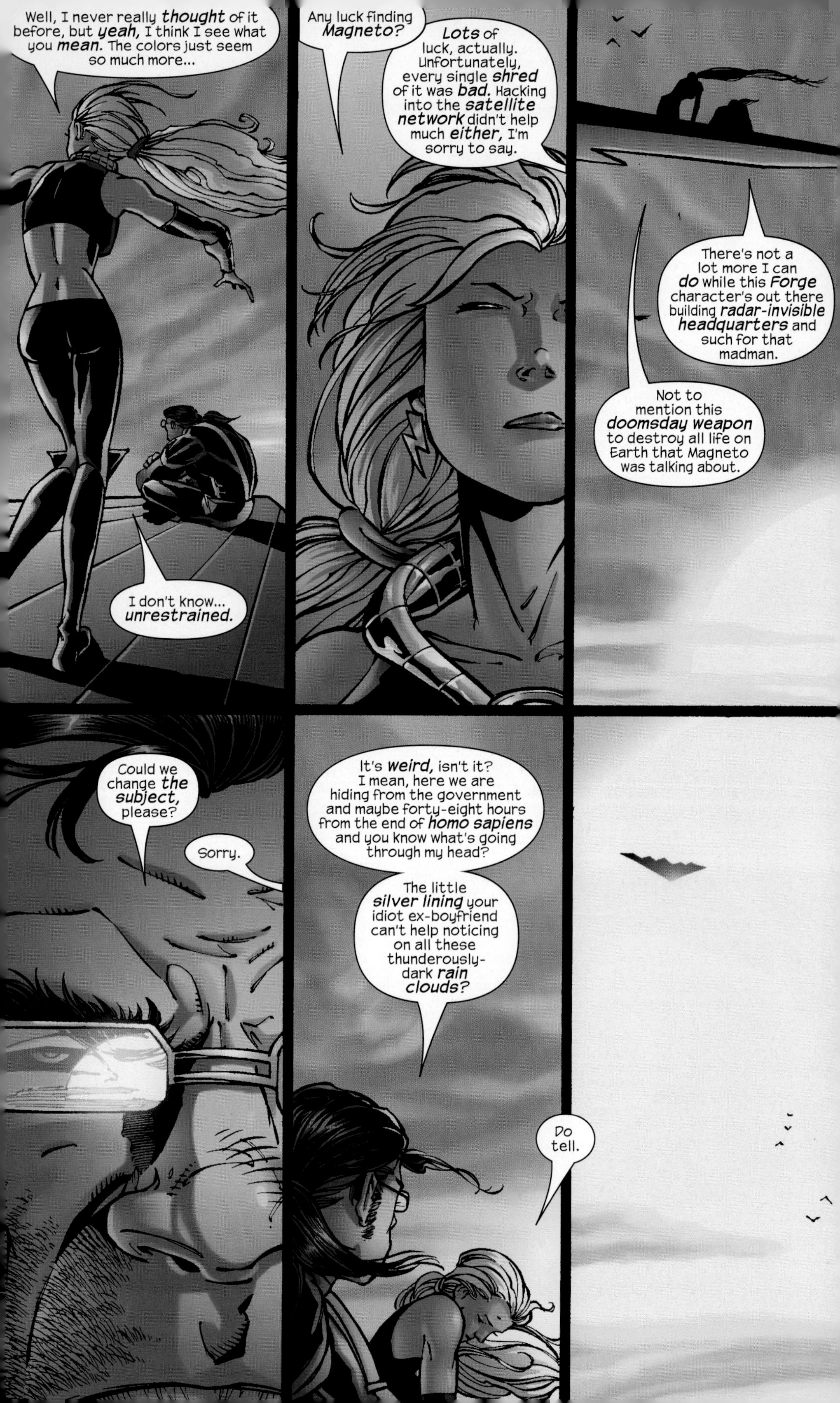
Well, I never really thought of it before, but yeah, I think I see what you mean. The colors just seem so much more...
I don't know... unrestrained.
Any luck finding Magneto?
Lots of luck, actually. Unfortunately, every single shred of it was bad. Hacking into the satellite network didn't help much either, I'm sorry to say.
There's not a lot more I can do while this Forge character's out there building radar-invisible headquarters and such for that madman.
Not to mention this doomsday weapon to destroy all life on Earth that Magneto was talking about.
Could we change the subject, please?
Sorry.
It's weird, isn't it? I mean, here we are hiding from the government and maybe forty-eight hours from the end of homo sapiens and you know what's going through my head?
The little silver lining your idiot ex-boyfriend can't help noticing on all these thunderously-dark rain clouds?
Do tell.

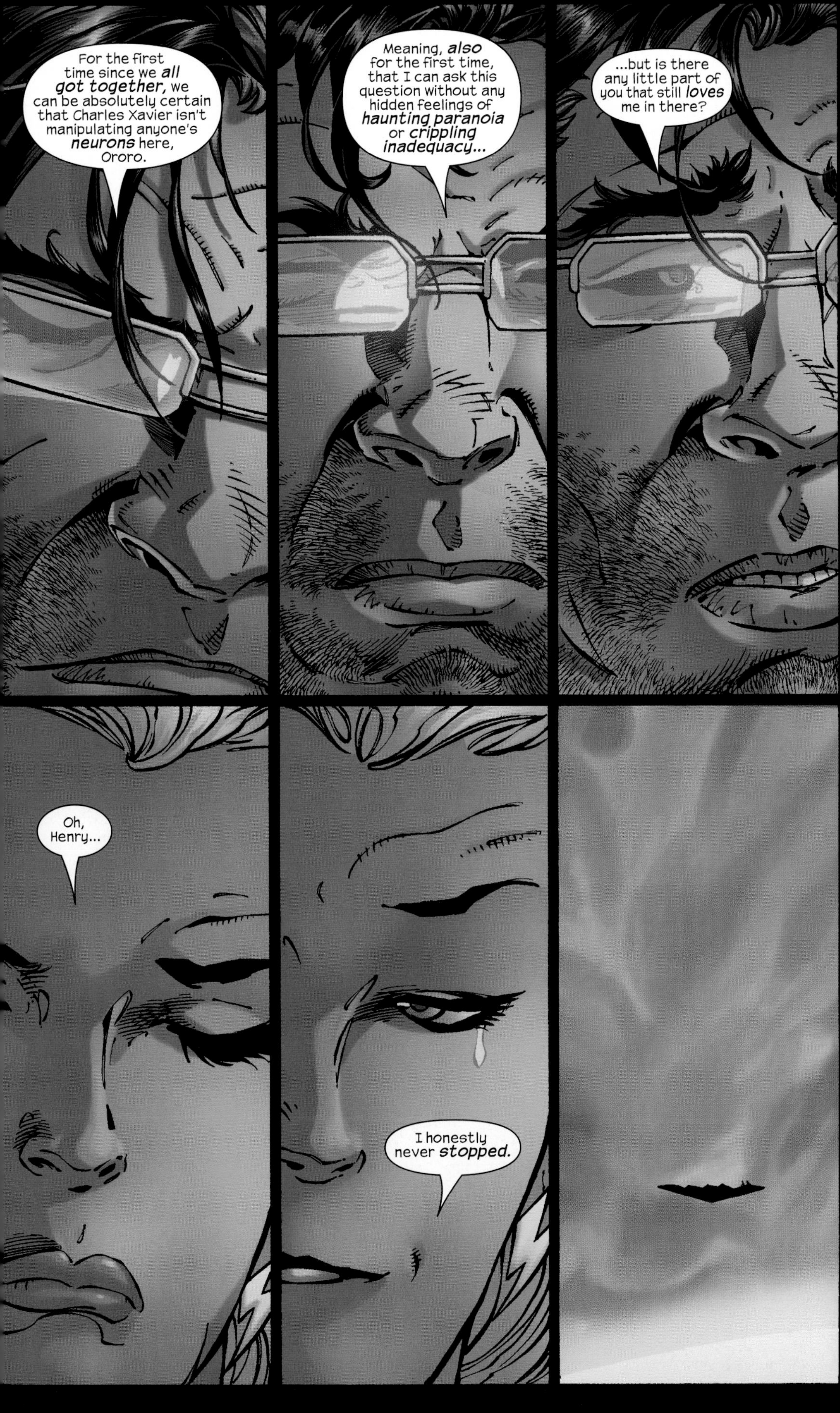
For the first time since we *all got together,* we can be absolutely certain that Charles Xavier isn't manipulating anyone's *neurons* here, Ororo.
Meaning, *also* for the first time, that I can ask this question without any hidden feelings of *haunting paranoia* or *crippling inadequacy...*
...but is there any little part of you that still *loves* me in there?
Oh, Henry...
I honestly never *stopped.*

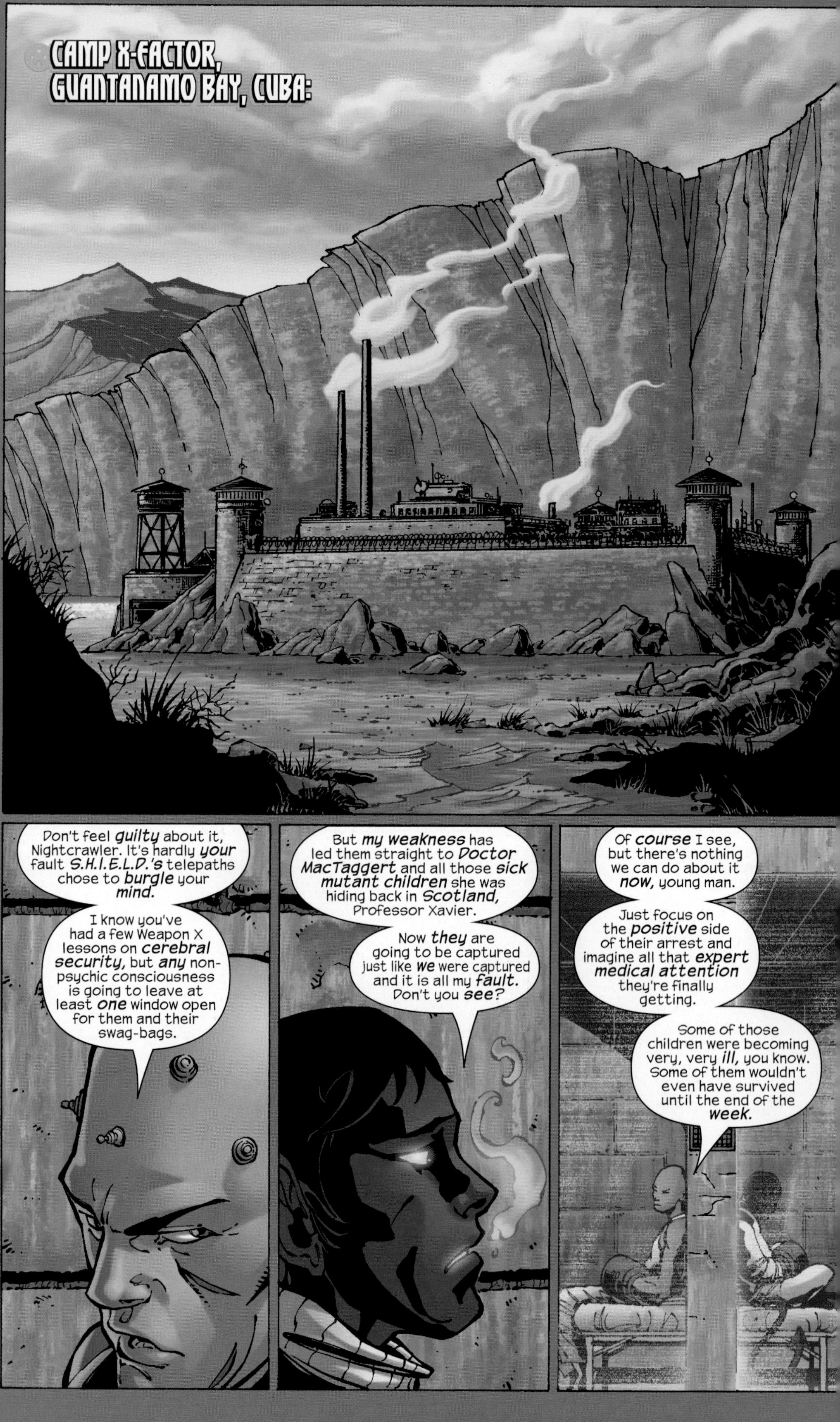
CAMP X-FACTOR, GUANTANAMO BAY, CUBA:
Don't feel guilty about it, Nightcrawler. It's hardly your fault S.H.I.E.L.D.'s telepaths chose to burgle your mind.
I know you've had a few Weapon X lessons on cerebral security, but any non-psychic consciousness is going to leave at least one window open for them and their swag-bags.
But my weakness has led them straight to Doctor MacTaggert and all those sick mutant children she was hiding back in Scotland, Professor Xavier.
Now they are going to be captured just like we were captured and it is all my fault. Don't you see?
Of course I see, but there's nothing we can do about it now, young man.
Just focus on the positive side of their arrest and imagine all that expert medical attention they're finally getting.
Some of those children were becoming very, very ill, you know. Some of them wouldn't even have survived until the end of the week.

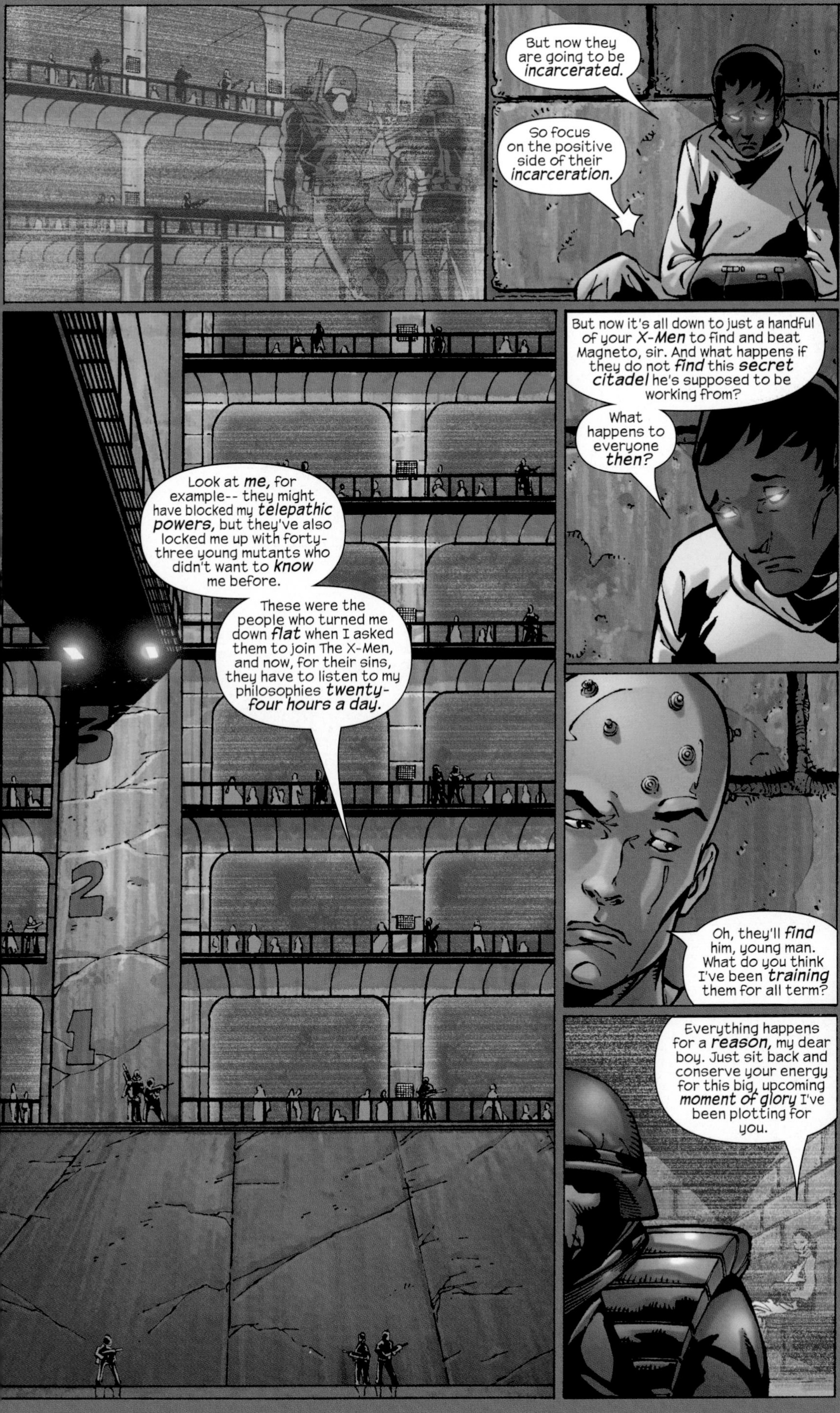
But now they are going to be *incarcerated.*
So focus on the positive side of their *incarceration.*
Look at *me,* for example-- they might have blocked my *telepathic powers,* but they've also locked me up with forty-three young mutants who didn't want to *know* me before.
These were the people who turned me down *flat* when I asked them to join The X-Men, and now, for their sins, they have to listen to my philosophies *twenty-four hours a day.*
But now it's all down to just a handful of your *X-Men* to find and beat Magneto, sir. And what happens if they do not *find* this *secret citadel* he's supposed to be working from?
What happens to everyone *then?*
Oh, they'll *find* him, young man. What do you think I've been *training* them for all term?
Everything happens for a *reason,* my dear boy. Just sit back and conserve your energy for this big, upcoming *moment of glory* I've been plotting for you.

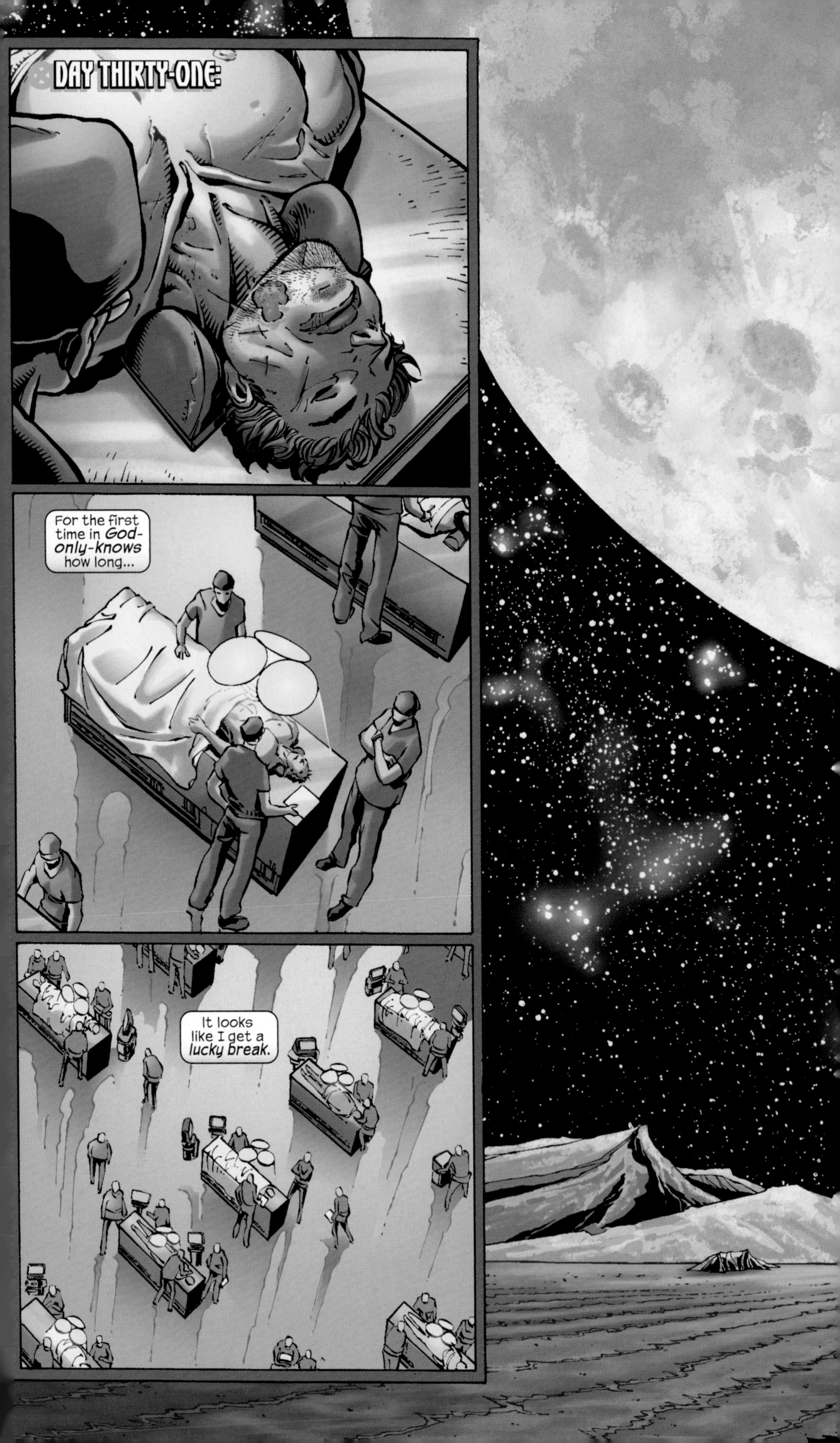
DAY THIRTY-ONE:
For the first time in *God-only-knows* how long...
It looks like I get a *lucky break.*

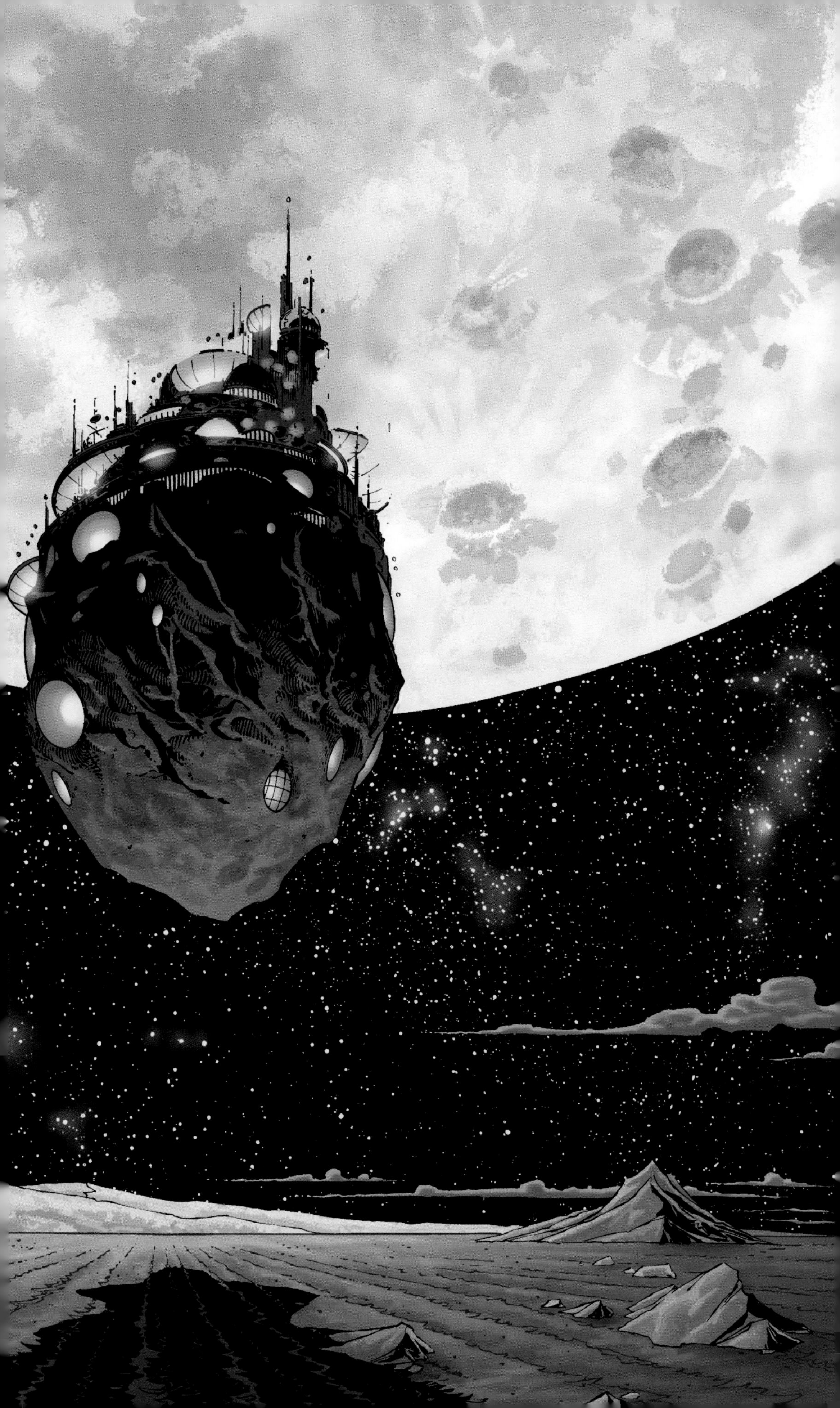

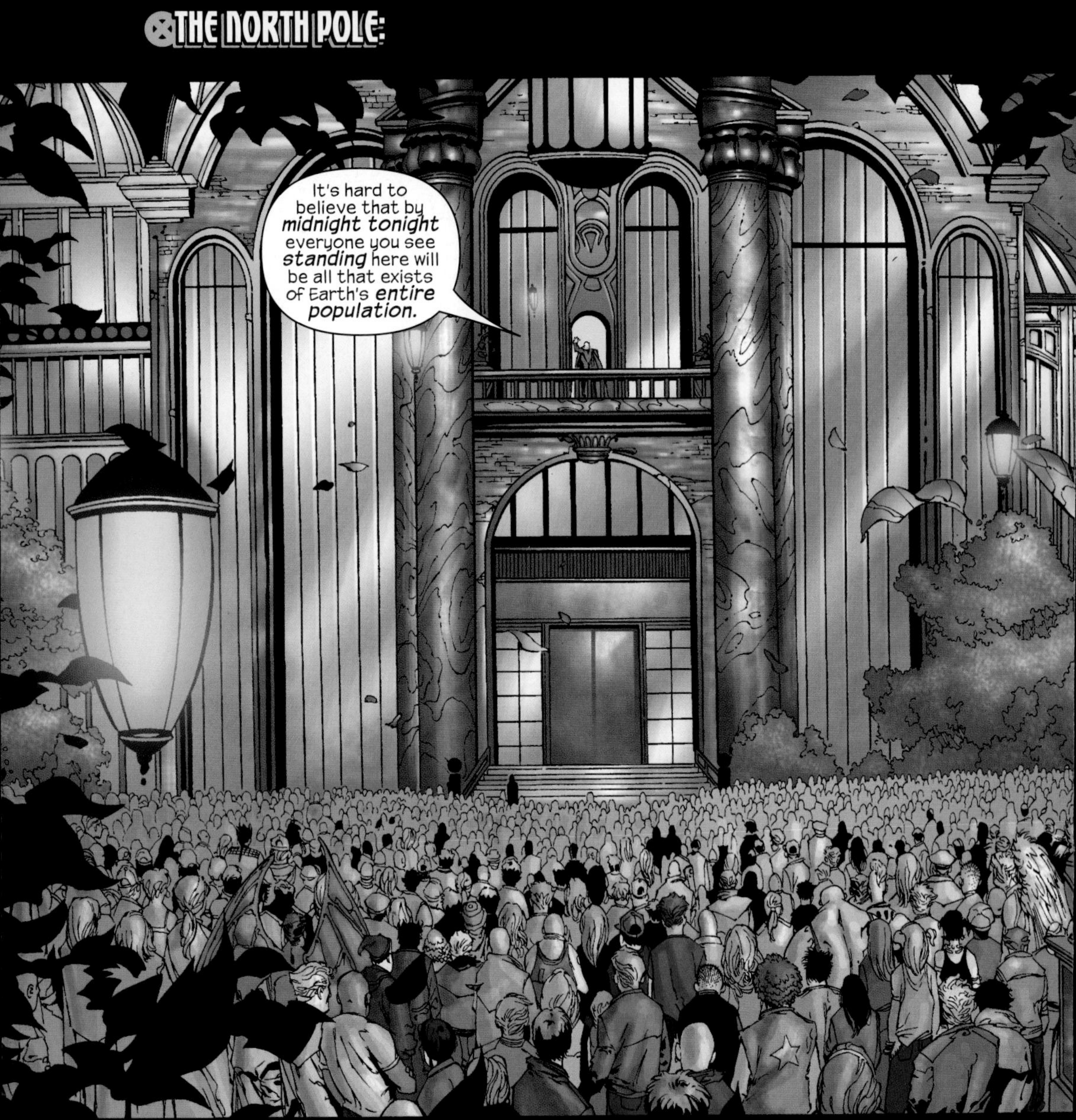
THE NORTH POLE:
It's hard to believe that by midnight tonight everyone you see standing here will be all that exists of Earth's entire population.

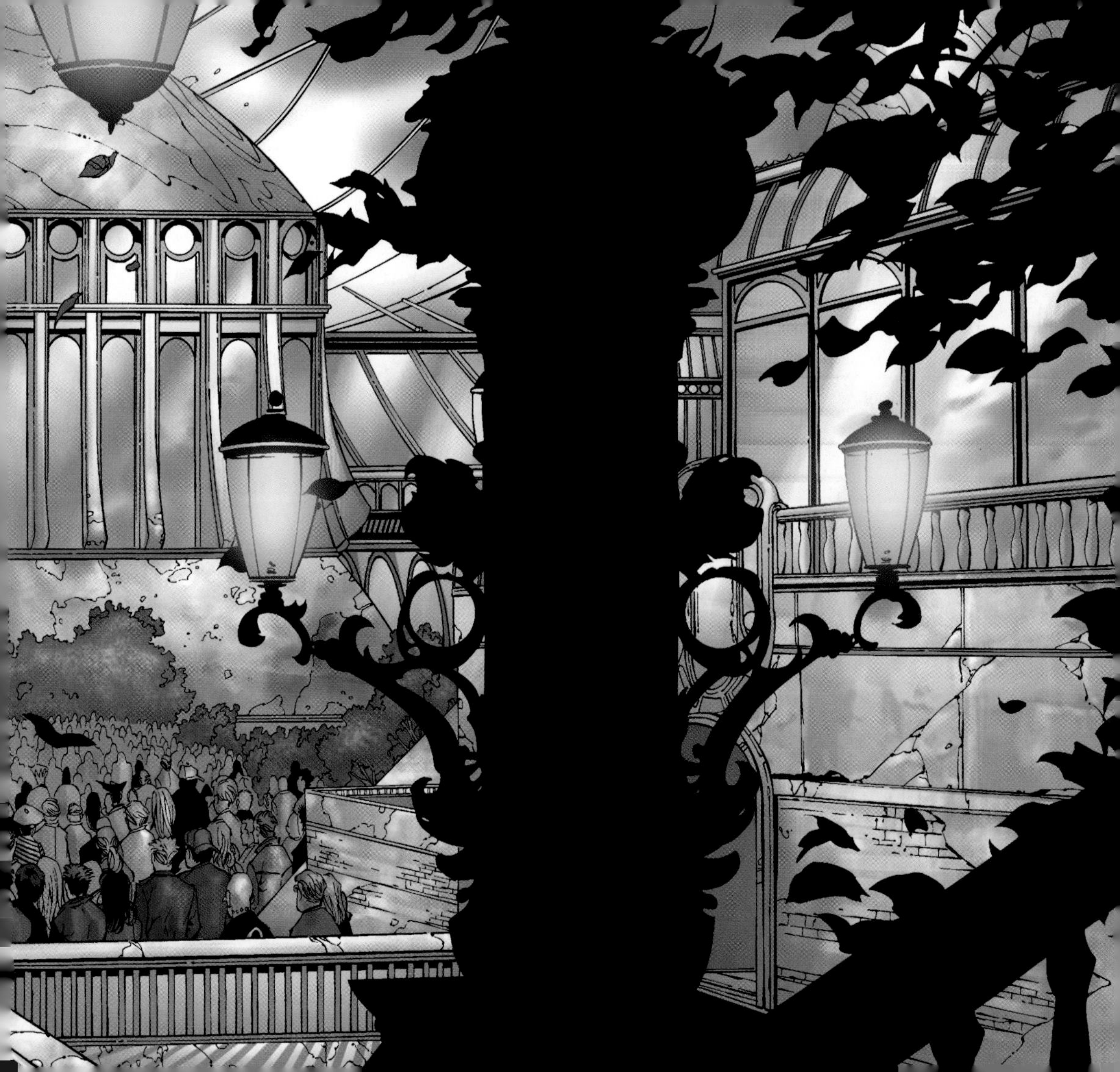

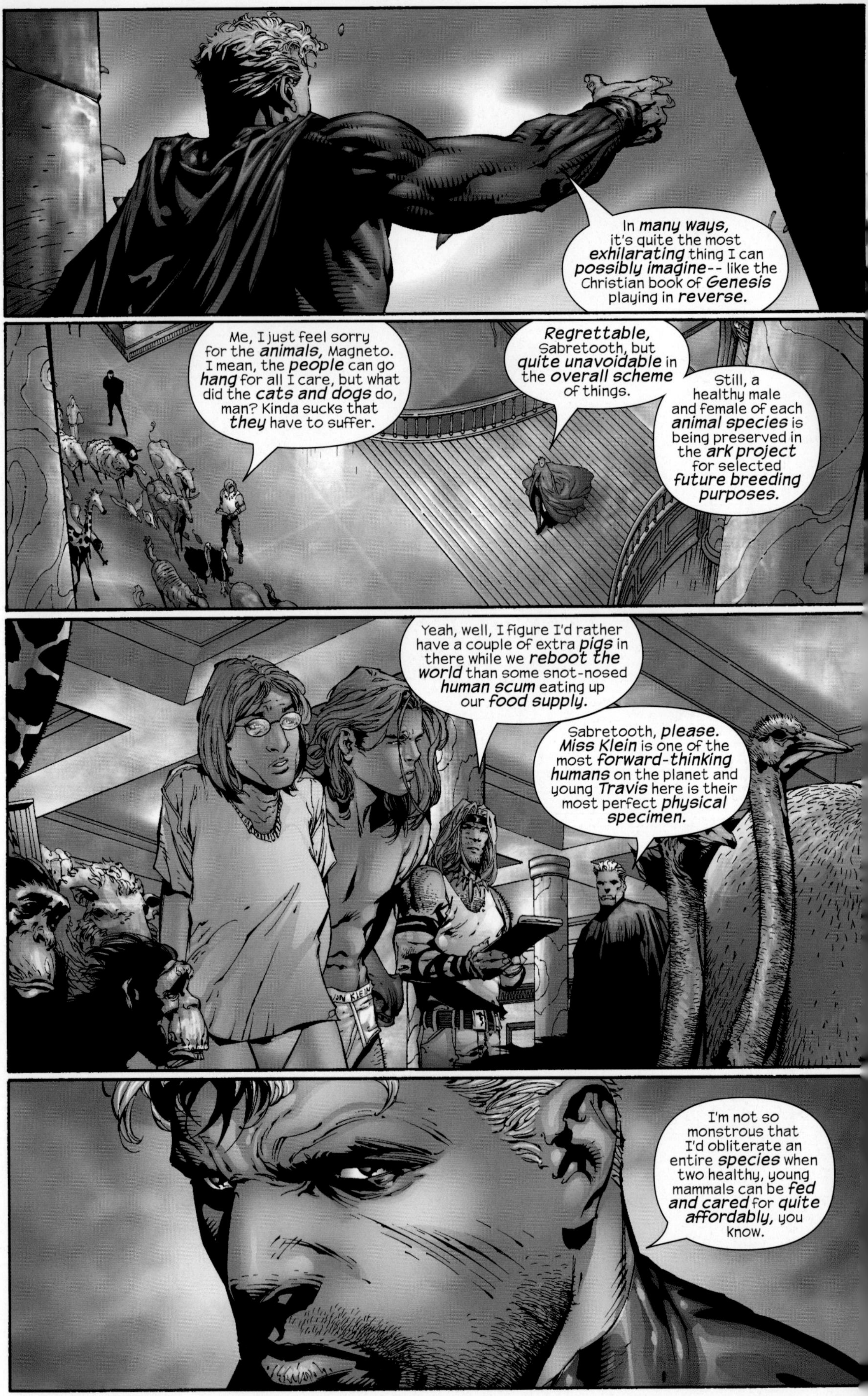
In many ways, it's quite the most exhilarating thing I can possibly imagine-- like the Christian book of Genesis playing in reverse.
Me, I just feel sorry for the animals, Magneto. I mean, the people can go hang for all I care, but what did the cats and dogs do, man? Kinda sucks that they have to suffer.
Regrettable, Sabretooth, but quite unavoidable in the overall scheme of things.
Still, a healthy male and female of each animal species is being preserved in the ark project for selected future breeding purposes.
Yeah, well, I figure I'd rather have a couple of extra pigs in there while we reboot the world than some snot-nosed human scum eating up our food supply.
Sabretooth, please. Miss Klein is one of the most forward-thinking humans on the planet and young Travis here is their most perfect physical specimen.
I'm not so monstrous that I'd obliterate an entire species when two healthy, young mammals can be fed and cared for quite affordably, you know.

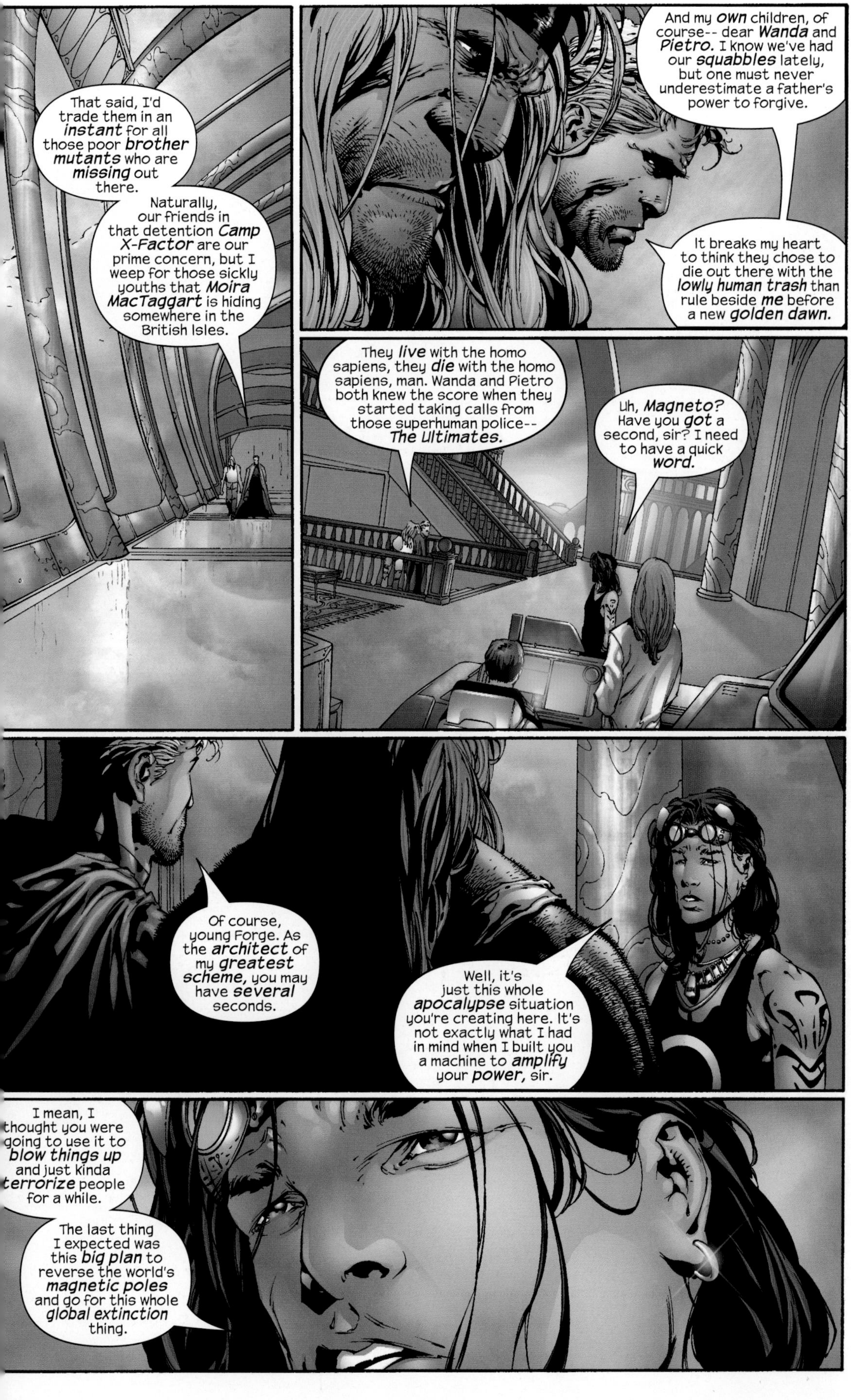
That said, I'd trade them in an instant for all those poor brother mutants who are missing out there.
Naturally, our friends in that detention Camp X-Factor are our prime concern, but I weep for those sickly youths that Moira MacTaggart is hiding somewhere in the British Isles.
And my own children, of course-- dear Wanda and Pietro. I know we've had our squabbles lately, but one must never underestimate a father's power to forgive.
It breaks my heart to think they chose to die out there with the lowly human trash than rule beside me before a new golden dawn.
They live with the homo sapiens, they die with the homo sapiens, man. Wanda and Pietro both knew the score when they started taking calls from those superhuman police-- The Ultimates.
Uh, Magneto? Have you got a second, sir? I need to have a quick word.
Of course, young Forge. As the architect of my greatest scheme, you may have several seconds.
Well, it's just this whole apocalypse situation you're creating here. It's not exactly what I had in mind when I built you a machine to amplify your power, sir.
I mean, I thought you were going to use it to blow things up and just kinda terrorize people for a while.
The last thing I expected was this big plan to reverse the world's magnetic poles and go for this whole global extinction thing.

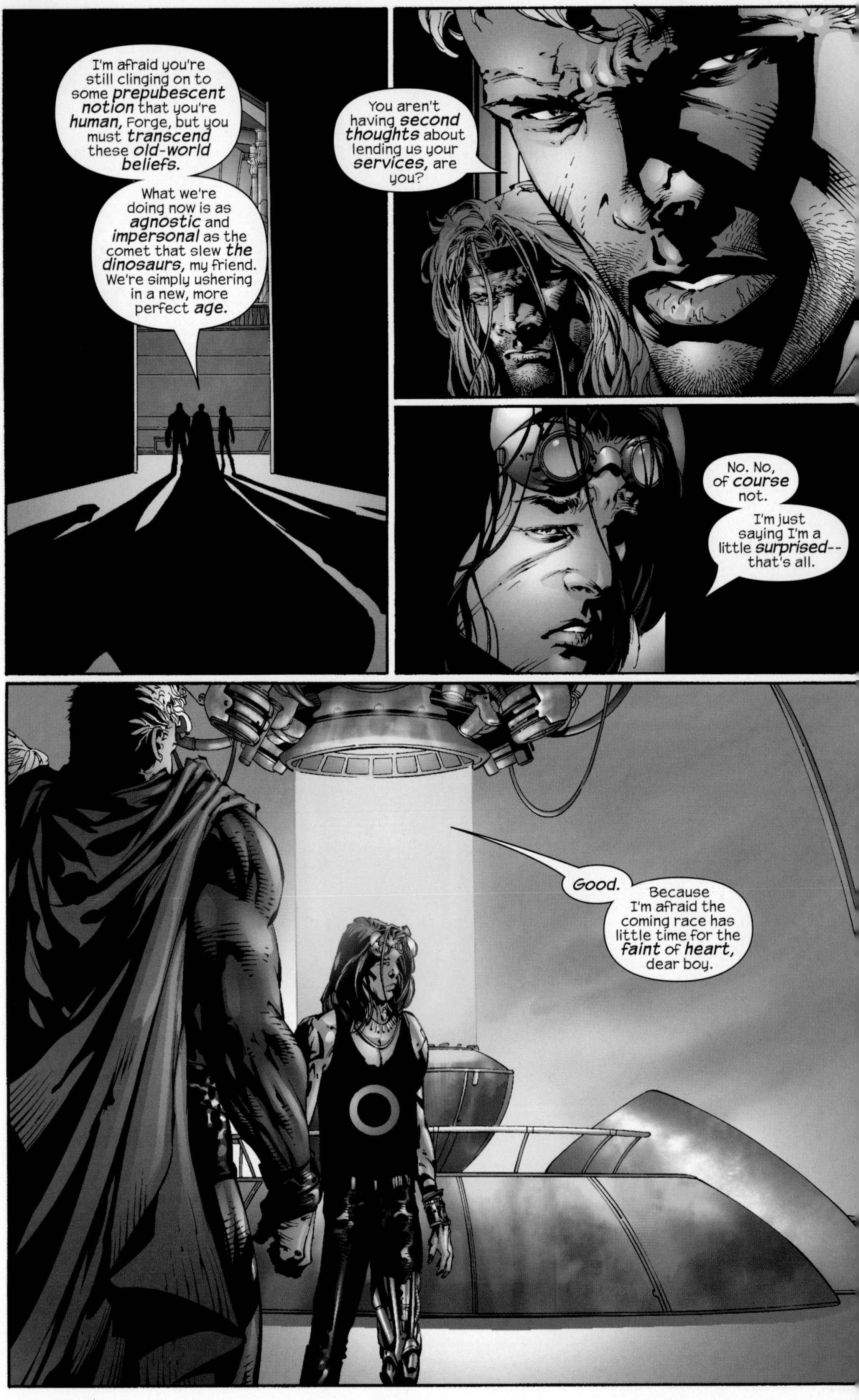
I'm afraid you're still clinging on to some *prepubescent notion* that you're *human,* Forge, but you must *transcend* these *old-world beliefs.*
What we're doing now is as *agnostic* and *impersonal* as the comet that slew *the dinosaurs,* my friend. We're simply ushering in a new, more perfect *age.*
You aren't having *second thoughts* about lending us your *services,* are you?
No. No, of *course* not.
I'm just saying I'm a little *surprised*-- that's all.
Good.
Because I'm afraid the coming race has little time for the *faint* of *heart,* dear boy.

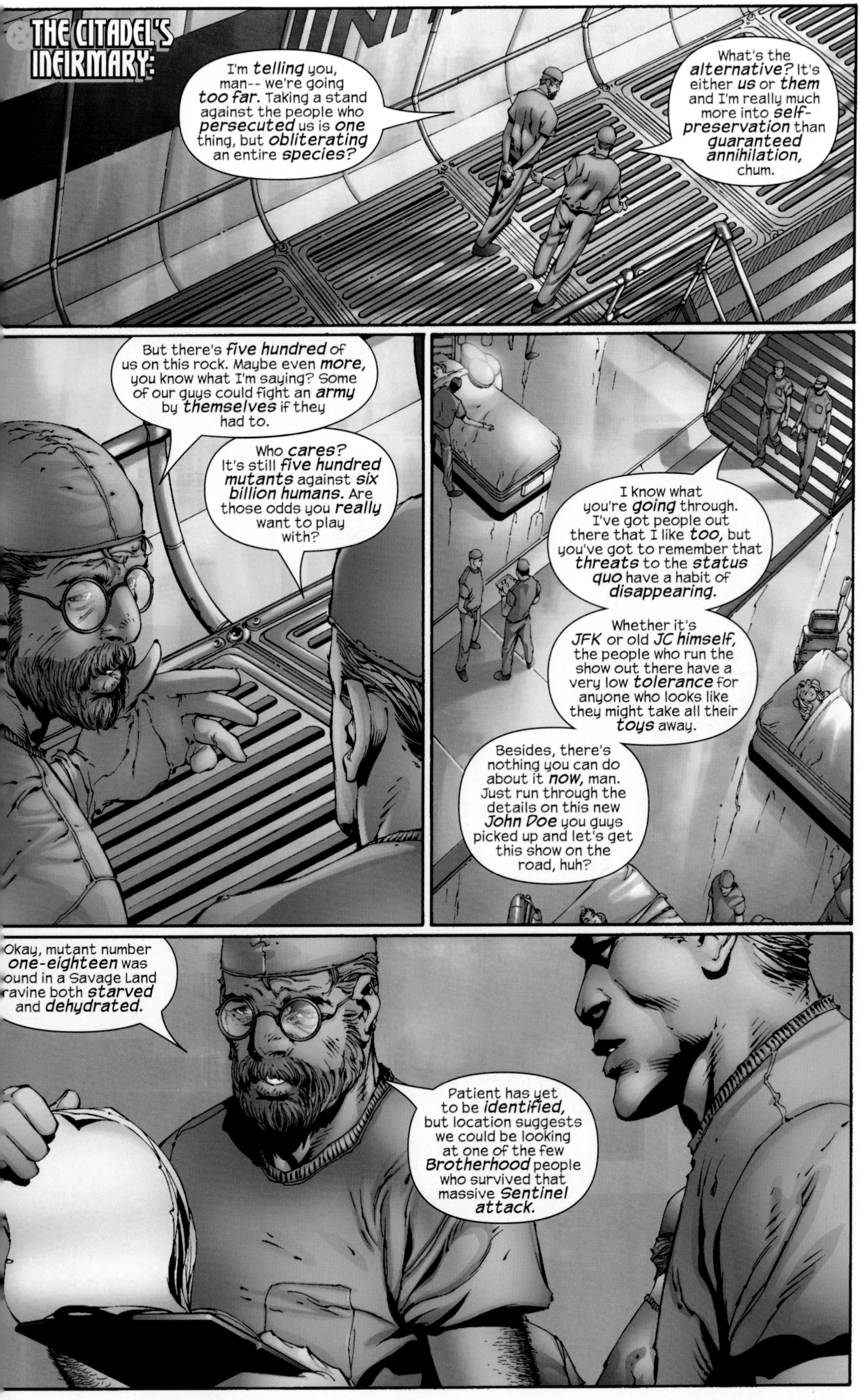
THE CITADEL'S INFIRMARY:
I'm telling you, man-- we're going too far. Taking a stand against the people who persecuted us is one thing, but obliterating an entire species?
What's the alternative? It's either us or them and I'm really much more into self-preservation than guaranteed annihilation, chum.
But there's five hundred of us on this rock. Maybe even more, you know what I'm saying? Some of our guys could fight an army by themselves if they had to.
Who cares? It's still five hundred mutants against six billion humans. Are those odds you really want to play with?
I know what you're going through. I've got people out there that I like too, but you've got to remember that threats to the status quo have a habit of disappearing.
Whether it's JFK or old JC himself, the people who run the show out there have a very low tolerance for anyone who looks like they might take all their toys away.
Besides, there's nothing you can do about it now, man. Just run through the details on this new John Doe you guys picked up and let's get this show on the road, huh?
Okay, mutant number one-eighteen was ound in a Savage Land ravine both starved and dehydrated.
Patient has yet to be identified, but location suggests we could be looking at one of the few Brotherhood people who survived that massive Sentinel attack.

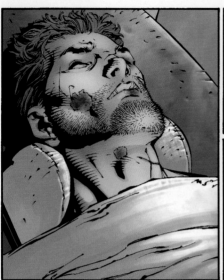

Are you out of your *mind*? Are you seriously telling me you don't *recognize* this traitor? It's...

Cyclops, baby.

Don't *wear* it out.

That's as far as you go, Mister! Another step and I'll burn that pretty head of yours clean off your shoulders!

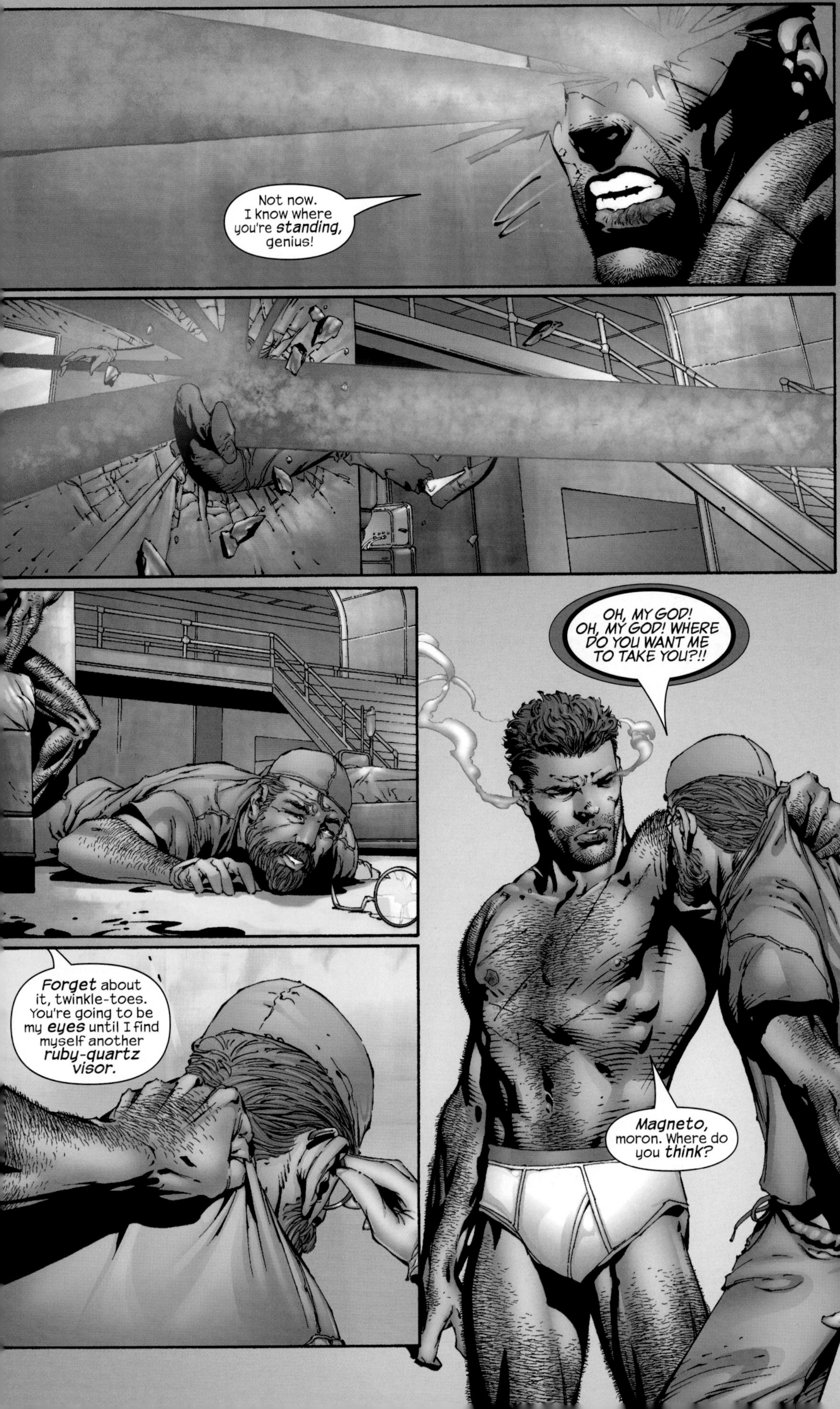
Not now. I know where you're standing, genius!
OH, MY GOD! OH, MY GOD! WHERE DO YOU WANT ME TO TAKE YOU?!!
Forget about it, twinkle-toes. You're going to be my eyes until I find myself another ruby-quartz visor.
Magneto, moron. Where do you think?

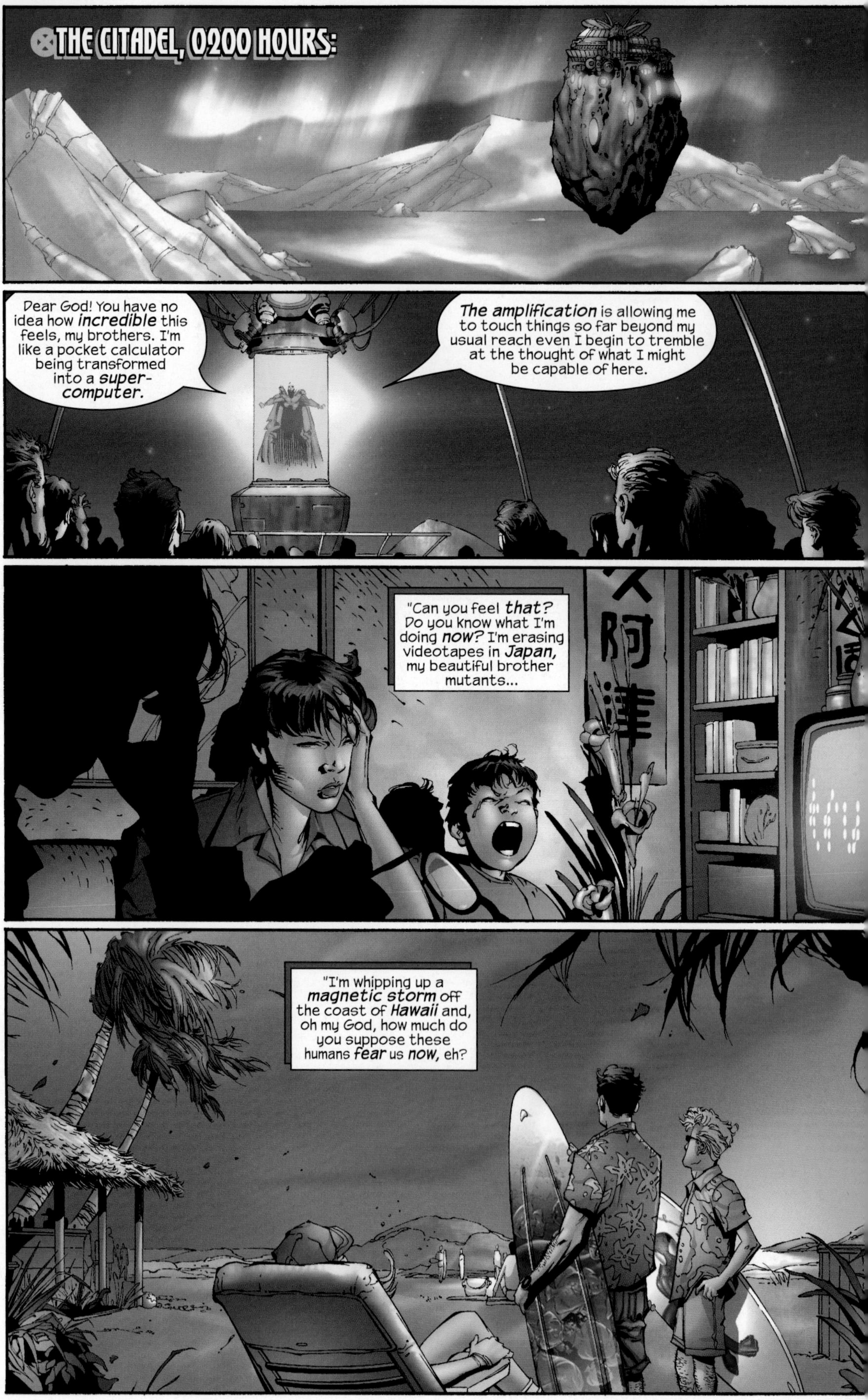
THE CITADEL, 0200 HOURS:
Dear God! You have no idea how *incredible* this feels, my brothers. I'm like a pocket calculator being transformed into a *super-computer.*
The amplification is allowing me to touch things so far beyond my usual reach even I begin to tremble at the thought of what I might be capable of here.
"Can you feel *that?* Do you know what I'm doing *now?* I'm erasing videotapes in *Japan,* my beautiful brother mutants...
"I'm whipping up a *magnetic storm* off the coast of *Hawaii* and, oh my God, how much do you suppose these humans *fear* us *now,* eh?

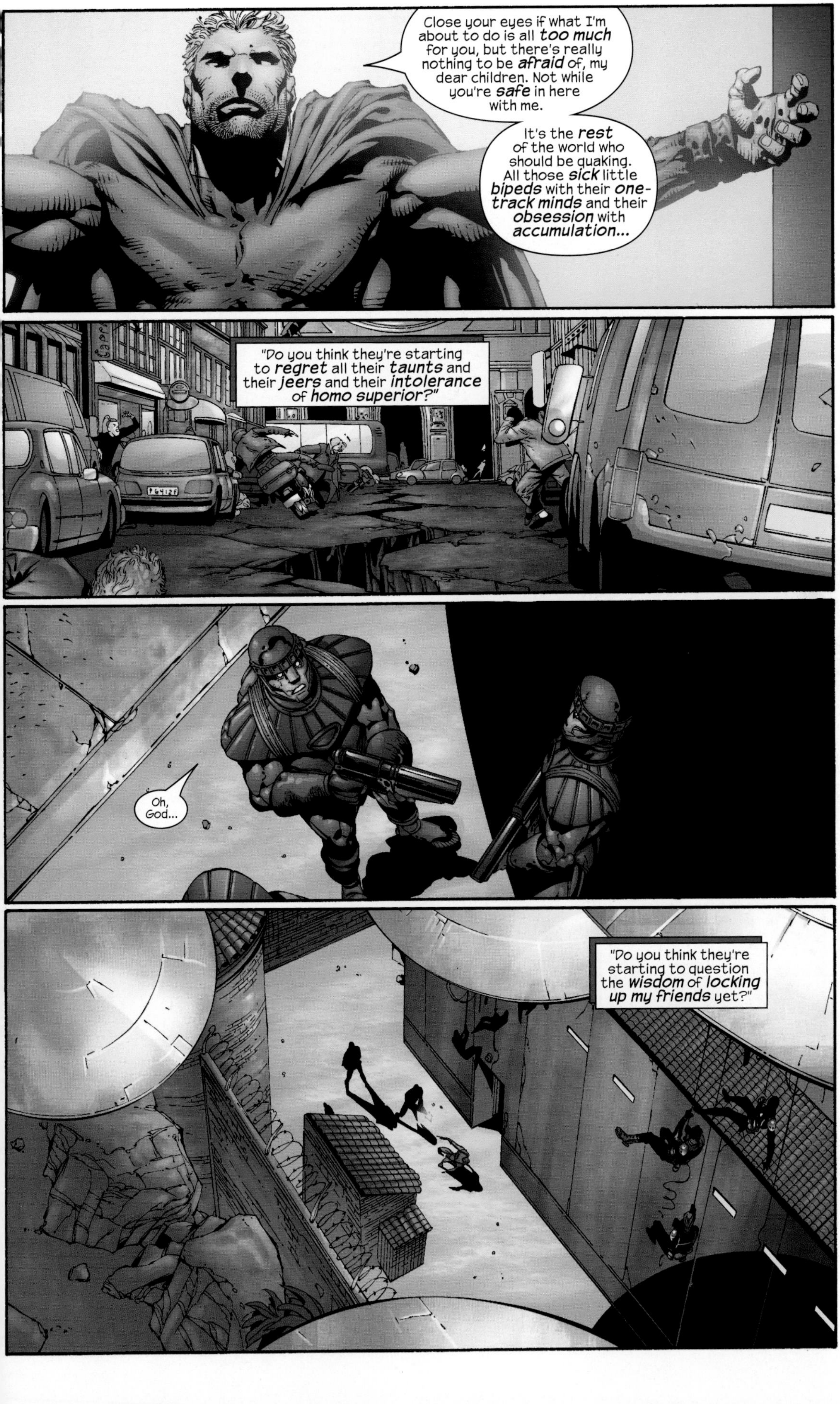

Close your eyes if what I'm about to do is all too much for you, but there's really nothing to be afraid of, my dear children. Not while you're safe in here with me.
It's the rest of the world who should be quaking. All those sick little bipeds with their one-track minds and their obsession with accumulation...
"Do you think they're starting to regret all their taunts and their jeers and their intolerance of homo superior?"
Oh, God...
"Do you think they're starting to question the wisdom of locking up my friends yet?"

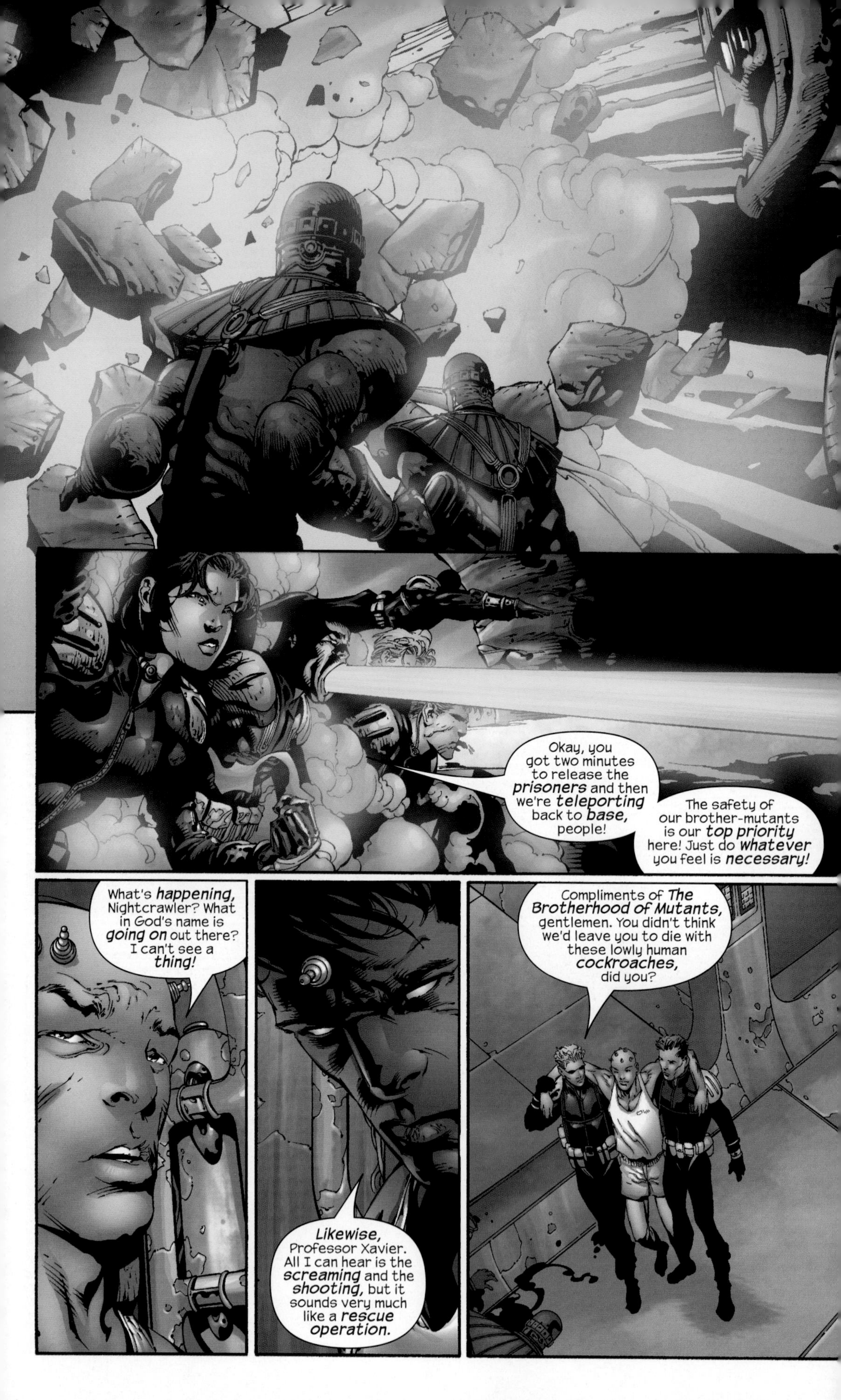
Okay, you got two minutes to release the prisoners and then we're teleporting back to base, people!
The safety of our brother-mutants is our top priority here! Just do whatever you feel is necessary!
What's happening, Nightcrawler? What in God's name is going on out there? I can't see a thing!
Likewise, Professor Xavier. All I can hear is the screaming and the shooting, but it sounds very much like a rescue operation.
Compliments of The Brotherhood of Mutants, gentlemen. You didn't think we'd leave you to die with these lowly human cockroaches, did you?

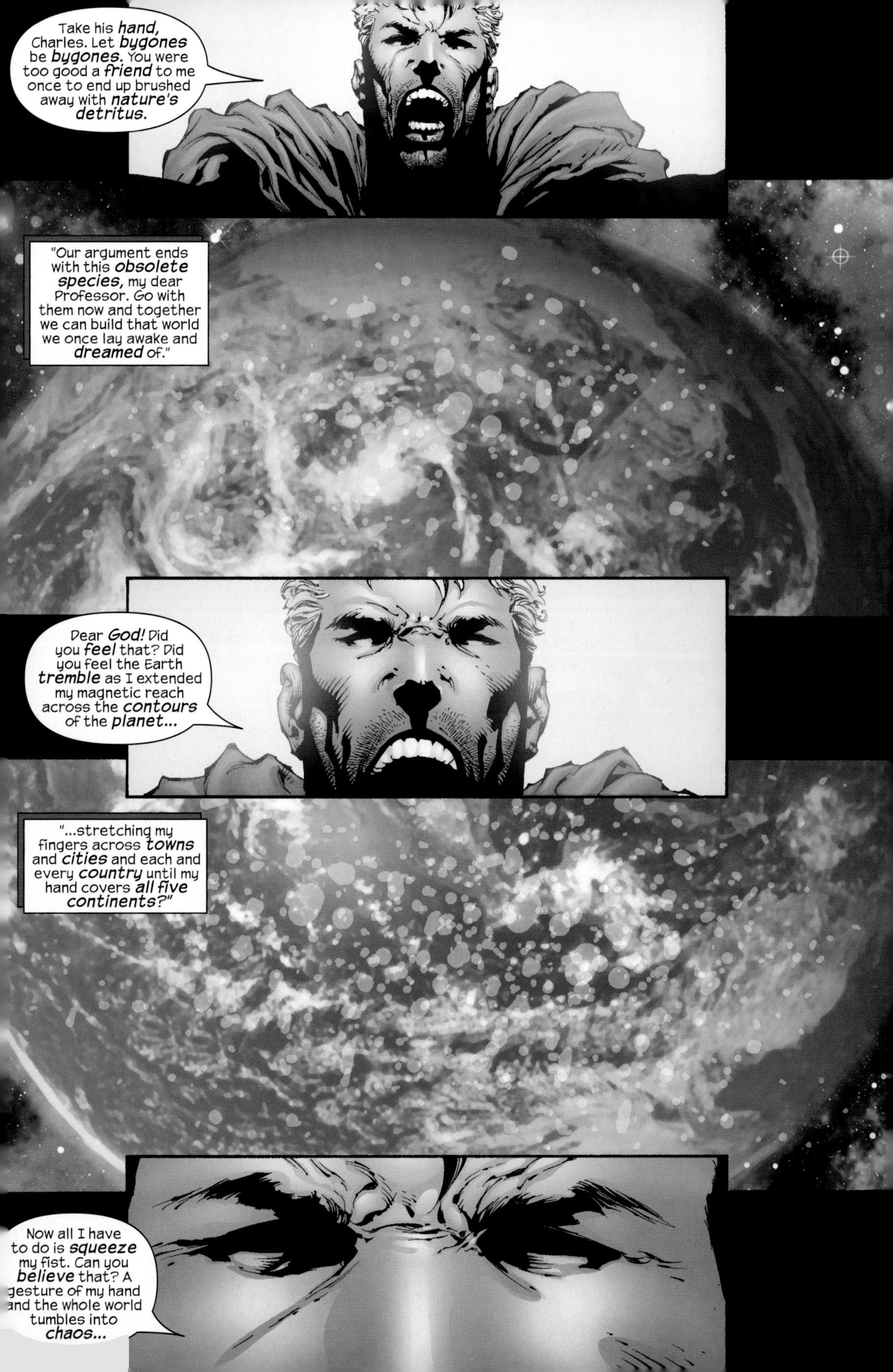

Take his *hand,* Charles. Let *bygones* be *bygones.* You were too good a *friend* to me once to end up brushed away with *nature's detritus.*
"Our argument ends with this *obsolete species,* my dear Professor. Go with them now and together we can build that world we once lay awake and *dreamed* of."
Dear *God!* Did you *feel* that? Did you feel the Earth *tremble* as I extended my magnetic reach across the *contours* of the *planet...*
"...stretching my fingers across *towns* and *cities* and each and every *country* until my hand covers *all five continents?"*
Now all I have to do is *squeeze* my fist. Can you *believe* that? A gesture of my hand and the whole world tumbles into *chaos...*

AARGH!

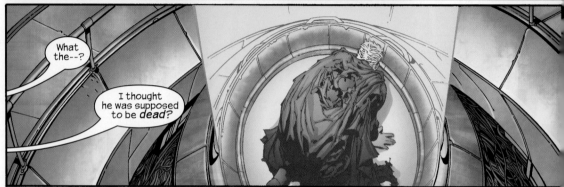

What the--?

I thought he was supposed to be *dead*?

Thought *wrong,* meatball. Now step away from that machine before someone gets seriously *hurt.*

Yeah, someone spelled C-Y-C-L-O-P-S.

No, Sabretooth. Put your *claws away* and leave him *alone.*

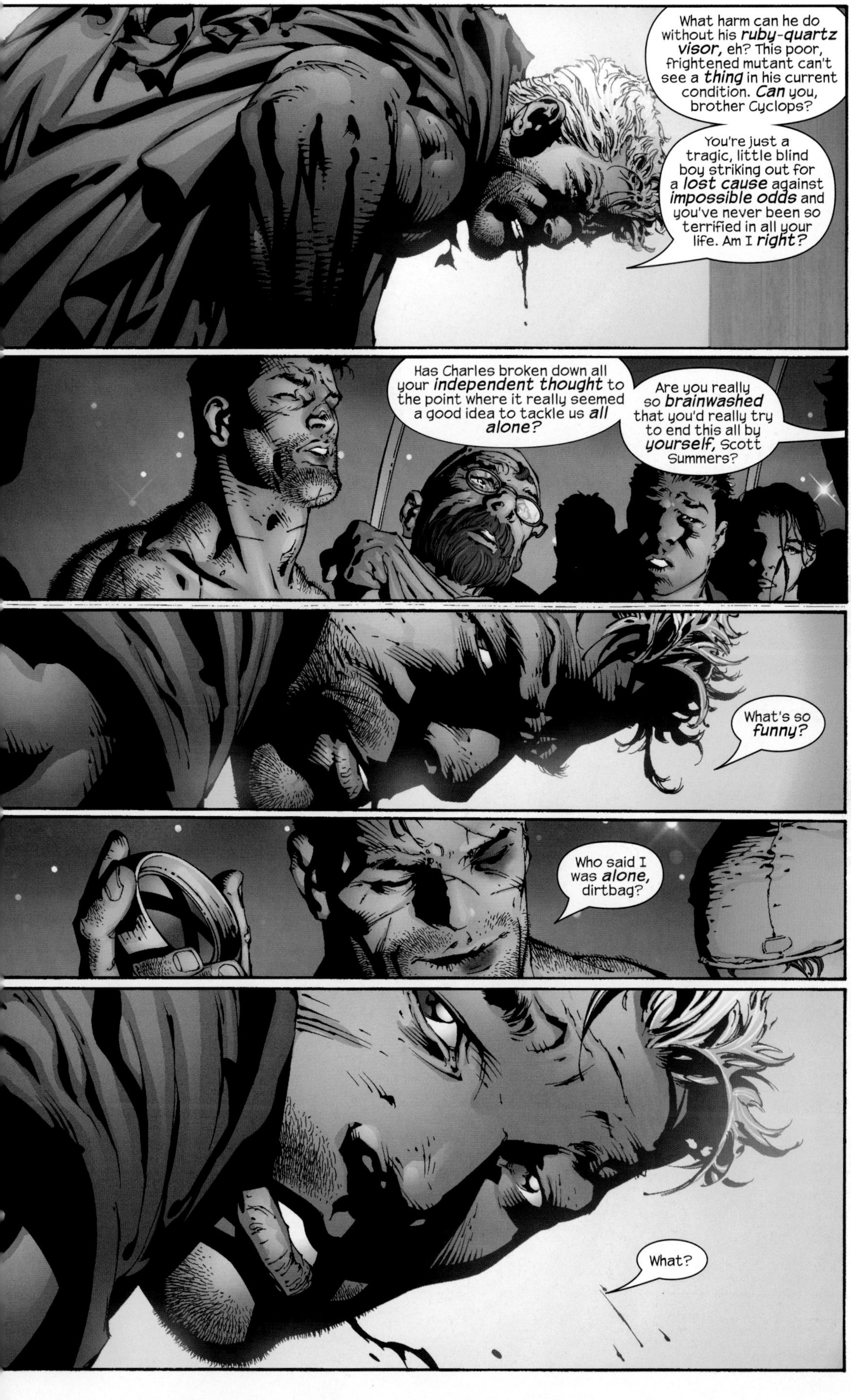
What harm can he do without his *ruby-quartz visor,* eh? This poor, frightened mutant can't see a *thing* in his current condition. *Can* you, brother Cyclops?
You're just a tragic, little blind boy striking out for a *lost cause* against *impossible odds* and you've never been so terrified in all your life. Am I *right?*
Has Charles broken down all your *independent thought* to the point where it really seemed a good idea to tackle us *all alone?*
Are you really so *brainwashed* that you'd really try to end this all by *yourself,* Scott Summers?
What's so *funny?*
Who said I was *alone,* dirtbag?
What?

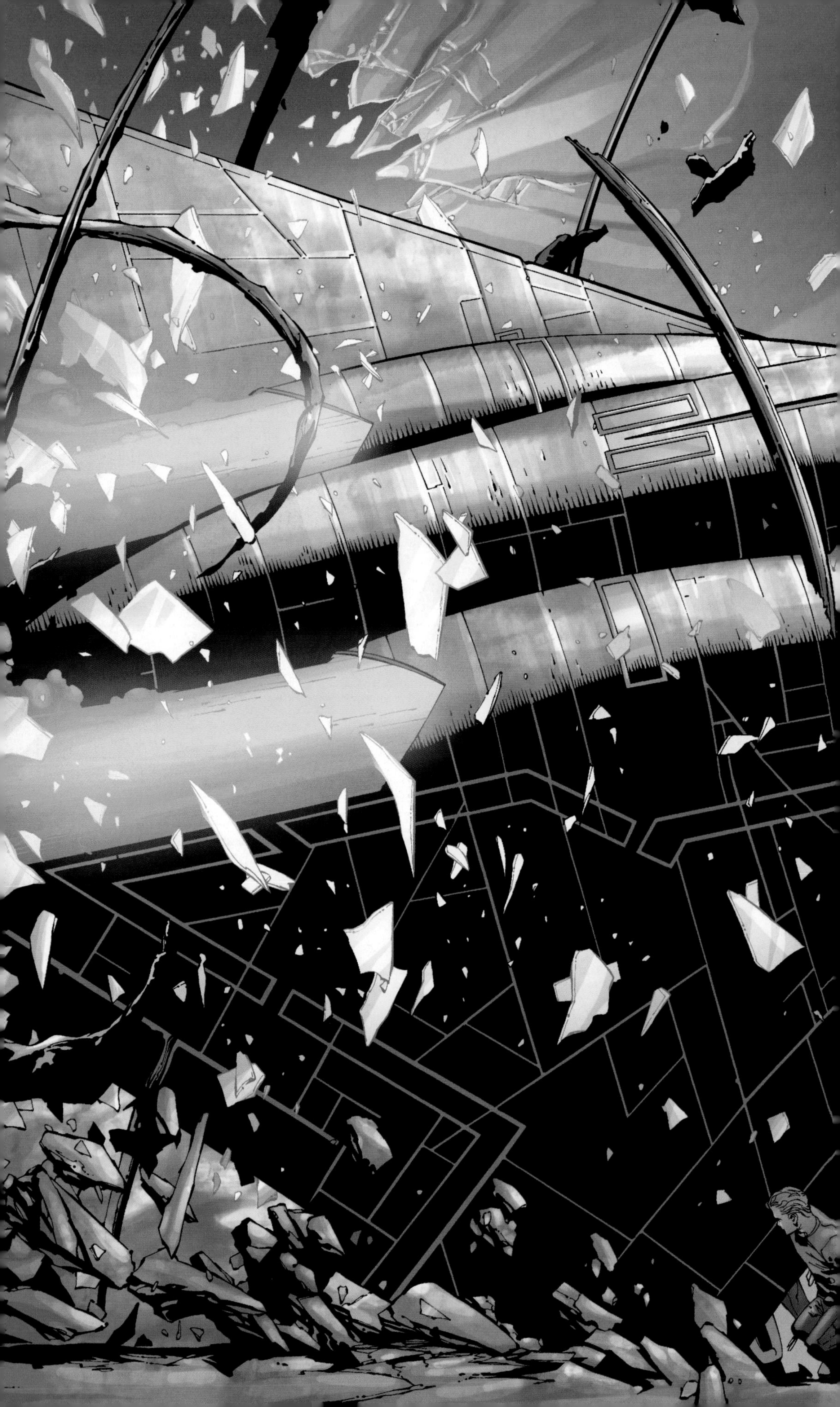

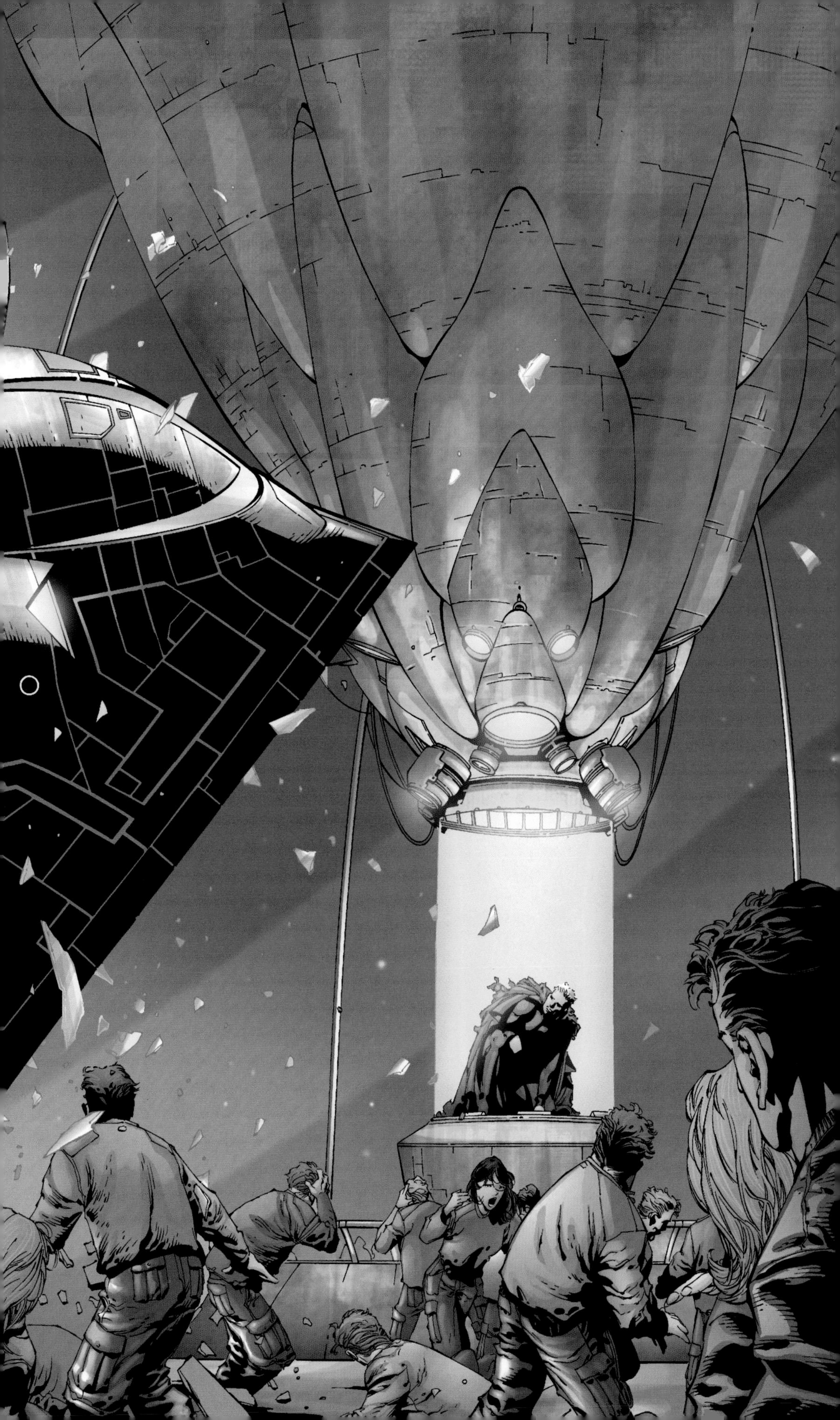

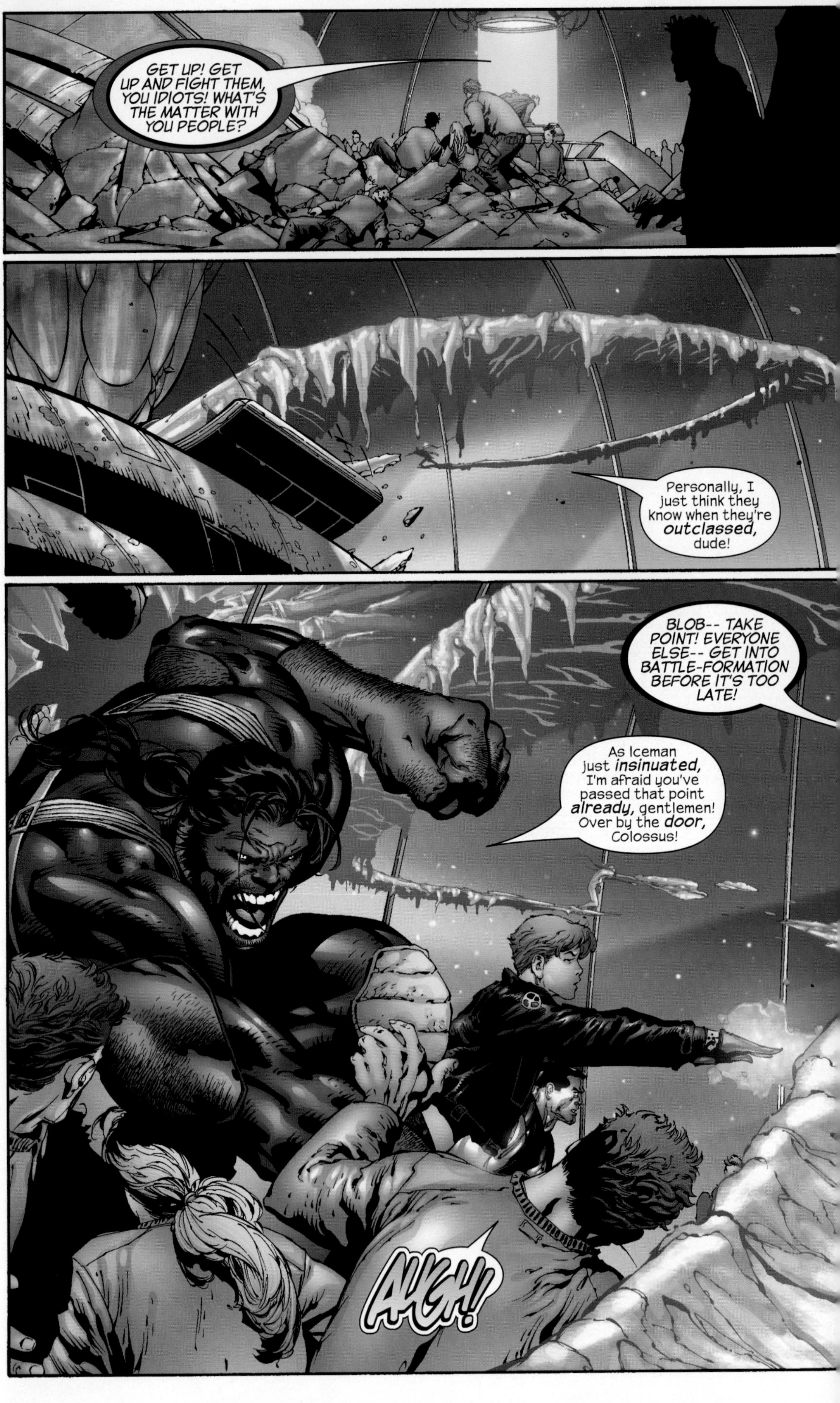
GET UP! GET UP AND FIGHT THEM, YOU IDIOTS! WHAT'S THE MATTER WITH YOU PEOPLE?
Personally, I just think they know when they're *outclassed,* dude!
BLOB-- TAKE POINT! EVERYONE ELSE-- GET INTO BATTLE-FORMATION BEFORE IT'S TOO LATE!
As Iceman just *insinuated,* I'm afraid you've passed that point *already,* gentlemen! Over by the *door,* Colossus!
AUGH!

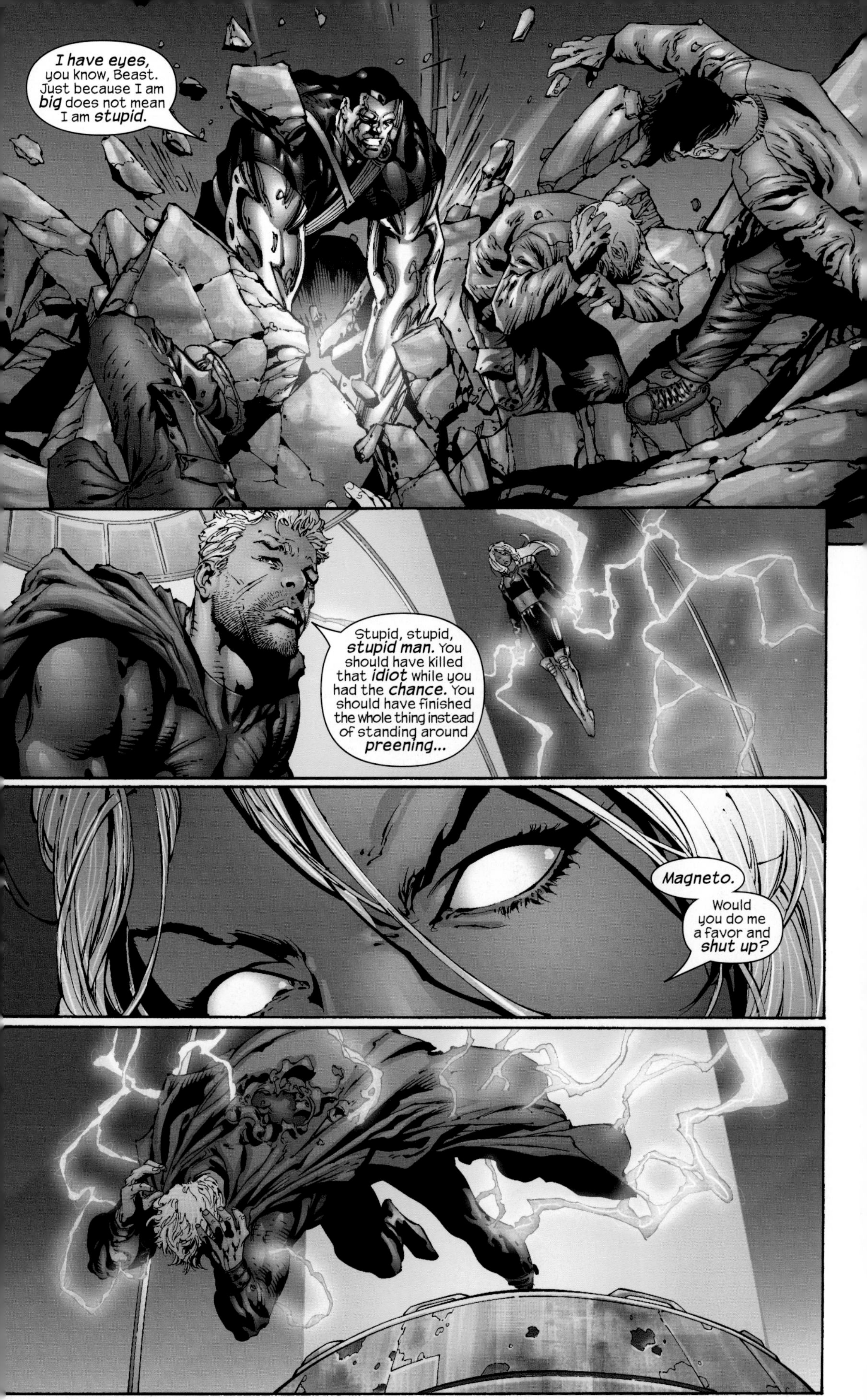

I have eyes, you know, Beast. Just because I am *big* does not mean I am *stupid.*
Stupid, stupid, *stupid man.* You should have killed that *idiot* while you had the *chance.* You should have finished the whole thing instead of standing around *preening...*
Magneto.
Would you do me a favor and *shut up?*

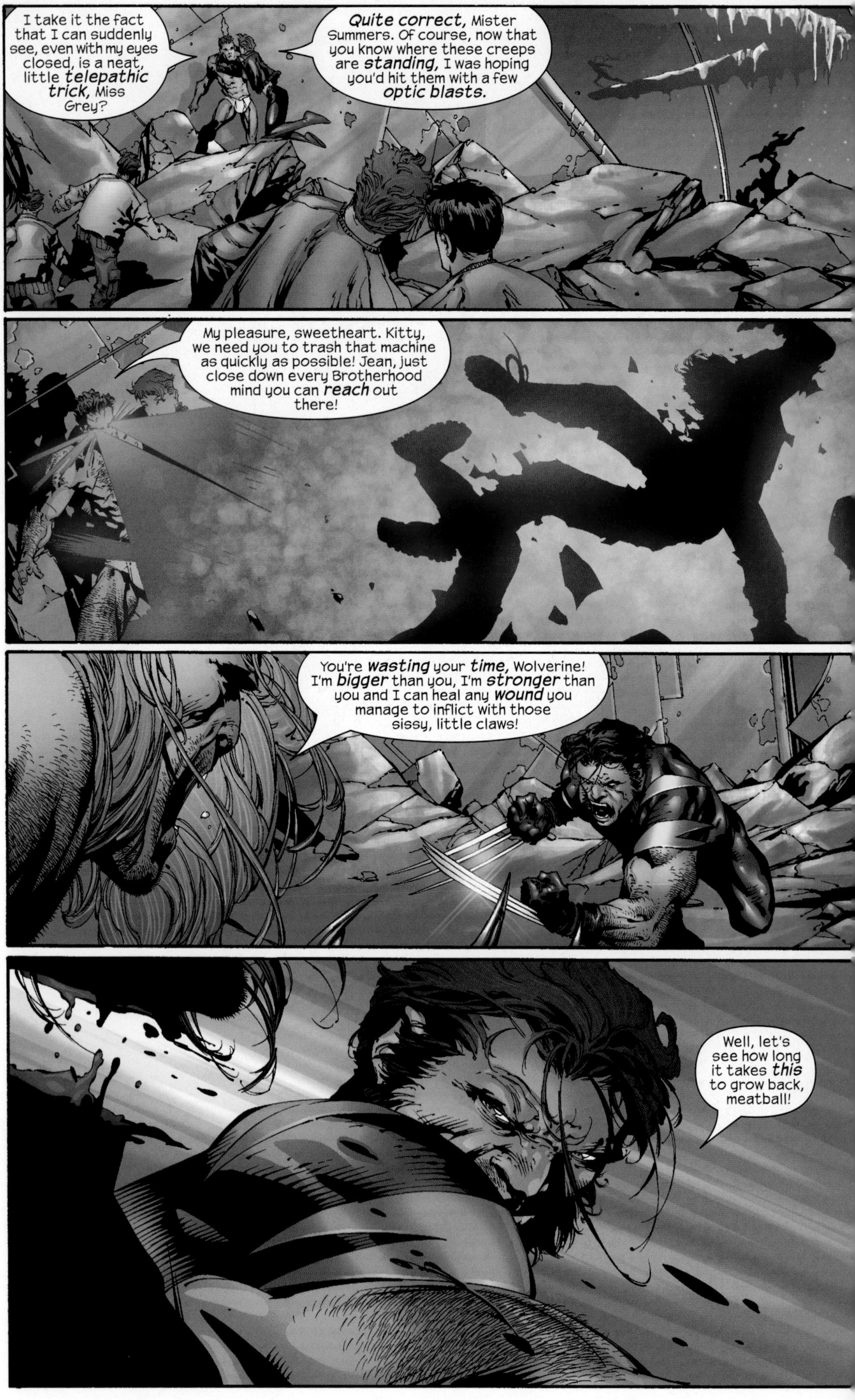
I take it the fact that I can suddenly see, even with my eyes closed, is a neat, little telepathic trick, Miss Grey?
Quite correct, Mister Summers. Of course, now that you know where these creeps are standing, I was hoping you'd hit them with a few optic blasts.
My pleasure, sweetheart. Kitty, we need you to trash that machine as quickly as possible! Jean, just close down every Brotherhood mind you can reach out there!
You're wasting your time, Wolverine! I'm bigger than you, I'm stronger than you and I can heal any wound you manage to inflict with those sissy, little claws!
Well, let's see how long it takes this to grow back, meatball!

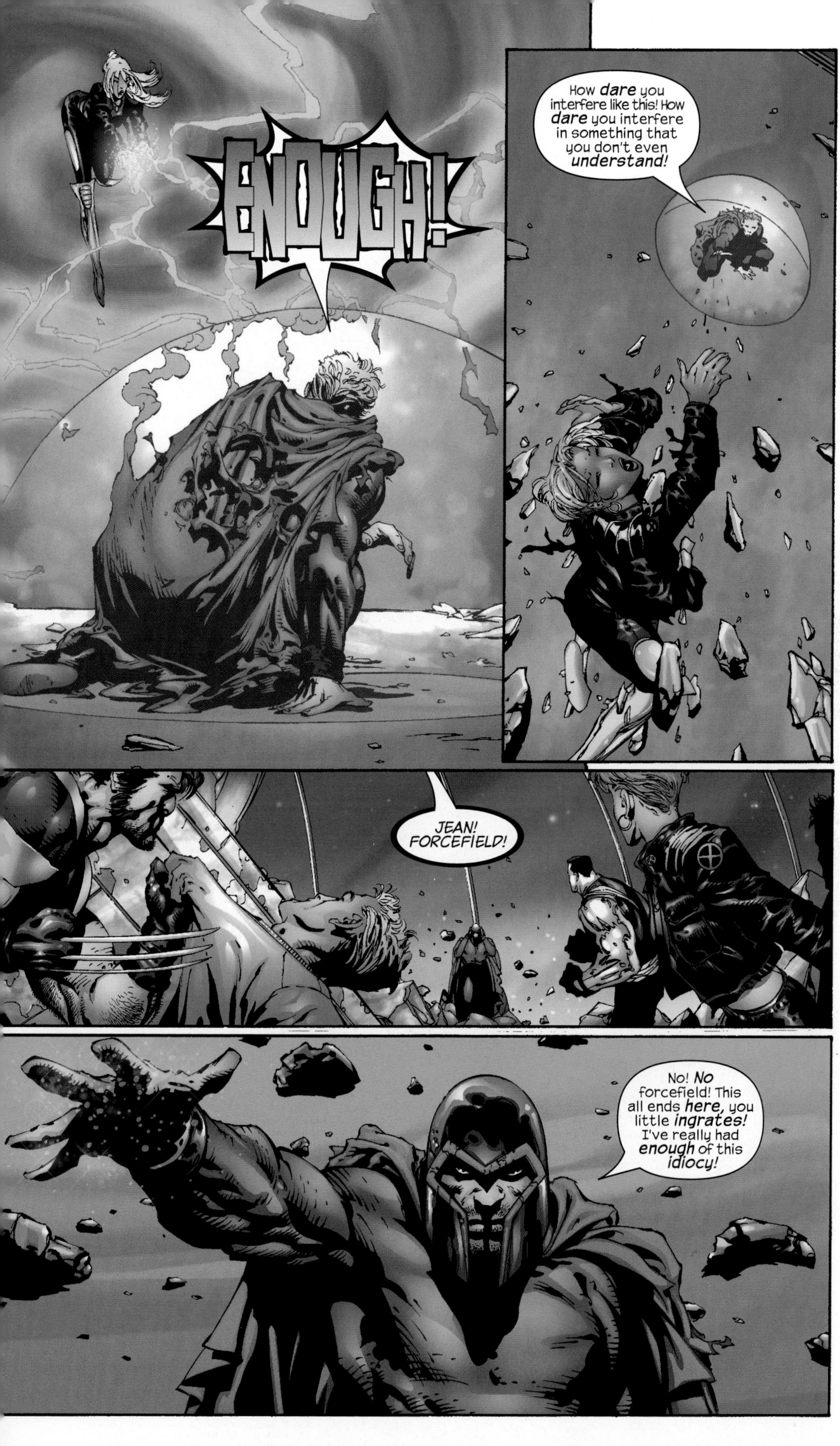
ENOUGH!
How dare you interfere like this! How dare you interfere in something that you don't even understand!
JEAN! FORCEFIELD!
No! No forcefield! This all ends here, you little ingrates! I've really had enough of this idiocy!

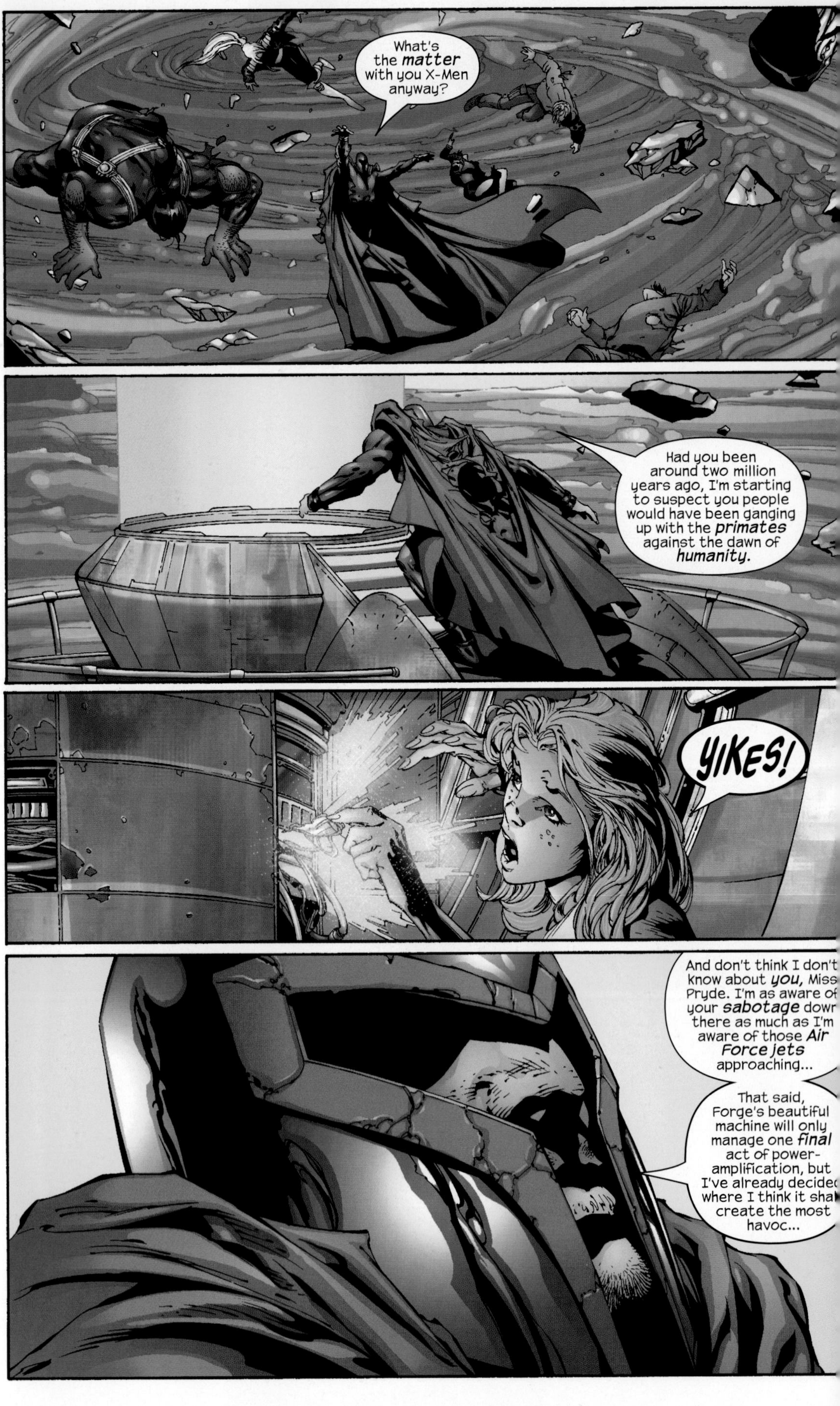
What's the *matter* with you X-Men anyway?
Had you been around two million years ago, I'm starting to suspect you people would have been ganging up with the *primates* against the dawn of *humanity.*
YIKES!
And don't think I don't know about *you,* Miss Pryde. I'm as aware of your *sabotage* down there as much as I'm aware of those *Air Force jets* approaching...
That said, Forge's beautiful machine will only manage one *final* act of power-amplification, but I've already decided where I think it sha create the most havoc...

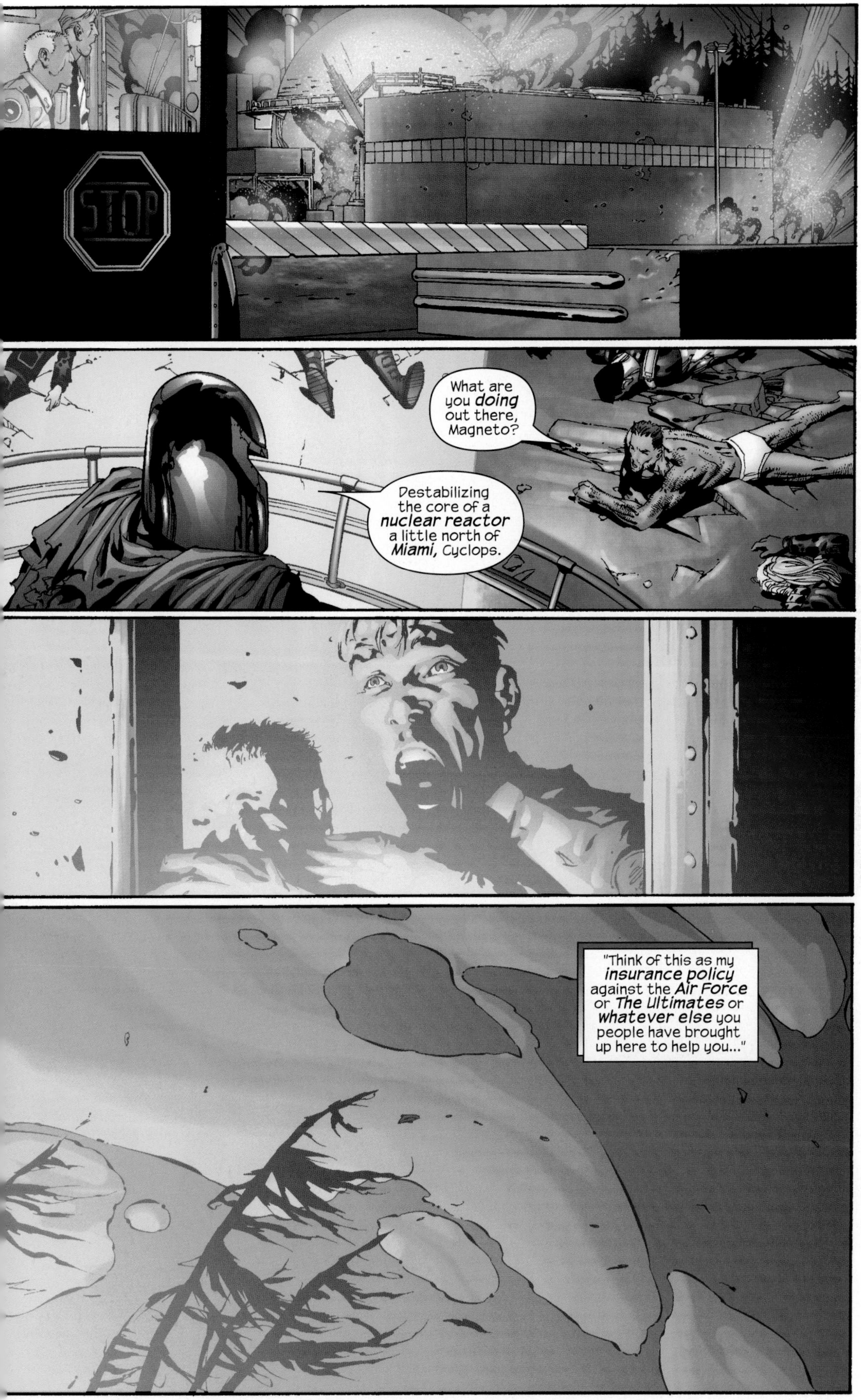

STOP
What are you *doing* out there, Magneto?
Destabilizing the core of a *nuclear reactor* a little north of *Miami*, Cyclops.
"Think of this as my *insurance policy* against the *Air Force* or *The Ultimates* or *whatever else* you people have brought up here to help you..."

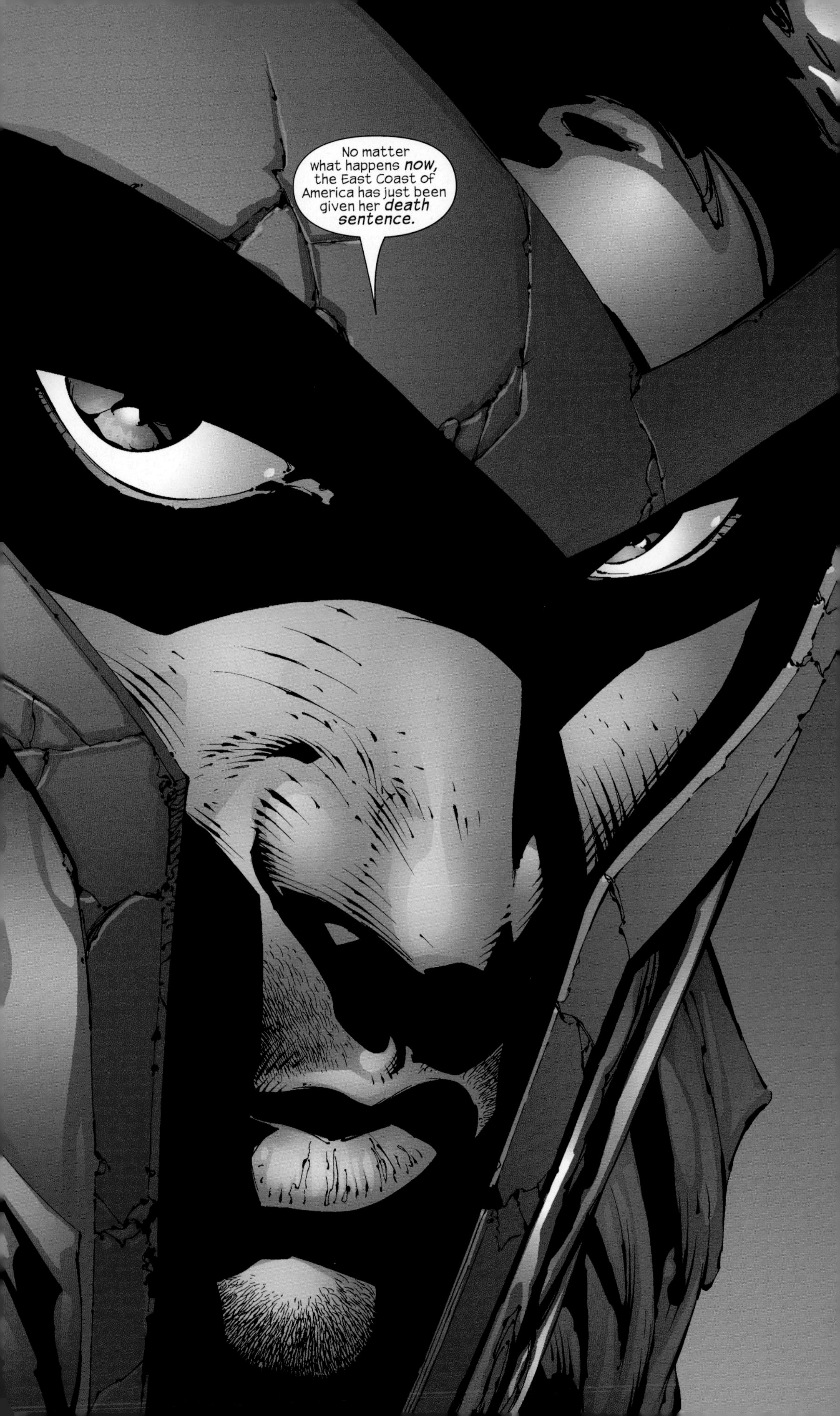
No matter what happens now, the East Coast of America has just been given her death sentence.

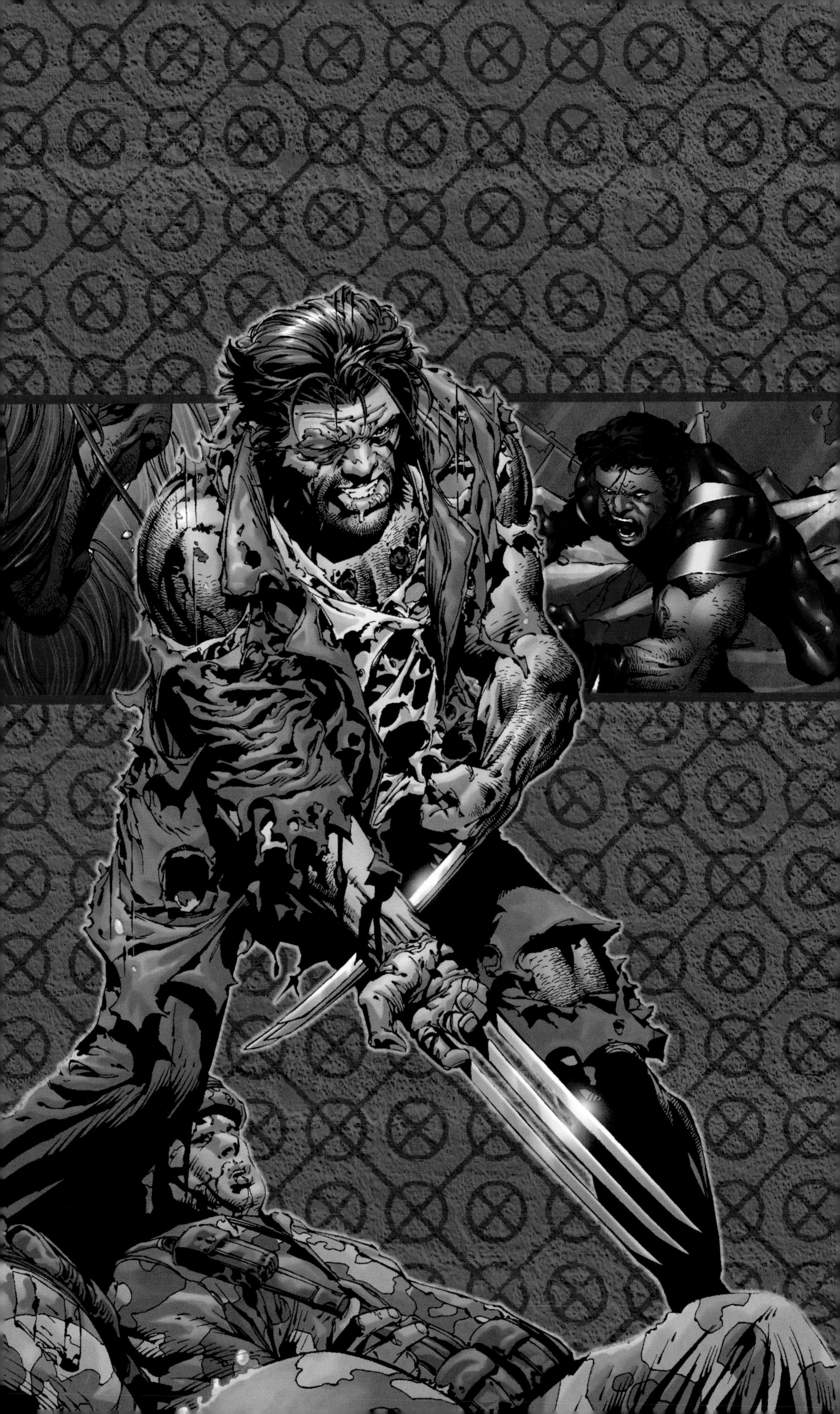

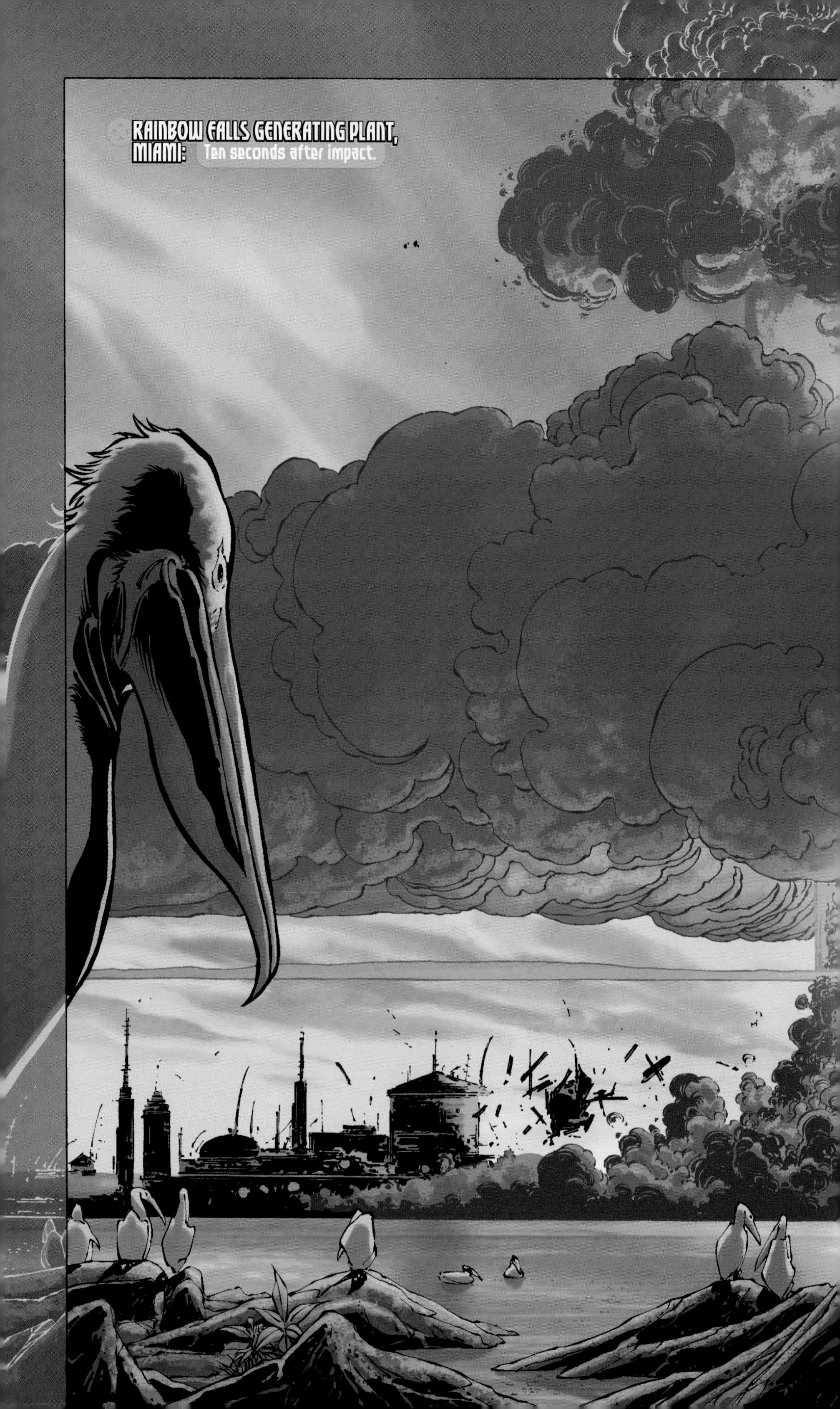
RAINBOW FALLS GENERATING PLANT, MIAMI:
Ten seconds after impact.

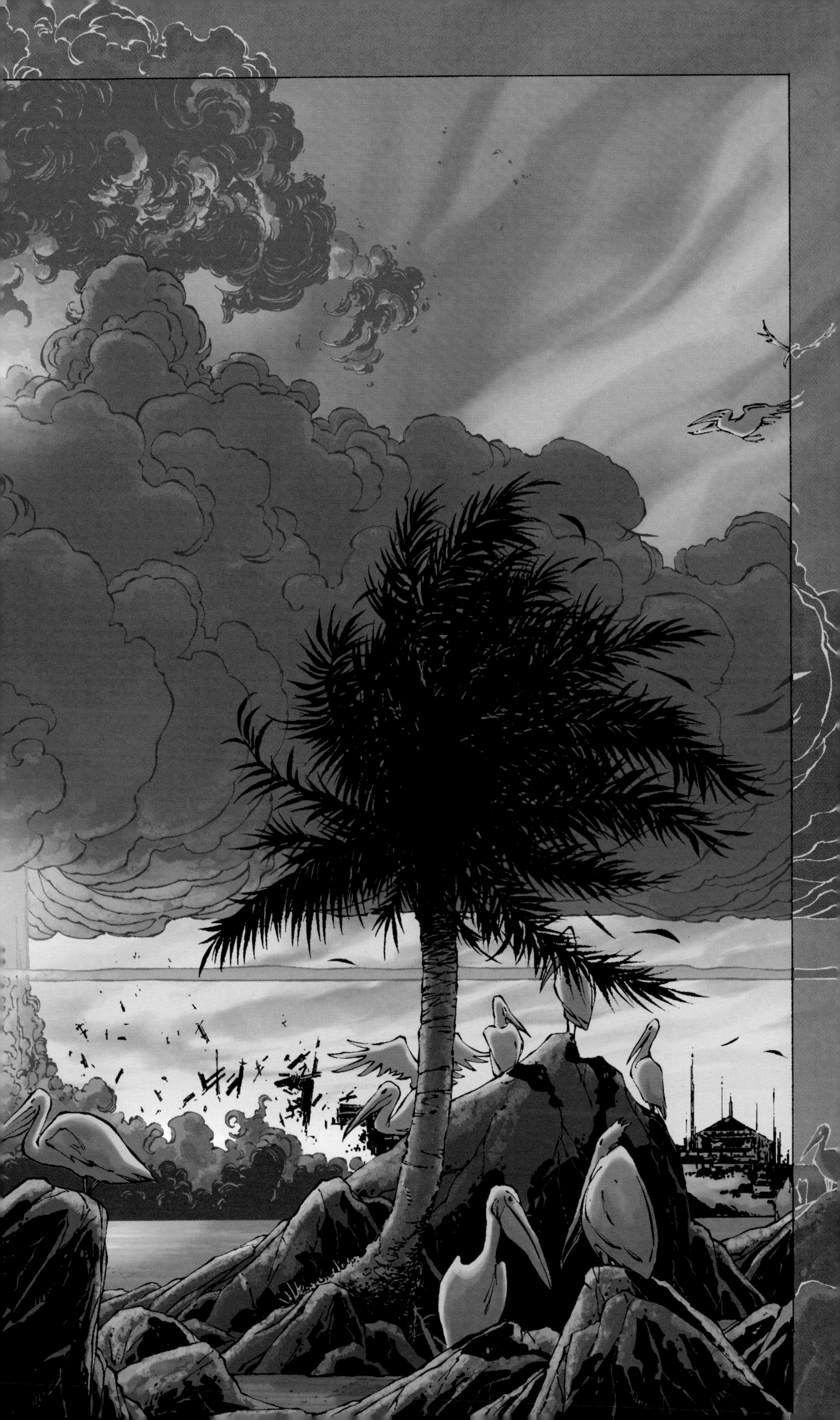

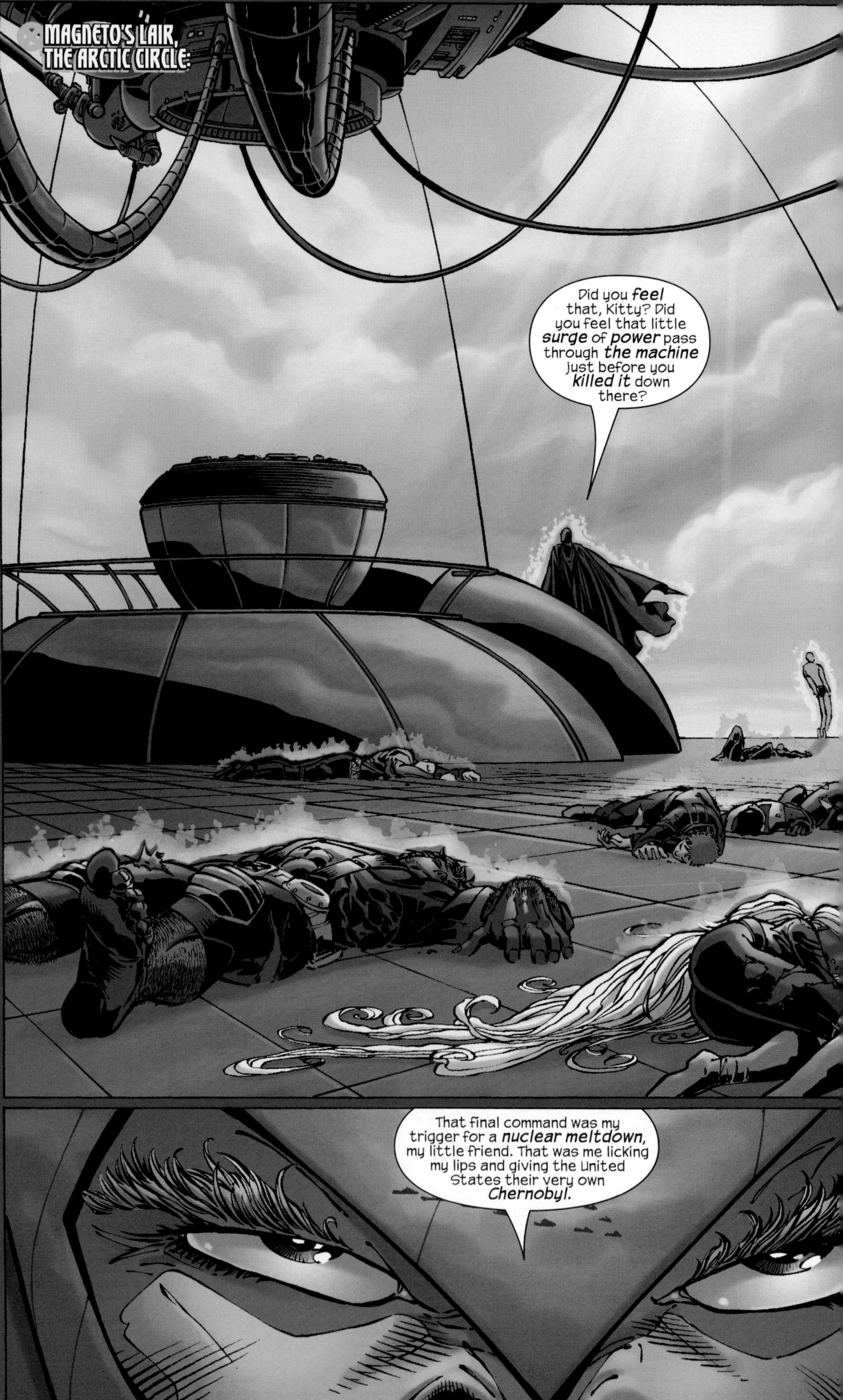
MAGNETO'S LAIR, THE ARCTIC CIRCLE:
Did you feel that, Kitty? Did you feel that little surge of power pass through the machine just before you killed it down there?
That final command was my trigger for a nuclear meltdown, my little friend. That was me licking my lips and giving the United States their very own Chernobyl.

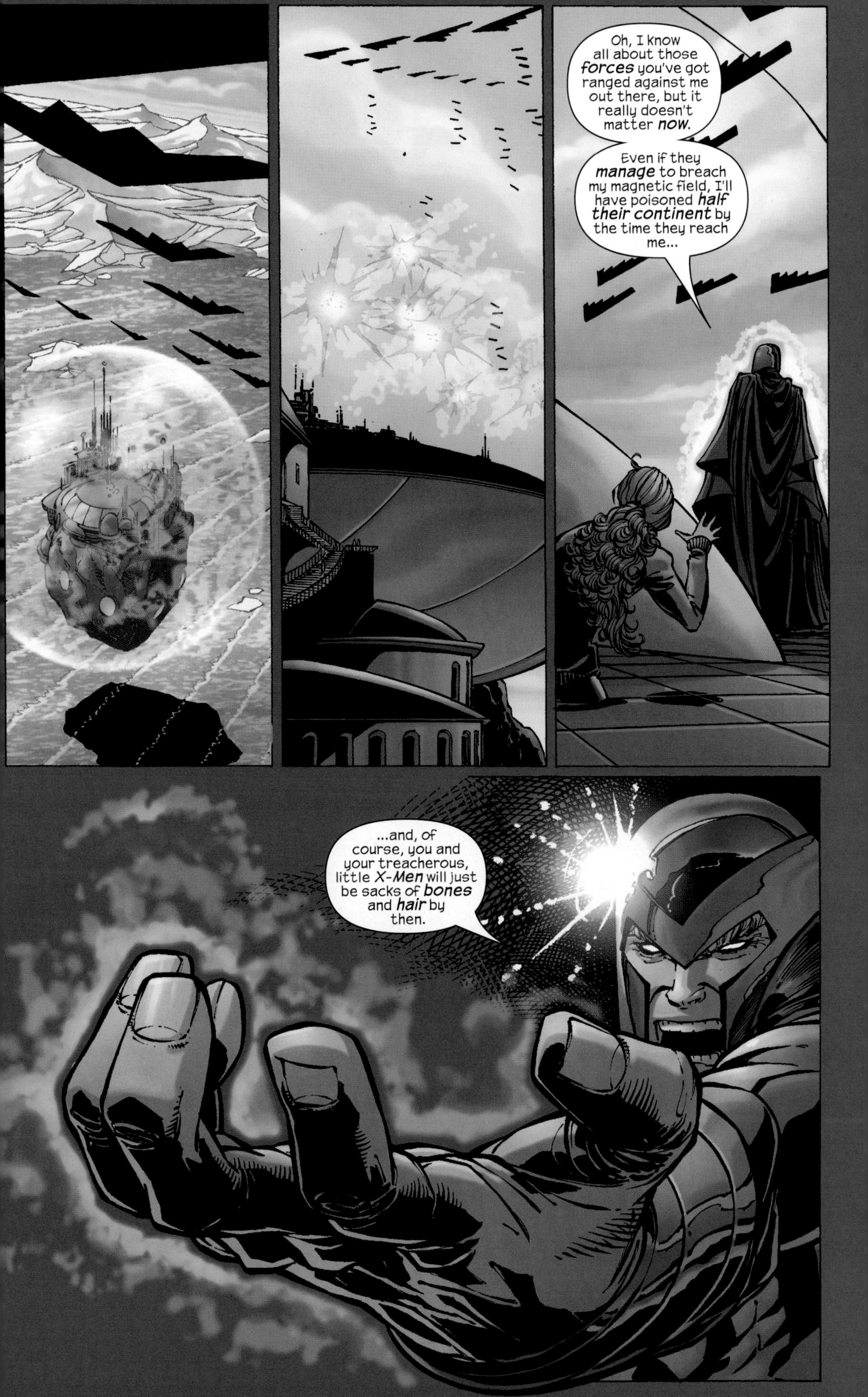

Oh, I know all about those *forces* you've got ranged against me out there, but it really doesn't matter *now*.
Even if they *manage* to breach my magnetic field, I'll have poisoned *half their continent* by the time they reach me...
...and, of course, you and your treacherous, little *X-Men* will just be sacks of *bones* and *hair* by then.

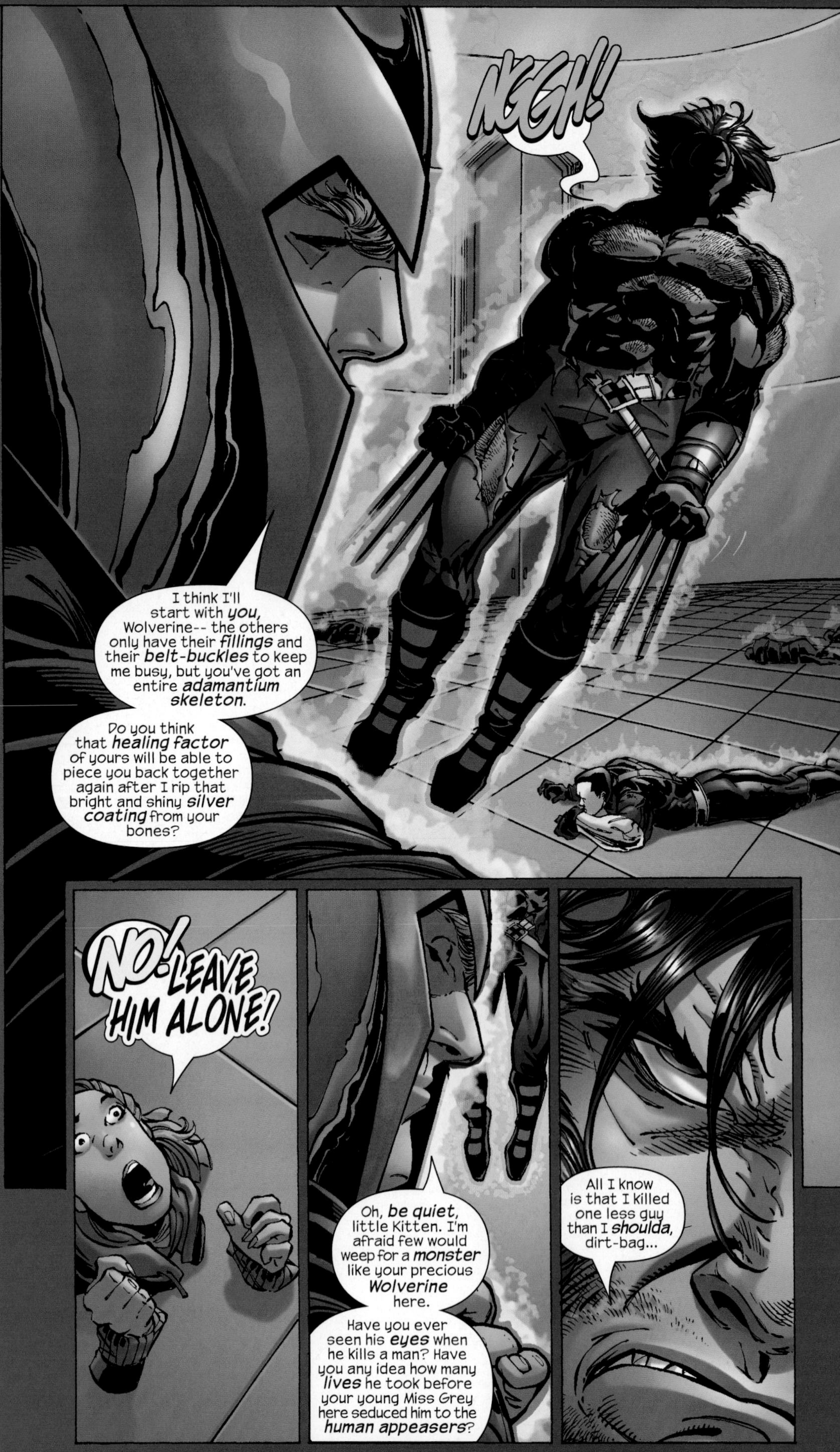
NGGH!!
I think I'll start with you, Wolverine-- the others only have their fillings and their belt-buckles to keep me busy, but you've got an entire adamantium skeleton.
Do you think that healing factor of yours will be able to piece you back together again after I rip that bright and shiny silver coating from your bones?
NO! LEAVE HIM ALONE!
Oh, be quiet, little Kitten. I'm afraid few would weep for a monster like your precious Wolverine here.
Have you ever seen his eyes when he kills a man? Have you any idea how many lives he took before your young Miss Grey here seduced him to the human appeasers?
All I know is that I killed one less guy than I shoulda, dirt-bag...

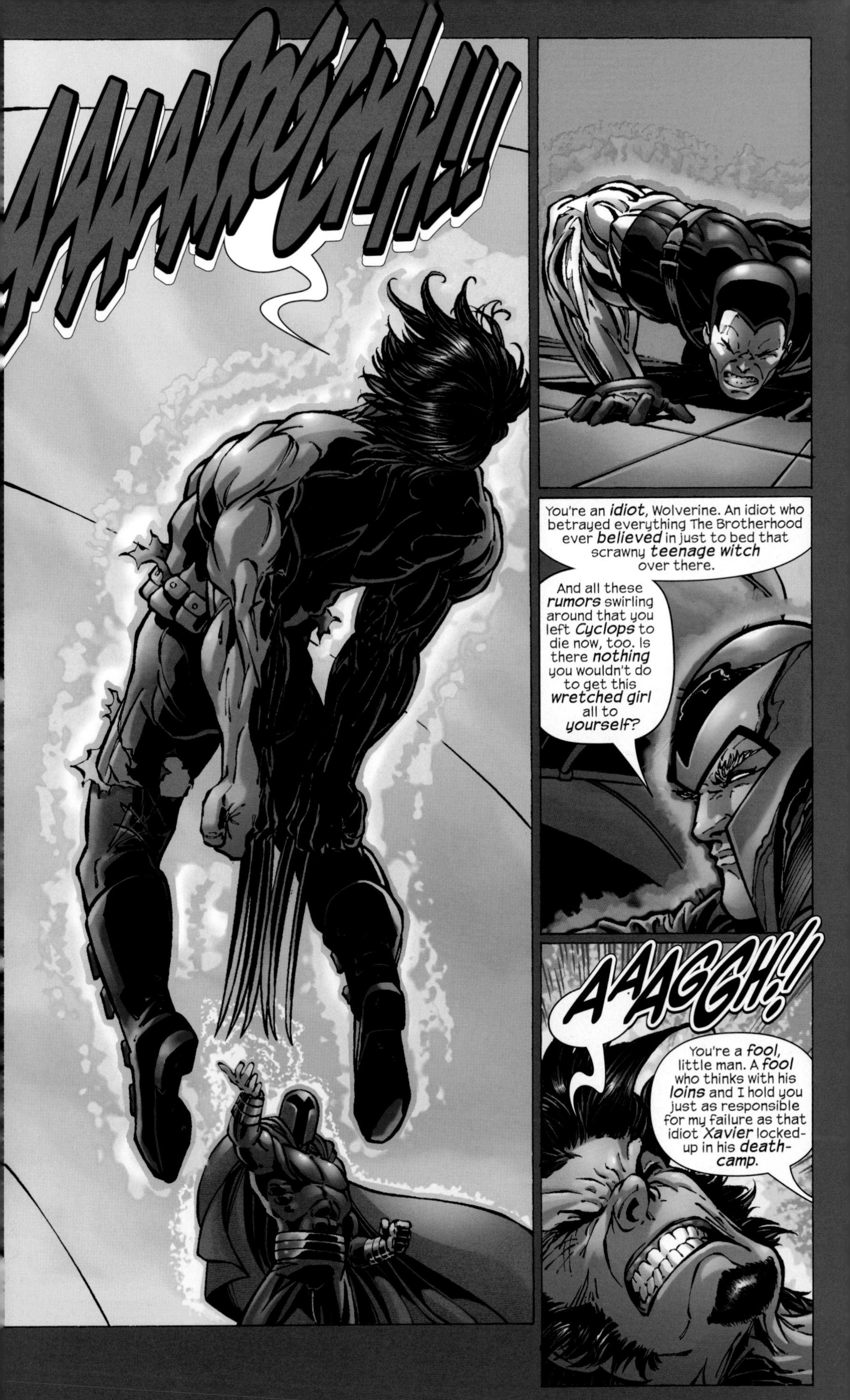
AAAARGGH!!!
You're an idiot, Wolverine. An idiot who betrayed everything The Brotherhood ever believed in just to bed that scrawny teenage witch over there.
And all these rumors swirling around that you left Cyclops to die now, too. Is there nothing you wouldn't do to get this wretched girl all to yourself?
AAAGGH!!
You're a fool, little man. A fool who thinks with his loins and I hold you just as responsible for my failure as that idiot Xavier locked-up in his death-camp.

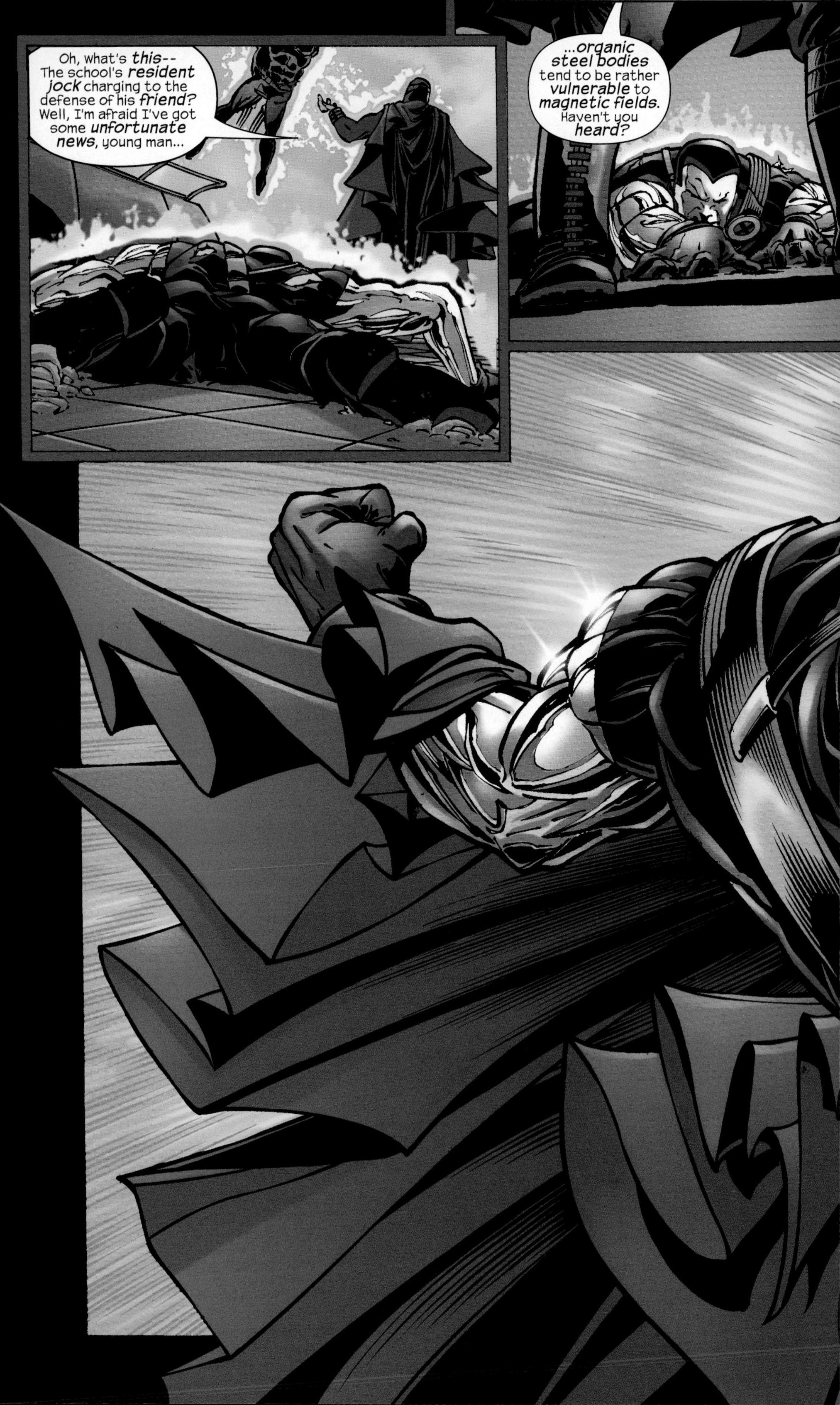
Oh, what's this-- The school's resident jock charging to the defense of his friend? Well, I'm afraid I've got some unfortunate news, young man...
...organic steel bodies tend to be rather vulnerable to magnetic fields. Haven't you heard?

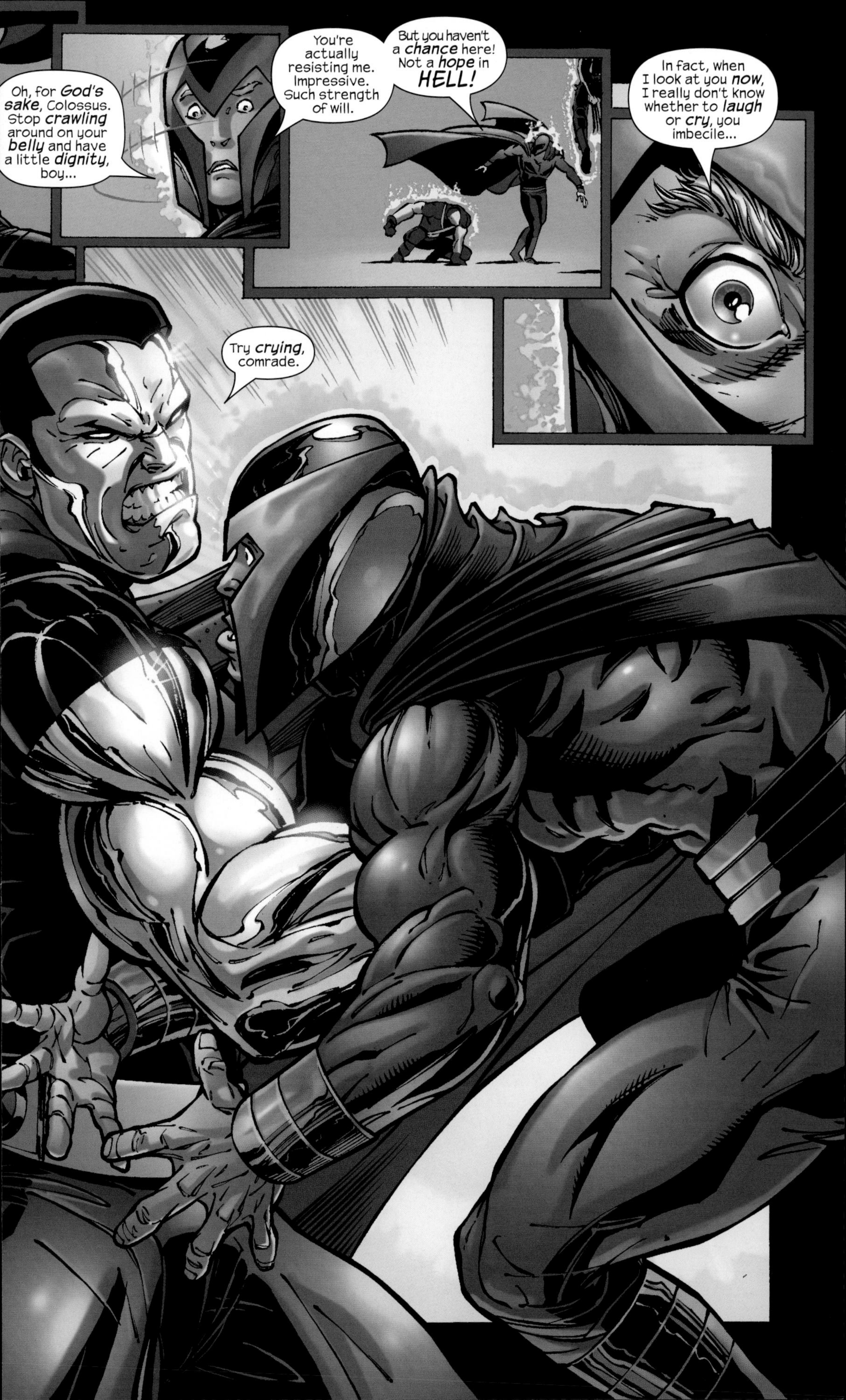

Oh, for God's sake, Colossus. Stop crawling around on your belly and have a little dignity, boy...
You're actually resisting me. Impressive. Such strength of will.
But you haven't a chance here! Not a hope in HELL!
In fact, when I look at you now, I really don't know whether to laugh or cry, you imbecile...
Try crying, comrade.

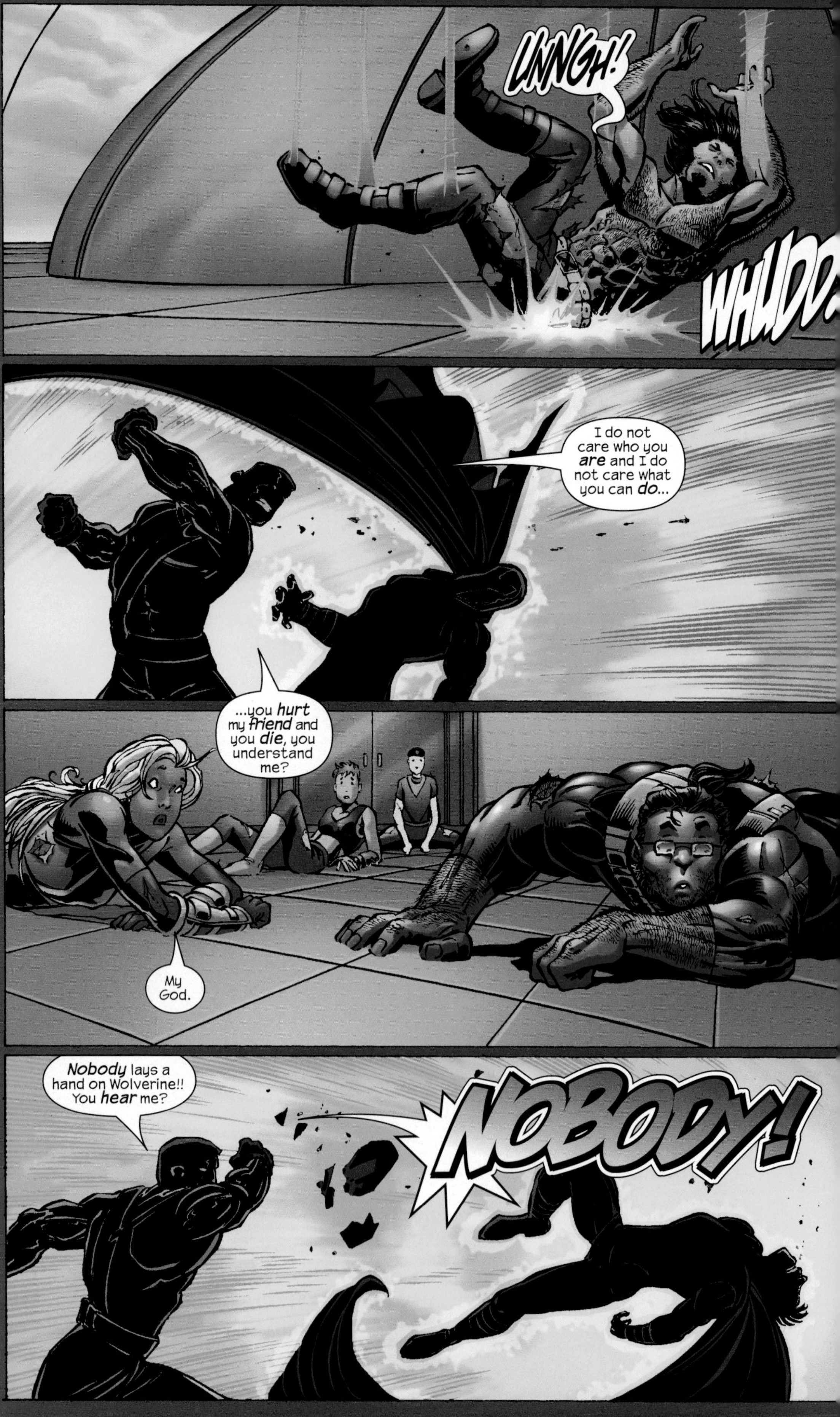
UNNGH!
WHUDD
I do not care who you are and I do not care what you can do...
...you hurt my friend and you die, you understand me?
My God.
Nobody lays a hand on Wolverine!! You hear me?
NOBODY!

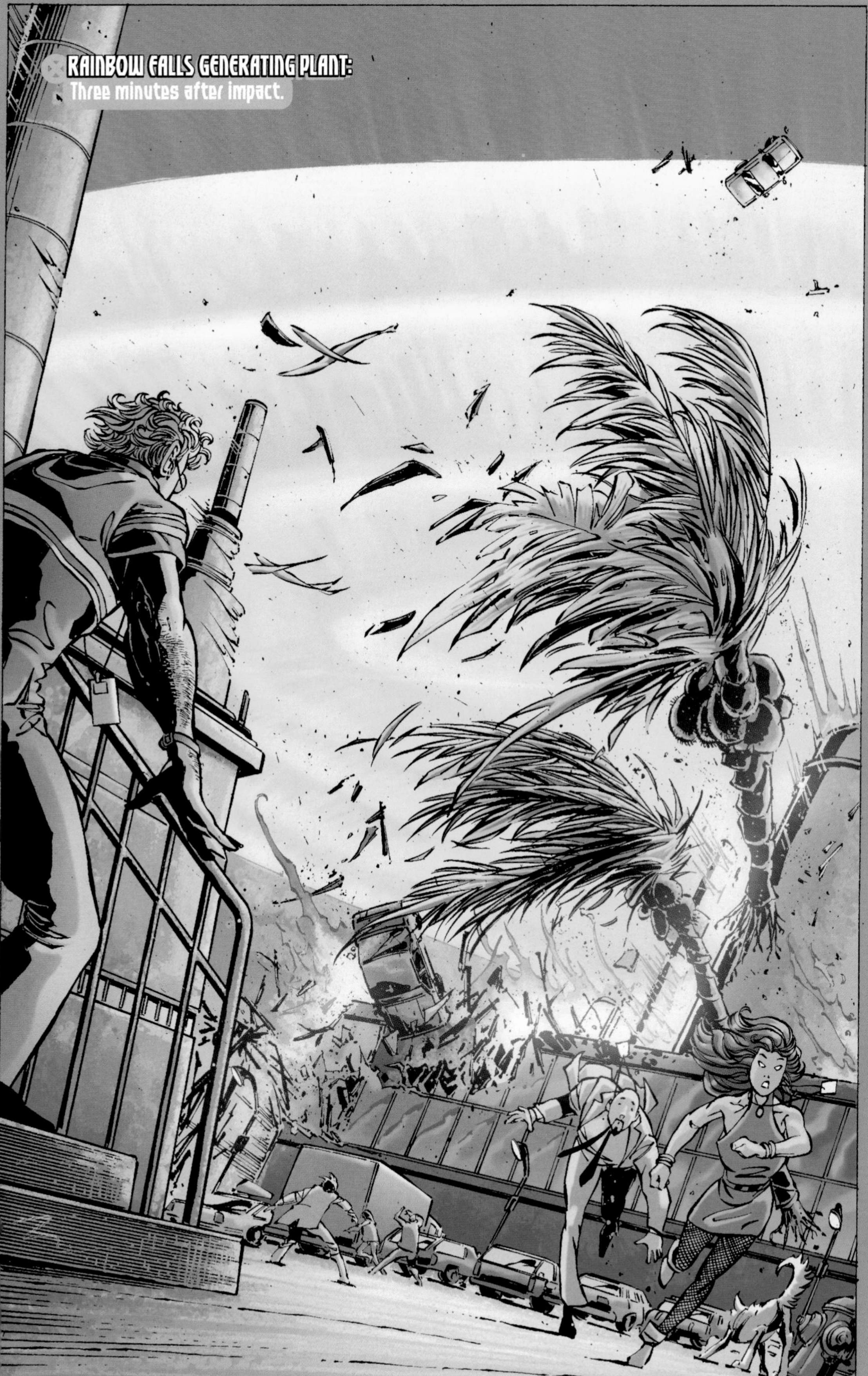
RAINBOW FALLS GENERATING PLANT:
Three minutes after impact.

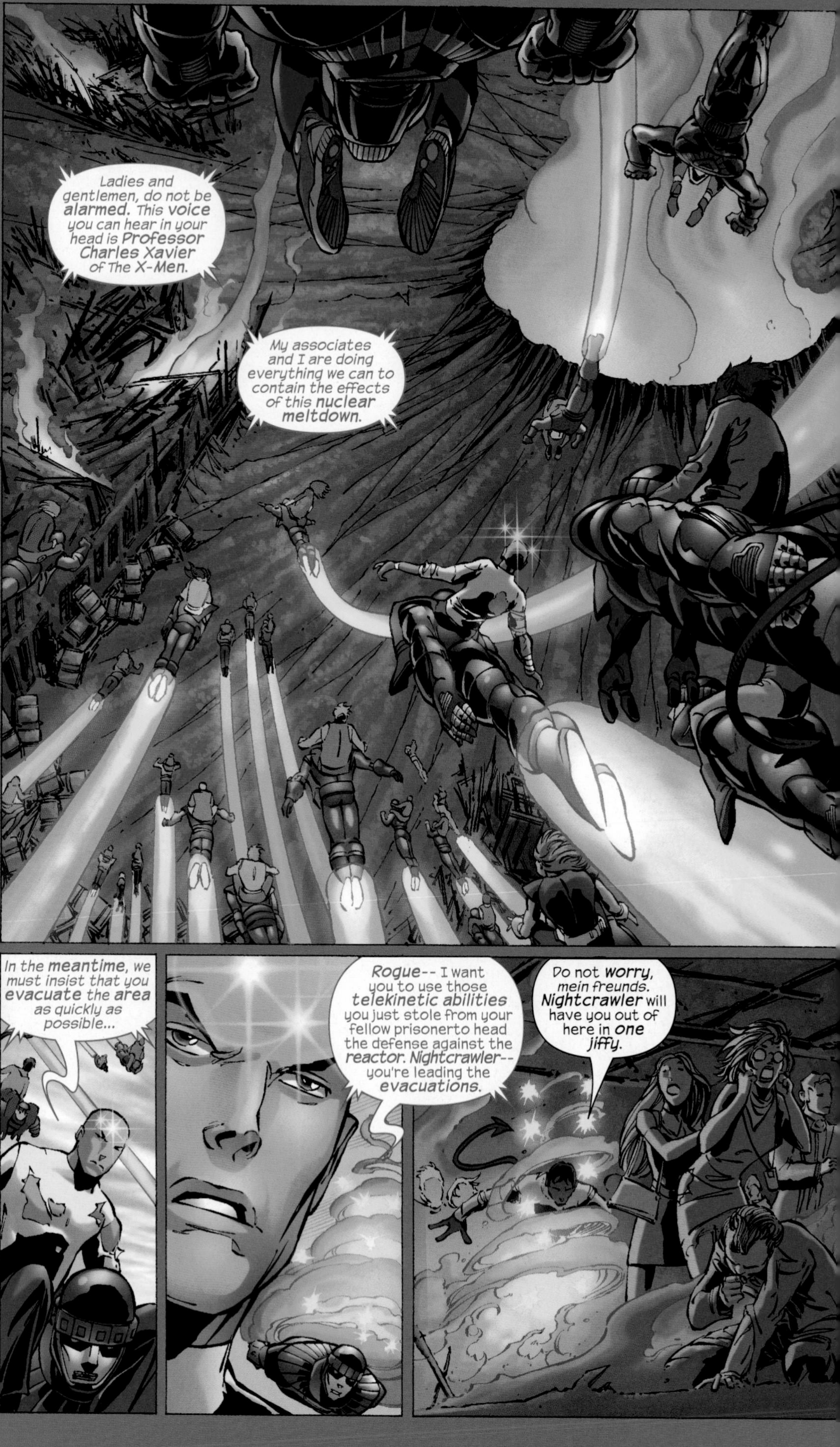
Ladies and gentlemen, do not be alarmed. This voice you can hear in your head is Professor Charles Xavier of The X-Men.
My associates and I are doing everything we can to contain the effects of this nuclear meltdown.
In the meantime, we must insist that you evacuate the area as quickly as possible...
Rogue-- I want you to use those telekinetic abilities you just stole from your fellow prisonerto head the defense against the reactor. Nightcrawler-- you're leading the evacuations.
Do not worry, mein freunds. Nightcrawler will have you out of here in one jiffy.

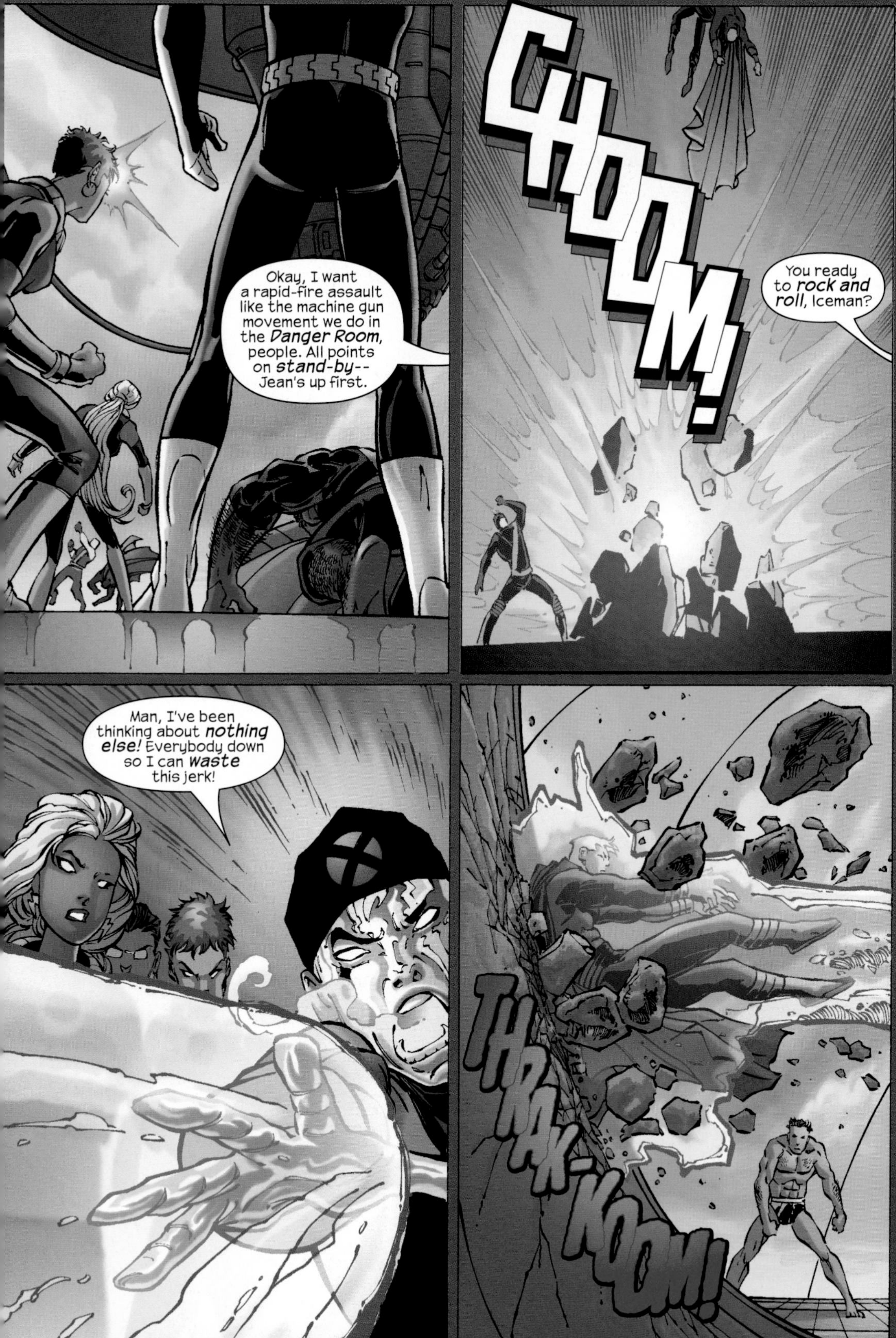
Okay, I want a rapid-fire assault like the machine gun movement we do in the Danger Room, people. All points on stand-by-- Jean's up first.
CHOOM!
You ready to rock and roll, Iceman?
Man, I've been thinking about nothing else! Everybody down so I can waste this jerk!
THRAK-KOOM!

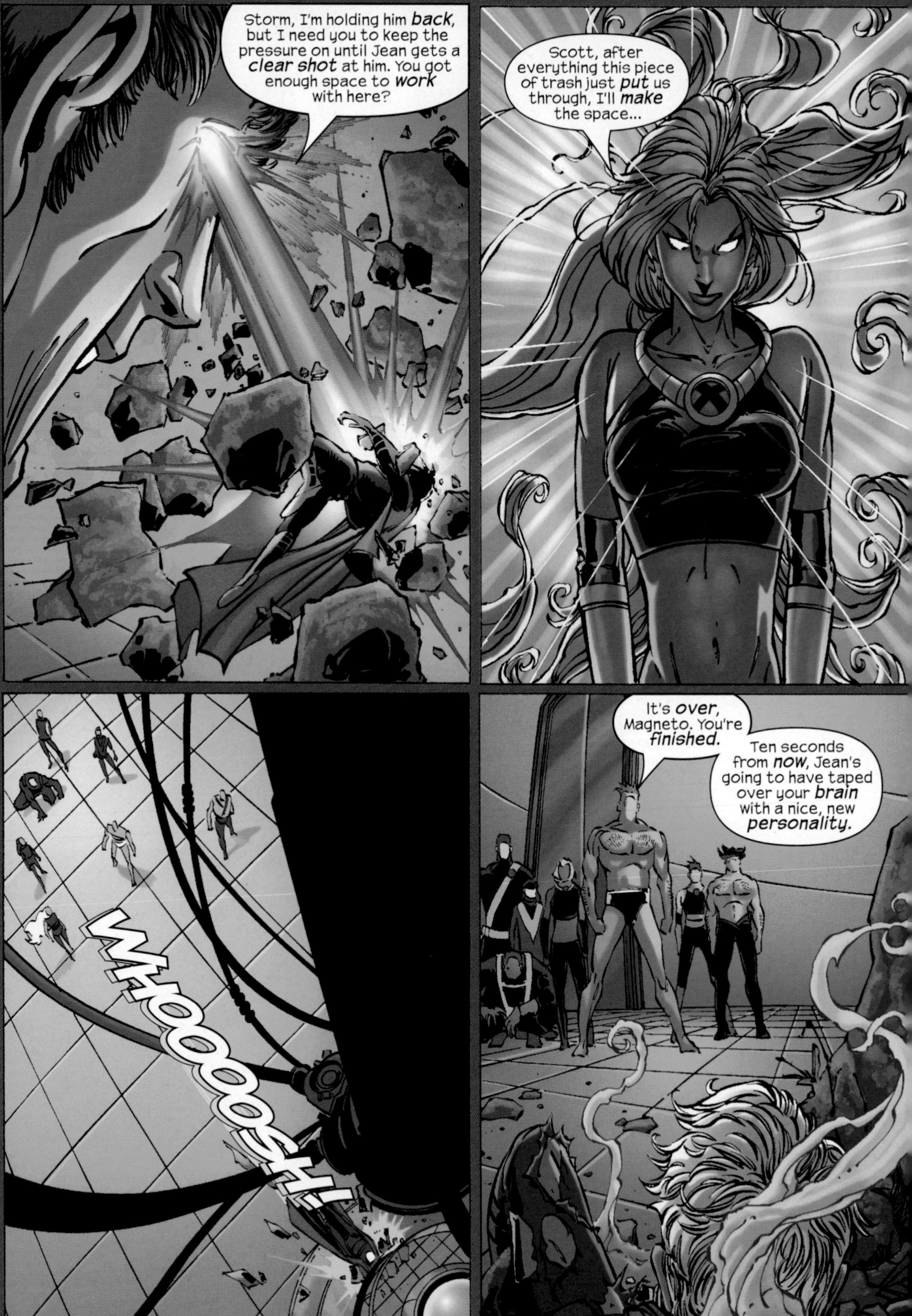
Storm, I'm holding him back, but I need you to keep the pressure on until Jean gets a clear shot at him. You got enough space to work with here?
Scott, after everything this piece of trash just put us through, I'll make the space...
WHOOOOSH!
It's over, Magneto. You're finished.
Ten seconds from now, Jean's going to have taped over your brain with a nice, new personality.

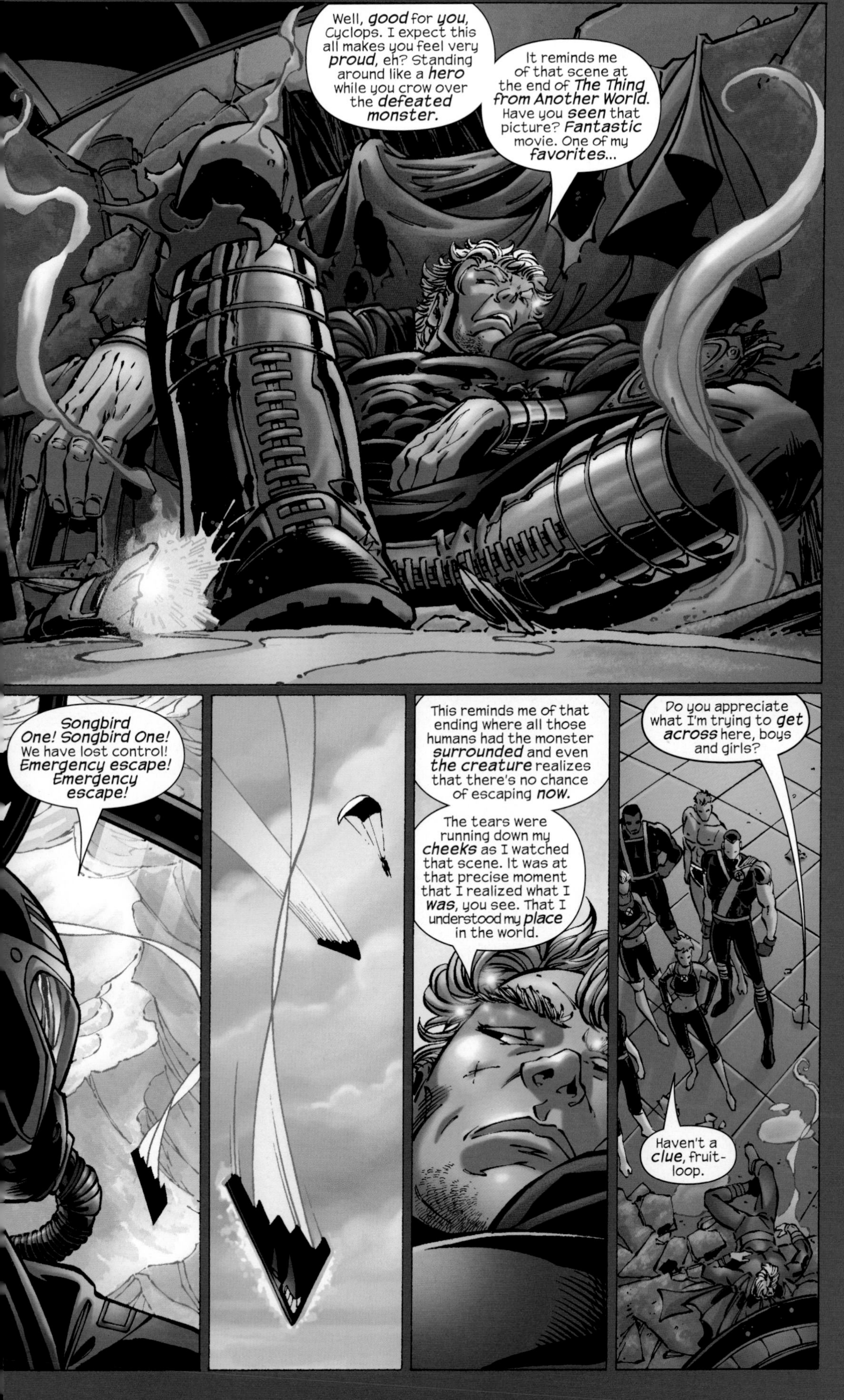
Well, good for you, Cyclops. I expect this all makes you feel very proud, eh? Standing around like a hero while you crow over the defeated monster.
It reminds me of that scene at the end of The Thing from Another World. Have you seen that picture? Fantastic movie. One of my favorites...
Songbird One! Songbird One! We have lost control! Emergency escape! Emergency escape!
This reminds me of that ending where all those humans had the monster surrounded and even the creature realizes that there's no chance of escaping now.
The tears were running down my cheeks as I watched that scene. It was at that precise moment that I realized what I was, you see. That I understood my place in the world.
Do you appreciate what I'm trying to get across here, boys and girls?
Haven't a clue, fruit-loop.

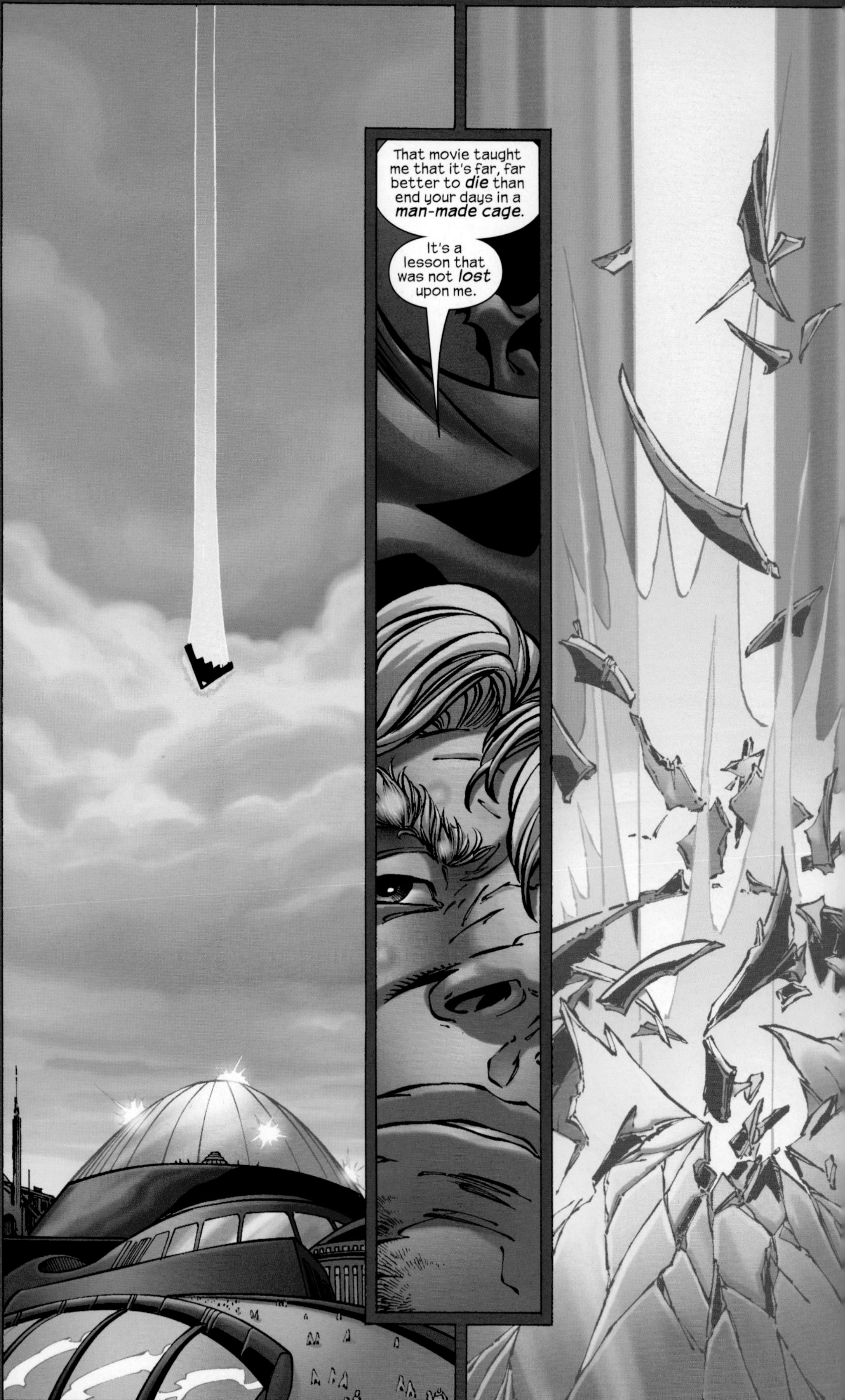

That movie taught me that it's far, far better to *die* than end your days in a *man-made cage*.
It's a lesson that was not *lost* upon me.

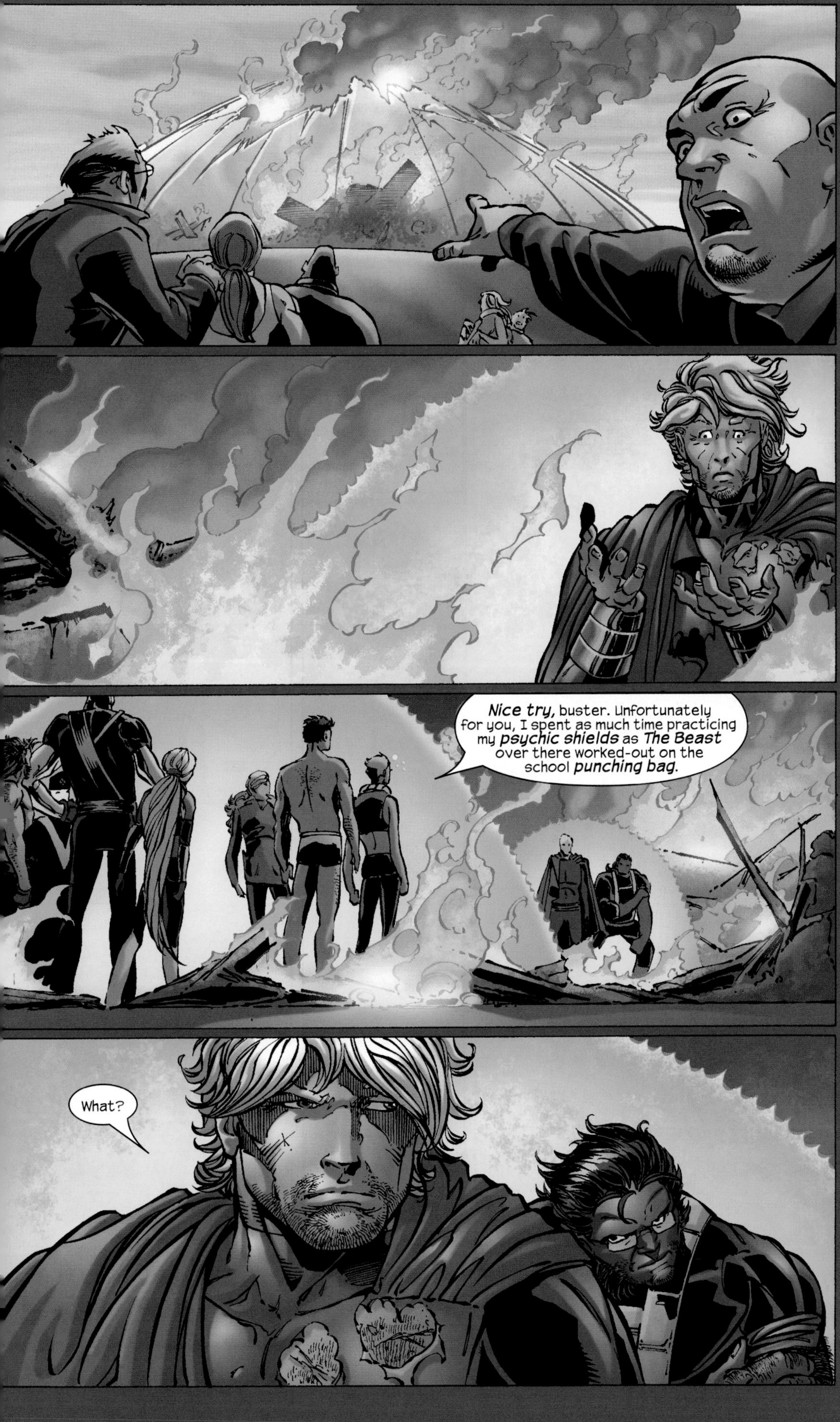

Nice try, buster. Unfortunately for you, I spent as much time practicing my psychic shields as The Beast over there worked-out on the school punching bag.
What?

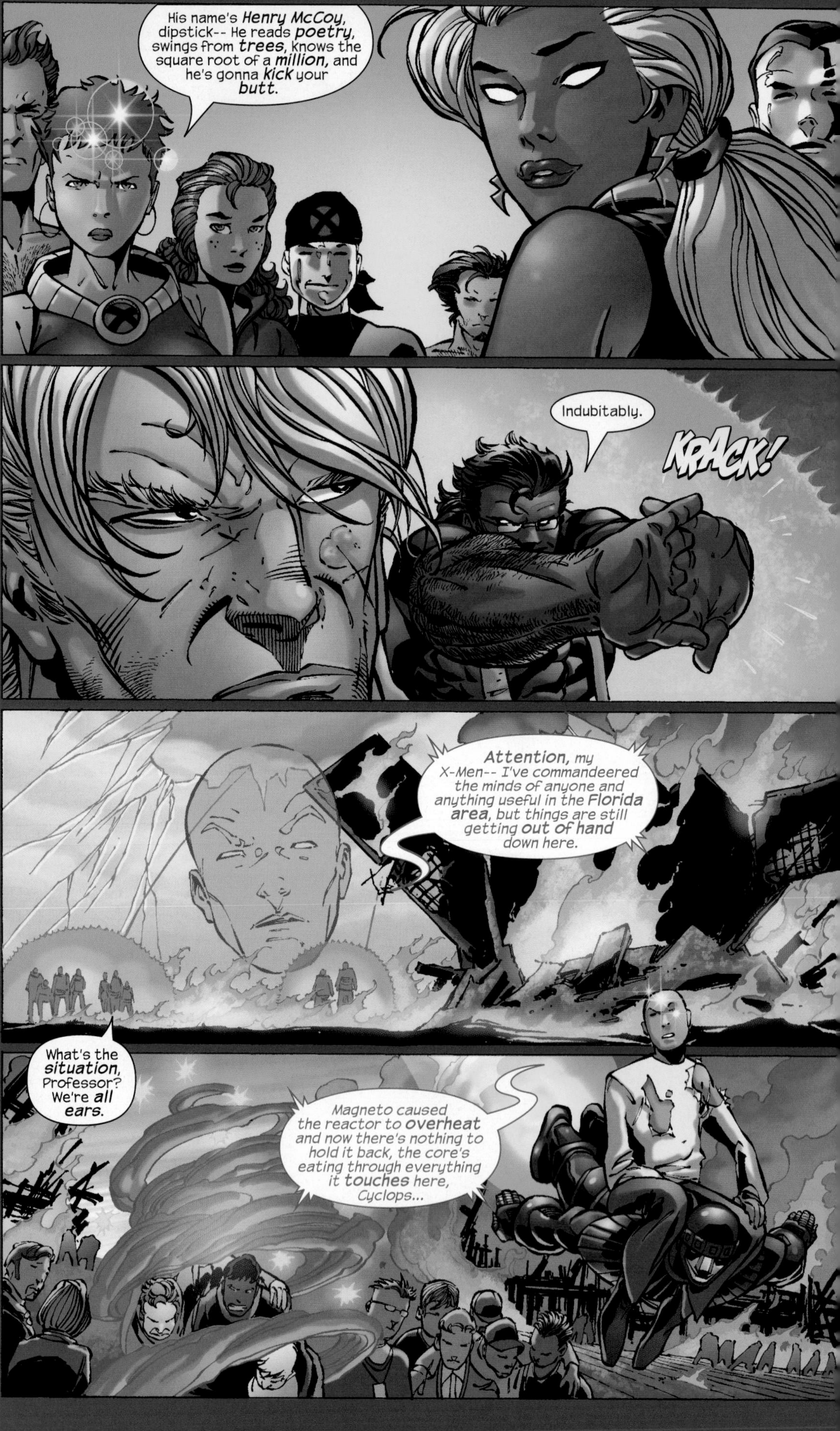
His name's Henry McCoy, dipstick-- He reads poetry, swings from trees, knows the square root of a million, and he's gonna kick your butt.
Indubitably.
KRACK!
Attention, my X-Men-- I've commandeered the minds of anyone and anything useful in the Florida area, but things are still getting out of hand down here.
What's the situation, Professor? We're all ears.
Magneto caused the reactor to overheat and now there's nothing to hold it back, the core's eating through everything it touches here, Cyclops...

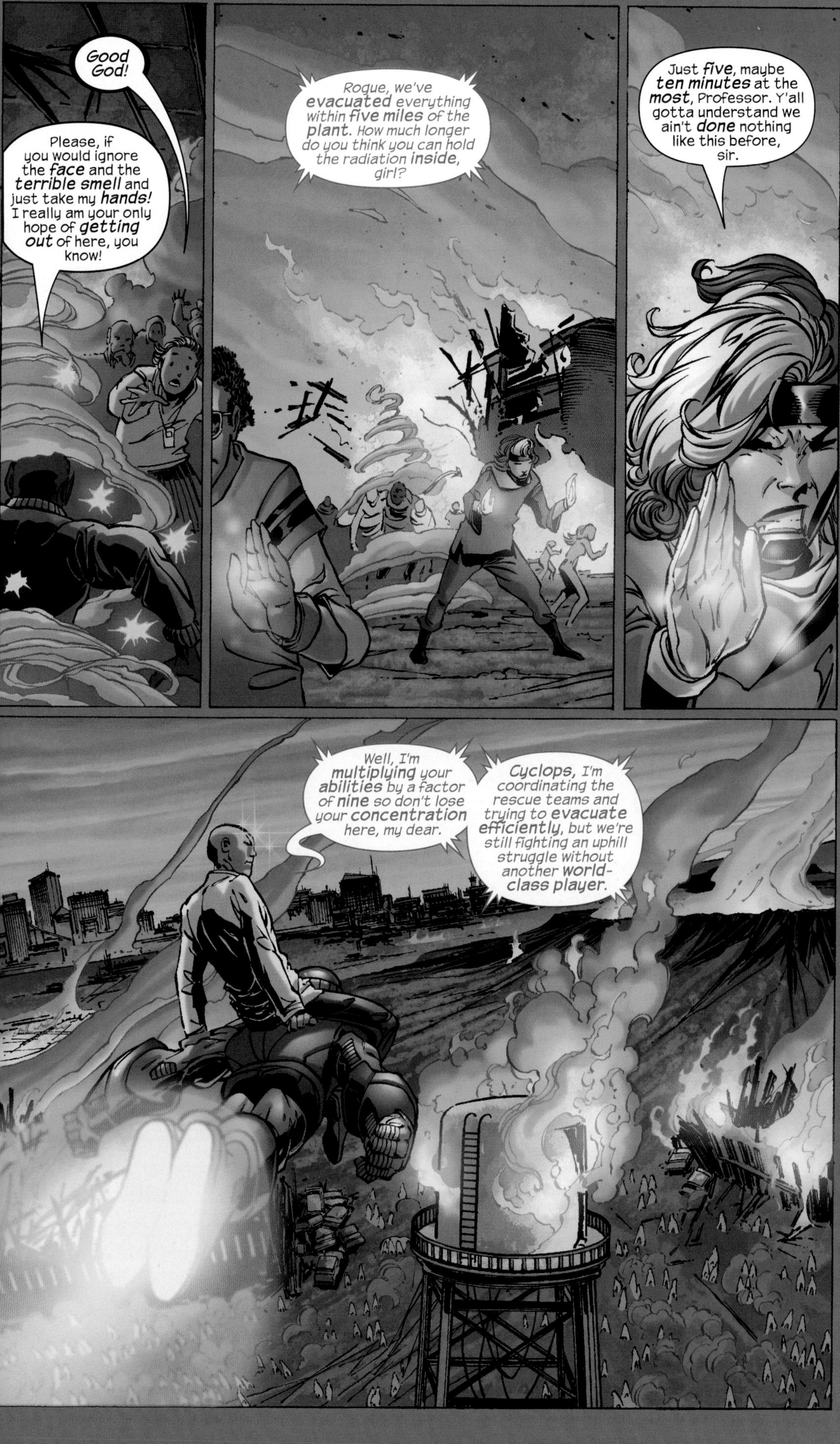
Good God!
Please, if you would ignore the face and the terrible smell and just take my hands! I really am your only hope of getting out of here, you know!
Rogue, we've evacuated everything within five miles of the plant. How much longer do you think you can hold the radiation inside, girl?
Just five, maybe ten minutes at the most, Professor. Y'all gotta understand we ain't done nothing like this before, sir.
Well, I'm multiplying your abilities by a factor of nine so don't lose your concentration here, my dear.
Cyclops, I'm coordinating the rescue teams and trying to evacuate efficiently, but we're still fighting an uphill struggle without another world-class player.

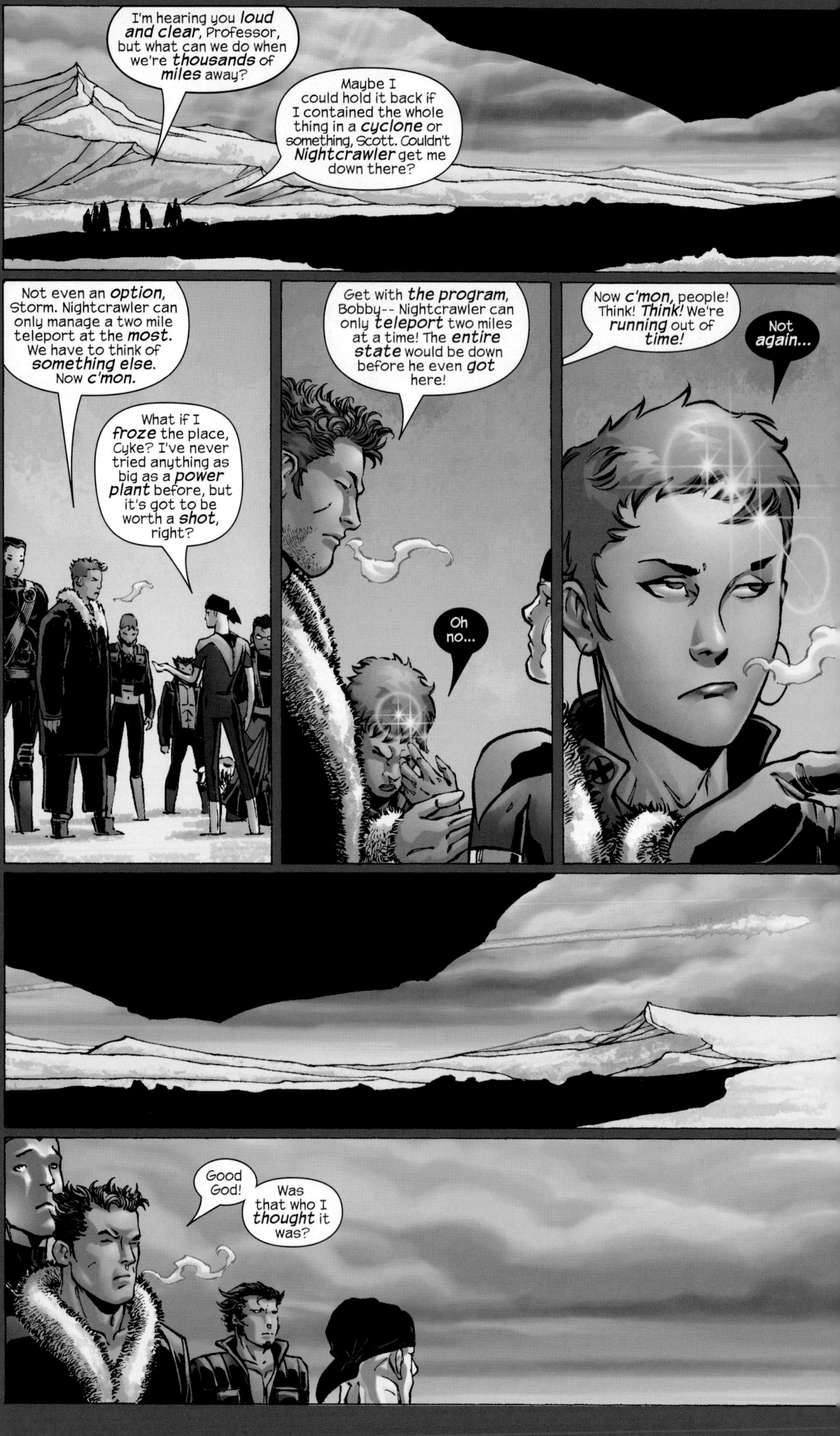
I'm hearing you loud and clear, Professor, but what can we do when we're thousands of miles away?
Maybe I could hold it back if I contained the whole thing in a cyclone or something, Scott. Couldn't Nightcrawler get me down there?
Not even an option, Storm. Nightcrawler can only manage a two mile teleport at the most. We have to think of something else. Now c'mon.
What if I froze the place, Cyke? I've never tried anything as big as a power plant before, but it's got to be worth a shot, right?
Get with the program, Bobby-- Nightcrawler can only teleport two miles at a time! The entire state would be down before he even got here!
Oh no...
Now c'mon, people! Think! Think! We're running out of time!
Not again...
Good God!
Was that who I thought it was?

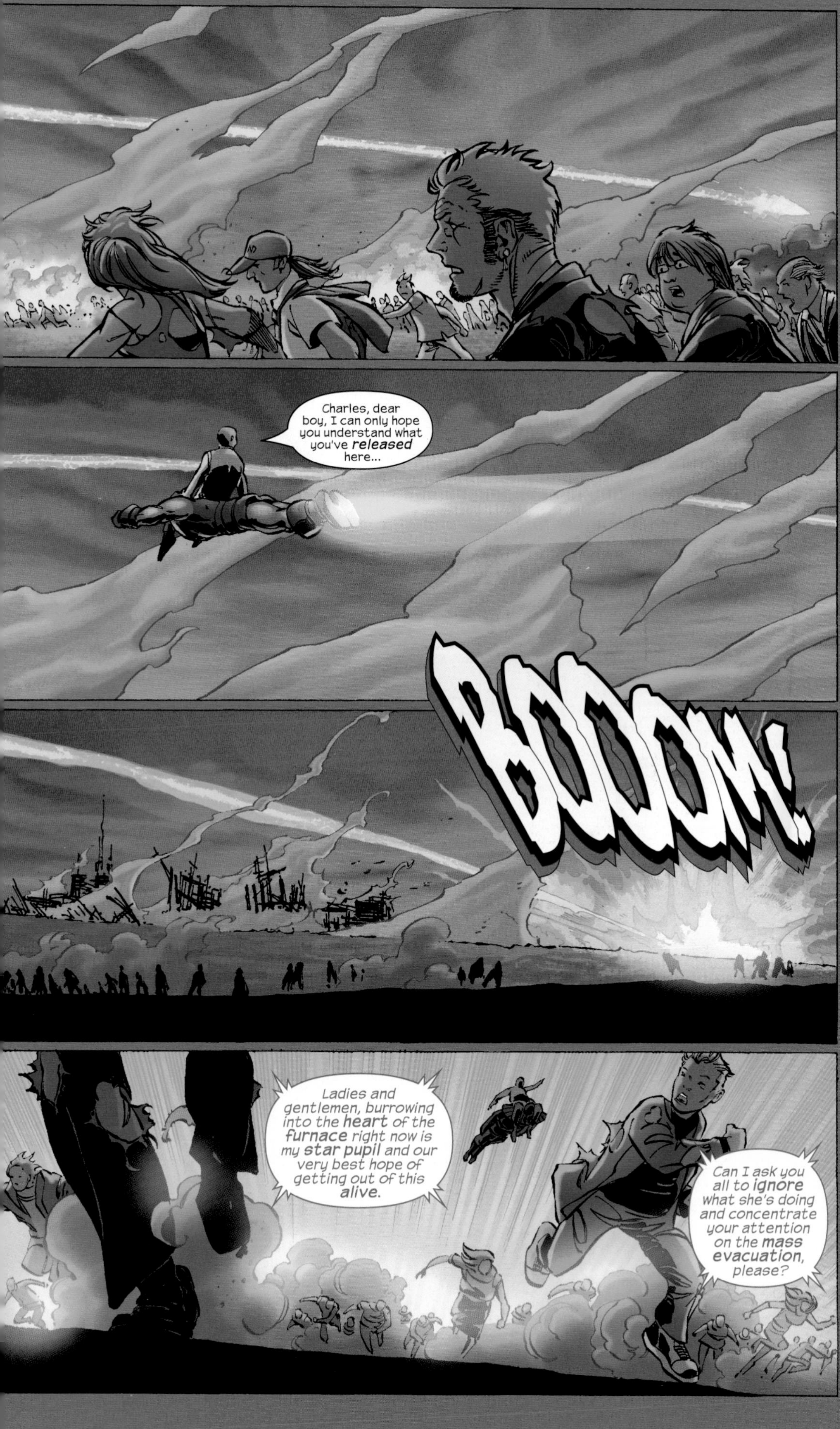

Charles, dear boy, I can only hope you understand what you've *released* here...
BOOOM!
Ladies and gentlemen, burrowing into the **heart** of the **furnace** right now is my **star pupil** and our very best hope of getting out of this **alive**.
Can I ask you all to **ignore** what she's doing and concentrate your attention on the **mass evacuation**, please?

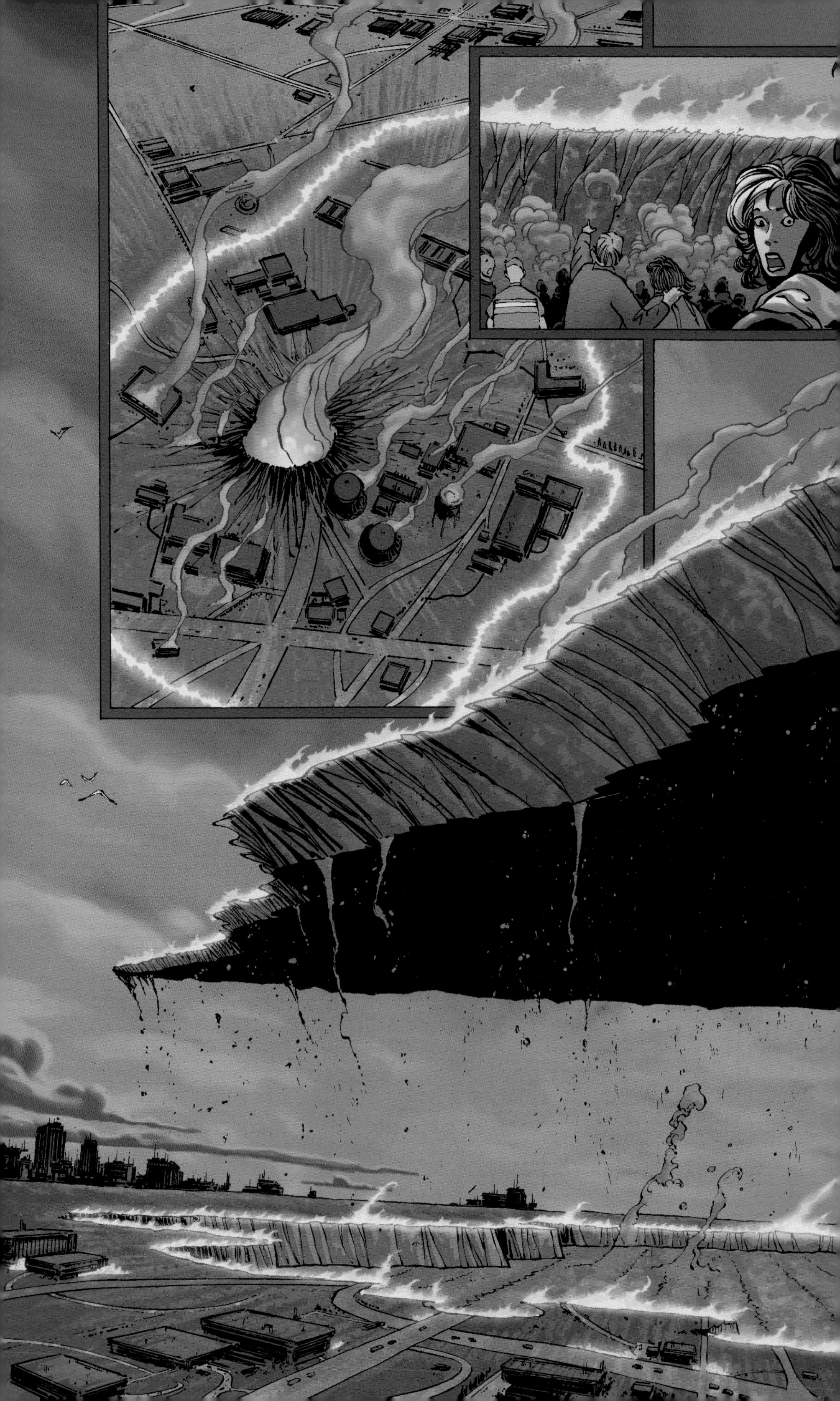

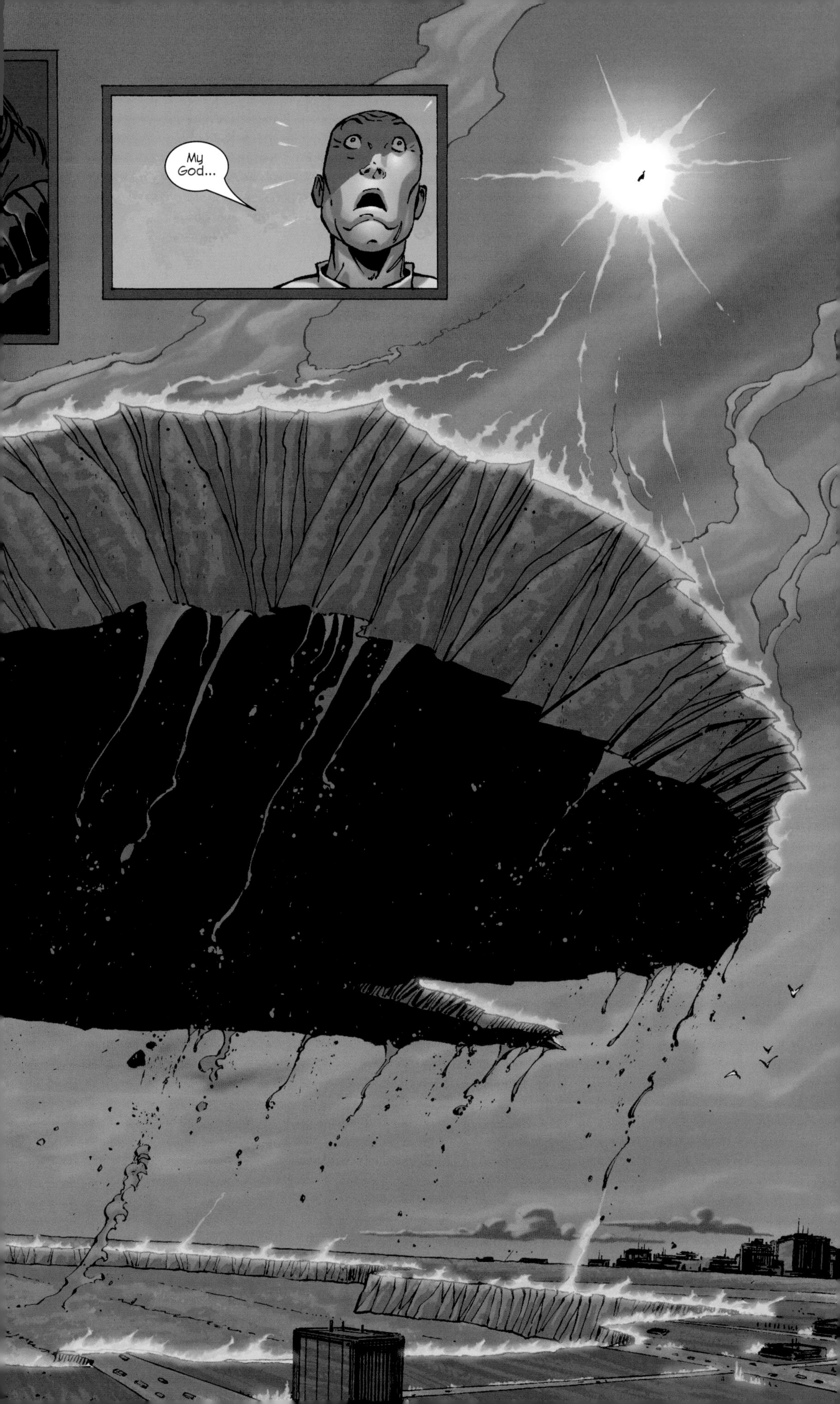
My God...

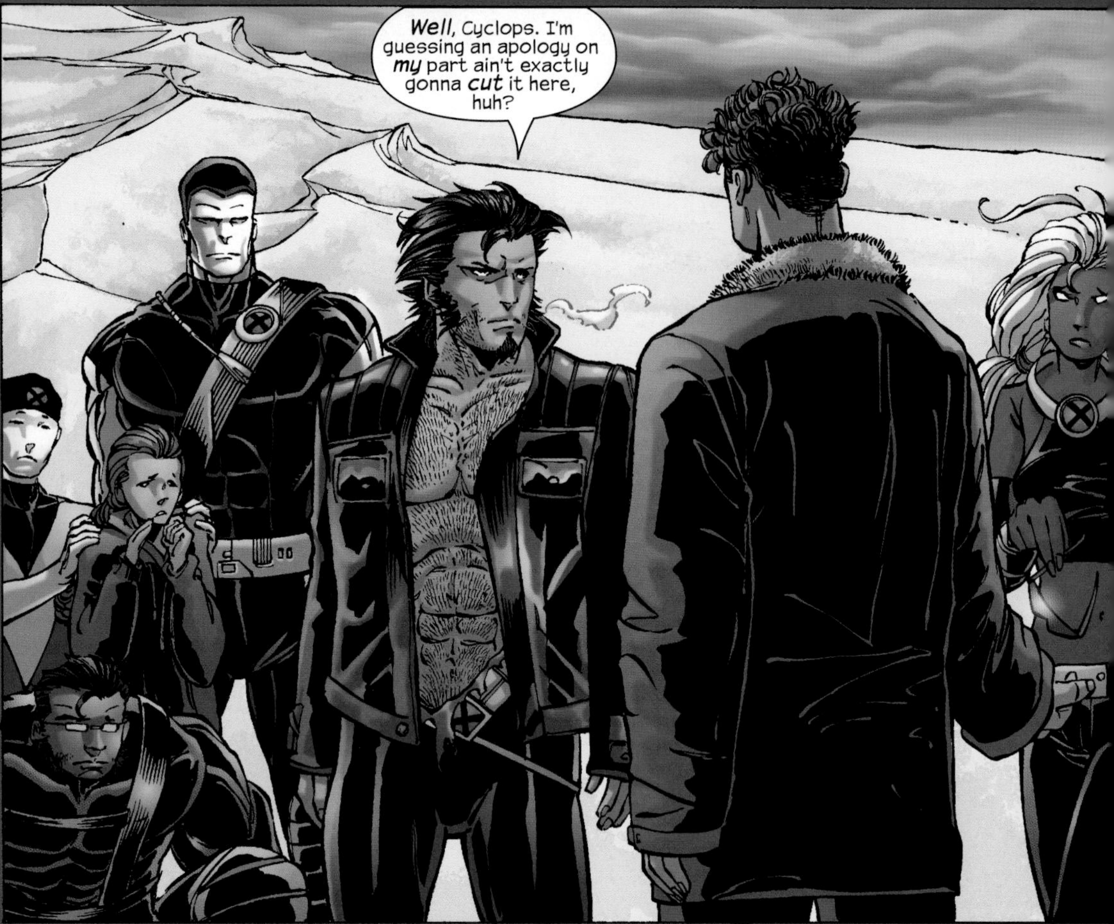
Well, Cyclops. I'm guessing an apology on *my* part ain't exactly gonna *cut* it here, huh?

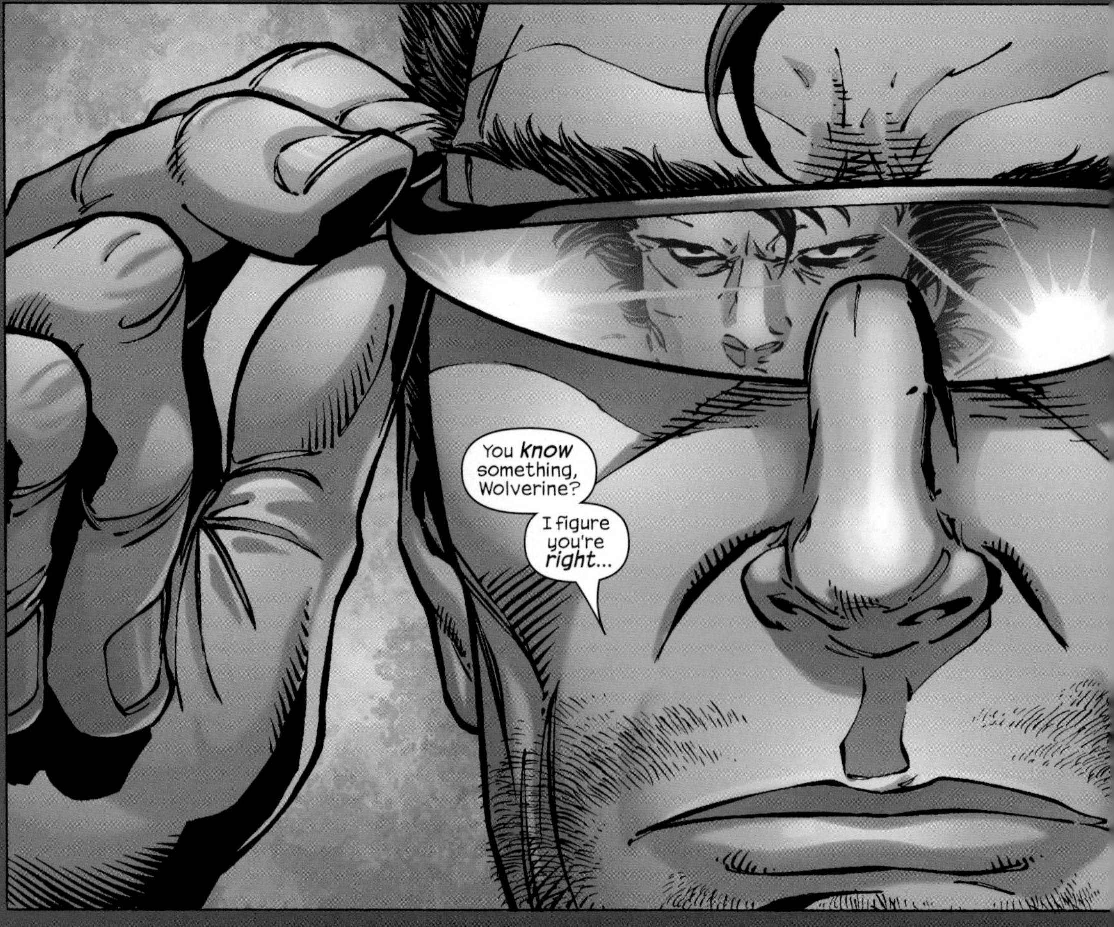
You *know* something, Wolverine?
I figure you're *right*...

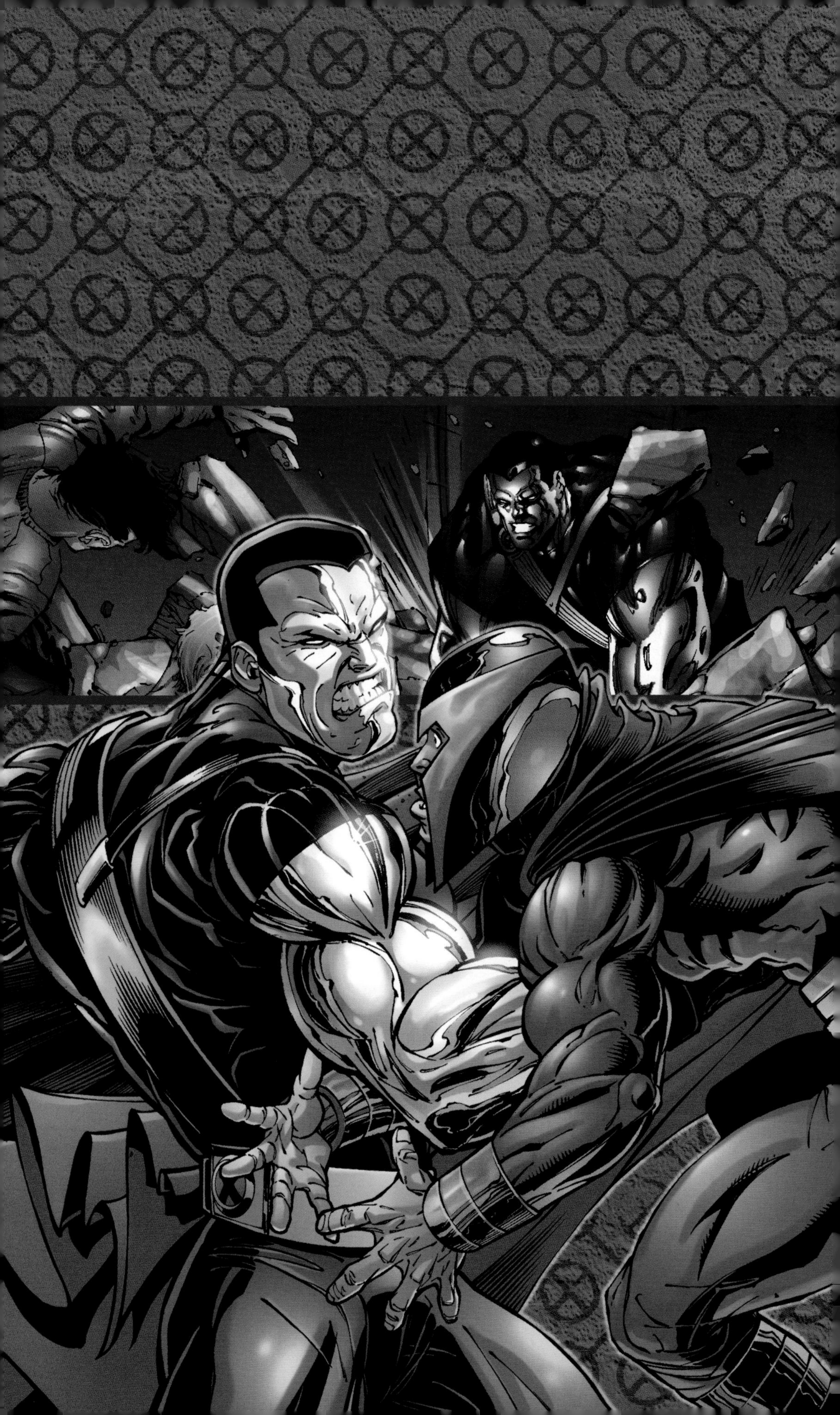

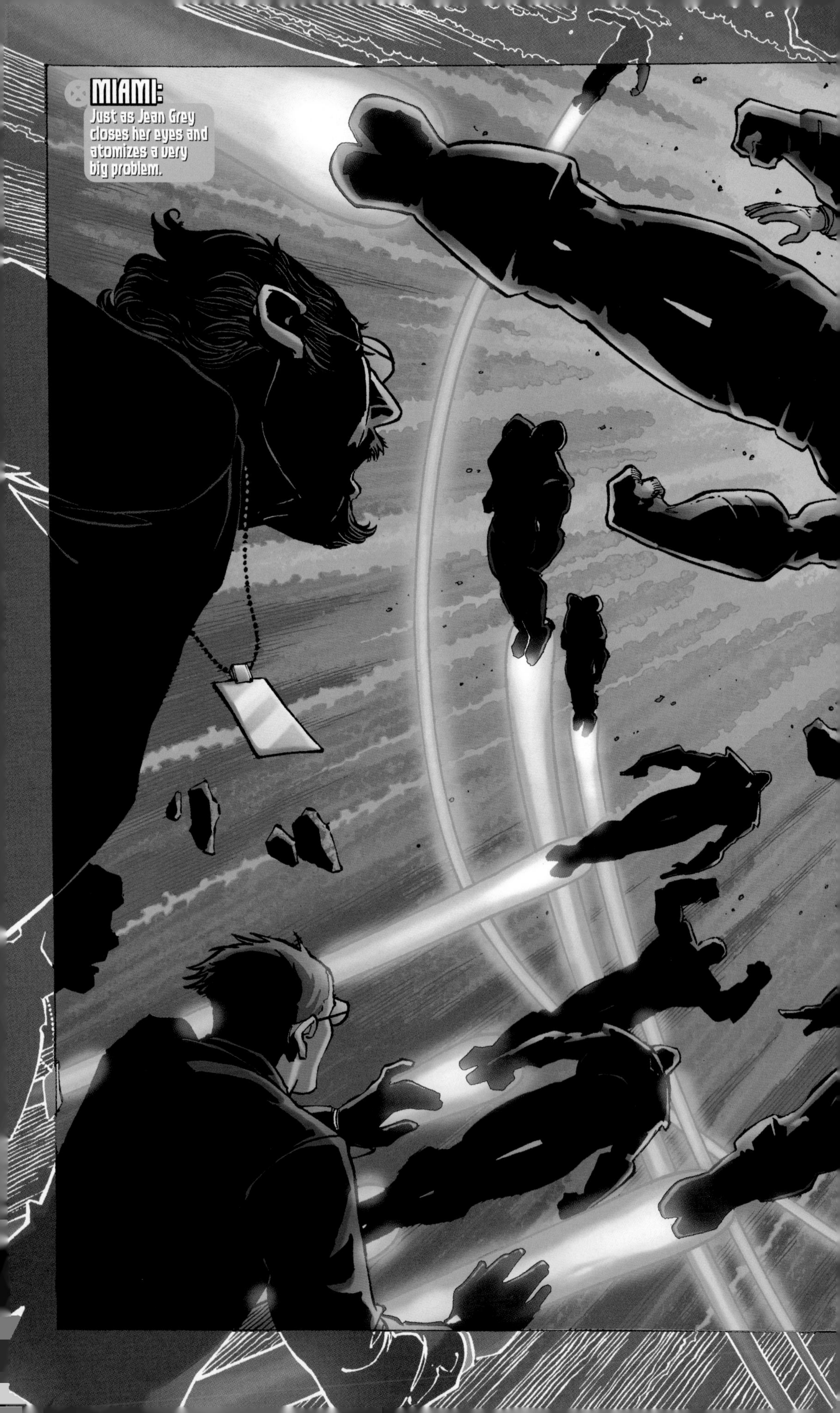
MIAMI:
Just as Jean Grey closes her eyes and atomizes a very big problem.

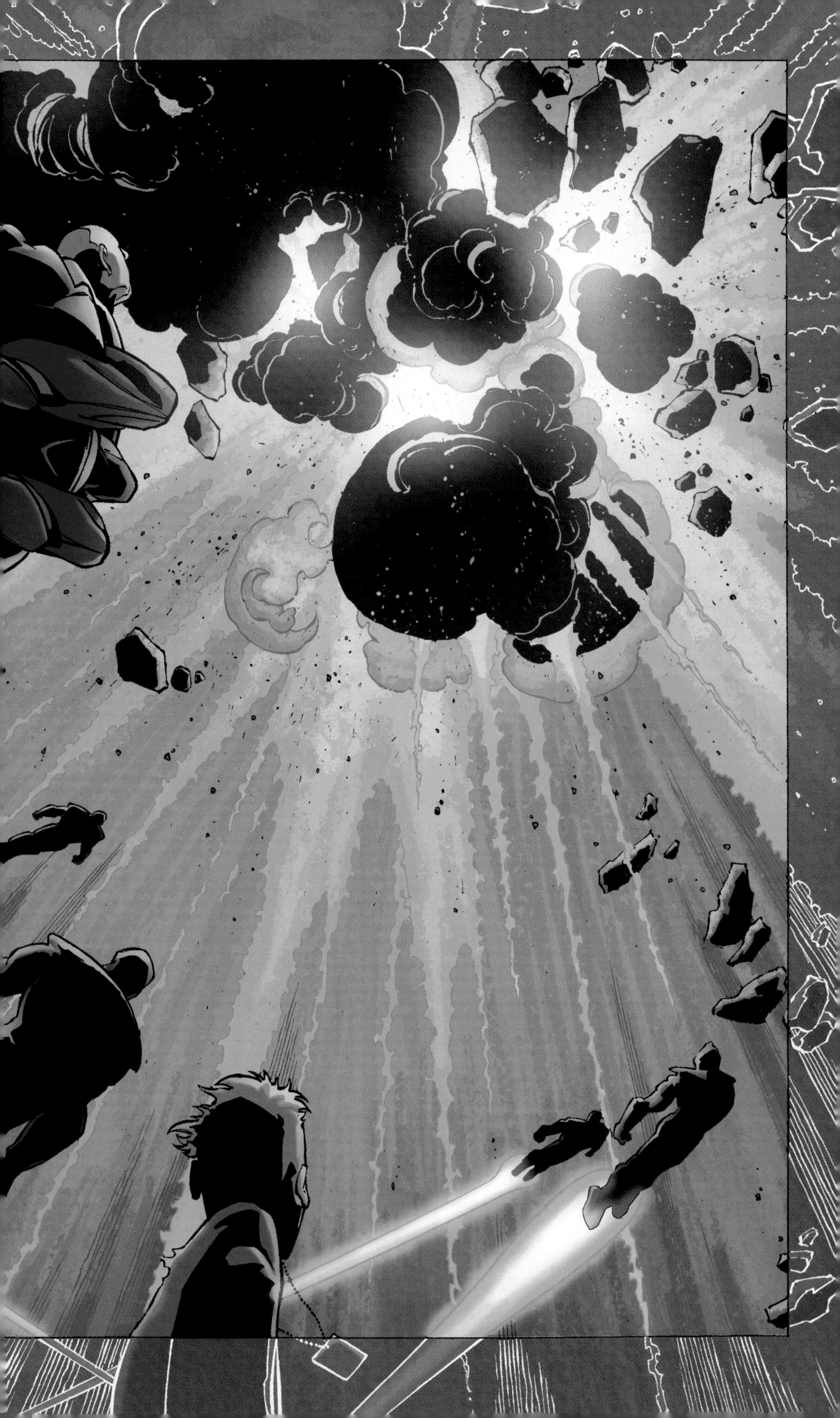

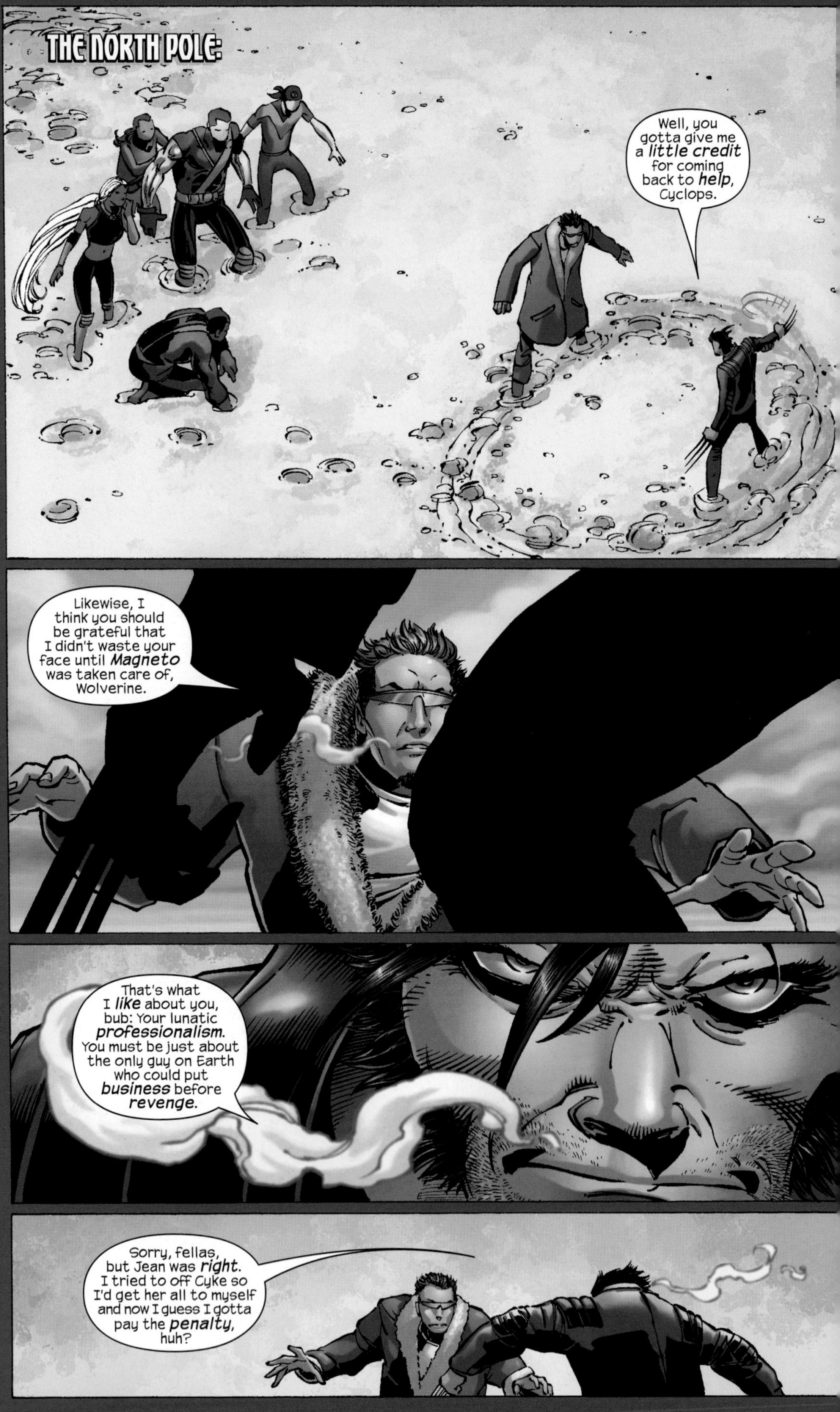
THE NORTH POLE:
Well, you gotta give me a *little credit* for coming back to *help*, Cyclops.
Likewise, I think you should be grateful that I didn't waste your face until *Magneto* was taken care of, Wolverine.
That's what I *like* about you, bub: Your lunatic *professionalism*. You must be just about the only guy on Earth who could put *business* before *revenge*.
Sorry, fellas, but Jean was *right*. I tried to off Cyke so I'd get her all to myself and now I guess I gotta pay the *penalty*, huh?

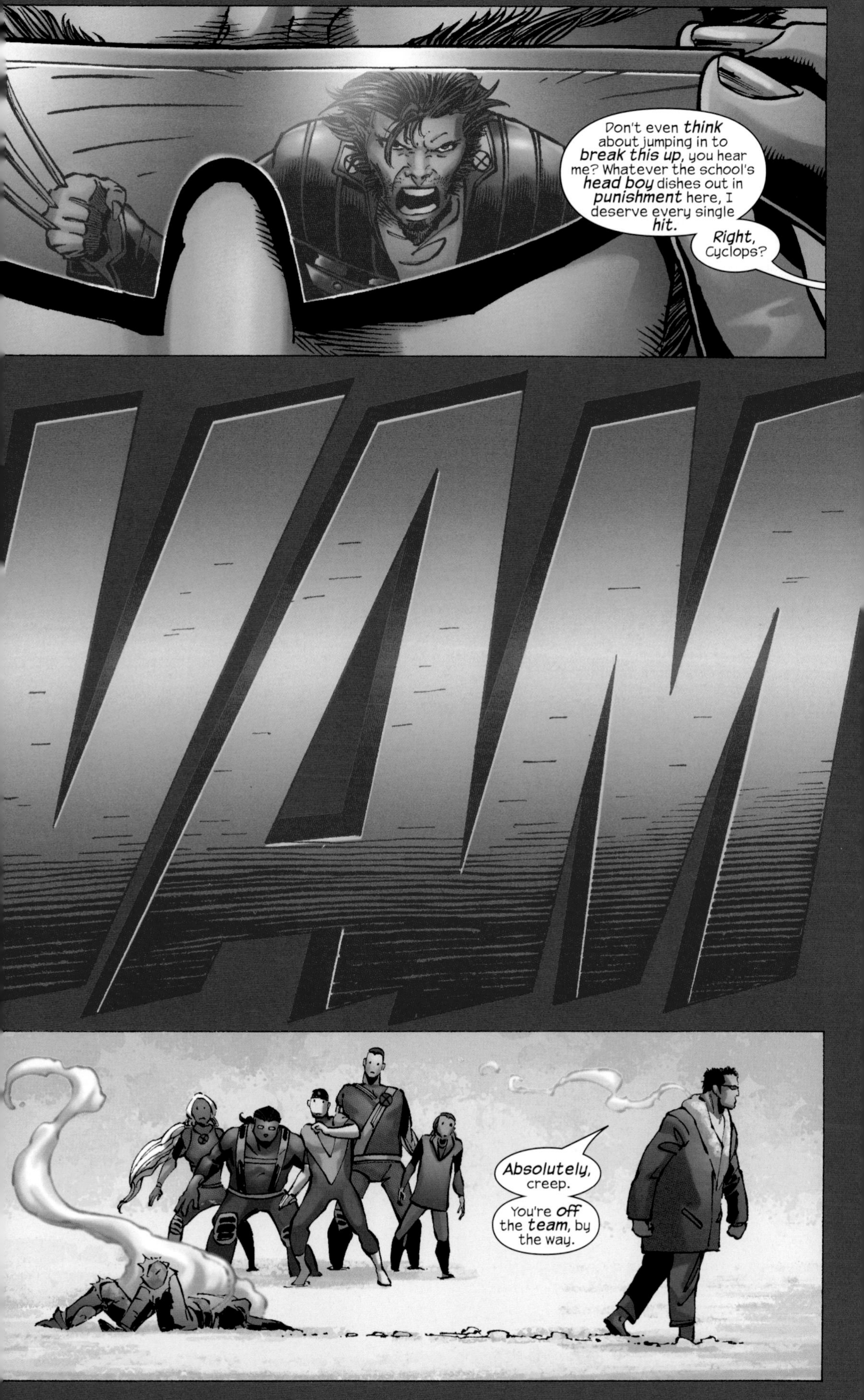
Don't even **think** about jumping in to **break this up**, you hear me? Whatever the school's **head boy** dishes out in **punishment** here, I deserve every single **hit.**
Right, Cyclops?
Absolutely, creep.
You're **off** the **team**, by the way.

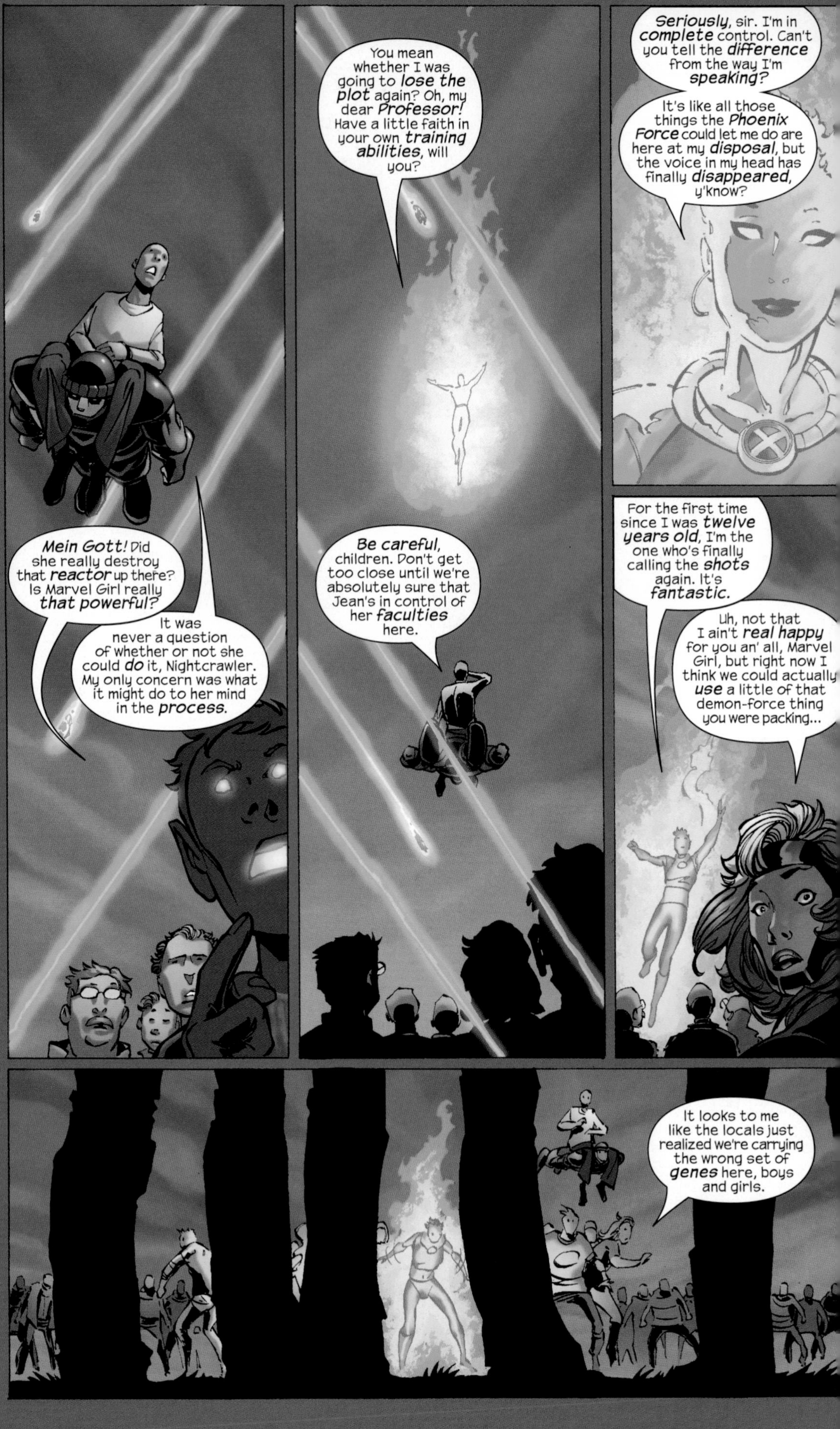
Mein Gott! Did she really destroy that reactor up there? Is Marvel Girl really that powerful?
It was never a question of whether or not she could do it, Nightcrawler. My only concern was what it might do to her mind in the process.
You mean whether I was going to lose the plot again? Oh, my dear Professor! Have a little faith in your own training abilities, will you?
Be careful, children. Don't get too close until we're absolutely sure that Jean's in control of her faculties here.
Seriously, sir. I'm in complete control. Can't you tell the difference from the way I'm speaking?
It's like all those things the Phoenix Force could let me do are here at my disposal, but the voice in my head has finally disappeared, y'know?
For the first time since I was twelve years old, I'm the one who's finally calling the shots again. It's fantastic.
Uh, not that I ain't real happy for you an' all, Marvel Girl, but right now I think we could actually use a little of that demon-force thing you were packing...
It looks to me like the locals just realized we're carrying the wrong set of genes here, boys and girls.

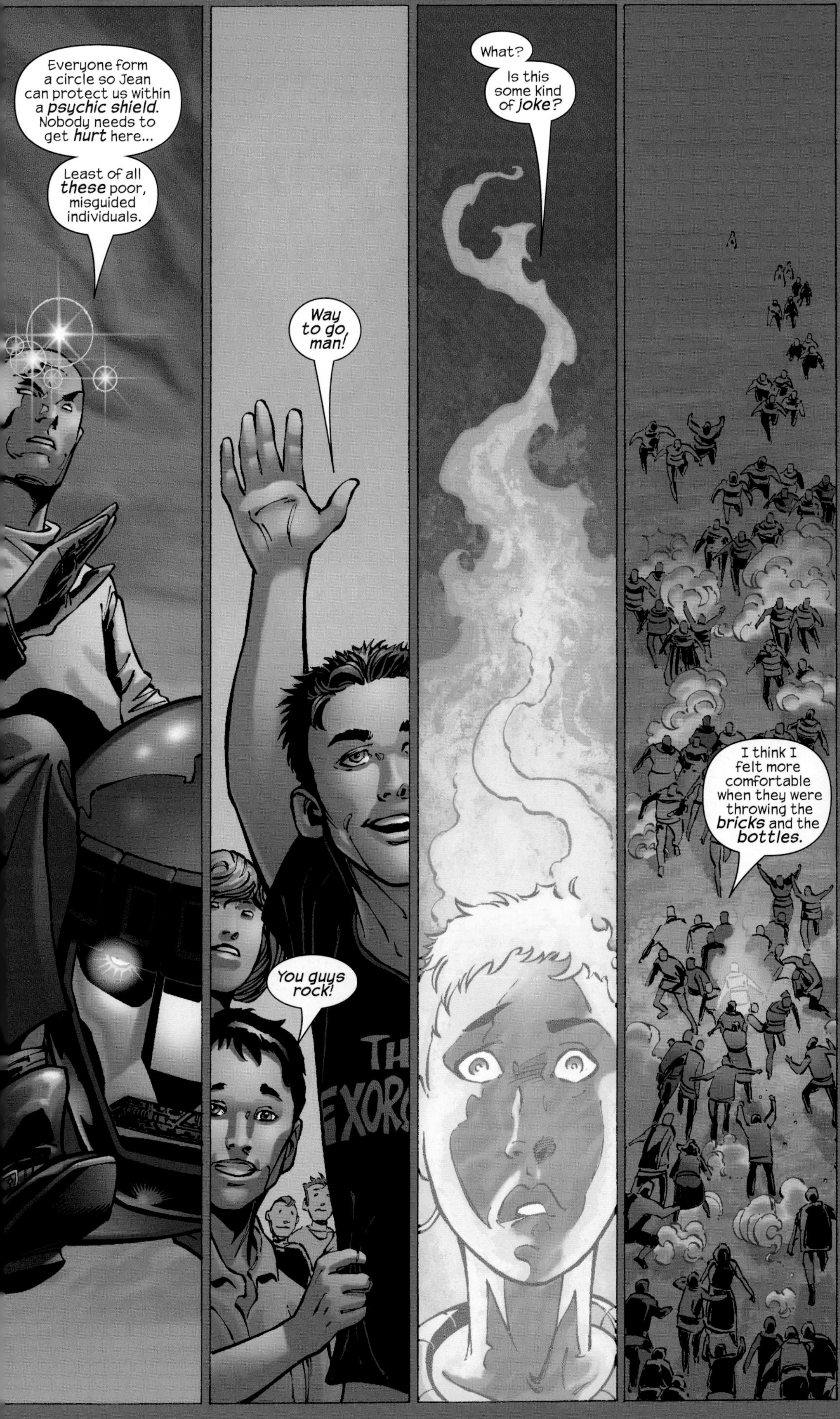

Everyone form a circle so Jean can protect us within a *psychic shield*. Nobody needs to get *hurt* here...
Least of all *these* poor, misguided individuals.
Way to go, man!
You guys rock!
What?
Is this some kind of *joke?*
I think I felt more comfortable when they were throwing the *bricks* and the *bottles*.

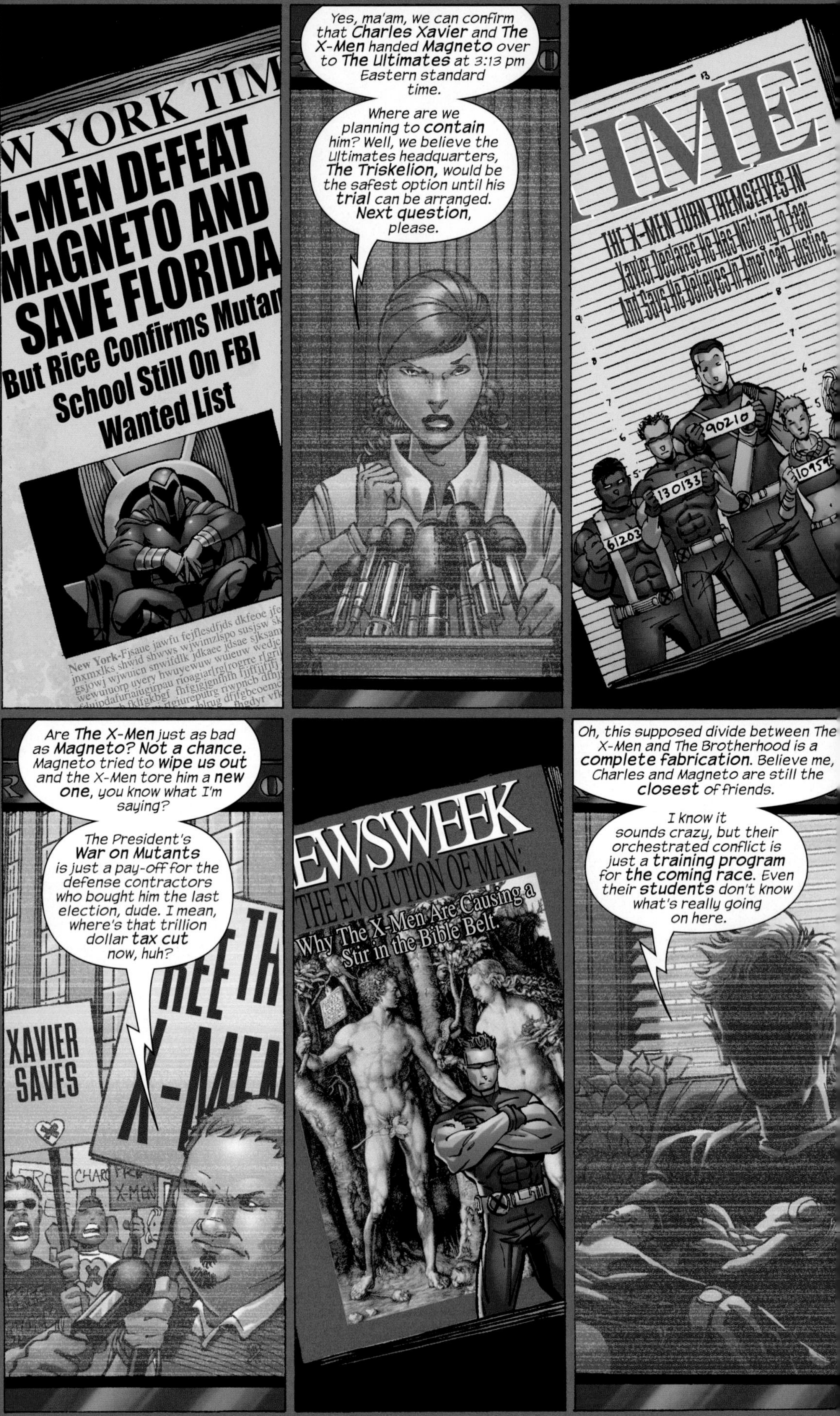
NEW YORK TIM
X-MEN DEFEAT MAGNETO AND SAVE FLORIDA
But Rice Confirms Mutan School Still On FBI Wanted List
Yes, ma'am, we can confirm that Charles Xavier and The X-Men handed Magneto over to The Ultimates at 3:13 pm Eastern standard time.
Where are we planning to contain him? Well, we believe the Ultimates headquarters, The Triskelion, would be the safest option until his trial can be arranged. Next question, please.
TIME
THE X-MEN TURN THEMSELVES IN
Xavier Declares He Has Nothing To Fear And Says He Believes In American Justice.
Are The X-Men just as bad as Magneto? Not a chance. Magneto tried to wipe us out and the X-Men tore him a new one, you know what I'm saying?
The President's War on Mutants is just a pay-off for the defense contractors who bought him the last election, dude. I mean, where's that trillion dollar tax cut now, huh?
XAVIER SAVES
X-MEN
EWSWEEK
THE EVOLUTION OF MAN:
Why The X-Men Are Causing a Stir in the Bible Belt.
Oh, this supposed divide between The X-Men and The Brotherhood is a complete fabrication. Believe me, Charles and Magneto are still the closest of friends.
I know it sounds crazy, but their orchestrated conflict is just a training program for the coming race. Even their students don't know what's really going on here.

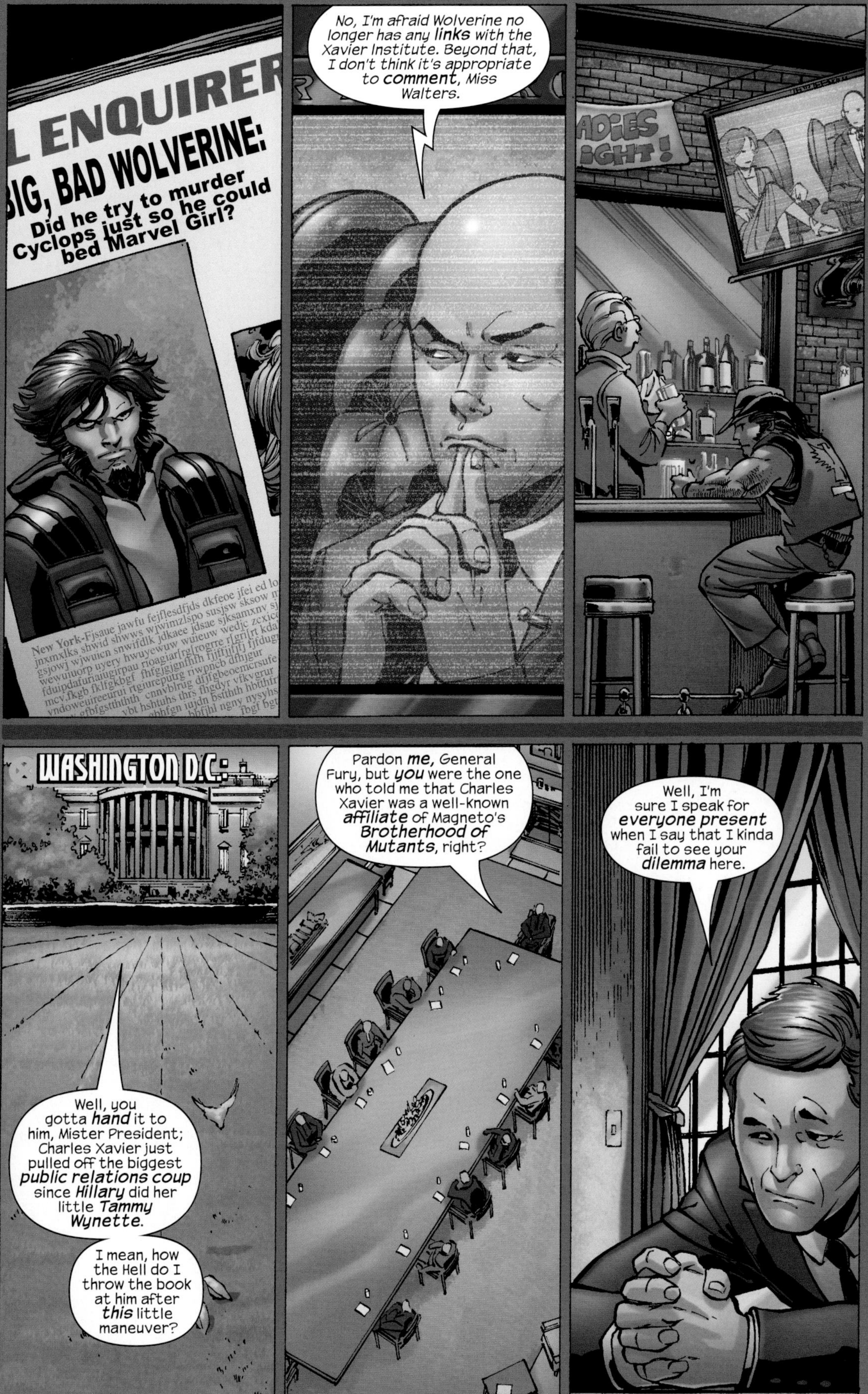

ENQUIRER
BIG, BAD WOLVERINE:
Did he try to murder Cyclops just so he could bed Marvel Girl?
No, I'm afraid Wolverine no longer has any links with the Xavier Institute. Beyond that, I don't think it's appropriate to comment, Miss Walters.
LADIES NIGHT!
WASHINGTON D.C.:
Well, you gotta hand it to him, Mister President; Charles Xavier just pulled off the biggest public relations coup since Hillary did her little Tammy Wynette.
I mean, how the Hell do I throw the book at him after this little maneuver?
Pardon me, General Fury, but you were the one who told me that Charles Xavier was a well-known affiliate of Magneto's Brotherhood of Mutants, right?
Well, I'm sure I speak for everyone present when I say that I kinda fail to see your dilemma here.

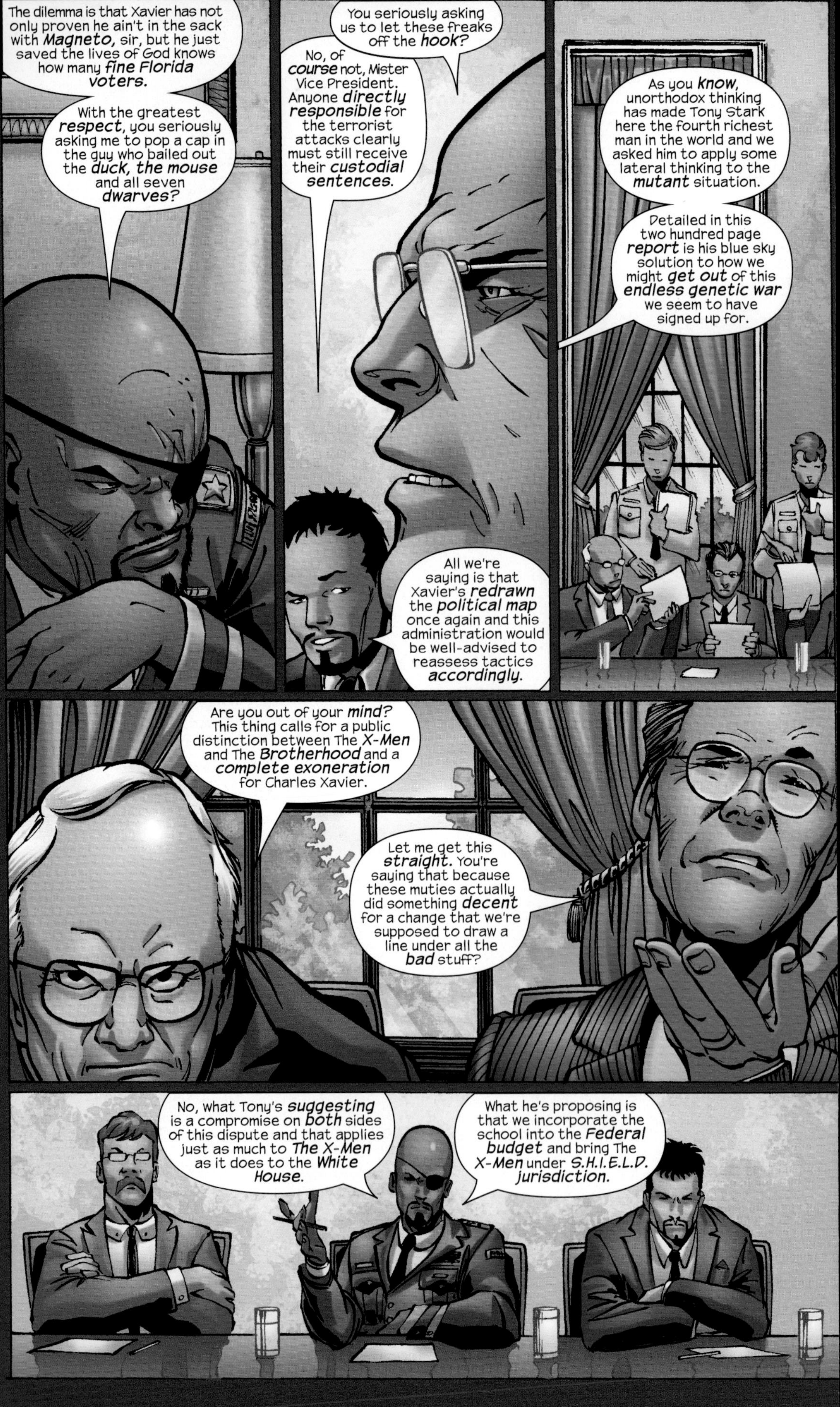

The dilemma is that Xavier has not only proven he ain't in the sack with Magneto, sir, but he just saved the lives of God knows how many fine Florida voters.
With the greatest respect, you seriously asking me to pop a cap in the guy who bailed out the duck, the mouse and all seven dwarves?
You seriously asking us to let these freaks off the hook?
No, of course not, Mister Vice President. Anyone directly responsible for the terrorist attacks clearly must still receive their custodial sentences.
All we're saying is that Xavier's redrawn the political map once again and this administration would be well-advised to reassess tactics accordingly.
As you know, unorthodox thinking has made Tony Stark here the fourth richest man in the world and we asked him to apply some lateral thinking to the mutant situation.
Detailed in this two hundred page report is his blue sky solution to how we might get out of this endless genetic war we seem to have signed up for.
Are you out of your mind? This thing calls for a public distinction between The X-Men and The Brotherhood and a complete exoneration for Charles Xavier.
Let me get this straight. You're saying that because these muties actually did something decent for a change that we're supposed to draw a line under all the bad stuff?
No, what Tony's suggesting is a compromise on both sides of this dispute and that applies just as much to The X-Men as it does to the White House.
What he's proposing is that we incorporate the school into the Federal budget and bring The X-Men under S.H.I.E.L.D. jurisdiction.

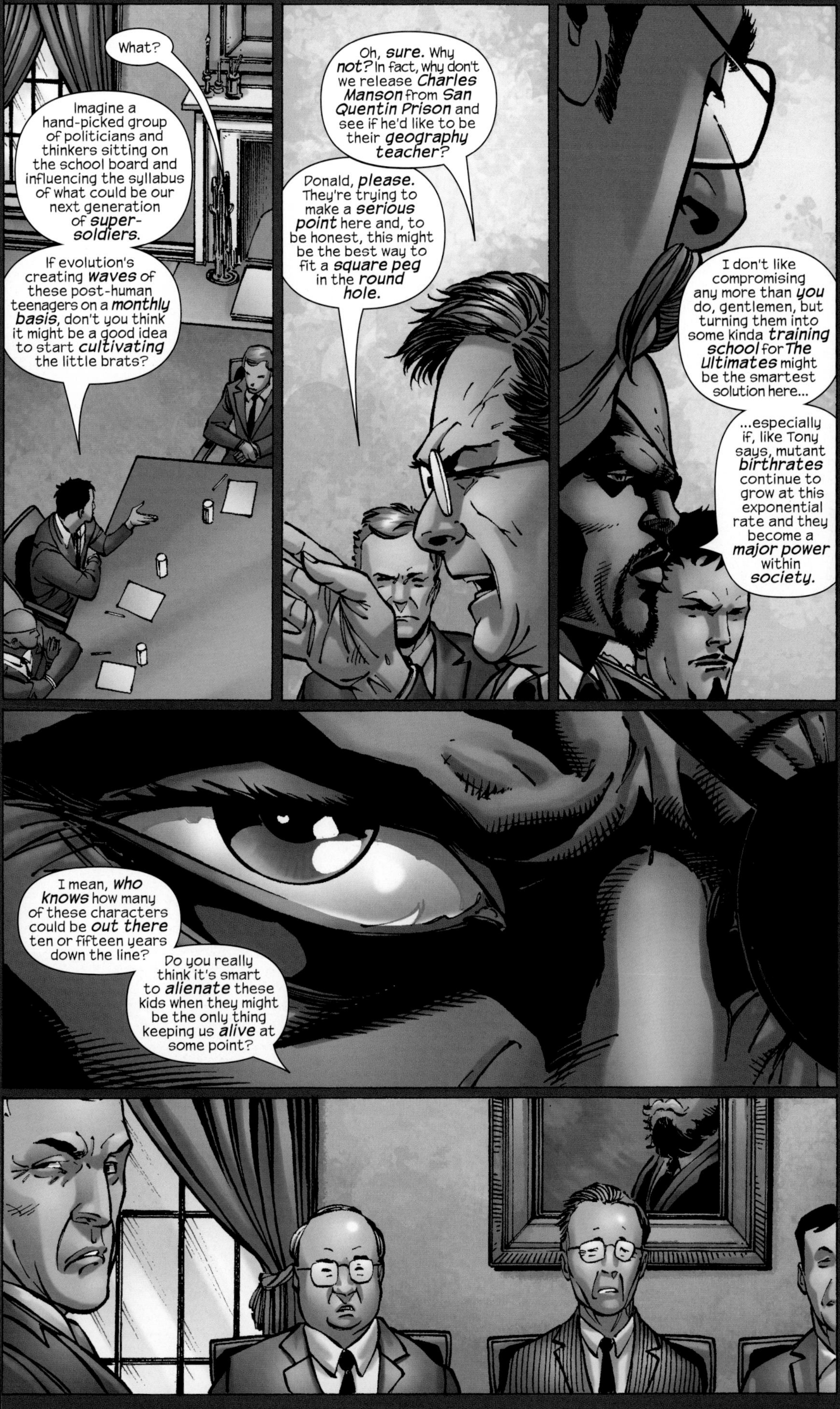
What?
Imagine a hand-picked group of politicians and thinkers sitting on the school board and influencing the syllabus of what could be our next generation of super-soldiers.
If evolution's creating waves of these post-human teenagers on a monthly basis, don't you think it might be a good idea to start cultivating the little brats?
Oh, sure. Why not? In fact, why don't we release Charles Manson from San Quentin Prison and see if he'd like to be their geography teacher?
Donald, please. They're trying to make a serious point here and, to be honest, this might be the best way to fit a square peg in the round hole.
I don't like compromising any more than you do, gentlemen, but turning them into some kinda training school for The Ultimates might be the smartest solution here...
...especially if, like Tony says, mutant birthrates continue to grow at this exponential rate and they become a major power within society.
I mean, who knows how many of these characters could be out there ten or fifteen years down the line?
Do you really think it's smart to alienate these kids when they might be the only thing keeping us alive at some point?

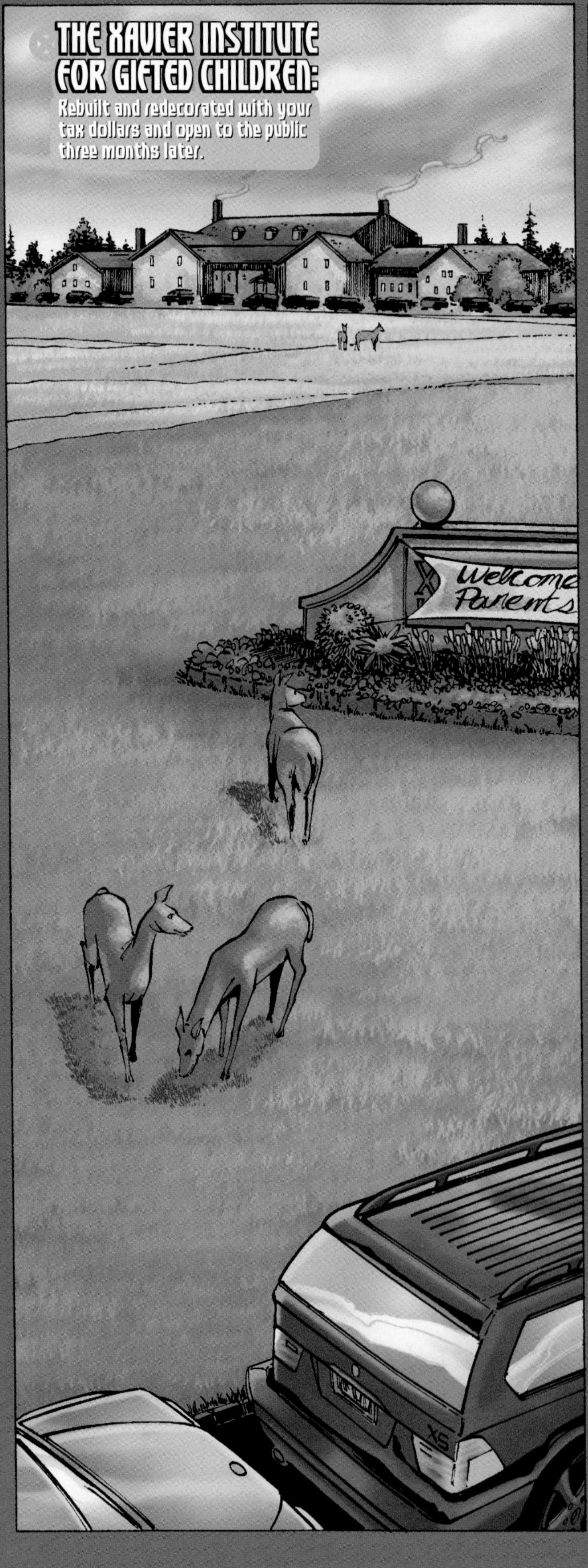
THE XAVIER INSTITUTE FOR GIFTED CHILDREN:
Rebuilt and redecorated with your tax dollars and open to the public three months later.
Welcome Parents

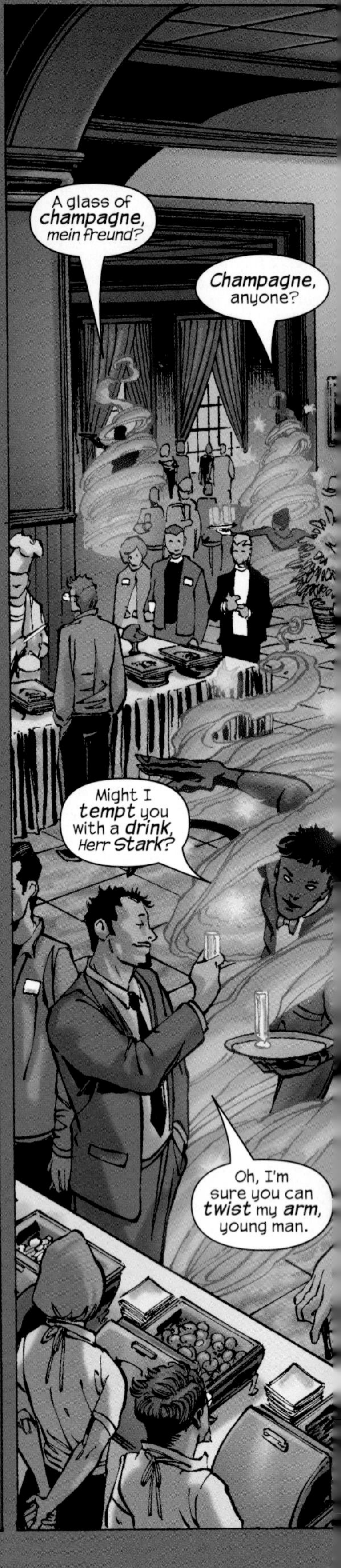
A glass of champagne, mein freund?
Champagne, anyone?
Might I tempt you with a drink, Herr Stark?
Oh, I'm sure you can twist my arm, young man.

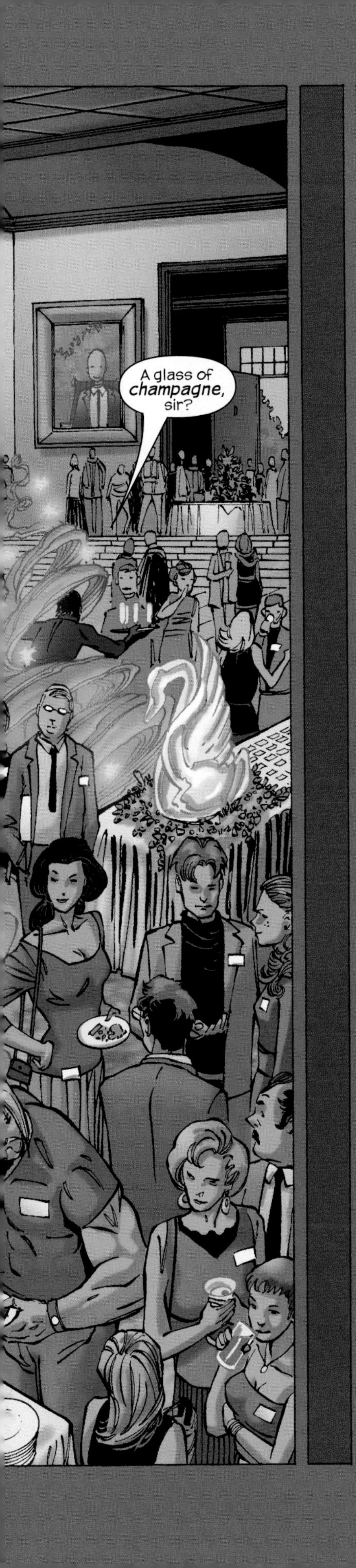

A glass of champagne, sir?

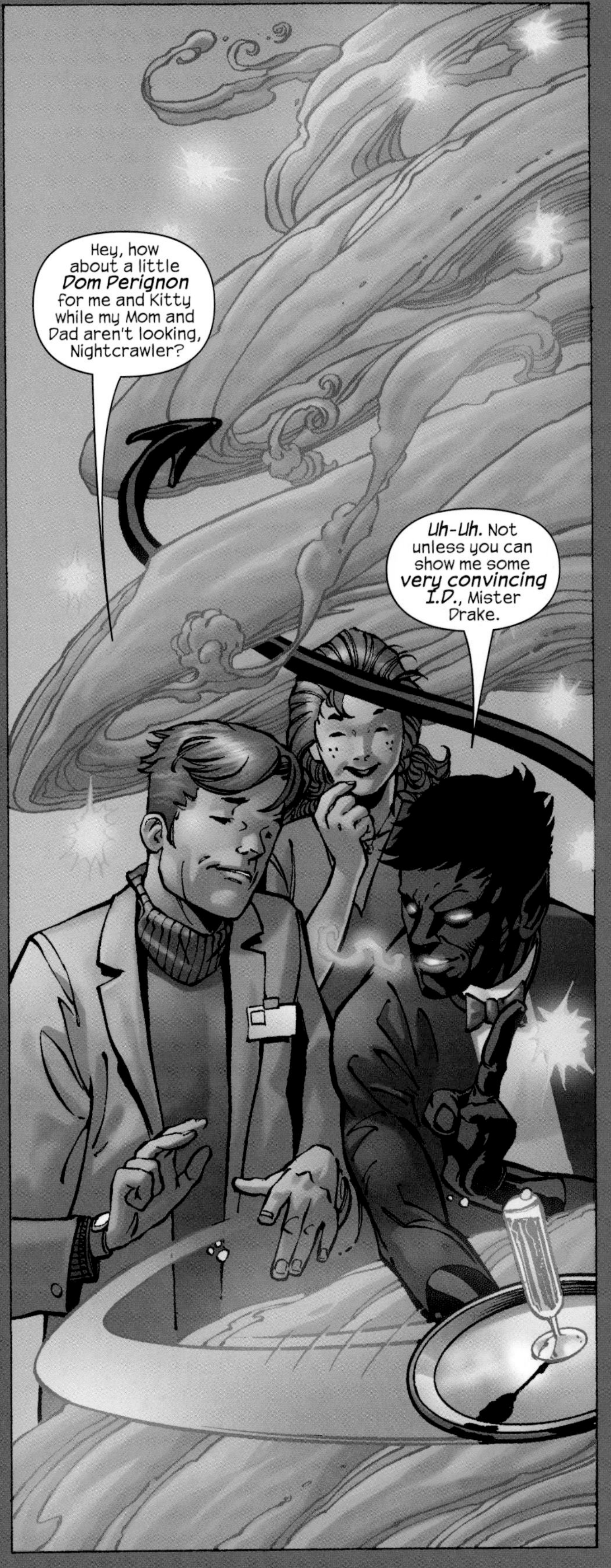

Hey, how about a little Dom Perignon for me and Kitty while my Mom and Dad aren't looking, Nightcrawler?
Uh-Uh. Not unless you can show me some very convincing I.D., Mister Drake.

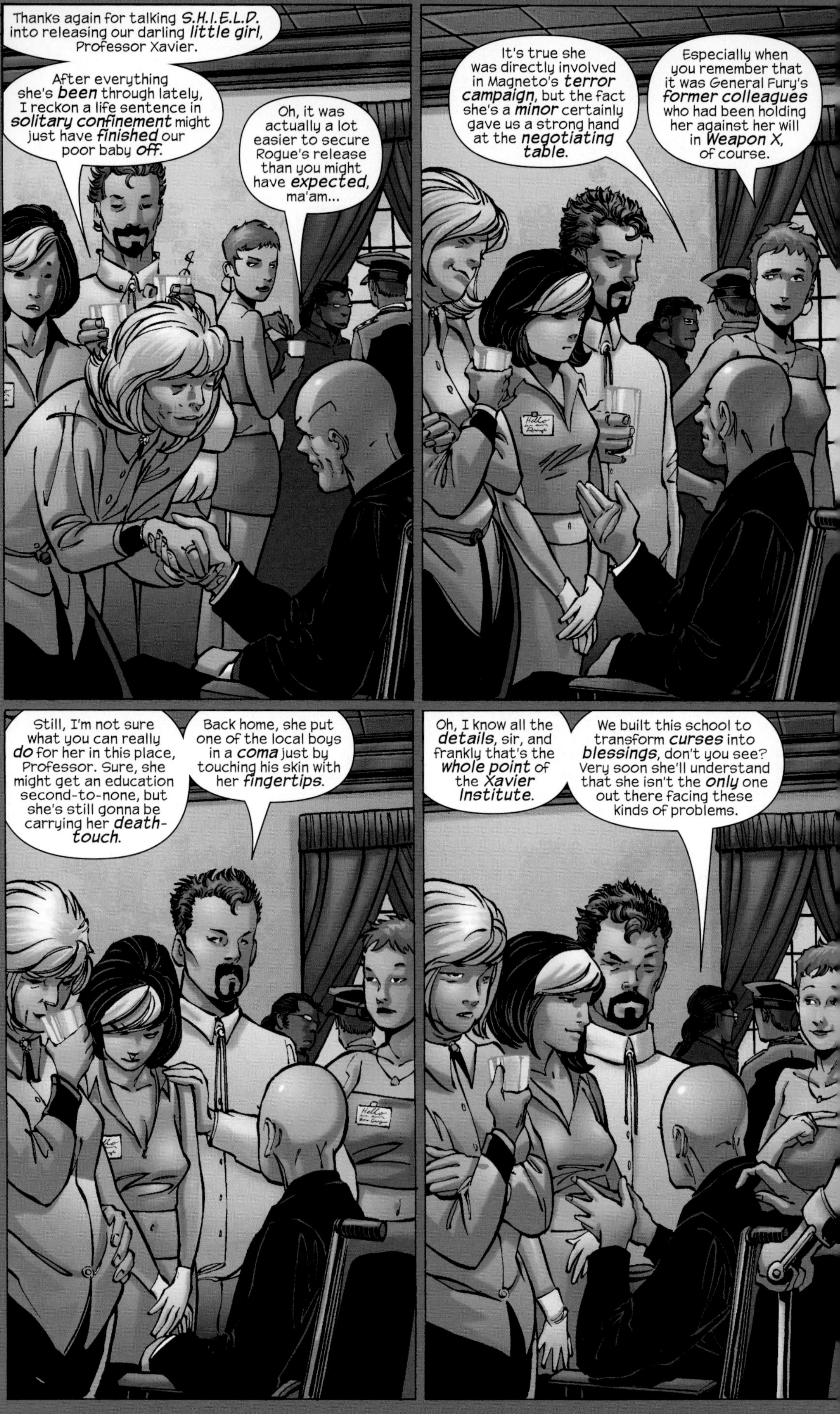

Thanks again for talking S.H.I.E.L.D. into releasing our darling little girl, Professor Xavier.
After everything she's been through lately, I reckon a life sentence in solitary confinement might just have finished our poor baby off.
Oh, it was actually a lot easier to secure Rogue's release than you might have expected, ma'am...
It's true she was directly involved in Magneto's terror campaign, but the fact she's a minor certainly gave us a strong hand at the negotiating table.
Especially when you remember that it was General Fury's former colleagues who had been holding her against her will in Weapon X, of course.
Still, I'm not sure what you can really do for her in this place, Professor. Sure, she might get an education second-to-none, but she's still gonna be carrying her death-touch.
Back home, she put one of the local boys in a coma just by touching his skin with her fingertips.
Oh, I know all the details, sir, and frankly that's the whole point of the Xavier Institute.
We built this school to transform curses into blessings, don't you see? Very soon she'll understand that she isn't the only one out there facing these kinds of problems.

He is **absolutely right**, you know.

Help yourself to a slice of **Battenburg** and let me tell you why I decided to lend my support to this **academy**.

Y'all just keep **smiling**, honey. Just **bite your lip** and graduation day's gonna come around **soon enough**, y'hear?

Hello the my autumn

Hello

Ah, **Professor Braddock**. I'm so delighted you could **make** it, sir. There honestly isn't a day goes by where I don't think about you and that lovely **wife** of yours.

You know I light a candle for your dear, departed **daughter** every time I light one for our poor **David**? She seemed like such a **special, special** girl.

I'm sure The Professor doesn't need to be **reminded** about everything that happened to **Betsy**, Charles. We're supposed to be having a **party** here, remember?

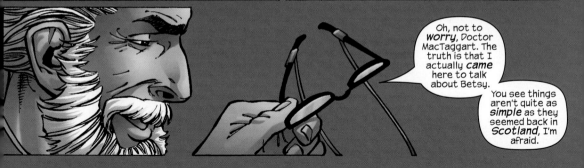

Oh, not to **worry**, Doctor MacTaggart. The truth is that I actually **came** here to talk about Betsy.

You see things aren't quite as **simple** as they seemed back in **Scotland**, I'm afraid.

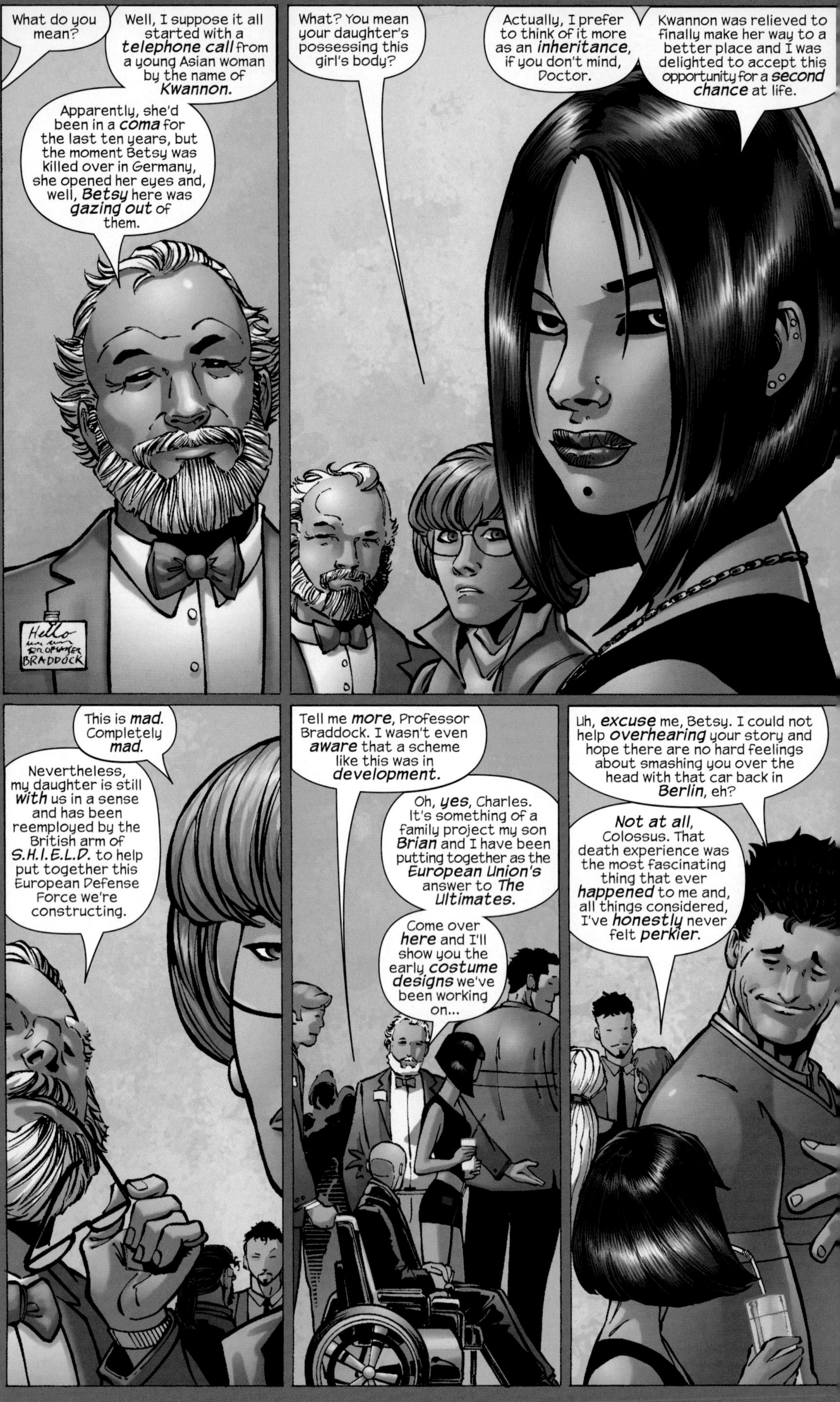

What do you mean?
Well, I suppose it all started with a telephone call from a young Asian woman by the name of Kwannon.
Apparently, she'd been in a coma for the last ten years, but the moment Betsy was killed over in Germany, she opened her eyes and, well, Betsy here was gazing out of them.
Hello
BRADDOCK
What? You mean your daughter's possessing this girl's body?
Actually, I prefer to think of it more as an inheritance, if you don't mind, Doctor.
Kwannon was relieved to finally make her way to a better place and I was delighted to accept this opportunity for a second chance at life.
This is mad. Completely mad.
Nevertheless, my daughter is still with us in a sense and has been reemployed by the British arm of S.H.I.E.L.D. to help put together this European Defense Force we're constructing.
Tell me more, Professor Braddock. I wasn't even aware that a scheme like this was in development.
Oh, yes, Charles. It's something of a family project my son Brian and I have been putting together as the European Union's answer to The Ultimates.
Come over here and I'll show you the early costume designs we've been working on...
Uh, excuse me, Betsy. I could not help overhearing your story and hope there are no hard feelings about smashing you over the head with that car back in Berlin, eh?
Not at all, Colossus. That death experience was the most fascinating thing that ever happened to me and, all things considered, I've honestly never felt perkier.

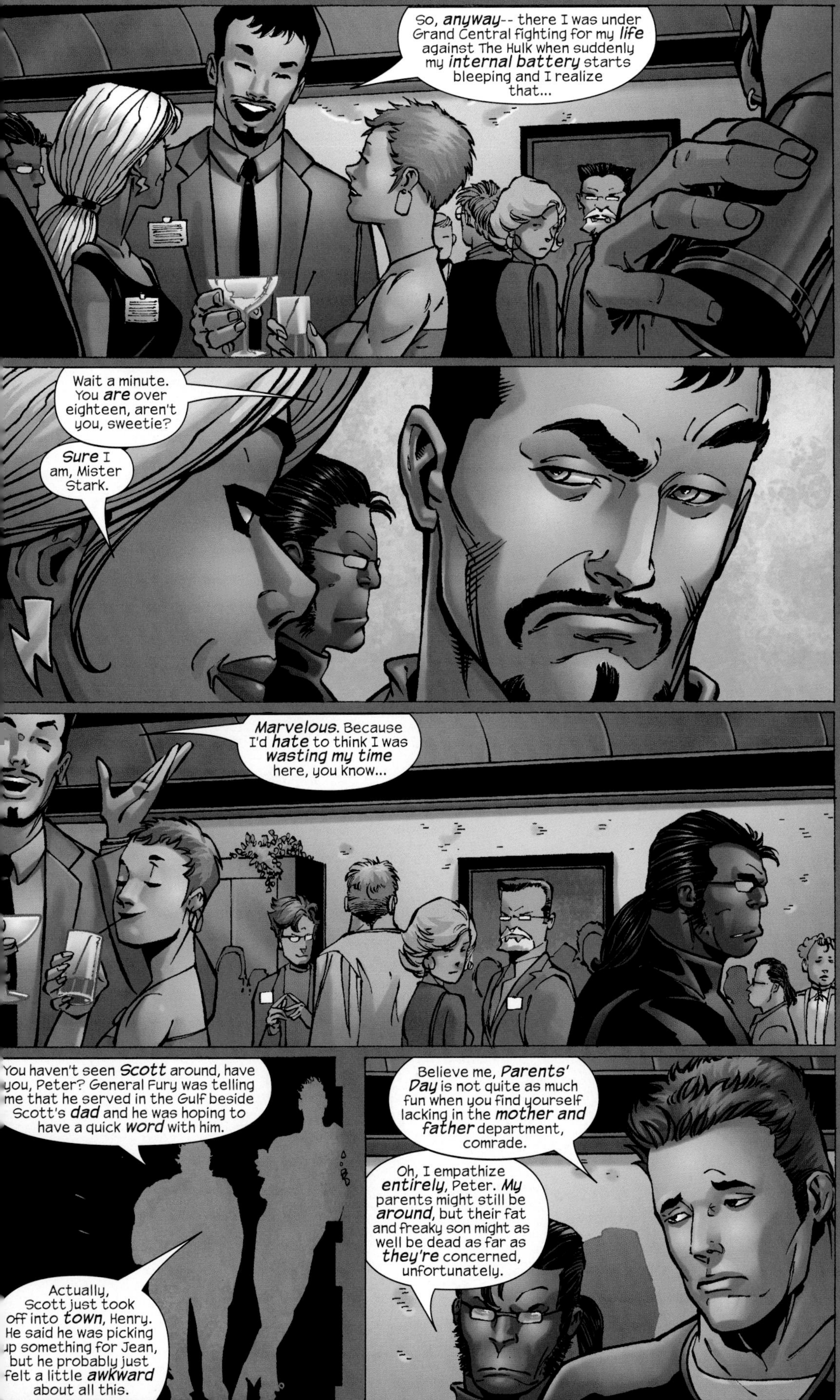

So, anyway-- there I was under Grand Central fighting for my life against The Hulk when suddenly my internal battery starts bleeping and I realize that...
Wait a minute. You are over eighteen, aren't you, sweetie?
Sure I am, Mister Stark.
Marvelous. Because I'd hate to think I was wasting my time here, you know...
You haven't seen Scott around, have you, Peter? General Fury was telling me that he served in the Gulf beside Scott's dad and he was hoping to have a quick word with him.
Actually, Scott just took off into town, Henry. He said he was picking up something for Jean, but he probably just felt a little awkward about all this.
Believe me, Parents' Day is not quite as much fun when you find yourself lacking in the mother and father department, comrade.
Oh, I empathize entirely, Peter. My parents might still be around, but their fat and freaky son might as well be dead as far as they're concerned, unfortunately.

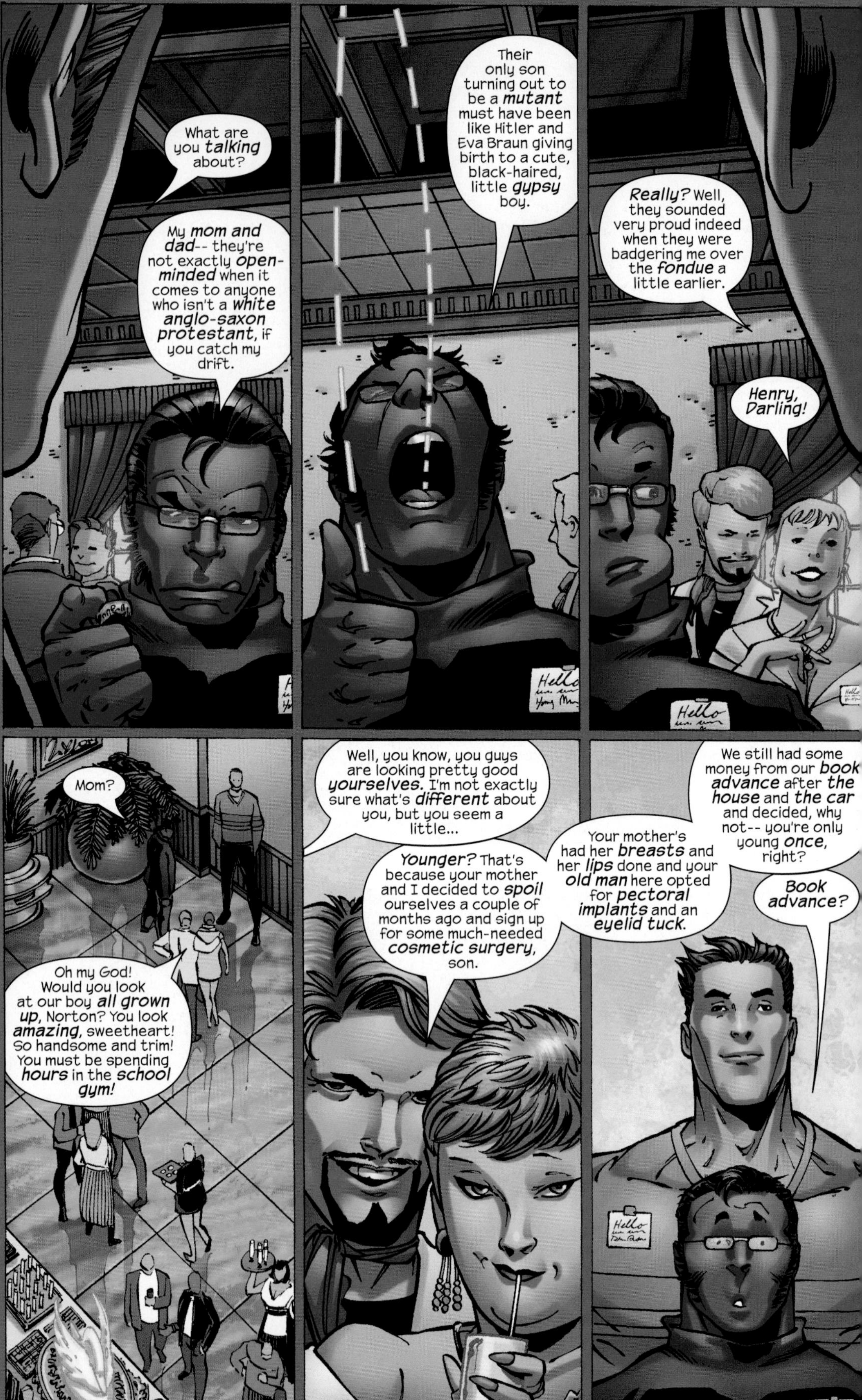
What are you talking about?
My mom and dad-- they're not exactly open-minded when it comes to anyone who isn't a white anglo-saxon protestant, if you catch my drift.
Their only son turning out to be a mutant must have been like Hitler and Eva Braun giving birth to a cute, black-haired, little gypsy boy.
Really? Well, they sounded very proud indeed when they were badgering me over the fondue a little earlier.
Henry, Darling!
Mom?
Oh my God! Would you look at our boy all grown up, Norton? You look amazing, sweetheart! So handsome and trim! You must be spending hours in the school gym!
Well, you know, you guys are looking pretty good yourselves. I'm not exactly sure what's different about you, but you seem a little...
Younger? That's because your mother and I decided to spoil ourselves a couple of months ago and sign up for some much-needed cosmetic surgery, son.
Your mother's had her breasts and her lips done and your old man here opted for pectoral implants and an eyelid tuck.
We still had some money from our book advance after the house and the car and decided, why not-- you're only young once, right?
Book advance?

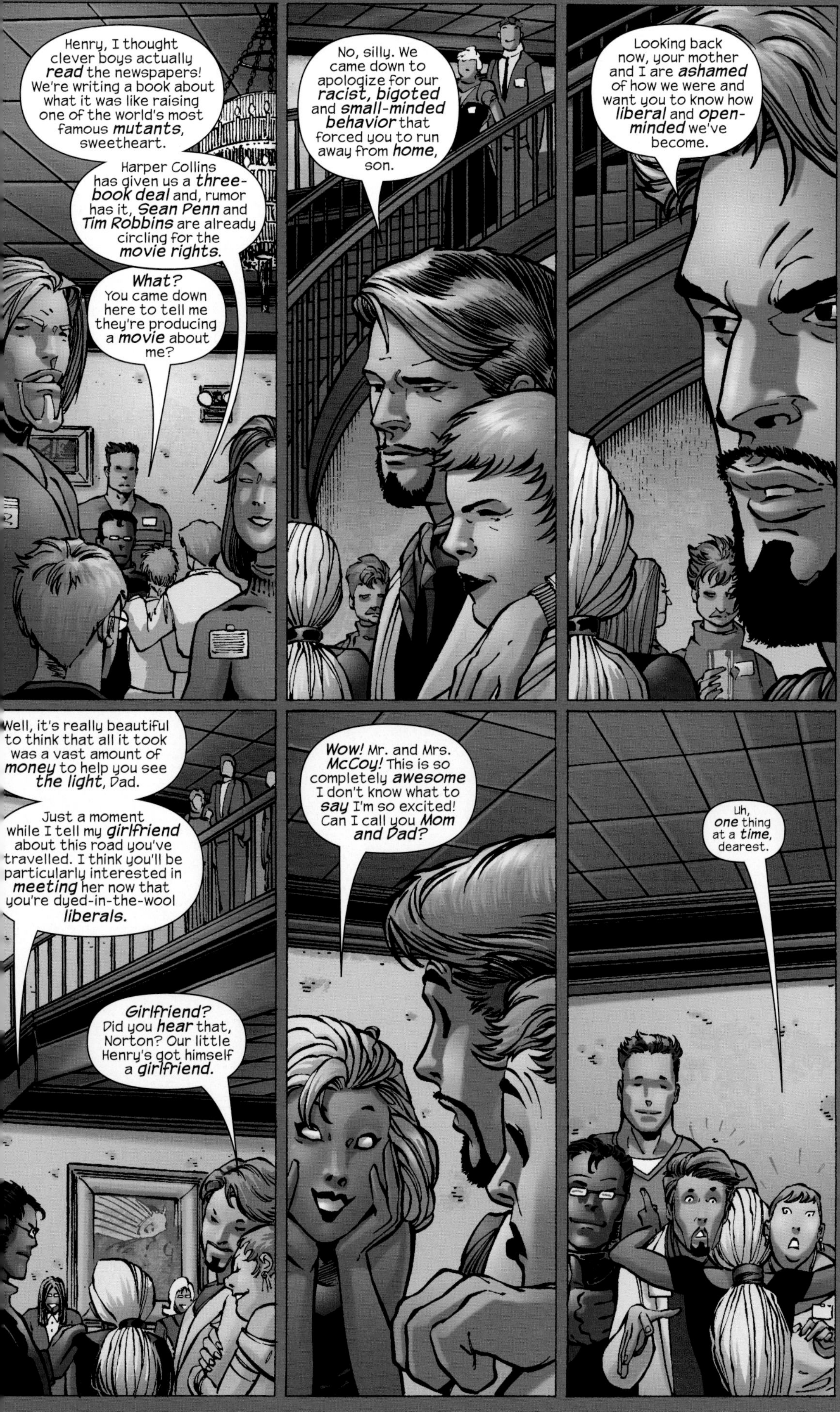
Henry, I thought clever boys actually read the newspapers! We're writing a book about what it was like raising one of the world's most famous mutants, sweetheart.
Harper Collins has given us a three-book deal and, rumor has it, Sean Penn and Tim Robbins are already circling for the movie rights.
What? You came down here to tell me they're producing a movie about me?
No, silly. We came down to apologize for our racist, bigoted and small-minded behavior that forced you to run away from home, son.
Looking back now, your mother and I are ashamed of how we were and want you to know how liberal and open-minded we've become.
Well, it's really beautiful to think that all it took was a vast amount of money to help you see the light, Dad.
Just a moment while I tell my girlfriend about this road you've travelled. I think you'll be particularly interested in meeting her now that you're dyed-in-the-wool liberals.
Girlfriend? Did you hear that, Norton? Our little Henry's got himself a girlfriend.
Wow! Mr. and Mrs. McCoy! This is so completely awesome I don't know what to say I'm so excited! Can I call you Mom and Dad?
Uh, one thing at a time, dearest.

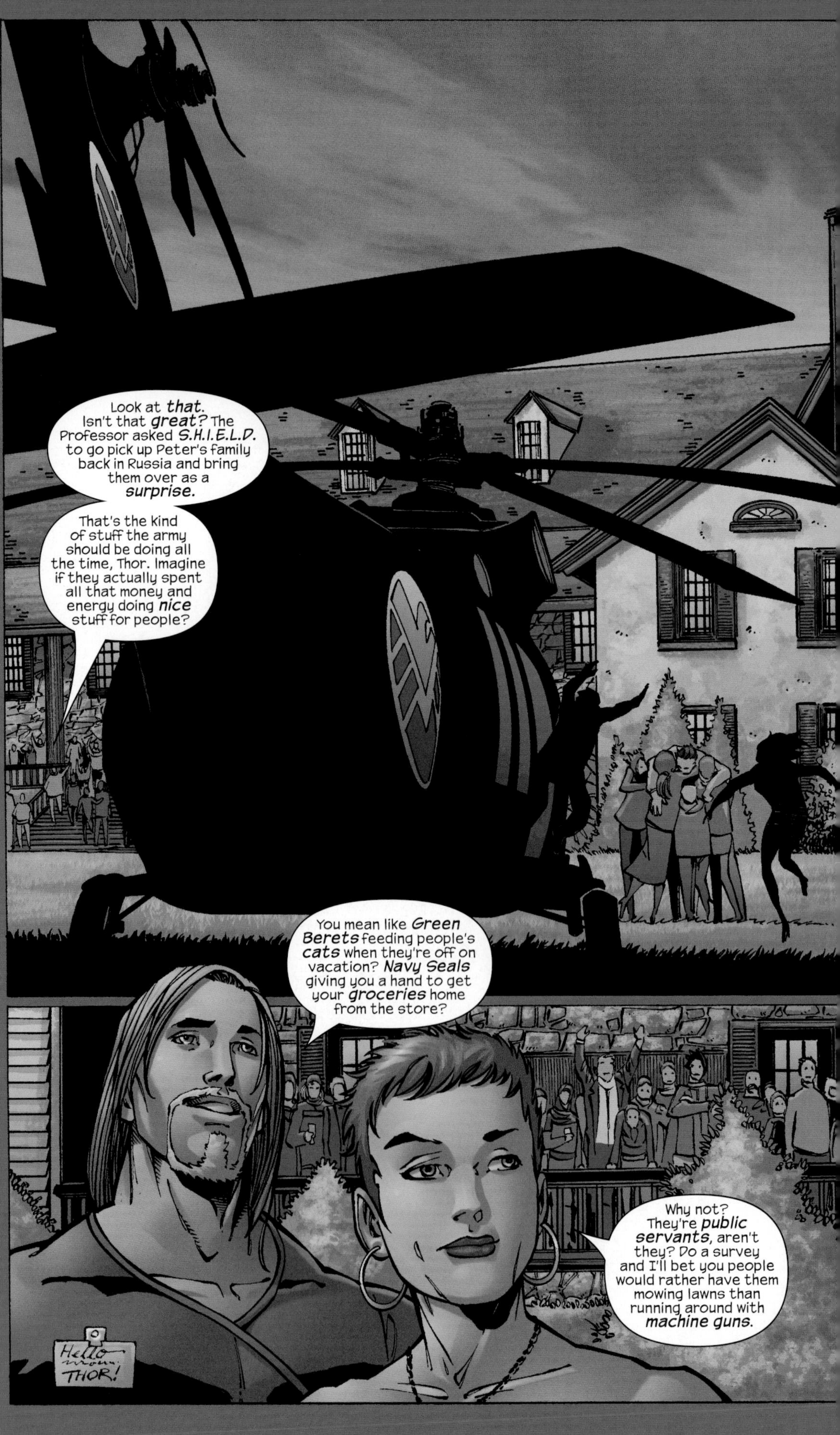
Look at *that*. Isn't that *great?* The Professor asked *S.H.I.E.L.D.* to go pick up Peter's family back in Russia and bring them over as a *surprise.*
That's the kind of stuff the army should be doing all the time, Thor. Imagine if they actually spent all that money and energy doing *nice* stuff for people?
You mean like *Green Berets* feeding people's *cats* when they're off on vacation? *Navy Seals* giving you a hand to get your *groceries* home from the store?
Why not? They're *public servants*, aren't they? Do a survey and I'll bet you people would rather have them mowing lawns than running around with *machine guns*.
Hello from THOR!

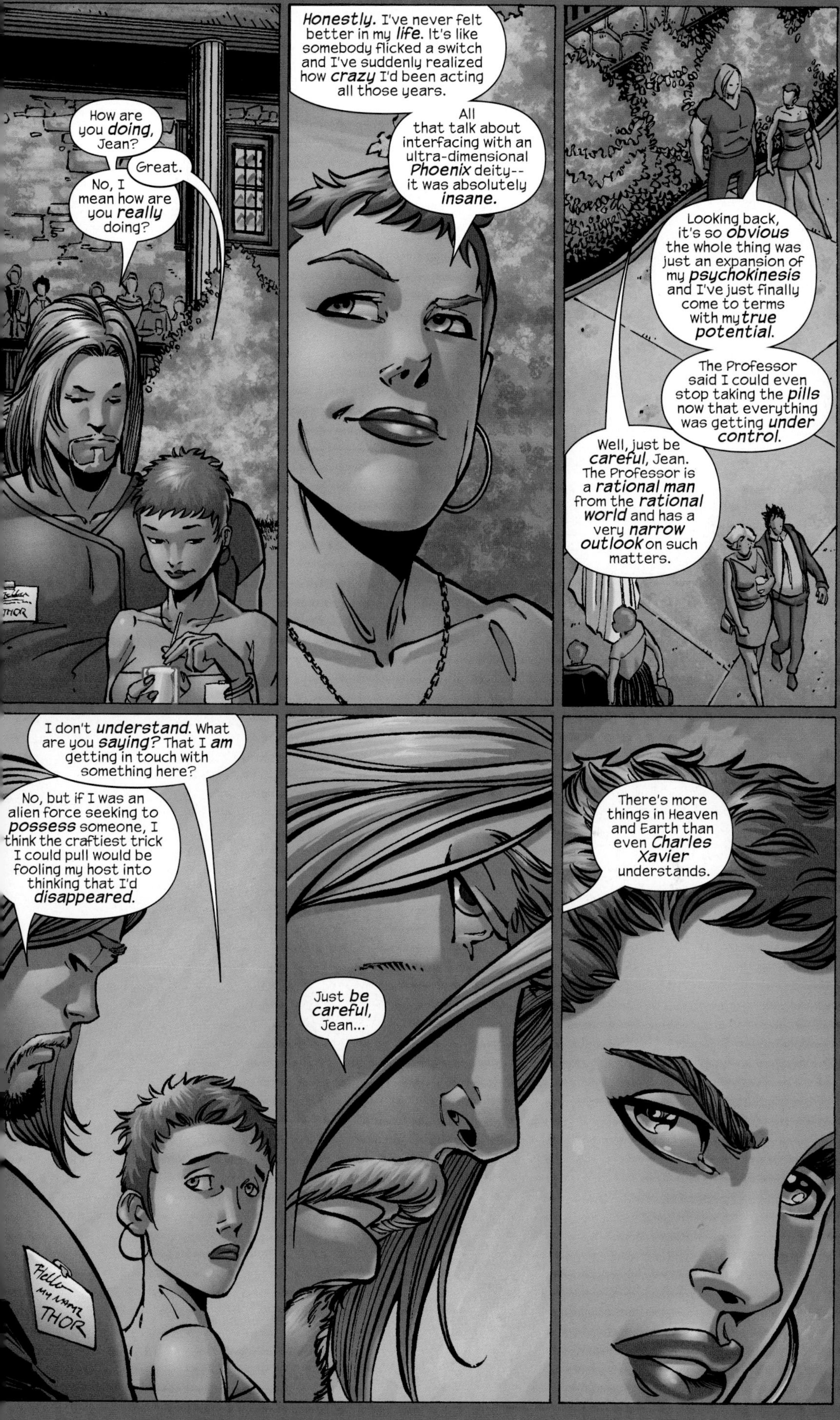

How are you doing, Jean?
Great.
No, I mean how are you really doing?
Honestly. I've never felt better in my life. It's like somebody flicked a switch and I've suddenly realized how crazy I'd been acting all those years.
All that talk about interfacing with an ultra-dimensional Phoenix deity-- it was absolutely insane.
Looking back, it's so obvious the whole thing was just an expansion of my psychokinesis and I've just finally come to terms with my true potential.
The Professor said I could even stop taking the pills now that everything was getting under control.
Well, just be careful, Jean. The Professor is a rational man from the rational world and has a very narrow outlook on such matters.
I don't understand. What are you saying? That I am getting in touch with something here?
No, but if I was an alien force seeking to possess someone, I think the craftiest trick I could pull would be fooling my host into thinking that I'd disappeared.
Just be careful, Jean...
There's more things in Heaven and Earth than even Charles Xavier understands.

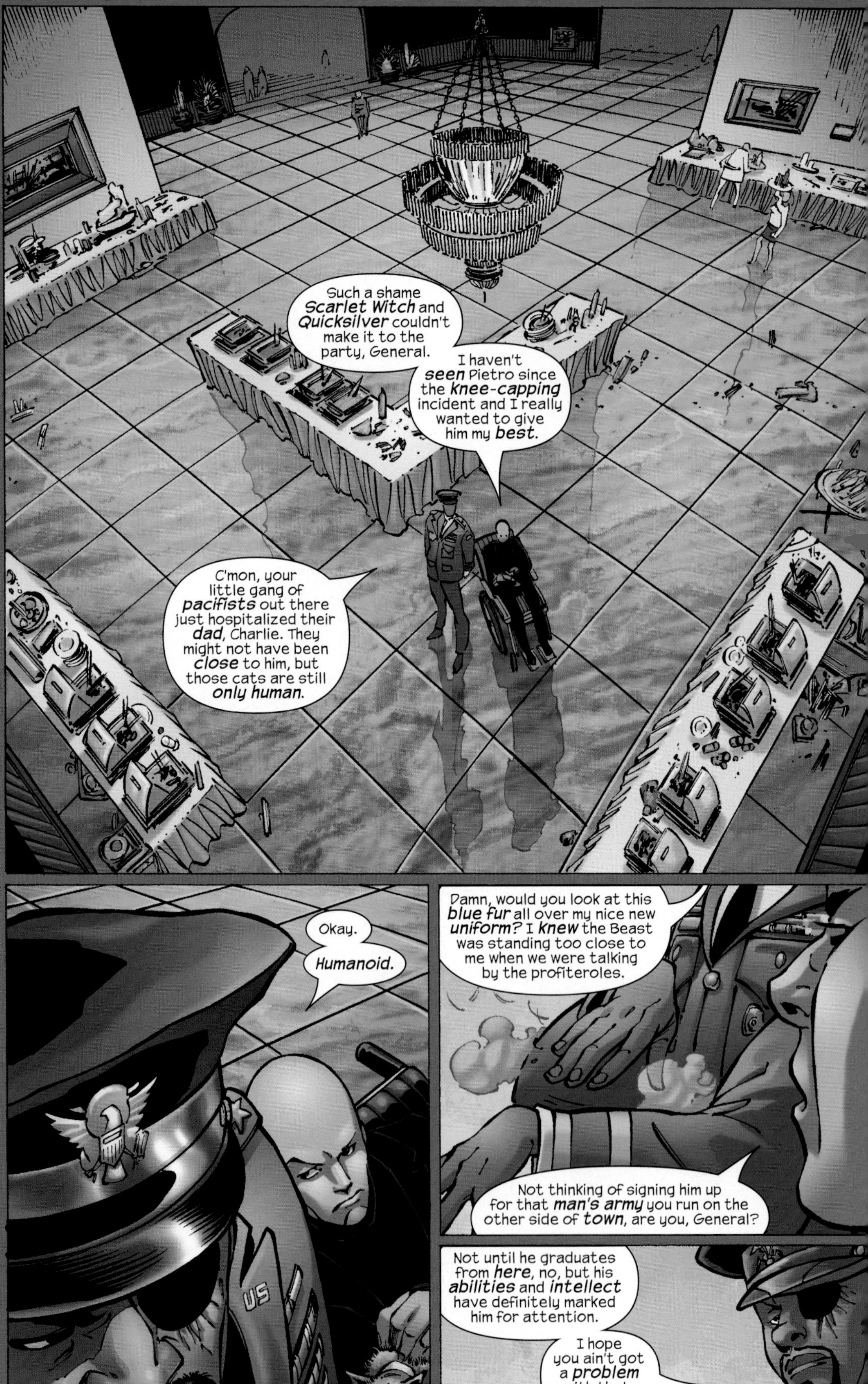
Such a shame Scarlet Witch and Quicksilver couldn't make it to the party, General.
I haven't seen Pietro since the knee-capping incident and I really wanted to give him my best.
C'mon, your little gang of pacifists out there just hospitalized their dad, Charlie. They might not have been close to him, but those cats are still only human.
Okay.
Humanoid.
Damn, would you look at this blue fur all over my nice new uniform? I knew the Beast was standing too close to me when we were talking by the profiteroles.
Not thinking of signing him up for that man's army you run on the other side of town, are you, General?
Not until he graduates from here, no, but his abilities and intellect have definitely marked him for attention.
I hope you ain't got a problem with that, Professor...

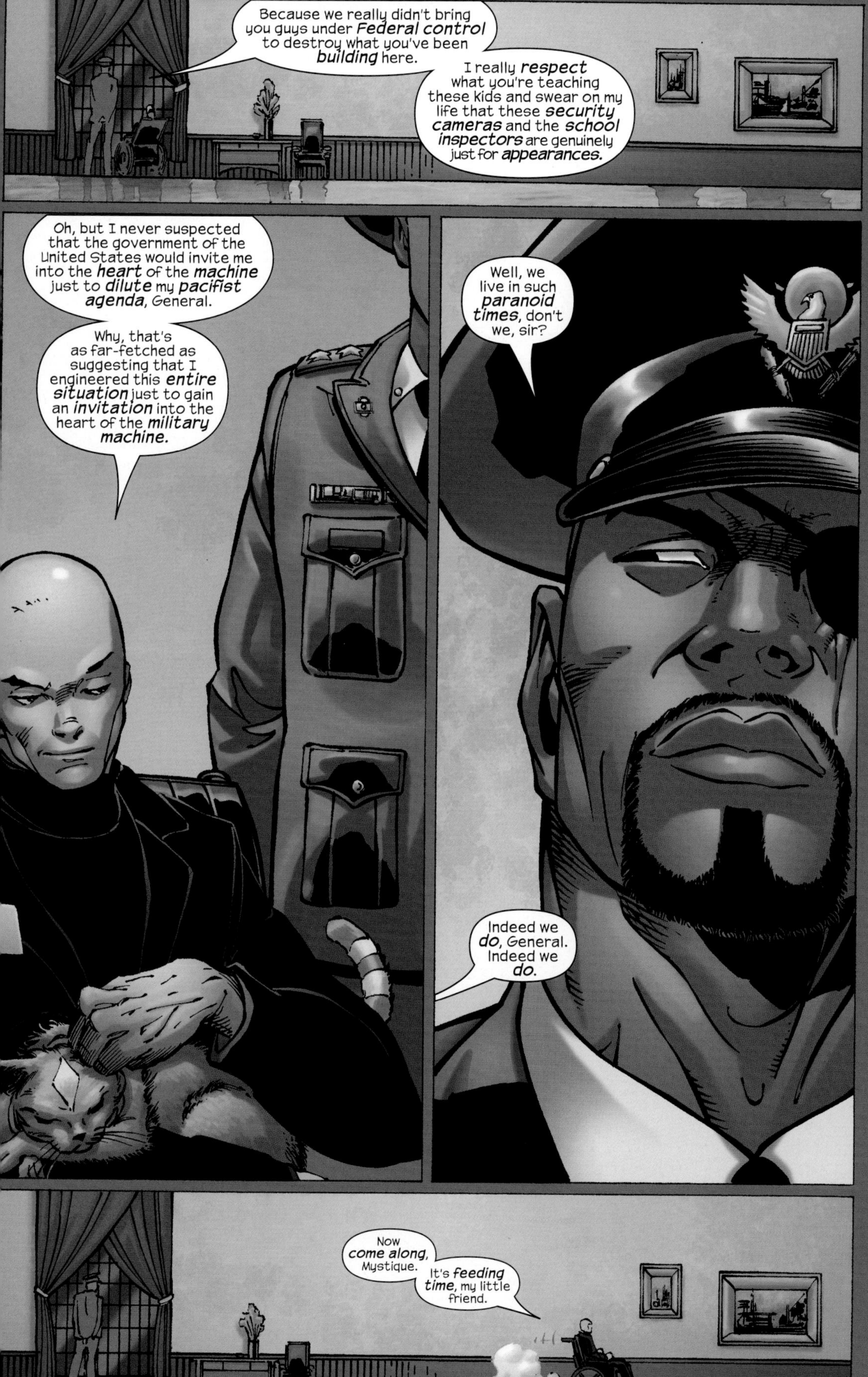
Because we really didn't bring you guys under Federal control to destroy what you've been building here.
I really respect what you're teaching these kids and swear on my life that these security cameras and the school inspectors are genuinely just for appearances.
Oh, but I never suspected that the government of the United States would invite me into the heart of the machine just to dilute my pacifist agenda, General.
Why, that's as far-fetched as suggesting that I engineered this entire situation just to gain an invitation into the heart of the military machine.
Well, we live in such paranoid times, don't we, sir?
Indeed we do, General. Indeed we do.
Now come along, Mystique.
It's feeding time, my little friend.

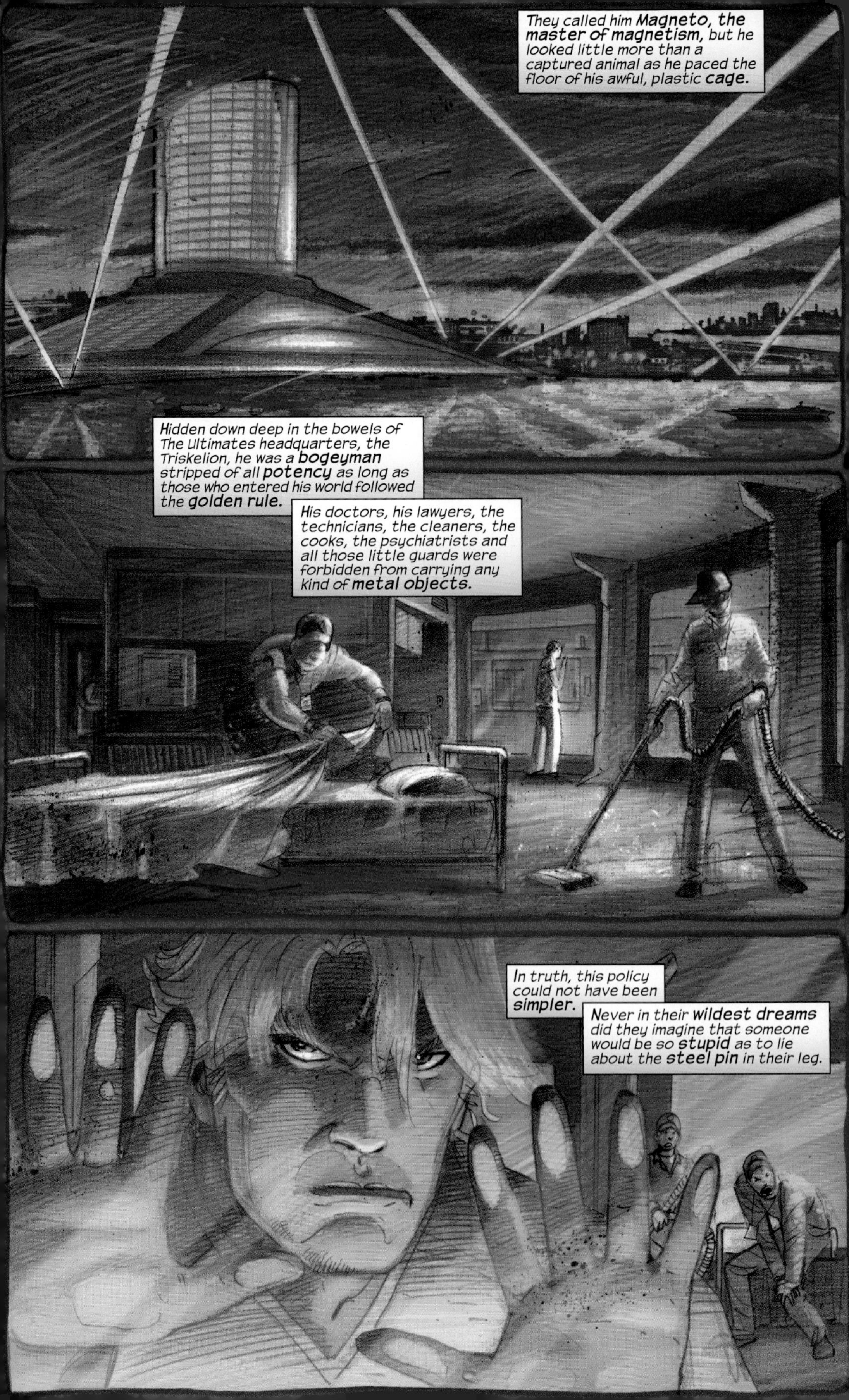
They called him Magneto, the master of magnetism, but he looked little more than a captured animal as he paced the floor of his awful, plastic cage.
Hidden down deep in the bowels of The Ultimates headquarters, the Triskelion, he was a bogeyman stripped of all potency as long as those who entered his world followed the golden rule.
His doctors, his lawyers, the technicians, the cleaners, the cooks, the psychiatrists and all those little guards were forbidden from carrying any kind of metal objects.
In truth, this policy could not have been simpler.
Never in their wildest dreams did they imagine that someone would be so stupid as to lie about the steel pin in their leg.

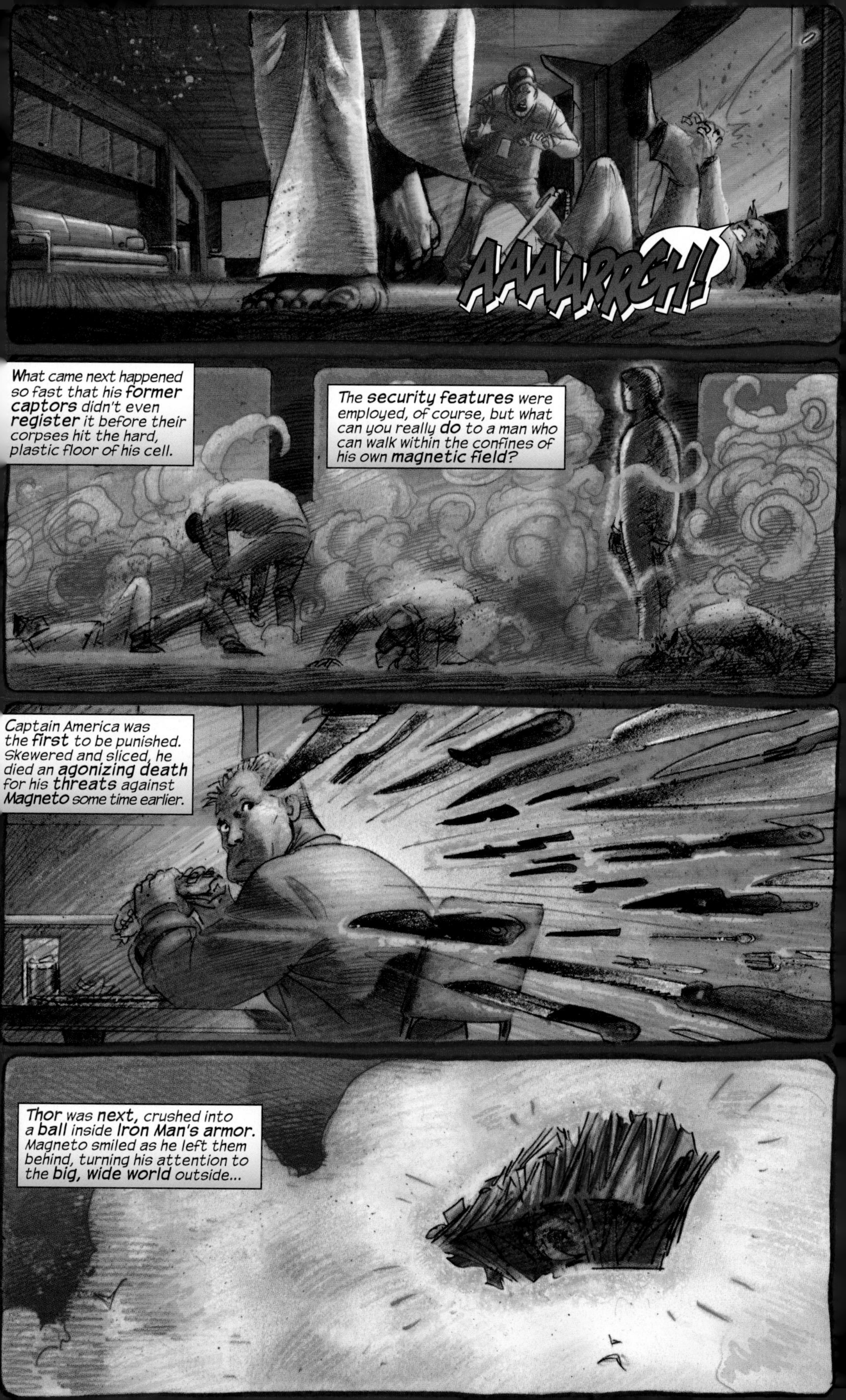
AAAARRGH!
What came next happened so fast that his former captors didn't even register it before their corpses hit the hard, plastic floor of his cell.
The security features were employed, of course, but what can you really do to a man who can walk within the confines of his own magnetic field?
Captain America was the first to be punished. Skewered and sliced, he died an agonizing death for his threats against Magneto some time earlier.
Thor was next, crushed into a ball inside Iron Man's armor. Magneto smiled as he left them behind, turning his attention to the big, wide world outside...

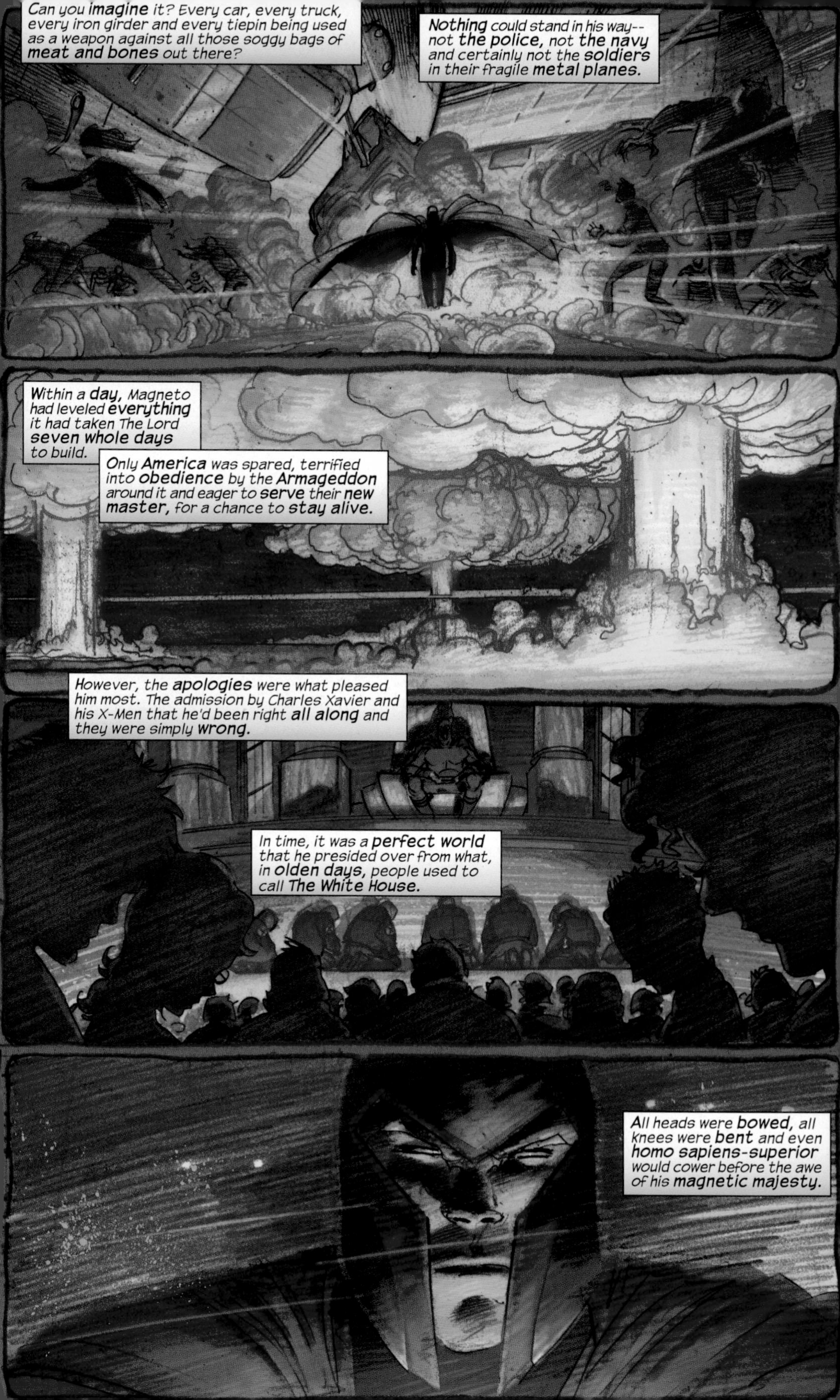
Can you imagine it? Every car, every truck, every iron girder and every tiepin being used as a weapon against all those soggy bags of meat and bones out there?
Nothing could stand in his way-- not the police, not the navy and certainly not the soldiers in their fragile metal planes.
Within a day, Magneto had leveled everything it had taken The Lord seven whole days to build.
Only America was spared, terrified into obedience by the Armageddon around it and eager to serve their new master, for a chance to stay alive.
However, the apologies were what pleased him most. The admission by Charles Xavier and his X-Men that he'd been right all along and they were simply wrong.
In time, it was a perfect world that he presided over from what, in olden days, people used to call The White House.
All heads were bowed, all knees were bent and even homo sapiens-superior would cower before the awe of his magnetic majesty.

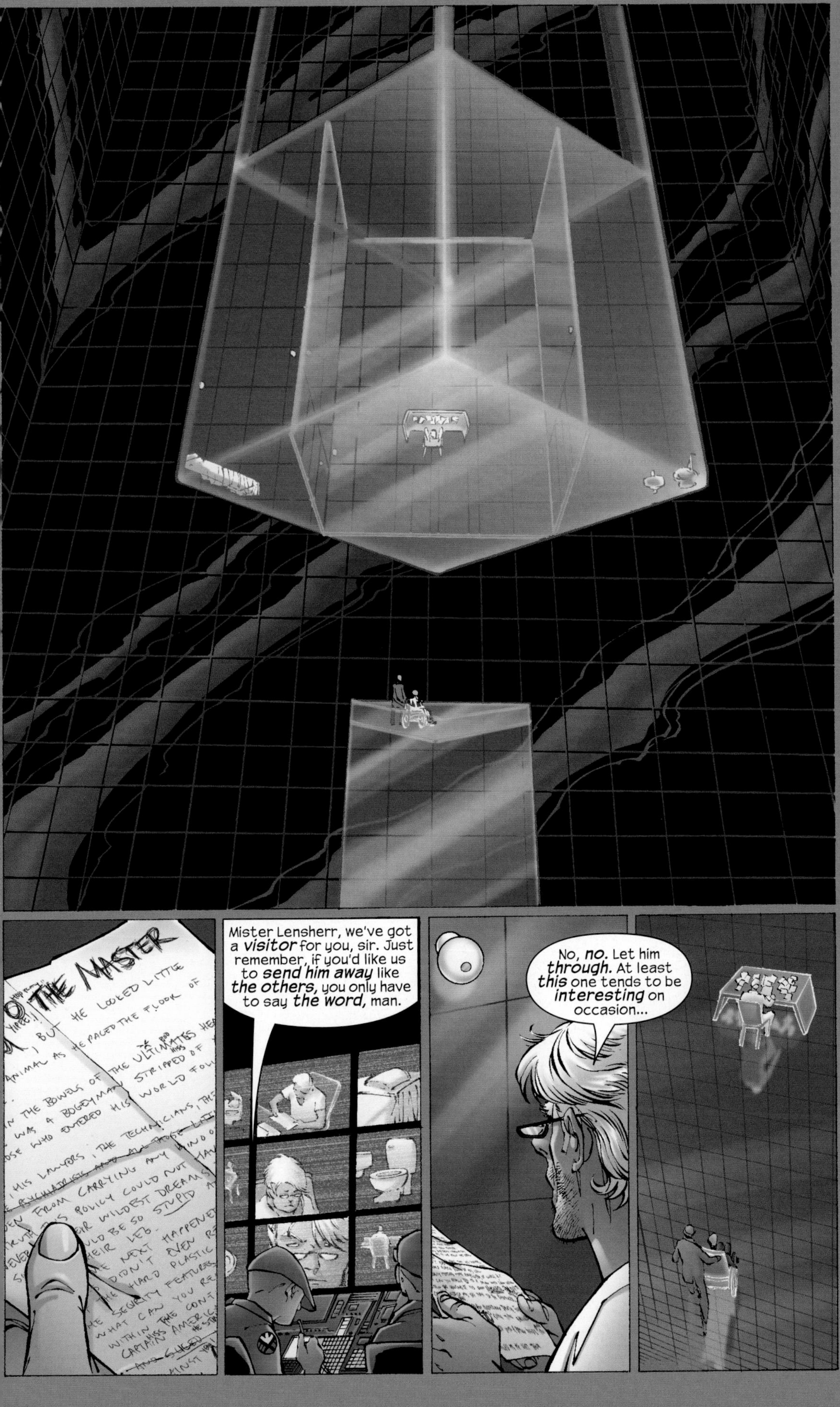
THE MASTER
Mister Lensherr, we've got a visitor for you, sir. Just remember, if you'd like us to send him away like the others, you only have to say the word, man.
No, no. Let him through. At least this one tends to be interesting on occasion...

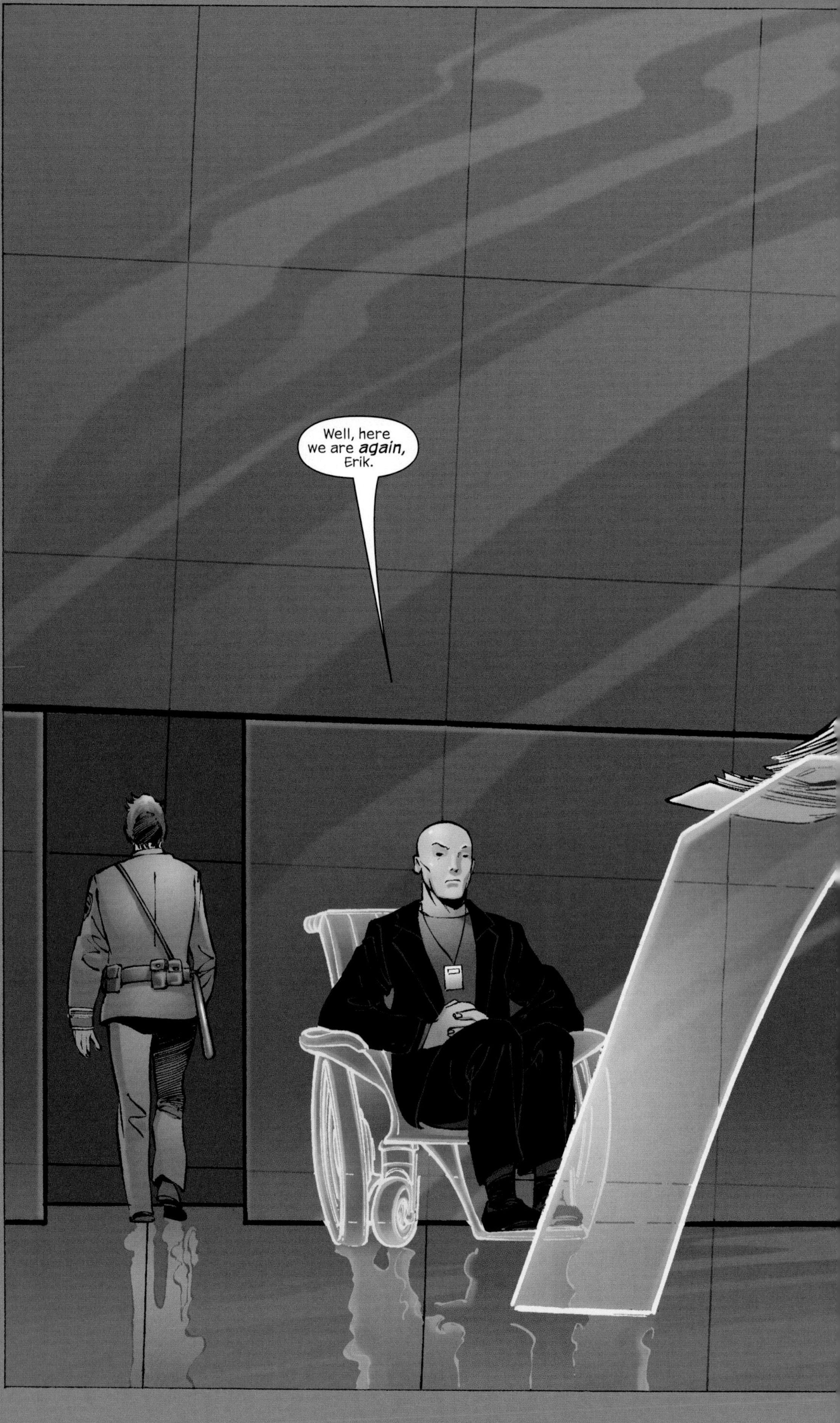
Well, here we are *again,* Erik.

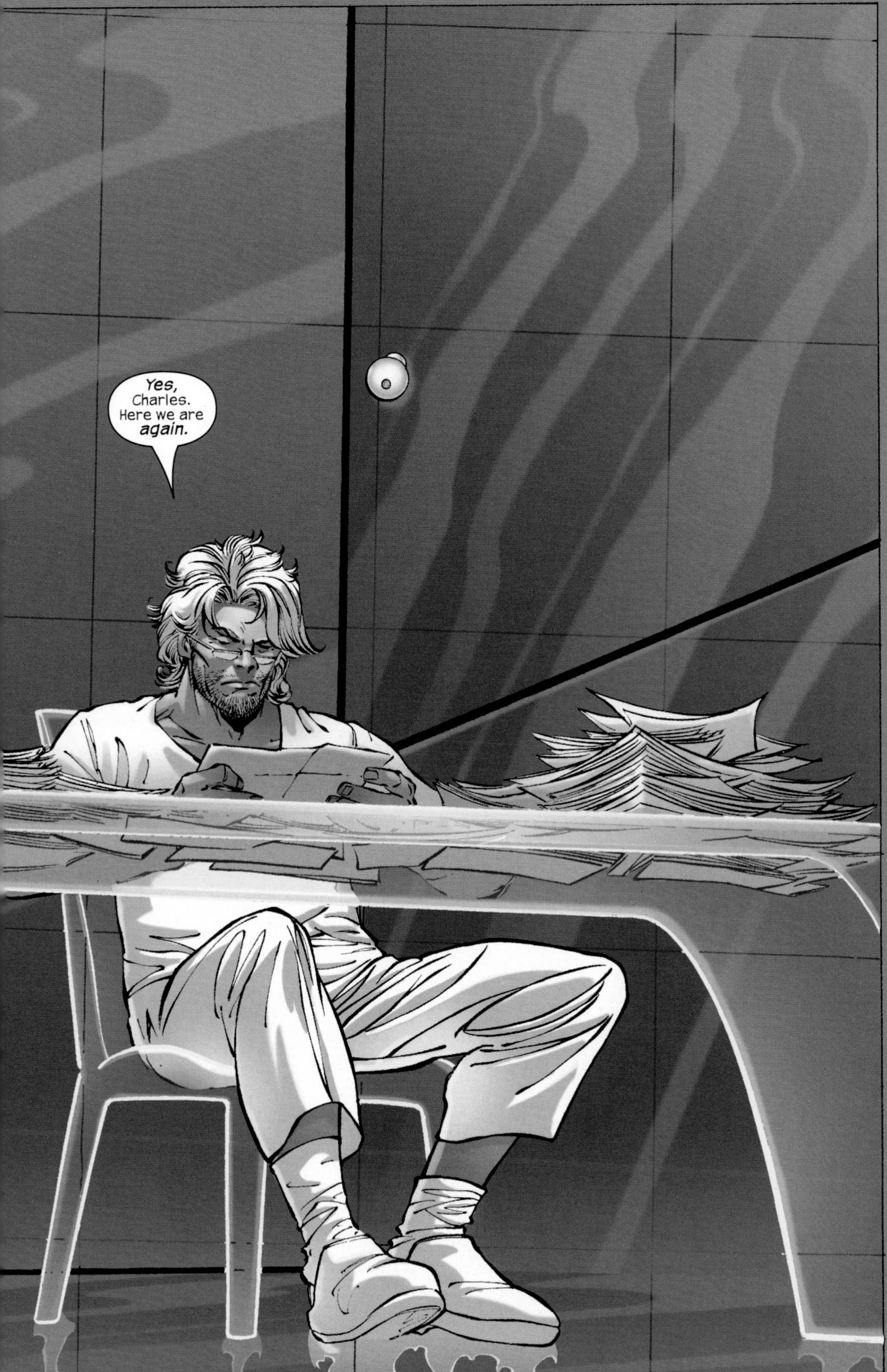
Yes, Charles. Here we are again.

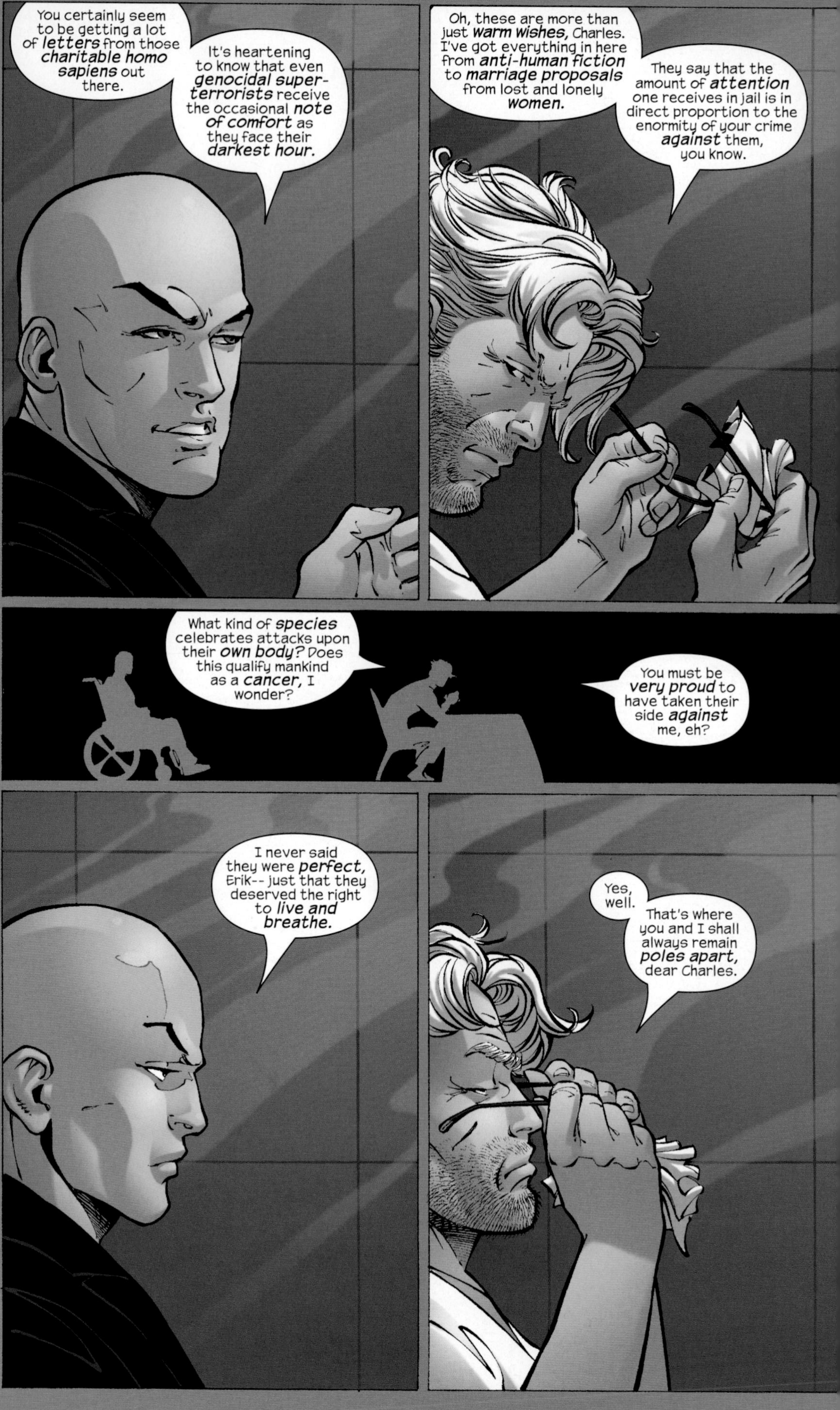
You certainly seem to be getting a lot of letters from those charitable homo sapiens out there.
It's heartening to know that even genocidal super-terrorists receive the occasional note of comfort as they face their darkest hour.
Oh, these are more than just warm wishes, Charles. I've got everything in here from anti-human fiction to marriage proposals from lost and lonely women.
They say that the amount of attention one receives in jail is in direct proportion to the enormity of your crime against them, you know.
What kind of species celebrates attacks upon their own body? Does this qualify mankind as a cancer, I wonder?
You must be very proud to have taken their side against me, eh?
I never said they were perfect, Erik-- just that they deserved the right to live and breathe.
Yes, well.
That's where you and I shall always remain poles apart, dear Charles.

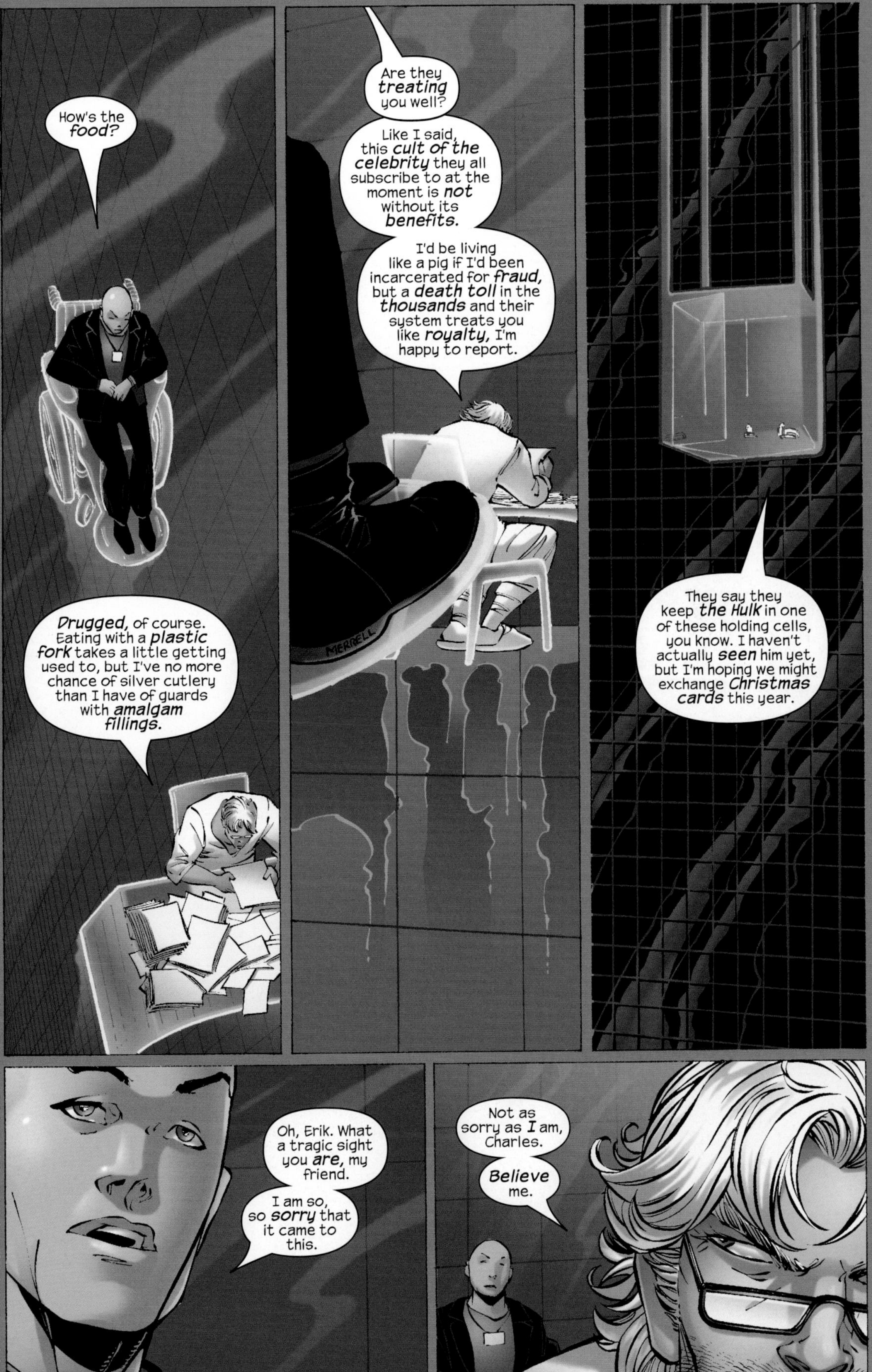
How's the food?
Drugged, of course. Eating with a plastic fork takes a little getting used to, but I've no more chance of silver cutlery than I have of guards with amalgam fillings.
Are they treating you well?
Like I said, this cult of the celebrity they all subscribe to at the moment is not without its benefits.
I'd be living like a pig if I'd been incarcerated for fraud, but a death toll in the thousands and their system treats you like royalty, I'm happy to report.
MERRELL
They say they keep the Hulk in one of these holding cells, you know. I haven't actually seen him yet, but I'm hoping we might exchange Christmas cards this year.
Oh, Erik. What a tragic sight you are, my friend.
I am so, so sorry that it came to this.
Not as sorry as I am, Charles.
Believe me.

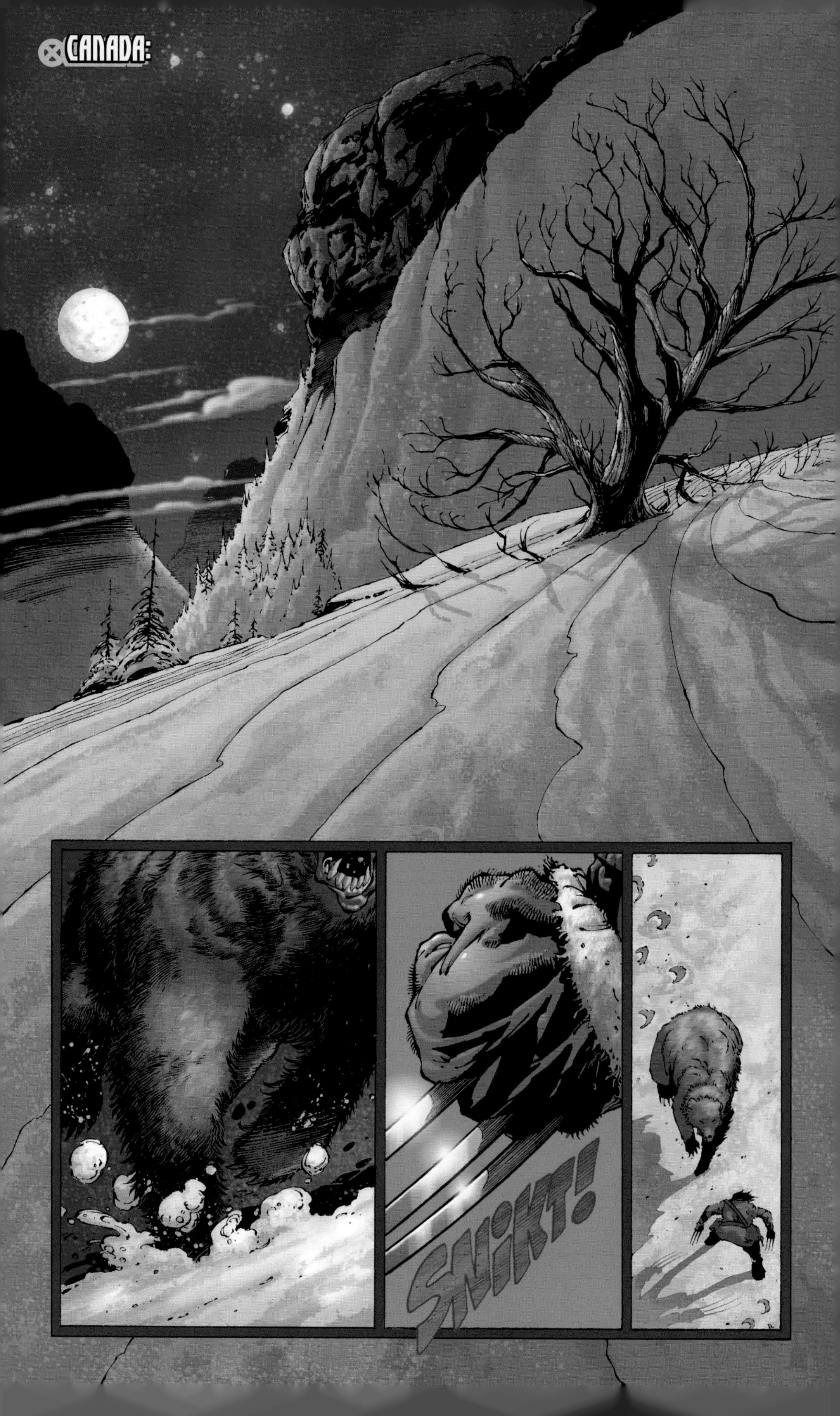
CANADA:
SNIKT!

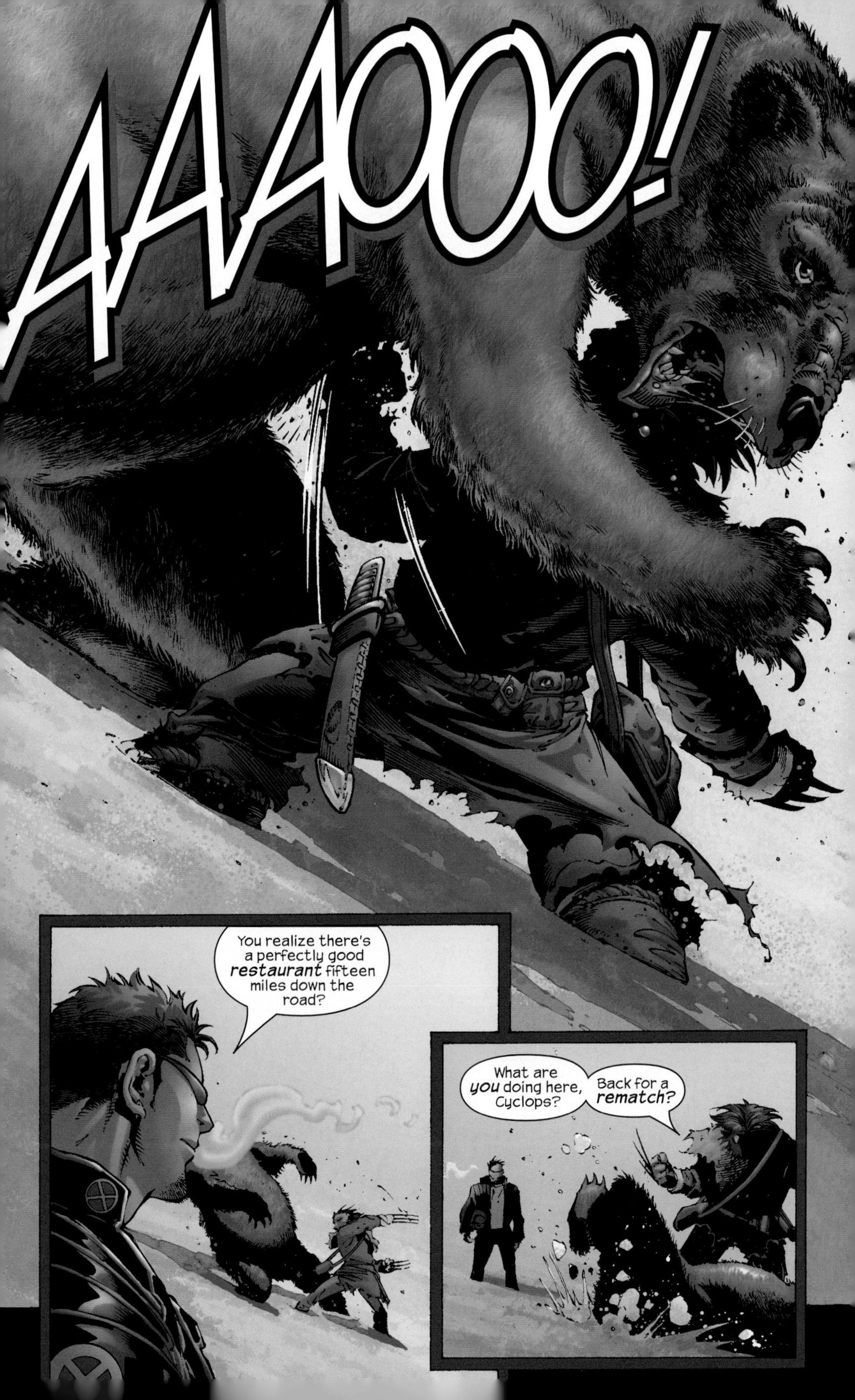
AAAOOO!
You realize there's a perfectly good *restaurant* fifteen miles down the road?
What are *you* doing here, Cyclops?
Back for a *rematch*?

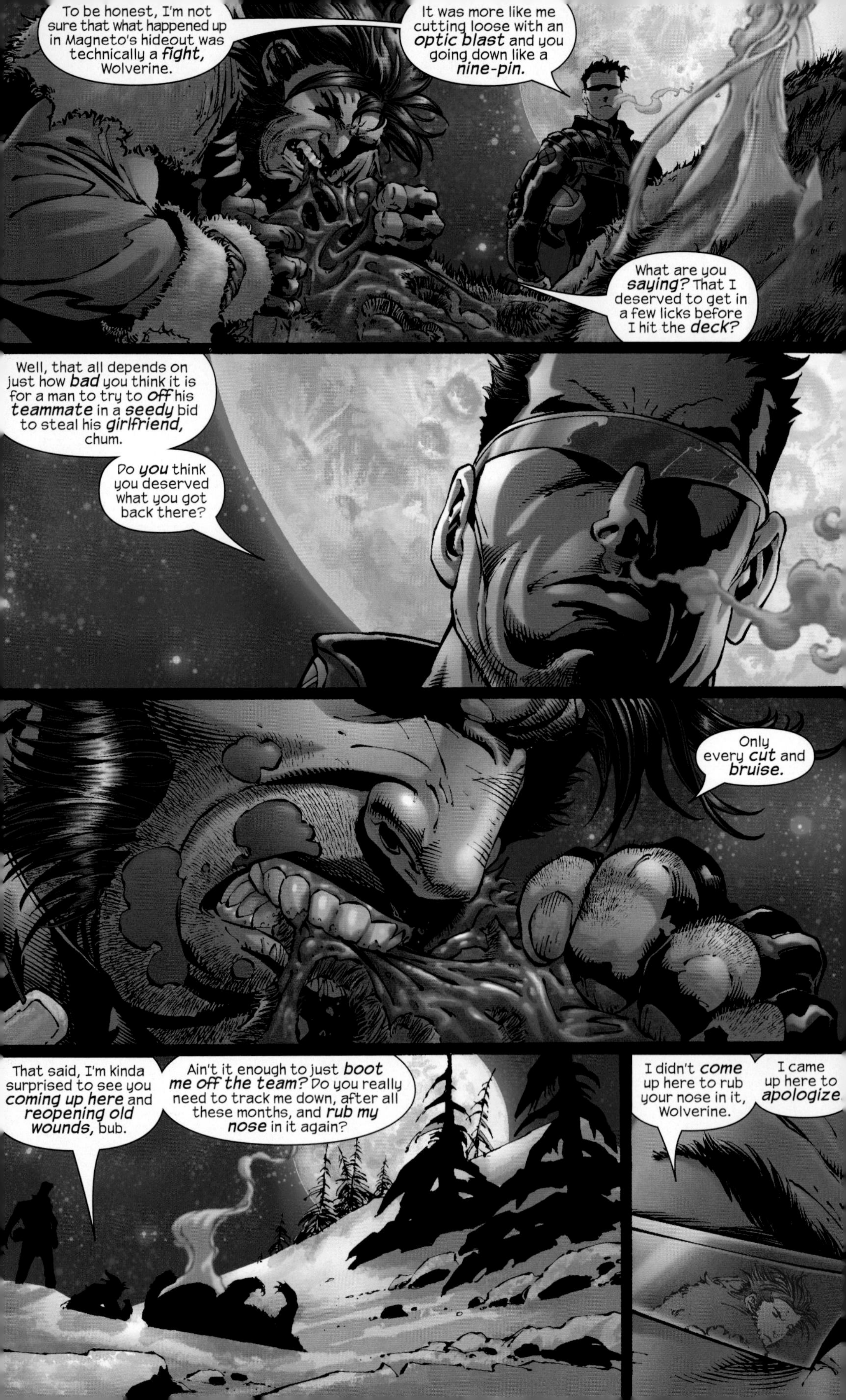
To be honest, I'm not sure that what happened up in Magneto's hideout was technically a *fight,* Wolverine.
It was more like me cutting loose with an *optic blast* and you going down like a *nine-pin.*
What are you *saying?* That I deserved to get in a few licks before I hit the *deck?*
Well, that all depends on just how *bad* you think it is for a man to try to *off* his *teammate* in a *seedy* bid to steal his *girlfriend,* chum.
Do *you* think you deserved what you got back there?
Only every *cut* and *bruise.*
That said, I'm kinda surprised to see you *coming up here* and *reopening old wounds,* bub.
Ain't it enough to just *boot me off the team?* Do you really need to track me down, after all these months, and *rub my nose* in it again?
I didn't *come* up here to rub your nose in it, Wolverine.
I came up here to *apologize.*

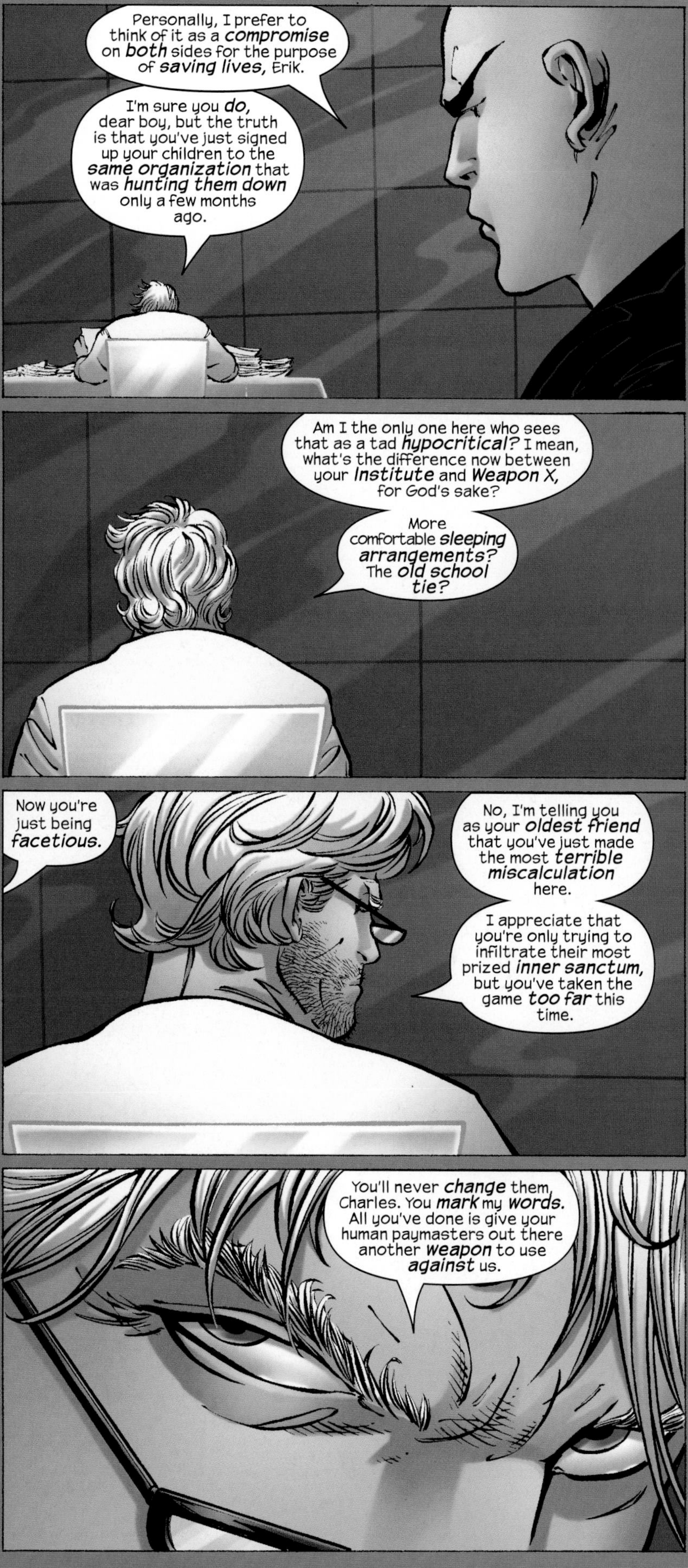

Personally, I prefer to think of it as a compromise on both sides for the purpose of saving lives, Erik.
I'm sure you do, dear boy, but the truth is that you've just signed up your children to the same organization that was hunting them down only a few months ago.
Am I the only one here who sees that as a tad hypocritical? I mean, what's the difference now between your Institute and Weapon X, for God's sake?
More comfortable sleeping arrangements? The old school tie?
Now you're just being facetious.
No, I'm telling you as your oldest friend that you've just made the most terrible miscalculation here.
I appreciate that you're only trying to infiltrate their most prized inner sanctum, but you've taken the game too far this time.
You'll never change them, Charles. You mark my words. All you've done is give your human paymasters out there another weapon to use against us.

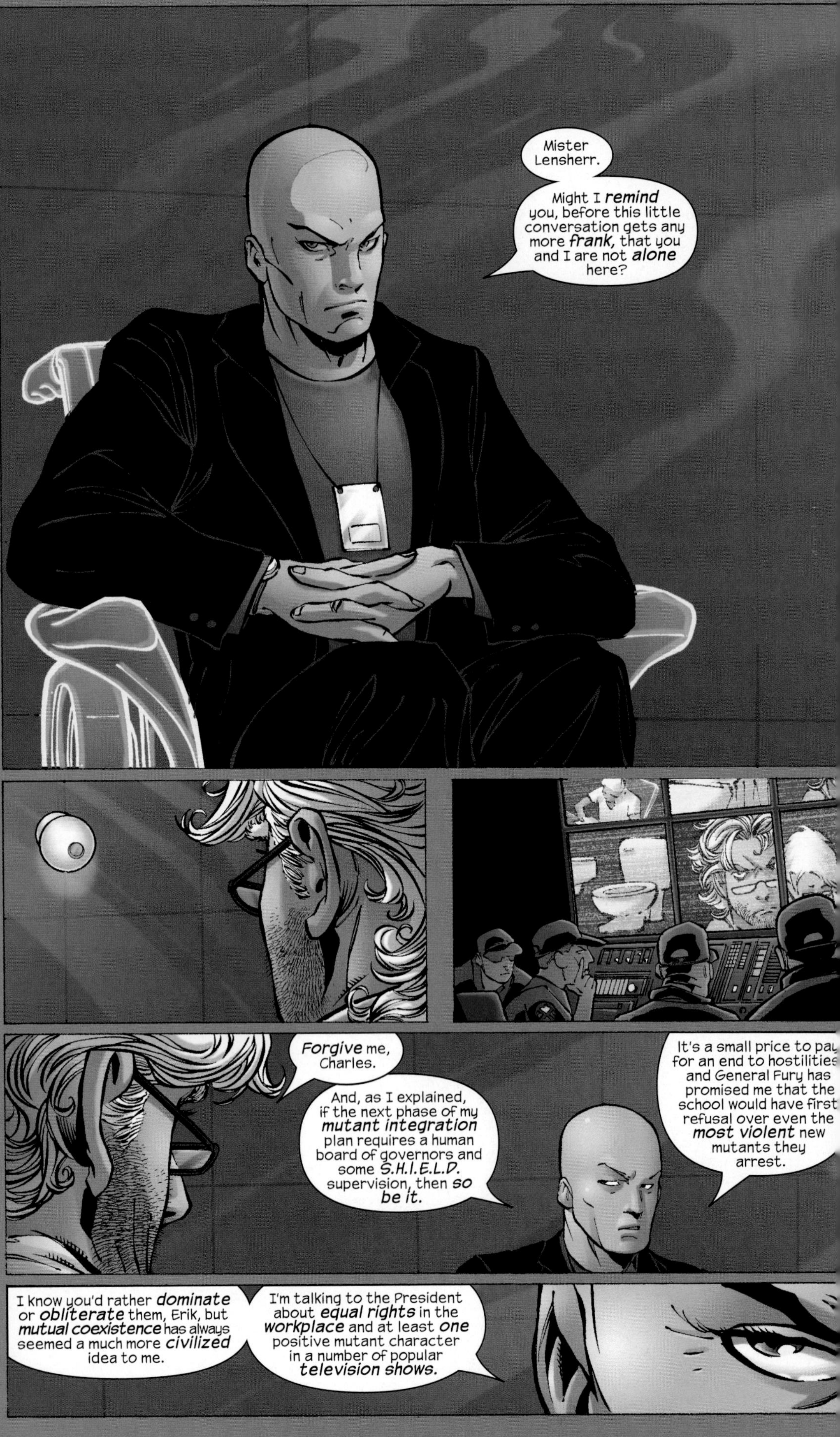
Mister Lensherr.
Might I *remind* you, before this little conversation gets any more *frank*, that you and I are not *alone* here?
Forgive me, Charles.
And, as I explained, if the next phase of my *mutant integration* plan requires a human board of governors and some *S.H.I.E.L.D.* supervision, then *so be it*.
It's a small price to pay for an end to hostilities and General Fury has promised me that the school would have first refusal over even the *most violent* new mutants they arrest.
I know you'd rather *dominate* or *obliterate* them, Erik, but *mutual coexistence* has always seemed a much more *civilized* idea to me.
I'm talking to the President about *equal rights* in the *workplace* and at least *one* positive mutant character in a number of popular *television shows*.

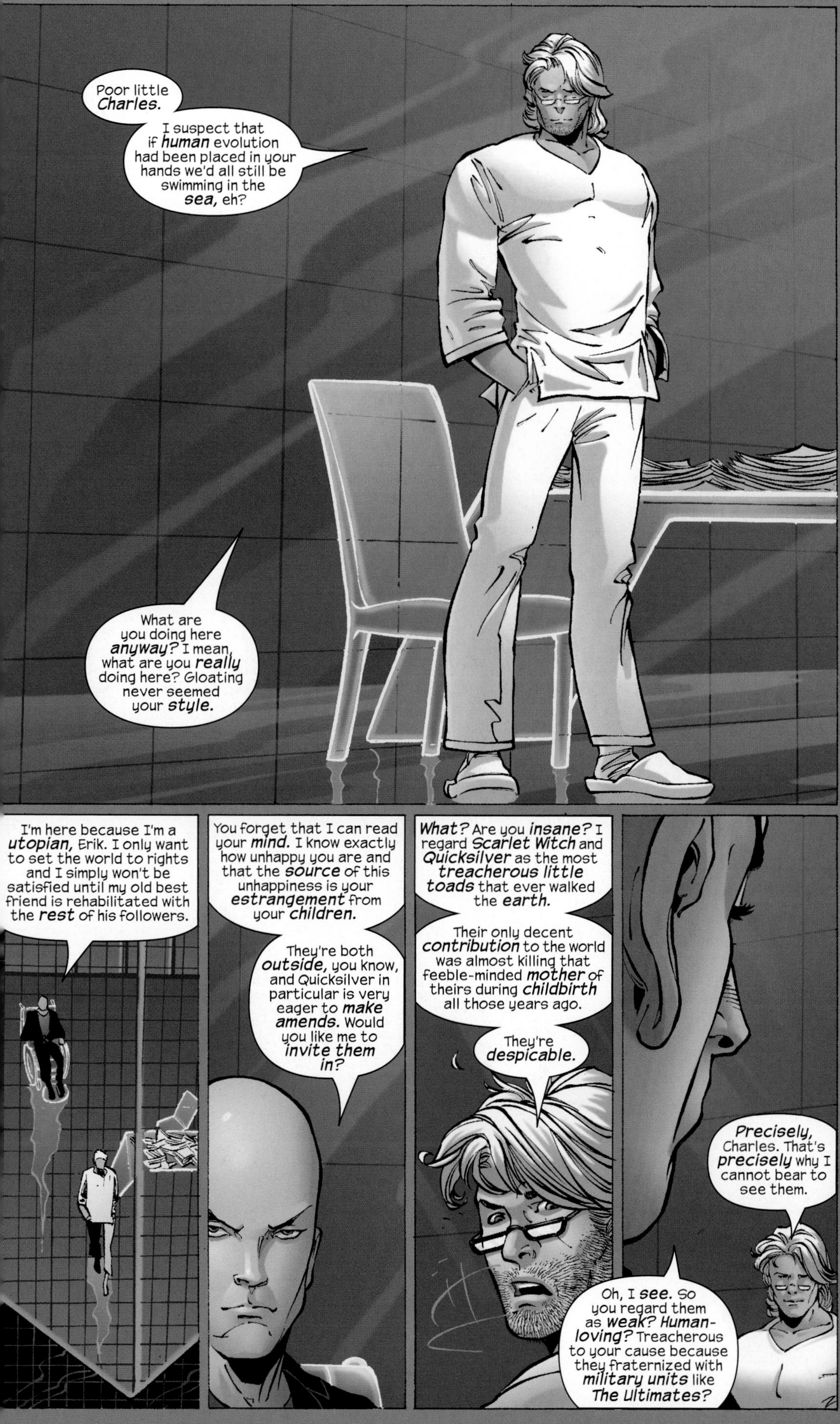
Poor little Charles.
I suspect that if human evolution had been placed in your hands we'd all still be swimming in the sea, eh?
What are you doing here anyway? I mean, what are you really doing here? Gloating never seemed your style.
I'm here because I'm a utopian, Erik. I only want to set the world to rights and I simply won't be satisfied until my old best friend is rehabilitated with the rest of his followers.
You forget that I can read your mind. I know exactly how unhappy you are and that the source of this unhappiness is your estrangement from your children.
They're both outside, you know, and Quicksilver in particular is very eager to make amends. Would you like me to invite them in?
What? Are you insane? I regard Scarlet Witch and Quicksilver as the most treacherous little toads that ever walked the earth.
Their only decent contribution to the world was almost killing that feeble-minded mother of theirs during childbirth all those years ago.
They're despicable.
Oh, I see. So you regard them as weak? Human-loving? Treacherous to your cause because they fraternized with military units like The Ultimates?
Precisely, Charles. That's precisely why I cannot bear to see them.

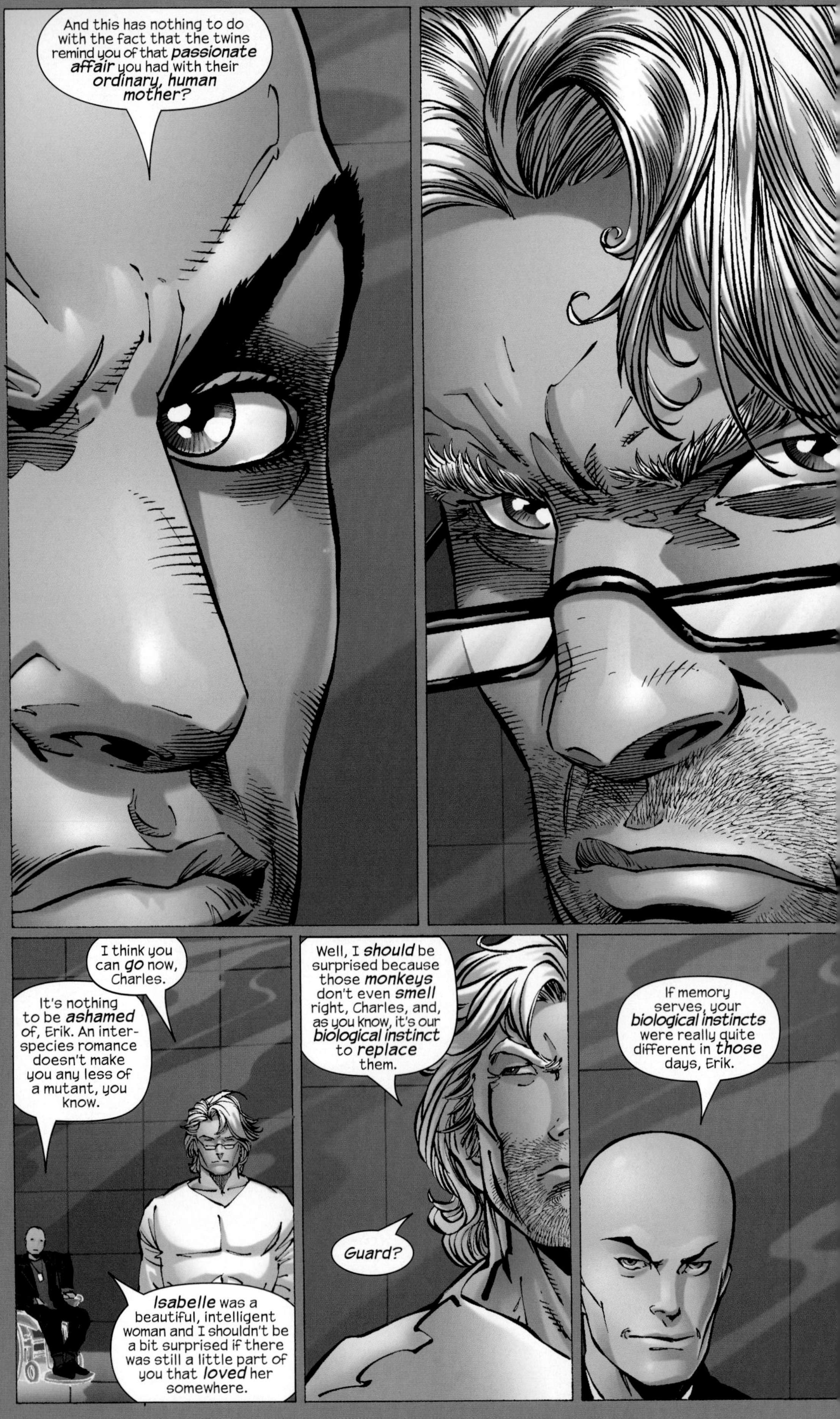
And this has nothing to do with the fact that the twins remind you of that *passionate affair* you had with their *ordinary, human mother?*
I think you can *go* now, Charles.
It's nothing to be *ashamed* of, Erik. An inter-species romance doesn't make you any less of a mutant, you know.
Isabelle was a beautiful, intelligent woman and I shouldn't be a bit surprised if there was still a little part of you that *loved* her somewhere.
Well, I *should* be surprised because those *monkeys* don't even *smell* right, Charles, and, as you know, it's our *biological instinct* to *replace* them.
Guard?
If memory serves, your *biological instincts* were really quite different in *those* days, Erik.

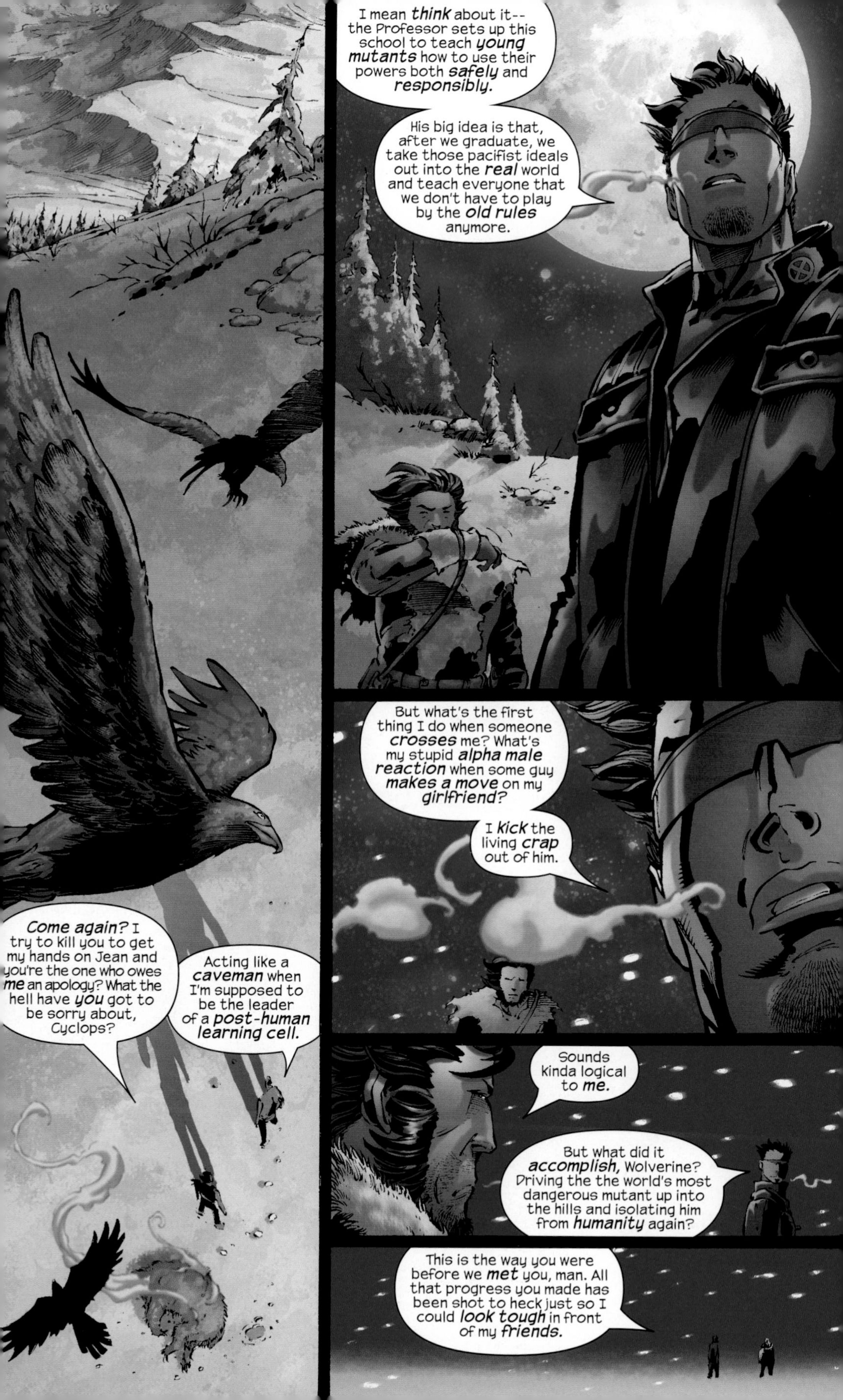

Come again? I try to kill you to get my hands on Jean and you're the one who owes me an apology? What the hell have you got to be sorry about, Cyclops?
Acting like a caveman when I'm supposed to be the leader of a post-human learning cell.
I mean think about it-- the Professor sets up this school to teach young mutants how to use their powers both safely and responsibly.
His big idea is that, after we graduate, we take those pacifist ideals out into the real world and teach everyone that we don't have to play by the old rules anymore.
But what's the first thing I do when someone crosses me? What's my stupid alpha male reaction when some guy makes a move on my girlfriend?
I kick the living crap out of him.
Sounds kinda logical to me.
But what did it accomplish, Wolverine? Driving the the world's most dangerous mutant up into the hills and isolating him from humanity again?
This is the way you were before we met you, man. All that progress you made has been shot to heck just so I could look tough in front of my friends.

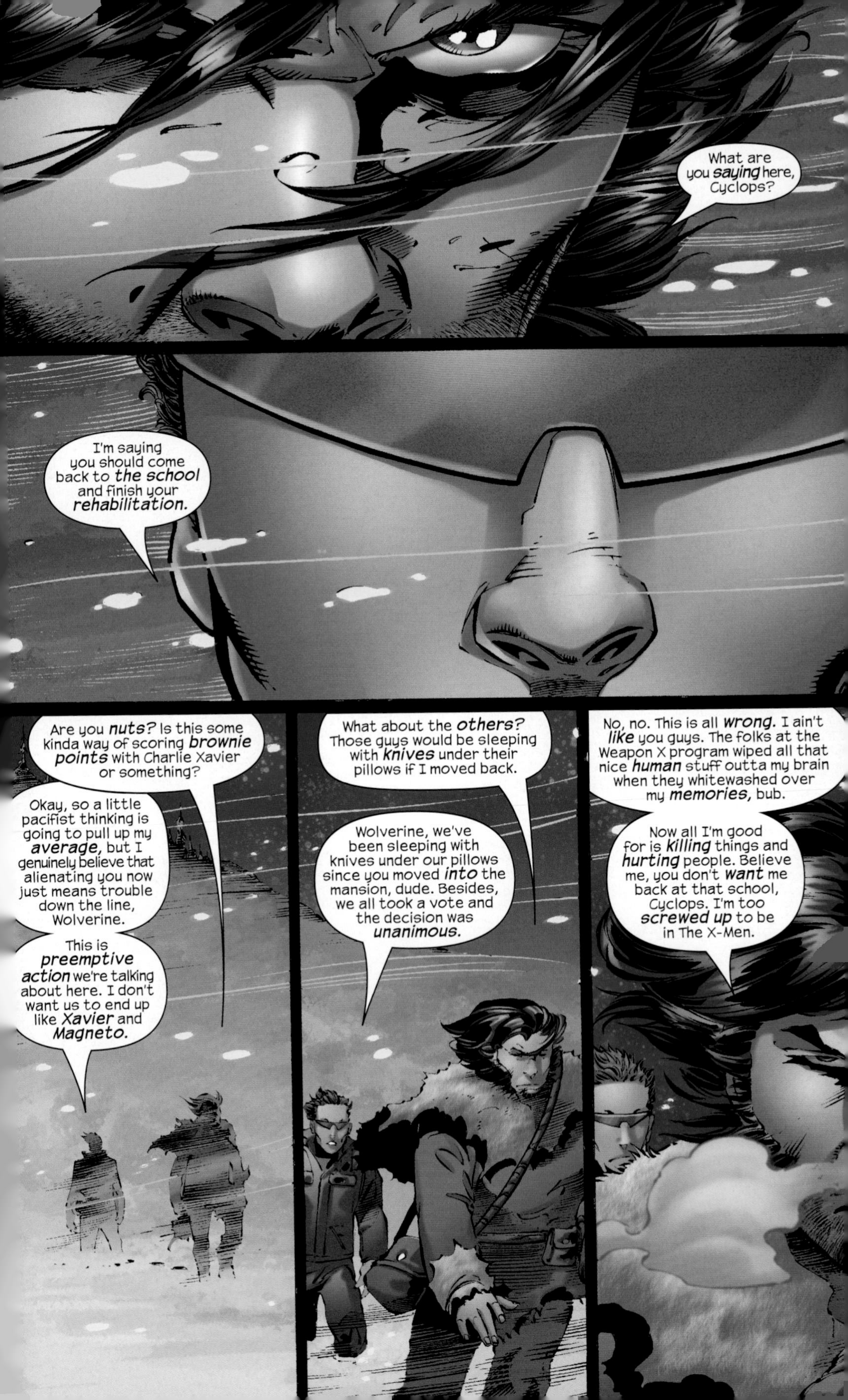
What are you saying here, Cyclops?
I'm saying you should come back to the school and finish your rehabilitation.
Are you nuts? Is this some kinda way of scoring brownie points with Charlie Xavier or something?
Okay, so a little pacifist thinking is going to pull up my average, but I genuinely believe that alienating you now just means trouble down the line, Wolverine.
This is preemptive action we're talking about here. I don't want us to end up like Xavier and Magneto.
What about the others? Those guys would be sleeping with knives under their pillows if I moved back.
Wolverine, we've been sleeping with knives under our pillows since you moved into the mansion, dude. Besides, we all took a vote and the decision was unanimous.
No, no. This is all wrong. I ain't like you guys. The folks at the Weapon X program wiped all that nice human stuff outta my brain when they whitewashed over my memories, bub.
Now all I'm good for is killing things and hurting people. Believe me, you don't want me back at that school, Cyclops. I'm too screwed up to be in The X-Men.

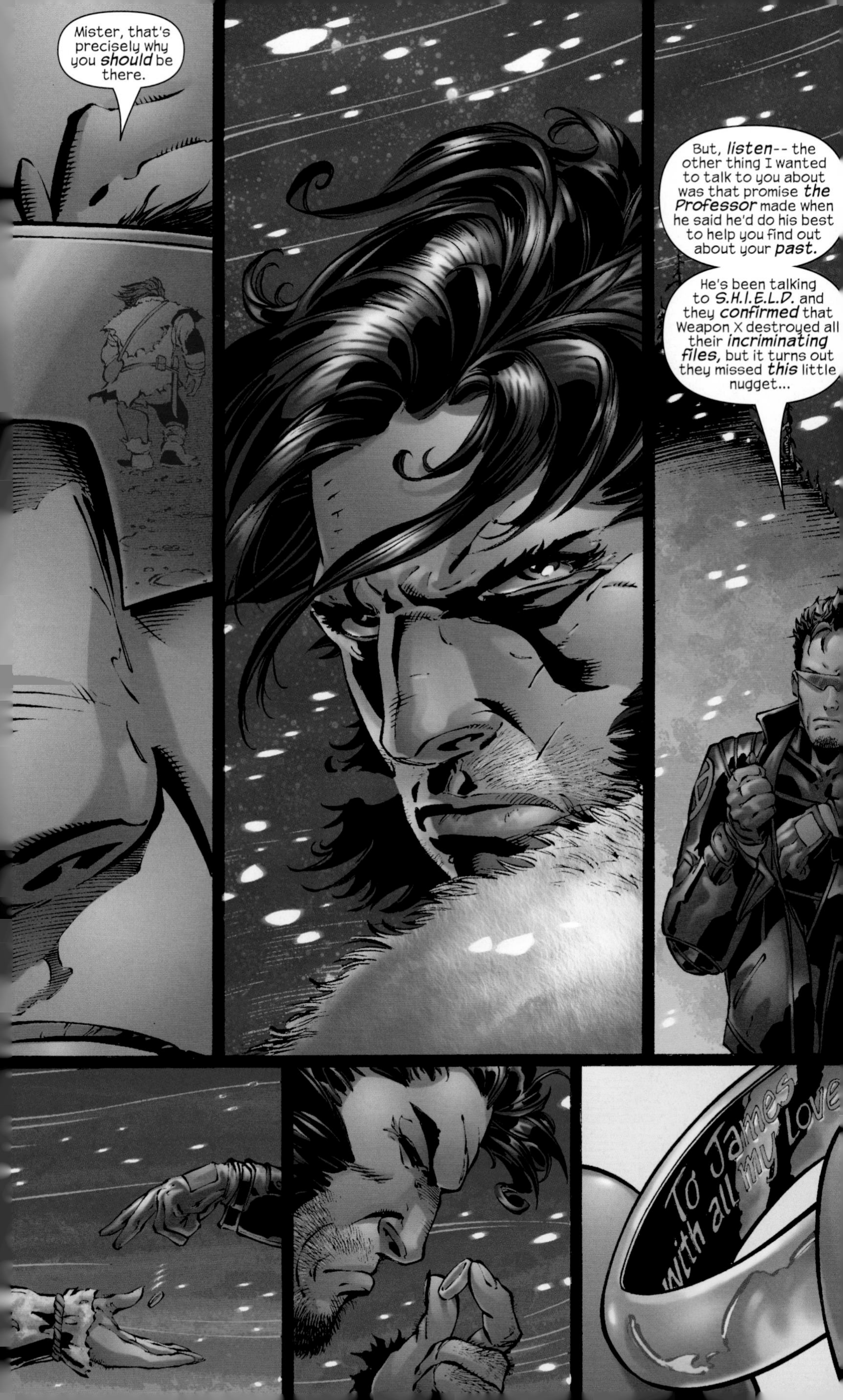
Mister, that's precisely why you *should* be there.
But, *listen*-- the other thing I wanted to talk to you about was that promise *the Professor* made when he said he'd do his best to help you find out about your *past.*
He's been talking to *S.H.I.E.L.D.* and they *confirmed* that Weapon X destroyed all their *incriminating files,* but it turns out they missed *this* little nugget...
To James with all my Love

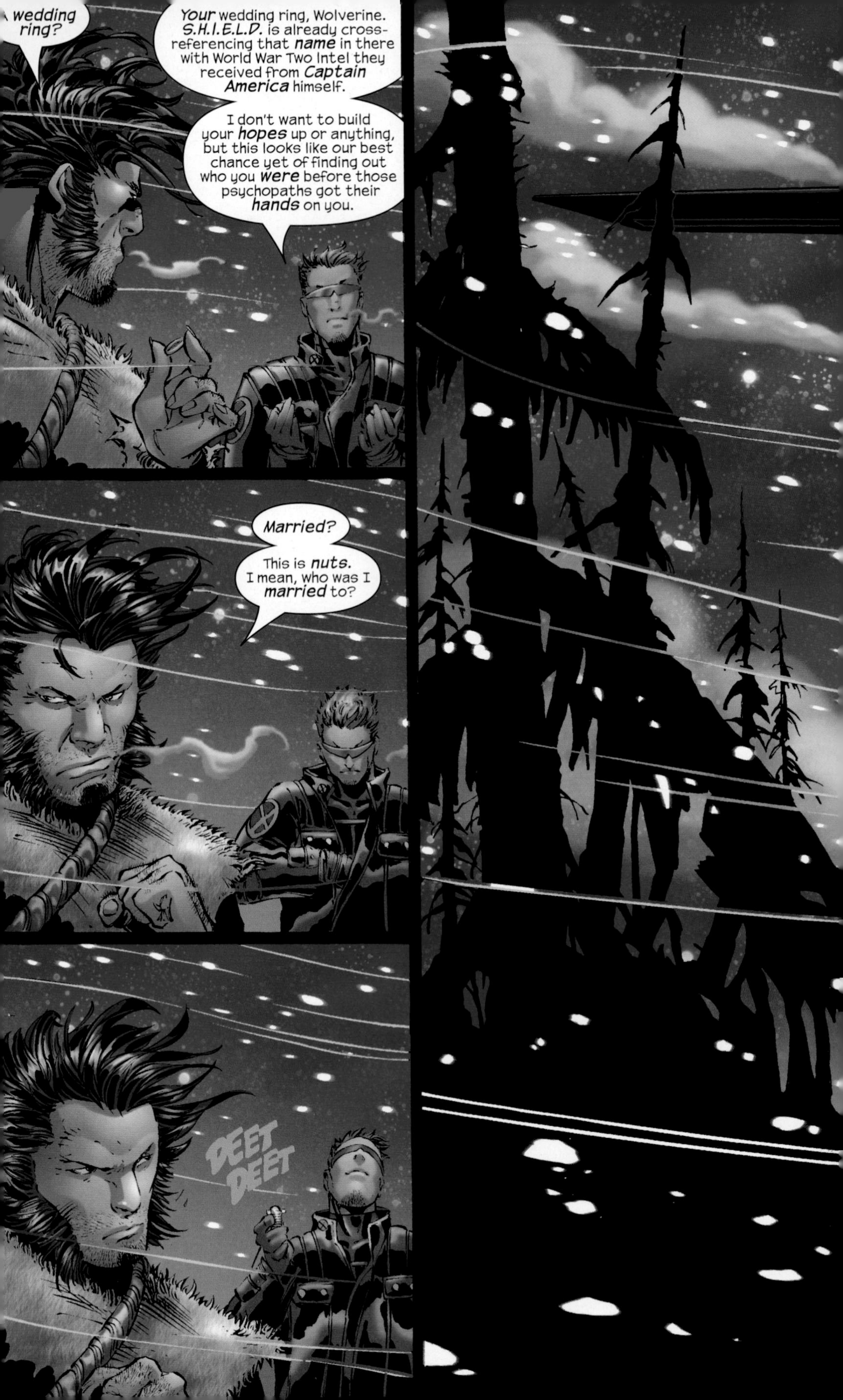

wedding ring?
Your wedding ring, Wolverine. S.H.I.E.L.D. is already cross-referencing that name in there with World War Two Intel they received from Captain America himself.
I don't want to build your hopes up or anything, but this looks like our best chance yet of finding out who you were before those psychopaths got their hands on you.
Married?
This is nuts. I mean, who was I married to?
DEET DEET

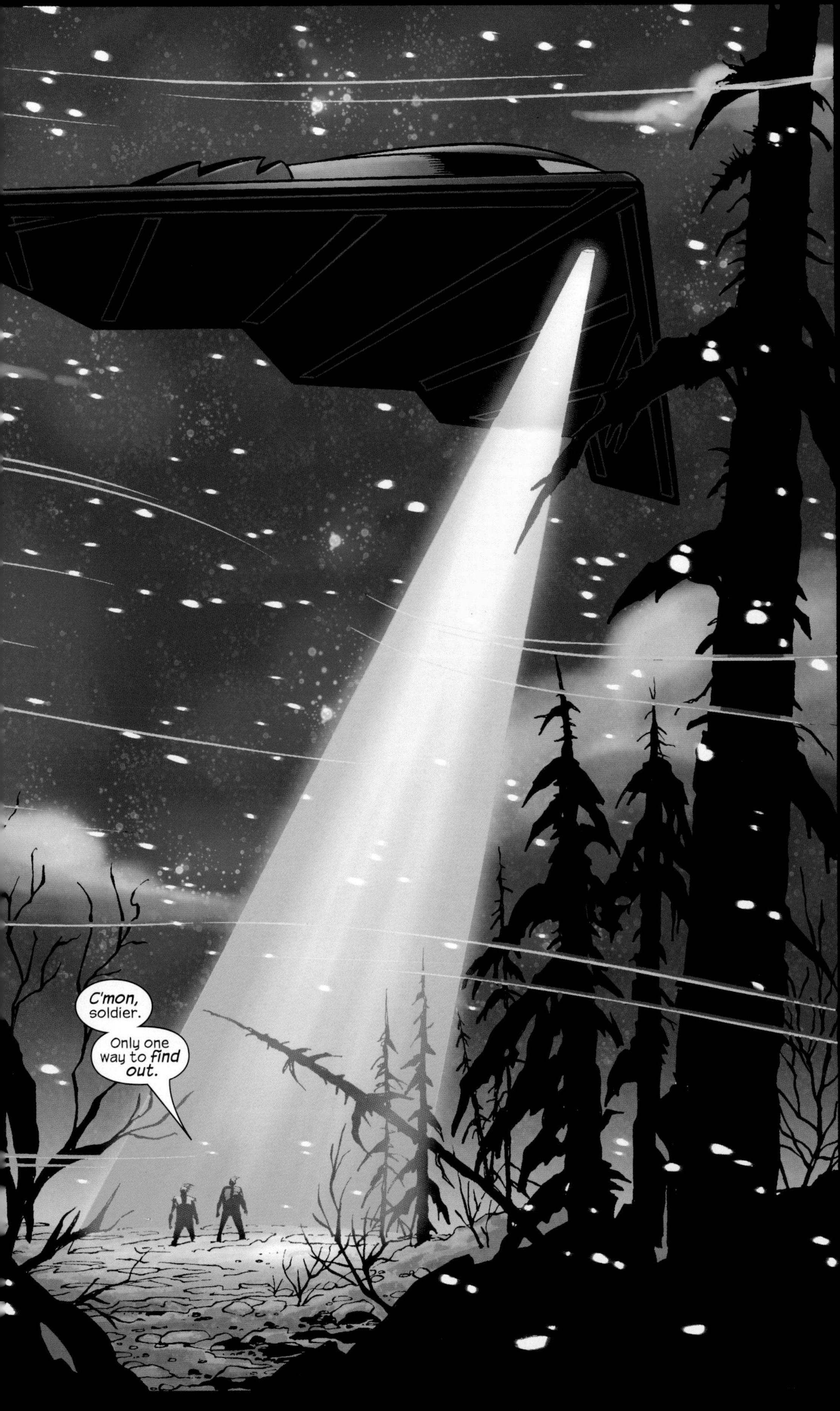
C'mon, soldier.
Only one way to find out.

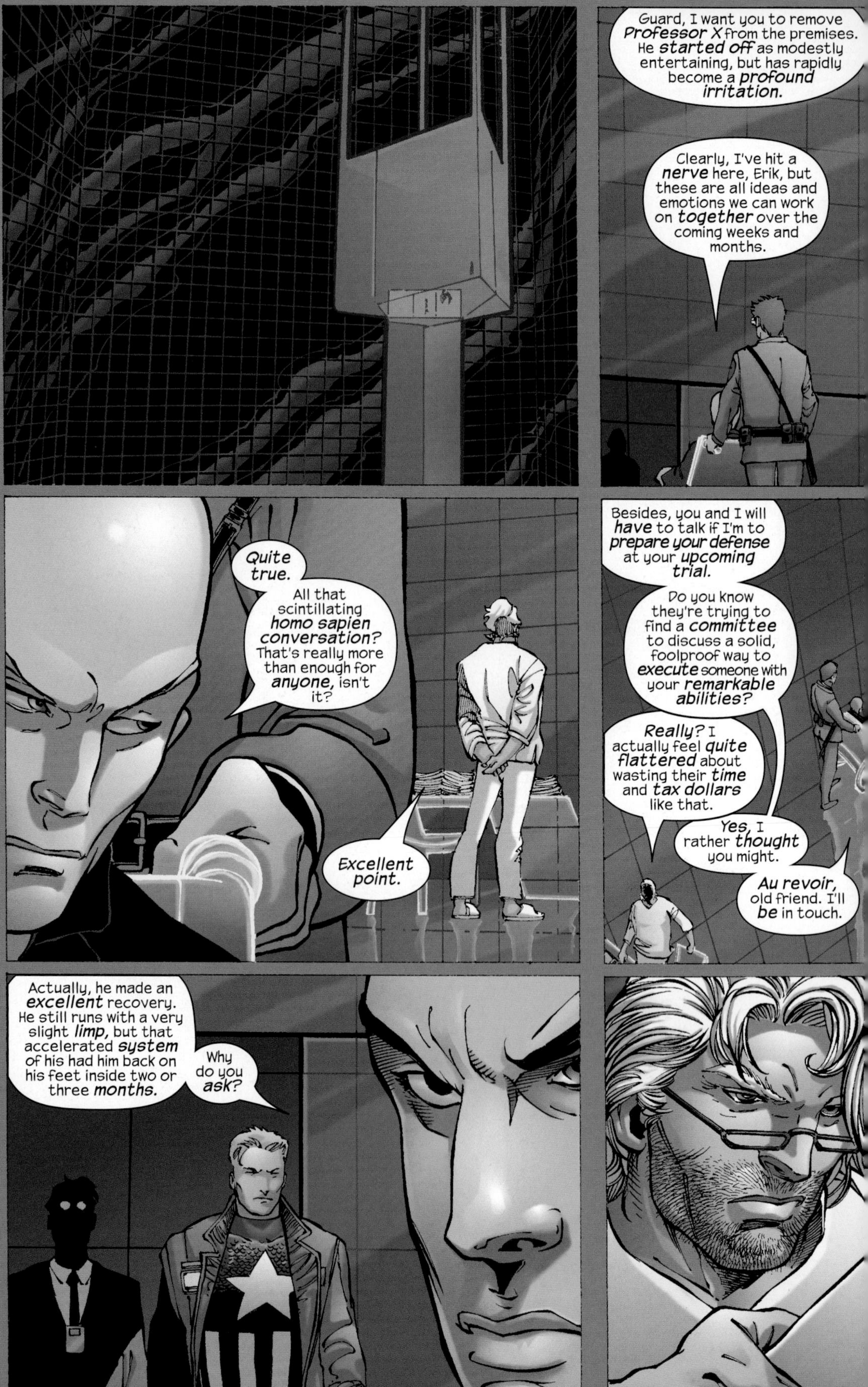

Guard, I want you to remove Professor X from the premises. He started off as modestly entertaining, but has rapidly become a profound irritation.
Clearly, I've hit a nerve here, Erik, but these are all ideas and emotions we can work on together over the coming weeks and months.
Quite true.
All that scintillating homo sapien conversation? That's really more than enough for anyone, isn't it?
Excellent point.
Besides, you and I will have to talk if I'm to prepare your defense at your upcoming trial.
Do you know they're trying to find a committee to discuss a solid, foolproof way to execute someone with your remarkable abilities?
Really? I actually feel quite flattered about wasting their time and tax dollars like that.
Yes, I rather thought you might.
Au revoir, old friend. I'll be in touch.
Actually, he made an excellent recovery. He still runs with a very slight limp, but that accelerated system of his had him back on his feet inside two or three months.
Why do you ask?

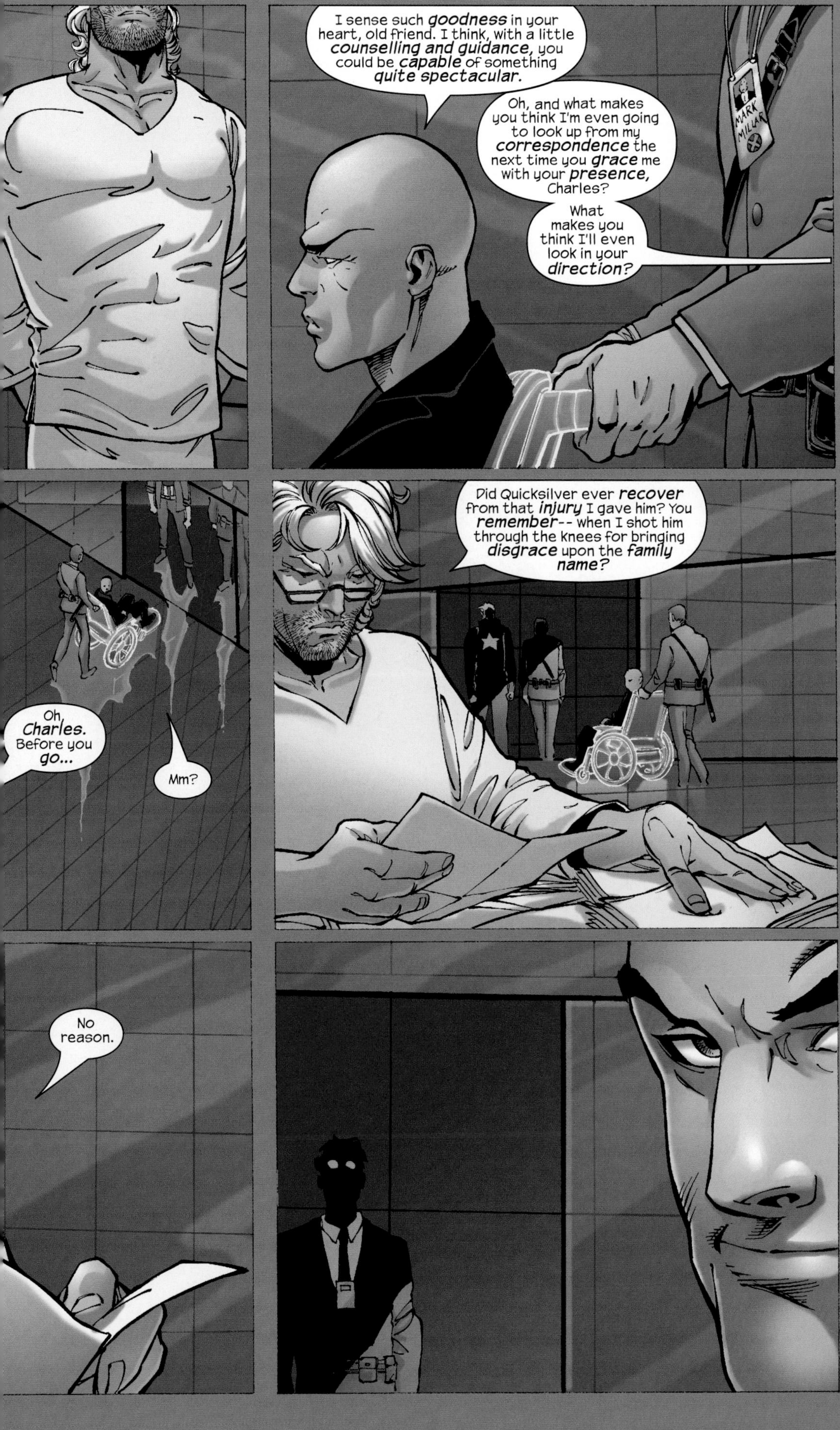

I sense such goodness in your heart, old friend. I think, with a little counselling and guidance, you could be capable of something quite spectacular.
Oh, and what makes you think I'm even going to look up from my correspondence the next time you grace me with your presence, Charles?
What makes you think I'll even look in your direction?
MARK MILLAR
Oh, Charles. Before you go...
Mm?
Did Quicksilver ever recover from that injury I gave him? You remember-- when I shot him through the knees for bringing disgrace upon the family name?
No reason.

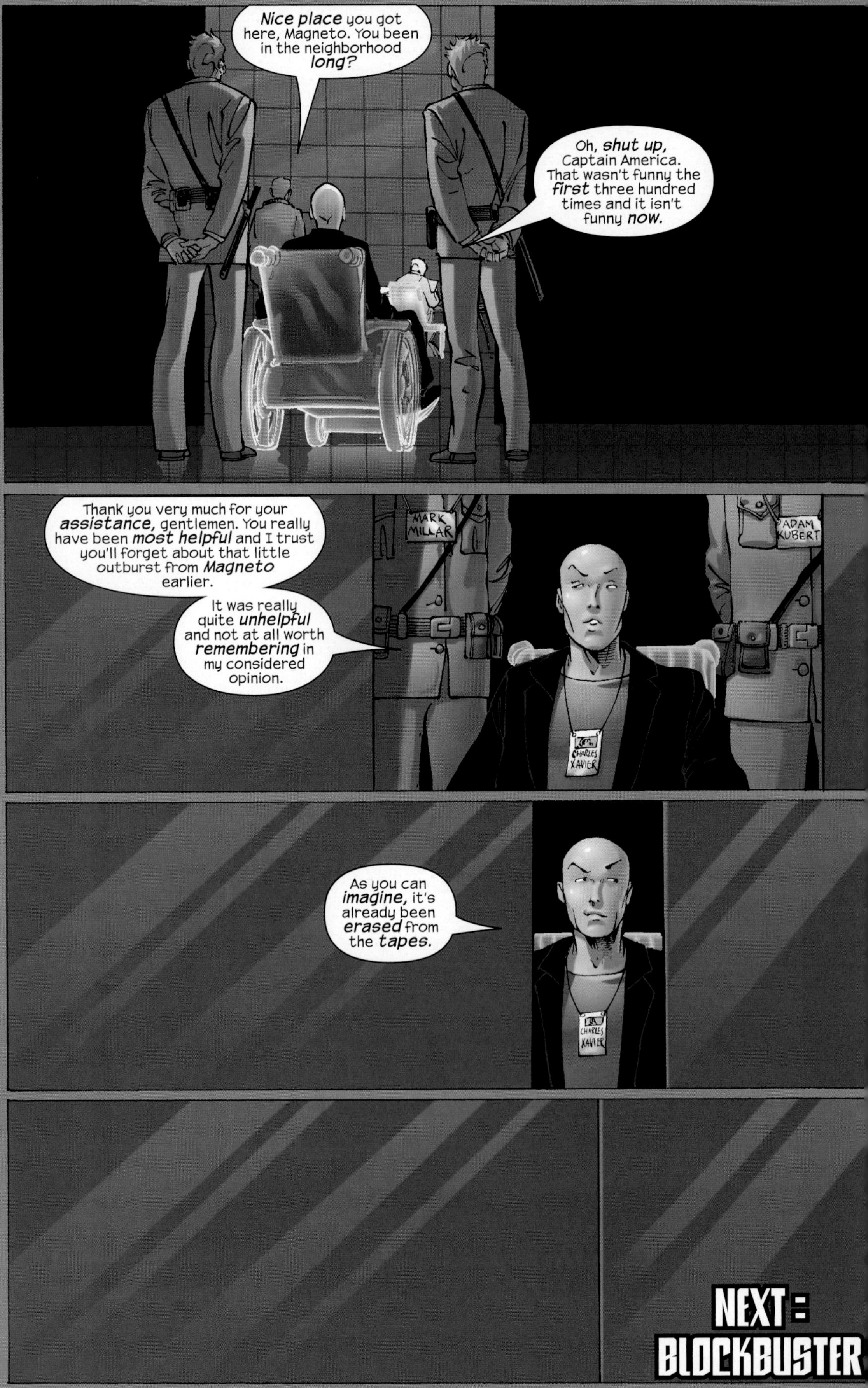
Nice place you got here, Magneto. You been in the neighborhood long?
Oh, shut up, Captain America. That wasn't funny the first three hundred times and it isn't funny now.
Thank you very much for your assistance, gentlemen. You really have been most helpful and I trust you'll forget about that little outburst from Magneto earlier.
It was really quite unhelpful and not at all worth remembering in my considered opinion.
MARK MILLAR
ADAM KUBERT
CHARLES XAVIER
As you can imagine, it's already been erased from the tapes.
CHARLES XAVIER
NEXT: BLOCKBUSTER

#26

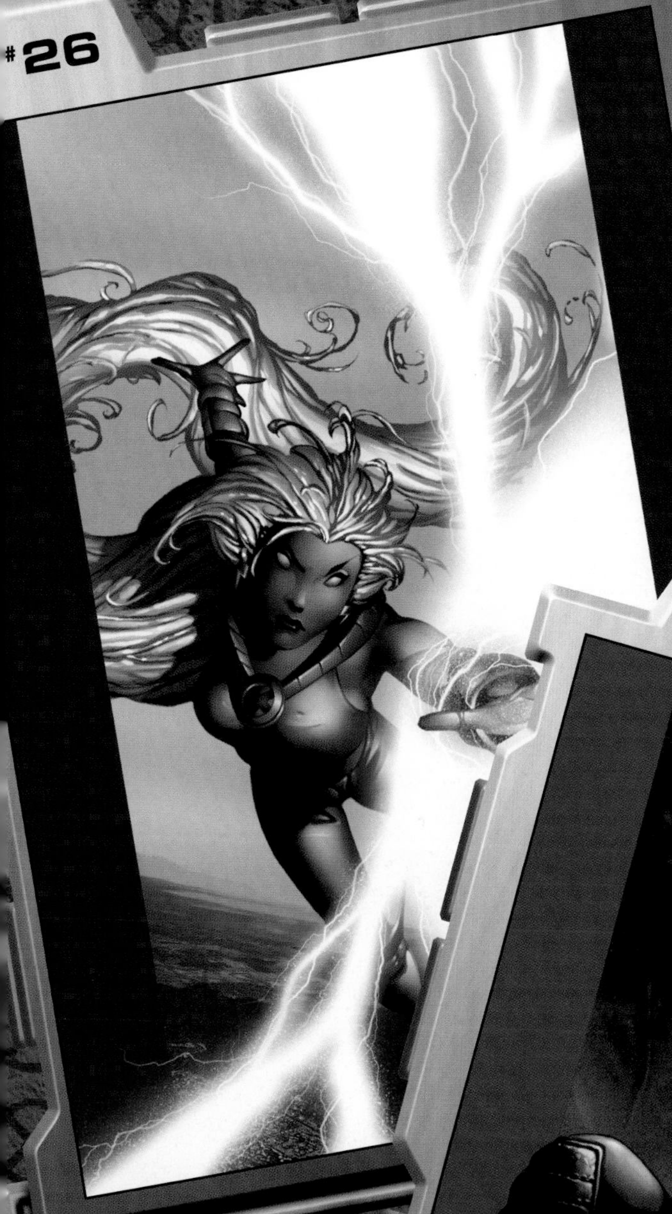

#27

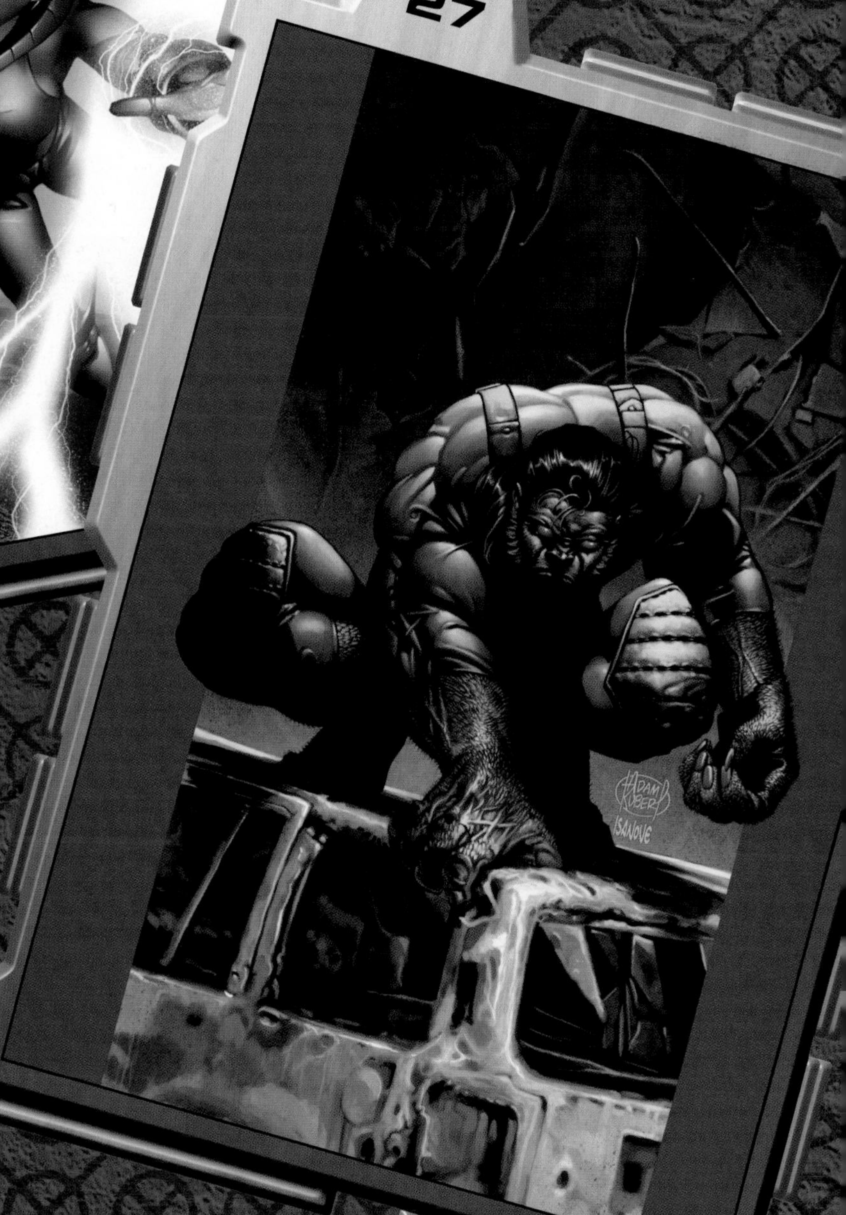
ADAM KUBERT
ISANOVE

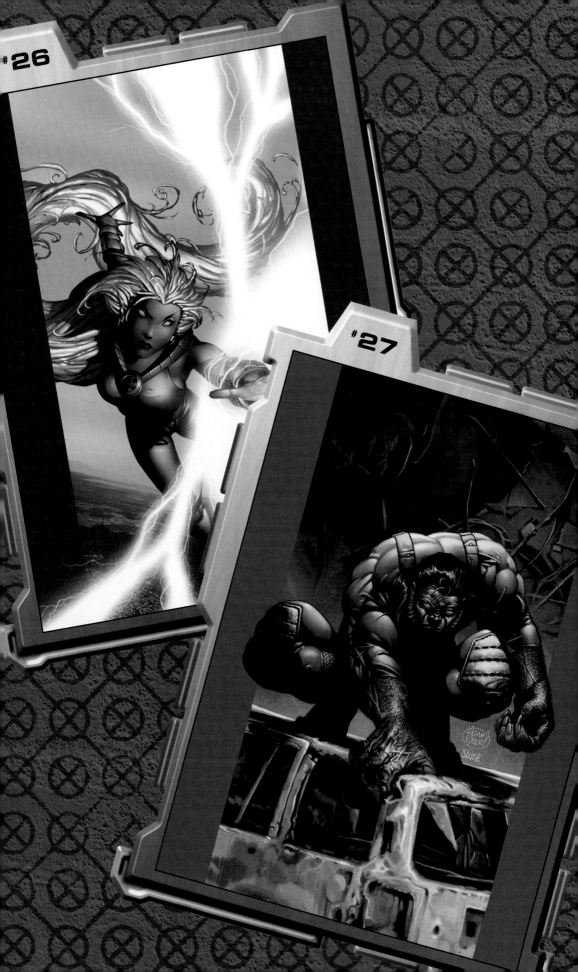

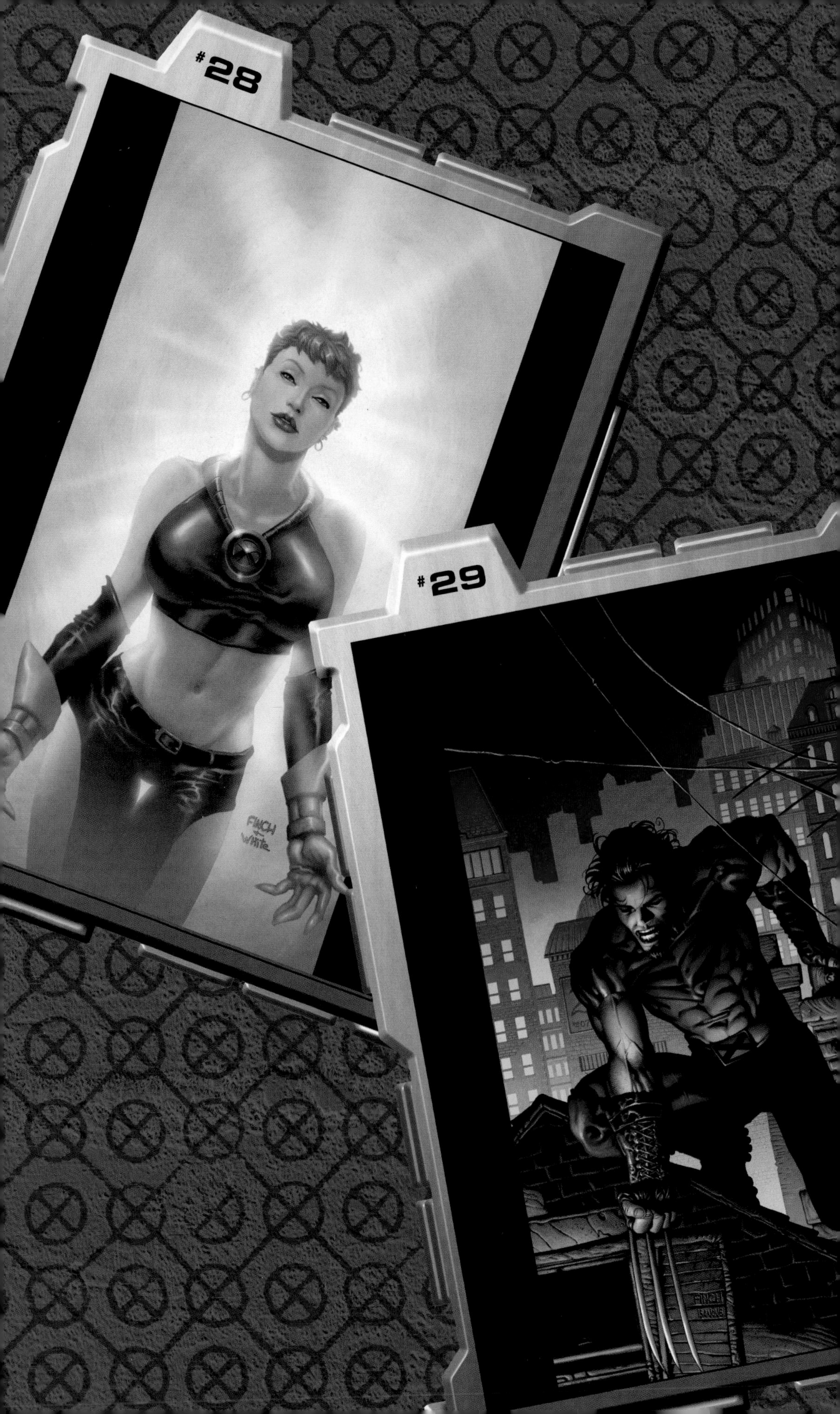
#28
FINCH
WHITE
#29
FINCH

#30

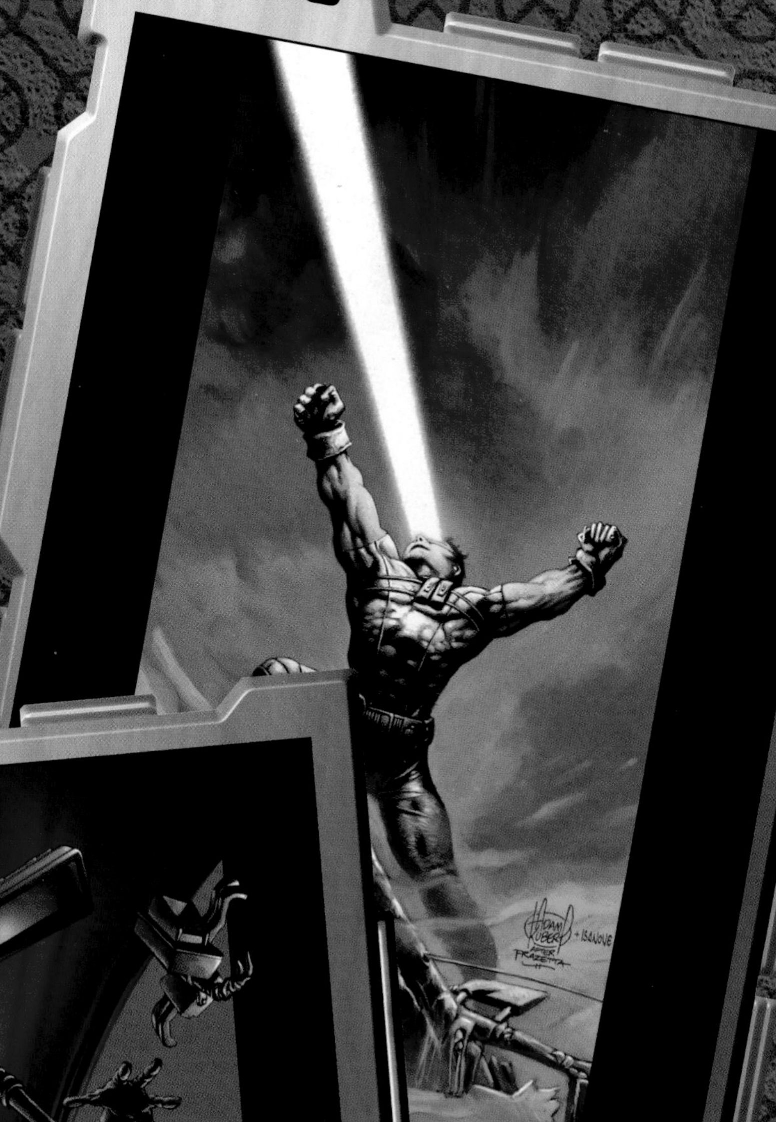

#31

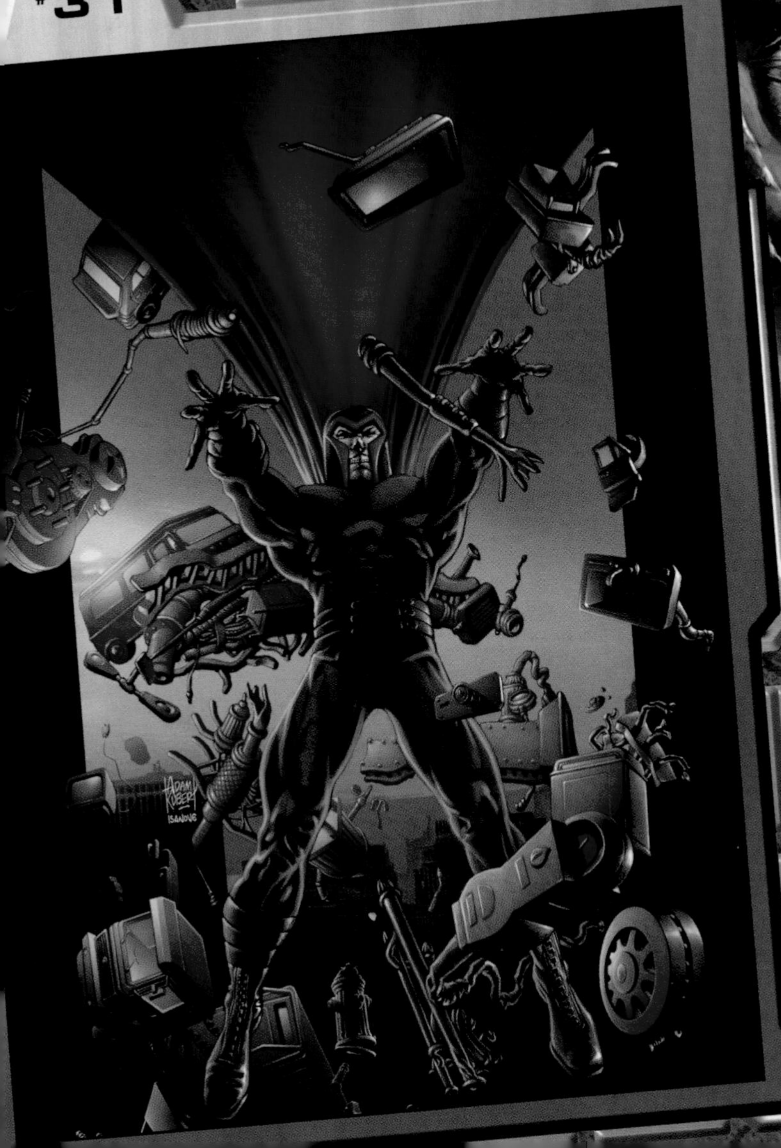

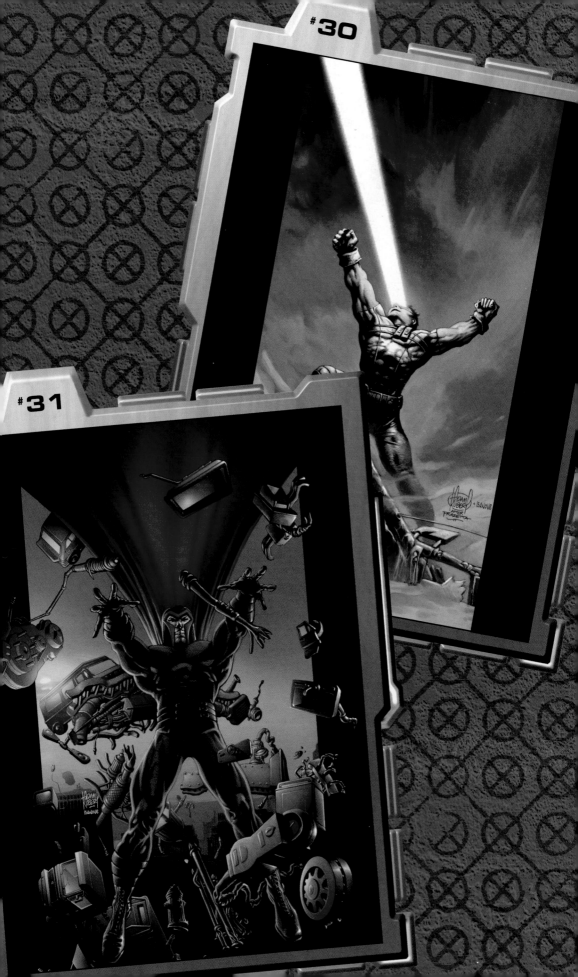

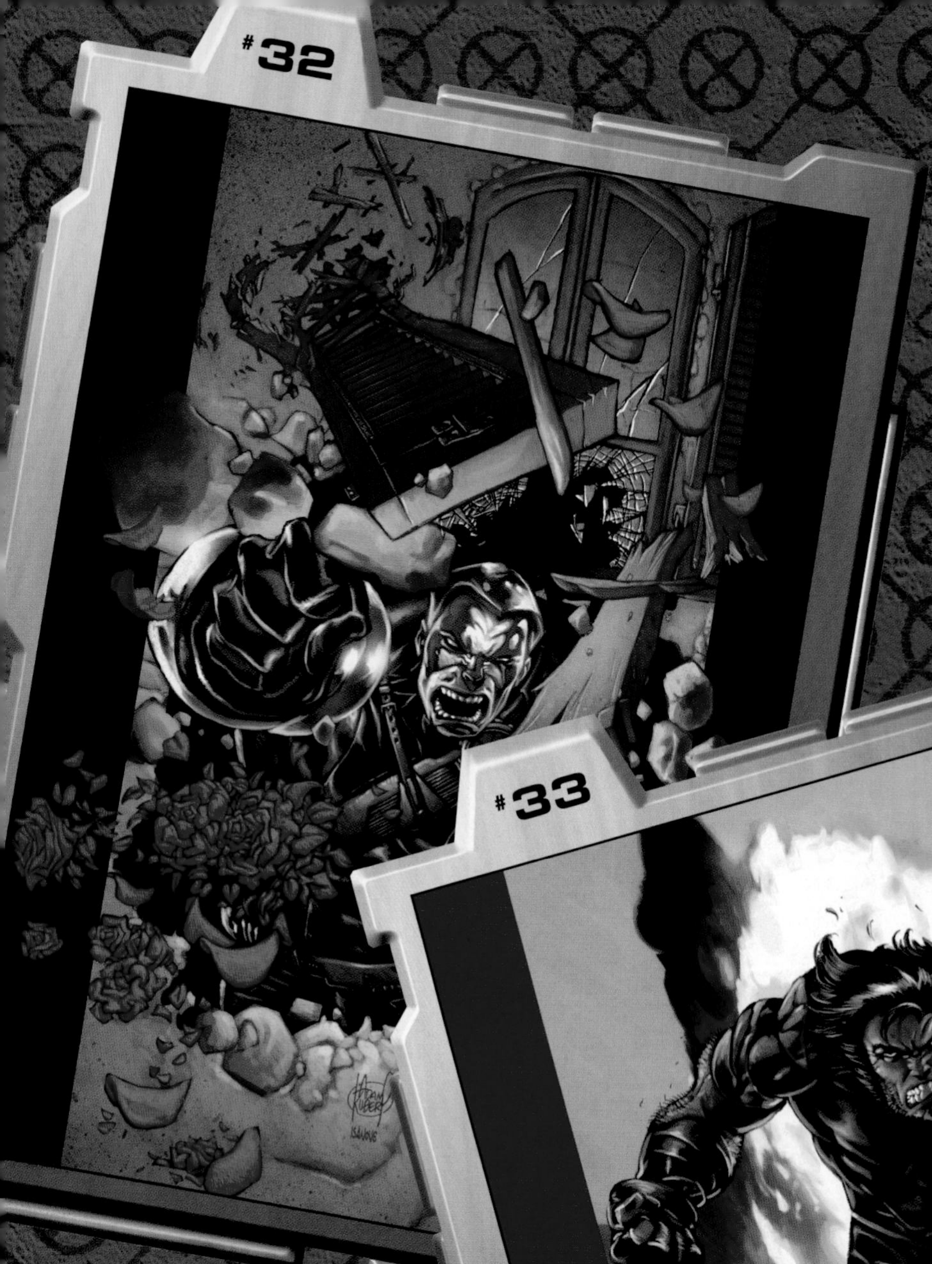
#32

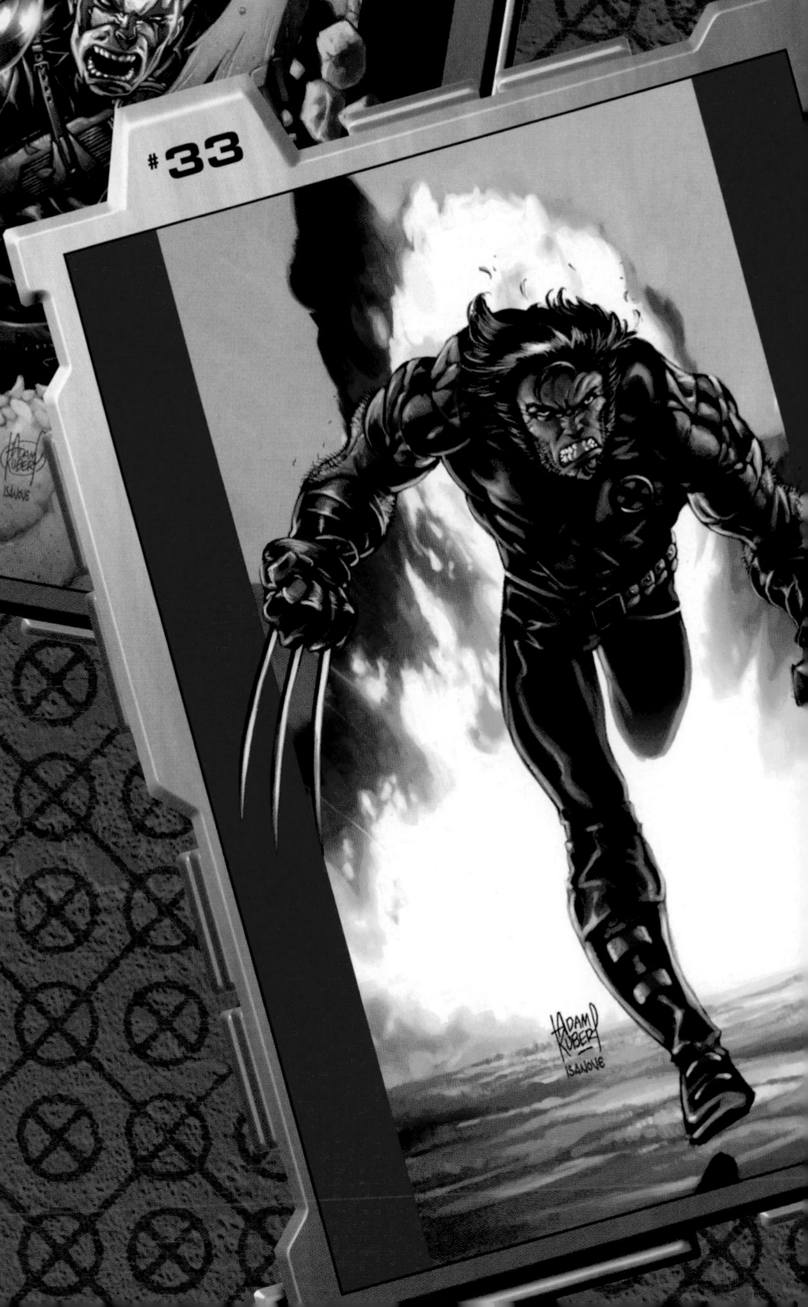
#33

MARVELS
10TH ANNIVERSARY EDITION

MARVEL®

CELEBRATE 10 YEARS OF MARVELS!
KURT BUSIEK · ALEX ROSS

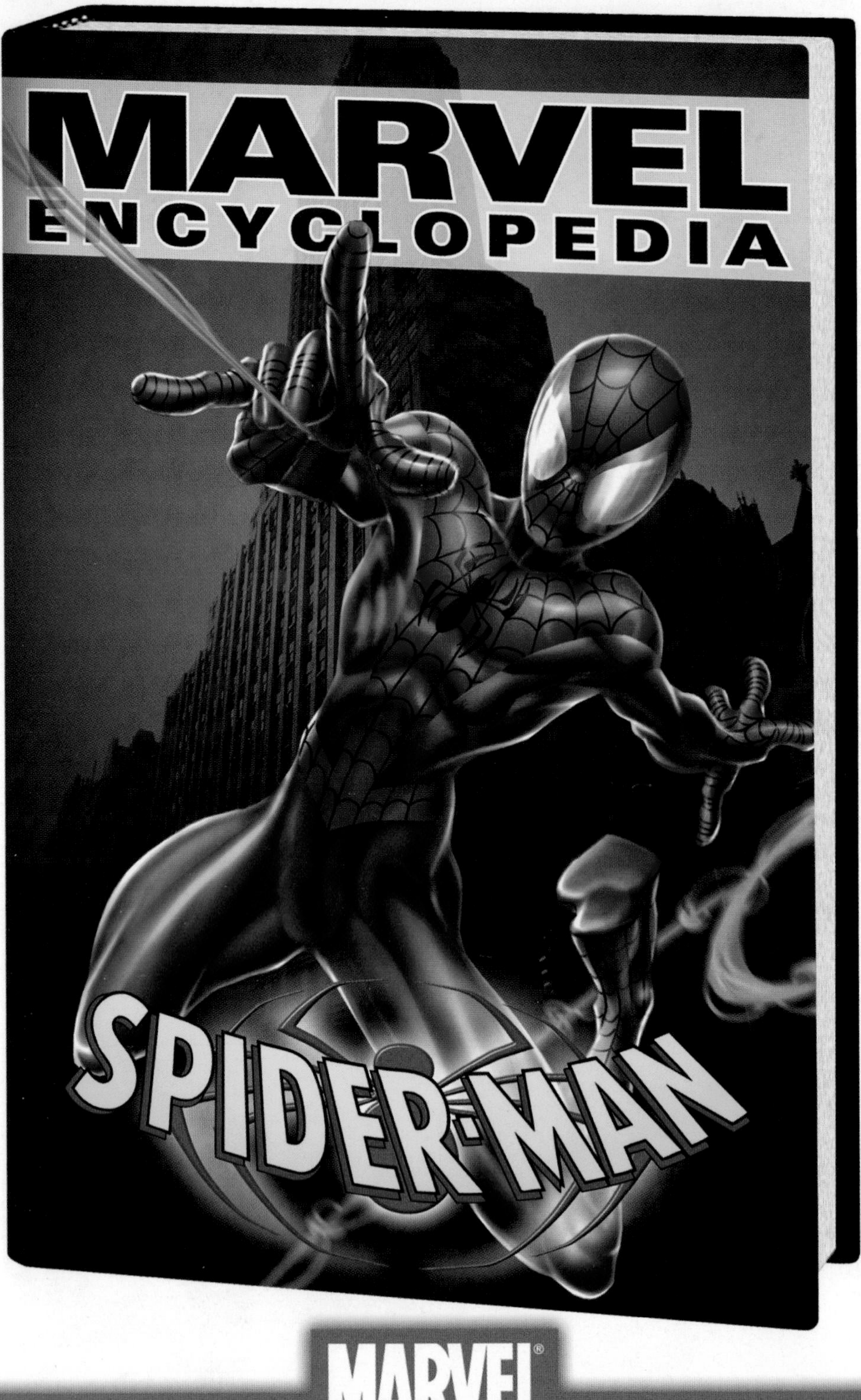
MARVEL
ENCYCLOPEDIA
SPIDER-MAN